Roland Barthes

Roland Barthes

A Biography

LOUIS-JEAN CALVET

Translated by Sarah Wykes

Indiana University Press
Bloomington and Indianapolis

This translation first published in North America in 1995 by Indiana University Press, 601 North Morton Street, Bloomington, Indiana, in association with Polity Press, 65 Bridge Street, Cambridge CB2 1UR, UK.

English translation copyright © 1994 by Polity Press
First published in France as *Roland Barthes* © 1990 by Flammarion

Published with the assistance of the French Ministry of Culture.

Manufactured in Great Britain

ISBN 0–253–34987–7

Library of Congress Cataloging in Publication Data
A CIP catalog record for this book is available from the Library of Congress

GIFT OF NATHAN LYONS
2017

Je lui dois, outre le bonheur de lecture, quelques intuitions latérales, et d'abord celle-ci: Ce n'est pas parce que Barthes aurait à l'avance récusé l'indiscrétion du geste biographique qu'il faut se fermer les yeux sur ce que son jeu d'ostentation et d'occultation pouvait signifier de désir d'être amicalement rudoyé.

(Apart from the pleasure of reading, I am also indebted to him for a few oblique insights, principally the following: even if Barthes himself rejected the indiscretion of the biographical gesture, the extent to which this show of ostentation and occultation concealed his desire for some intrusive yet friendly bullying should not be overlooked.)

Max Genève, 'Les nuits magnétiques',
France-Culture, 13 May 1986

Si j'étais écrivain, et mort, comme j'aimerais que ma vie se réduisît, par les soins d'un biographe amical et désinvolte, à quelques détails, à quelques goûts, à quelques inflexions, disons: des 'biographèmes', dont la distinction et la mobilité pourraient voyager hors de tout destin et venir toucher, à la façon des atomes épicuriens, quelque corps futur, promis à la même dispersion; une vie trouée, en somme, comme Proust a su écrire la sienne dans son oeuvre . . .

(Were I a writer, and dead, how I would love it if my life, through the pains of some friendly and detached biographer, were to reduce itself to a few details, a few preferences, a few inflections, let us say: to 'biographemes' whose distinction and mobility might go beyond any fate and come to touch, like Epicurean atoms, some future body, destined to the same dispersion; a marked life, in sum, as Proust succeeded in writing his in his work.)

Roland Barthes, *Sade, Fourier, Loyola*
(trans. R. Miller)

Contents

Preliminary Note

This book is the result of a great deal of work: making inquiries, searching in archives, interviewing people, tracking down references, reading. Among the texts I read were a large number of letters. Roland Barthes wrote a great many letters, several per day, and, a loyal friend, he corresponded with many different people for many years. Practically everyone I approached – from the President, François Mitterrand, who granted me an interview at the Elysée Palace, down to the anonymous student who entrusted me with his memories of the seminar – was more than willing to talk to me about Barthes. I should point out that among the numerous people I interviewed, two were particularly helpful. One is Philippe Rebeyrol, who from 1932 to 1980 received hundreds of letters from Barthes. Rebeyrol and Barthes first met in the third form at secondary school, and their friendship lasted almost fifty years until Barthes's death. The other is Robert David, who was a patient at the same sanatorium as Barthes during the war and who also remained a lifelong friend. The two men exchanged dozens of letters.

These two sets of interviews provided me with a remarkable account of the evolution of Barthes's ideas and feelings, and I would like to thank both Philippe Rebeyrol and Robert David for talking to me. Unfortunately, Barthes's heirs refused to allow me to quote from their letters. Because I have respected their wishes, at times the narrative may seem a little vague. I hope the reader will bear with me.

Philippe Rebeyrol also informed me about the following unpublished texts by Barthes: a short one-act piece called 'Le voyage d'Arion' ('The voyage of Arion'), dated December 1934; an apologue, 'Les aventures d'un jeune crétois' ('The adventures of a young Cretan'), dated February 1935; a poem, 'La ballade des susceptiblitiés' ('The ballad of sensitivities'), dated March 1935. In 1974, in the review *L'Arc*, Barthes published and introduced 'En marge du Criton' ('In the margin of the Crito'), his very first text, written at the age of seventeen during the summer of 1933. The three unpublished texts complete the Barthes file and illustrate his earliest phase of writing. Unfortunately, I am once again unable to quote from these texts out of respect for the wishes of Barthes's heirs. I only hope that one day researchers will have access to these texts.

This book may also seem vague in one other respect, but in this case the vagueness is intentional. Roland Barthes, as everyone is aware since his editor's publication of *Incidents* in 1987, was a homosexual. As will be seen, he never publicly admitted his homosexuality and – in an era when (especially after 1968) his friends were becoming passionately involved in a series of struggles against the intolerance and repression homosexuals had been subject to for centuries – he never campaigned about it. If this book is the history of a life, it is also a book of History with a capital H, and History has a duty to seek out and reveal the truth at all times. However, I did not think it my place to mention any names, with two exceptions. Barthes had love affairs, like everyone else, but if he did not want them to become public knowledge, and if, after his death, his lovers choose not to discuss them, then there is no reason why I should deliver up their names to the public. Especially when they would not contribute in any real way to the book's interest. The two exceptions are, first, someone who has been dead for a long time and, second, someone Barthes was very much in love with but who never responded to his advances. He has agreed, in view of the importance of his testimony, to allow his name to appear here in print.

Preface:
The Genealogical Silence

Before reading on, the reader should be warned that this book bears a rather strange relation to its subject. Barthes, who in his own work often dealt with oeuvres (for instance those of Jules Michelet and Racine, and even his own, as will be seen later), always expressed certain reservations about the notion of biography, and naturally he found theoretical justifications for his reticence. These arguments will be examined in due course. But at the same time, when it came to himself, it sometimes seems as if there is something else behind his reticence, different reasons for it, and that it cannot simply be understood as the end result of an analysis or as a theoretical choice.

In the miniature photo album which opens *Roland Barthes by Roland Barthes*, the book of which he is both author and subject, there are portraits of his two grandfathers, with a comment on each one added on the facing page. Opposite the portrait of his maternal grandfather (a lithograph of Captain Binger in uniform, with his moustache and medals), he writes: 'In his old age, he grew bored. Always coming early to table (though the dinner hour was constantly moved), he lived further and further ahead of time, more and more bored. He had no part in language.' Opposite the photo of Léon Barthes, with his white beard and wing collar, is written. 'He liked writing out the programmes for musicals, or mending the choir music stands, boxes, anything made of wood. He, too, had no part in language.'[1]

This insistence on his grandfathers' *silence* is odd, and it seems to express another, generic silence: that of biography or genealogy, whichever one wishes to call it. There is nothing to look for, nothing to find in such a genre, Barthes thinks. There is a person born at the same time as him on 12 November 1915, who in the accounts of his life told by others – or by himself – cannot help but become a third person ('he'), or an 'imaginary' first person ('I'). Throughout *Roland Barthes*, he switches between this third and first person, sometimes within the same passage. Thus there is the phrase 'Saussure's *bête noire* was the *arbitrary* (nature of the sign). His is *analogy*'[2] where one would have expected him to put 'Mine' not 'His', which is followed a few lines later by 'When I resist analogy'. *He, I*: Barthes switches around the personal pronouns so as to keep a reasonable distance between him and himself, some might think, or between the oeuvre and the life, as he would probably have preferred to put it.

Such a mistrust of biography, which explains the reluctance of a handful of those who knew him (and who regard themselves as his intelletual heirs) to talk about him, could mean that in its turn this book is condemned to becoming another novel. 'The only biography is of an unproductive life,' he wrote,[3] remaining faithful in this respect to the structural approach which, in the case of Racine, made him avoid 'inferring from the work to the author and from the author to the work'.[4] Here he went on to explain that his analysis is not concerned with Racine at all but only with the Racinian hero. In other words, there is no need to go and search for Racine's laundry bills or for the traces of his contingent love affairs in order to be able to discuss his tragedies, since 'unproductive' life has hardly anything to do with his oeuvre.

Without wishing to embark on a discussion with an absent author or to argue against a theory with which, on many points, I agree, I must, however, say that in my own view a life is a whole, and between a man and his oeuvre, between the *body* and what it *produces*, there are connections to be deciphered, close – and sometimes bizarre – links and filiations.

Thus these grandfathers who 'had no part in language' and who nevertheless have a great deal to say cannot be disposed of so easily. The very fact that their photographs appear alongside those of his mother, his aunt, his great-grandparents and his brother, in the opening pages of a somewhat provocative book (in a collection with the generic title of X by himself, by Y, we have a Roland Barthes by himself, by Roland Barthes) cannot be overlooked. I have absolutely no way of knowing what Roland Barthes would have made of this current undertaking. I have before me a letter written by him dated

10 September 1973. He had just read a book which I had written about his work and his theories, and he had kindly written to me. In his letter he referred precisely to *Roland Barthes by Roland Barthes*, which he was in the process of working on: 'It's all so good that frankly I'm going to find it extremely difficult to write the little book about myself which Seuil have asked me for.' In the letters which followed (of which there were many, but that does not mean much because Barthes wrote a lot of letters) and at our meetings (which were rarer), we always touched on other subjects. Perhaps he would have reproached me for transgressing, for entering a prohibited area which a handful of those close to him have taken it on themselves to guard zealously. Or perhaps he would write once again: 'It's all so good that . . .'

This book is therefore a biography, with all the risks that entails, and I cannot claim not to have been warned. It is a biography: that is, both a piece of historical research (and sometimes a piece of journalism) and the translation of an affinity. 'Every biography is a novel that dares not admit it,' Barthes wrote.[5] On this point, I disagree with him slightly: a novel is in fact a double adventure, in the sense that it is both a formal creation which works on language and at the same time a product of the imagination. However much interpretation it contains, a biography does not have this problem, because even if the life it relates is fictional, the history of that life is already written and the principal task of the biographer is to uncover this history and give an account of it. The account you are about to read is intended to be the story of a life in the full sense of the term, that is, to reiterate, the history of a *body* and what it has *produced*.

Roland Barthes was, on his own admission, a believer in the index card, and he described how his *Michelet par lui même* was born precisely from an almost chance ordering of these bits of paper.[6] 'I copied the phrases I liked, on whatever grounds, or which kept recurring, onto index cards, and by classifying these cards rather in the way one amuses oneself by playing a game of cards, I was bound to come up with a thematic structure.'

Twenty-one years later, writing for the same series the *Michelet* appeared in, but this time really a *Roland Barthes by Roland Barthes*, he published an example of one of these cards with notes on 'the stereotype' along with the following comment: 'Still warm, nothing is yet to be determined of its quality: stupid? dangerous? insignificant? worth keeping? to be thrown away? to be focused? to be protected?'[7]

Without wishing to indulge in pastiche, which I am not at all good at, I still could not resist jotting down my own notes on a card, accompanied by the same questions:

GRANDPARENTS

Paternal grandfather: Léon Barthes, official of the Midi Railway Company, from a family of notaries from Mazamet (Tarn). Grandmother's parents from Tarbes.

Maternal grandfather: Louis Binger, soldier, descendant of master glassmakers from the Alsace, grandmother from Lorraine, her parents the owners of a smelting works in Paris.

On his father's side, Catholic and from the south-west, on his mother's Protestant and from the east. He was to inherit the religion of his mother but choose the region of his father.

It could be that one of the grandfathers spoke Alsatian and the other Occitan: Barthes himself was never really interested in languages.

The grandfathers' silence: 'They had no part in language.'

Still warm, as can be seen, that is to say in its raw state.
Insignificant? Who knows. Stupid? Without a doubt at this stage.
Dangerous? To whom?
Worth keeping? To be thrown away? Rather to be focused. And protected, no doubt. To be developed.

The reader can rest assured that I shall not overuse this falsely parodic style and that even if I have also had to rely on numerous index cards to write this book, the reader will not see any of them. They will simply have served as a base on which to reconstruct a story. In his approach to signs, Barthes showed that he loved at least two things. Firstly neologisms, those made-up words which are like illegitimate children one has by language, and secondly etymology, which allowed him to cheat a bit sometimes with the arbitrary nature of the sign by restoring a lost sense to words. Thus, before embarking on this story, and history, of a life, I would like to remind you that etymologically the word 'history' is derived from a Greek word meaning 'inquiry'. This is how these pages should be read, as an attempt to reconstruct a journey. An inquiry into a man, a way of thinking, and also into a century, this century, since Roland Barthes's oeuvre is so deeply rooted in our time, in its conflicts, myths, and its systems of producing meaning. It is an attempt to collect together some 'biographemes', in the sense in which the ethnographer 'collects' the elements in his corpus from oral tradition.

Acknowledgements

I would like to thank all those who agreed to respond to my questions, either in person or by letter, or who have helped me in various ways in the course of my lengthy inquiries, in particular the following: Marc Avelot, Norbert Bensaïd, Fernand Bentolila, Abdallah Bounfour, Jean-Louis Bouttes, Michel Bouvard, Olivier Burgelin, Claude Courrouve, Michel Dalifard, Jean Daniel, Robert David, Daniel Defert, Bernard Dort, Jean-Paul Enthoven, Didier Eribon, Jacqueline Fournié, Max Genève, Françoise Giroud, Algirdas Greimas, Noura Kaddour, Jean-Claude Klein, Julia Kristeva, Hervé Landry, Jack Lang, Annette Lavers, Monique Lulin, François Mitterrand, Laurent Morelle, Edgar Morin, Violette Morin, Vincent Mouchez, François Moulonguet, Maurice Nadeau, François Neel, Josette Pacaly, Christian Parat, Georges Péninou, Philippe Rebeyrol, François Ricci, Jean-Loup Rivière, Alain Robbe-Grillet, Josyane Savigneau, Charles Singevin, Jean Sirinelli, Phillippe Sollers, Raphaël Sorin, Jacques Staes, Romaric Sulger-Büel, André Téchiné, Aimée Vigneron.

Finally, I would like to thank Monique Nemer and Françoise Verny for their help throughout this project.

1

A Ward of the Nation

Roland Gérard Barthes was born on 12 November 1915, at 107, Rue de la Bucaille in Cherbourg. His mother, Henriette Barthes, née Binger, from the Alsace, was twenty-two years old. His father, naval lieutenant Louis Barthes, was from Gascony, and was ten years older. Louis chose two of his naval colleagues as witnesses at the registration of his son's birth: Maurice Göerende, 'leading seaman gunner', and Pierre Duval, 'ordinary seaman', accompanied him to the town hall to sign the birth certificate. Thus it was under maritime auspices and in a naval town that Barthes came into the world, and into a household – comprising a sailor father and a non-working mother – which was far from well-off.

How important are families? What role does the family play in shaping an individual's personality? Before beginning to tell someone's life story, we may wonder where it starts. What is its point of departure? Is it a birth, a biological relationship? Does one's ancestry – this 'prehistory of the body'[1] – really have any great significance? I will assume that being born into a particular milieu and culture does have certain consequences and that these ramifications of the genealogical tree can help our understanding. Our understanding of what? Those minute reflexes of belonging which, when they are added up, help to shape a personality. And when, as in this case, the two branches of the family are so different, an incursion into genealogy becomes a necessary part of the journey.

Thus, by way of a preamble, here are two profiles: the first of an omnipresent maternal grandfather – present even in dictionaries and

history books; the second of an absent father – absent from the very
earliest days of childhood.

On his mother's side

Barthes's maternal grandfather, Louis Gustave Binger, was born in
Strasburg on 14 October 1856 (at the time the town was French,
coming under German control from 1870 to 1918) and he died in
1936 at Isle-Adam. He had what is usually known as a 'colonial
career' during which he made a far from negligible contribution to
our knowledge of West African geography.

In fact, for a long time the Niger and the Senegal rivers were
mistakenly thought to be one and cartographers attributed one
course to both rivers. It was not until after a reconnaissance
expedition in 1690 that La Courbe, inspector general of the colony
of Senegal, claimed that they were in fact two different rivers. But
the geographers remained unconvinced, and in 1707, in the maps of
Guillaume Delisle, the two river courses were once again merged.
After this they were separated, but in 1795, on the eve of his first
expedition, Mungo Park believed that the Niger flowed into the
Congo. When he died on his second expedition in 1805, the Niger
had still not revealed its secret. In 1817, James Riby claimed that it
flowed into the Gulf of Guinea and this intuition was confirmed by
Richard Lander's voyage in 1830. However, the river's source was
still undiscovered, while the exact course of another river, the Volta,
was also a mystery.

On 3 September 1887, naval infantry captain Binger, who had
formerly been aide-de-camp to Louis Faidherbe, had served in
Senegal and was regarded as having a sound knowledge of Africa,
crossed the Niger at Bamako and set off alone on a long journey of
exploration. The funds for his expedition had been provided by the
Foreign Office, thanks to the support of Faidherbe but against the
advice of the naval minister, from whom he normally took his
orders. He travelled through Sikasso, where he was received by the
almamy Samory. The latter was a self-proclaimed religious leader
and also a war chief fighting a very effective campaign against the
invading French. At the time, he was laying siege to the town. The
main part of Binger's African career was to unfold in the shadow of
the epic of this Malinké chief, whose campaign against the colonial
troops lasted from 1883 to 1898. The young officer spent several
weeks with him, delivered a letter from Gallieni (at the time

governor of the French Sudan), and then continued his journey towards Kong, reaching it on 10 February 1888. Leaving politics aside, he turned his attention once again to exploring, and was able to prove that the mountains of Kong did not exist. This discovery shed light on the course of the Volta. He pushed on to Ouagadougou, where he was received by Sanom, the Moro Naba (the Mossi emperor), then headed back south. On 5 January 1889 he arrived back in Kong where, exhausted after his long and difficult journey, he collapsed tearfully into the arms of Marcel Treich-Laplène, a young sales representative for the Verdier firm of La Rochelle and a French resident of Grand-Bassam. The two men travelled on to the Ivory Coast together, reaching Grand-Bassam on 20 March 1889. Binger was thirty-three years old and would live for another forty-seven years. Treich-Laplène was twenty and would be dead the following year. Both men gave their names to towns on the Ivory Coast – Treich-Ville and Bingerville respectively.

Binger then returned to France, where the following year he published a two-volume account of his explorations, *Du Niger au golfe de Guinée par le pays de Kong et le Mossi*.[2] Maurice Delafosse, himself a colonial administrator and the author of reference works on the French Sudan, commented in 1912: 'Not only did he reconnoitre the upper basin of the Volta and the previously unexplored western part of the Niger loop . . . but he brought back such a plentiful and accurate mass of information, and such precisely detailed itineraries, that today there are still things to be learnt from reading his account of his journey.'[3]

It is true that Binger took an interest in everything. He had his own theory about the origin of the name of the Soninké people ('supporter of the Sonni') and he studied the history of the Dioula tribe – according to Delafosse he was 'the first person to have studied them and the person who knows most about them'. He provided extremely precise descriptions of the places he visited, which is why contemporary Africanists so often quote him on points of detail. In short, he was a typical example of those 'explorers' of the last century, of the dawn of colonization, and it was by this term – 'the explorer' – that Roland Barthes later referred to his grandfather when talking about him with friends. A more contemporary view is that of the historian Yves Person, a Samory expert. He pays tribute to Binger's sense of observation and precision, while at the same time pointing out Binger's prejudices and his lack of objectivity. In short, he considers Binger to have been slightly racist.

But in 1889, when Binger returned to France, his book was given a very different reception. The popular press published a map of his journey and the opening of this window on previously unknown territories aroused commercial appetites. The general feeling was that there were good business opportunities to be had over there, and Binger was the first to be convinced of it. Was he already thinking of leaving the army at this point? Louis Faidherbe, his former patron, had just died and he had lost his support in high circles. The African policy he was attempting to promote raised scarcely a ripple of response from the corridors of power.

At the time, of course, France was celebrating the first centenary of the French revolution or *the* centenary as it was then known. In May, the Eiffel tower had been inaugurated, an event which had at first caused some controversy. Nevertheless, within three months it had attracted two million visitors. For its part, the Great Universal Exhibition was to attract close to fifty million visitors. In this atmosphere of republican celebration, Binger met a beautiful, elegant young woman from the Lorraine, whose parents owned a smelting works in Paris. Noémie Élise Georgette Lepet had been born in 1872, and was therefore sixteen years his junior. He married Noémie and in 1891 a son, Philippe, was born.

Binger went back to Africa for several months, but returned home to France in 1892, uncertain what to do about his future. He considered leaving the army and going into business. Indeed, his knowledge of the region gave him access to groups who dreamt of extending economic imperialism towards the Gulf of Guinea. But, in March 1893 Delcassé decided to create the colony of the Ivory Coast and he needed a governor capable of taking this new territory in hand. On 20 March he appointed Binger to the post, and Binger promptly resigned from the army. He was to serve as civil governor of the Ivory Coast from 1893 to 1896. For the time being, however, he was in no hurry to take up his post: Noémie was pregnant again, and on 18 July 1893 she gave birth to a daughter, who was baptized Henriette. Her father, 'officier de la Légion d'honneur et de l'instruction publique' and governor of the Ivory Coast, as stated on the civil register of Chennevières-sur-Marne, registered her birth with the mayor, Jules Viéjo, in the presence of two witnesses, Claude Pierre Bouquet, gardener, and Joseph Désiré Guillemin, gentleman landowner. In this small village east of Paris, Commander Binger was regarded as a hero of colonization, an adventurer who had journeyed to the furthest frontiers of the empire.

However, the genuine popularity of the colonial adventure among the general public was being overshadowed by events closer to home.

For over a year, in fact, the country had been living under the threat of anarchist terrorism. Profoundly influenced by the Russian nihilists, the French movement had begun to engage in direct individual action. On 11 March 1892, Ravachol had planted a bomb at 136, Boulevard Saint-Germain, the block of flats where the president of the Crown Court lived. On 15 March, the Lobau barracks had been blown up, and on 27 March a block of flats in the Rue de Clichy where Bulot, the state prosecutor lived, was hit. Ravachol was finally arrested in the Very restaurant on the Boulevard Magenta, where he had been recognized and denounced by the waiter. His sensational trial began on 26 April, surrounded by a mass of security precautions. On the eve of the trial, a bomb went off in the Very restaurant in revenge for his arrest. Ravachol was sentenced to death and his execution set for 11 July 1892 at Montbrison. On the day of his execution, having refused the ministrations of a priest ('I don't give a damn about your Christ, don't show him to me or I'll spit on him'), he mounted the scaffold singing a song from *Père Duchêne*, the very revolutionary broadsheet which, sixty years later, Roland Barthes was to quote in the introduction to *Le Degré zéro de l'écriture* (*Writing Degree Zero*):

> Si tu veux être heurex, nom de Dieu!
> Pends ton proprietaire
> Coupe les curés en deux, nom de Dieu!
> Fous les églises par terre, Sang-Dieu!
> Et l'bon Dieu dans la merde, nom de Dieu
> Et l'bon Dieu dans la merde.
>
> (If you want to be happy,
> Then bloody well hang your landlord!
> Chop up the bloody clergy!
> Burn down the bloody churches!
> And throw God in the shit!
> Throw God in the shit!)

Then Ravachol toppled over, his final cry interrupted by the guillotine, 'Long live the re-'. Probably he meant 'the revolution' or the 'rebellion', but in the telegram which the prefect sent to the chancellor after the execution, his cry was turned into 'Long live the republic!':

Justice was done this morning at 4.05 a.m. without any incidents or demonstrations. The condemned man was woken at 3.40 a.m. He refused

the ministrations of the chaplain, declaring that he had nothing to confess.
Although at first pale and trembling, he tried to affect cynicism in front of
me. At the foot of the scaffold in the minutes preceding the execution, he
appeared exasperated. In a hoarse voice, he sang several verses of a
blasphemous and revoltingly obscene nature. He did not mention the
word anarchy and, with his head on the block, the final words he cried
were, 'Long live the republic'. Absolute calm has reigned without incident
in the town. Report to follow.

On 20 July 1893, two days after the birth of his daughter,
Governor Binger took leave of his family and boarded the sloop
Capitaine Ménard in Bordeaux. He arrived in Bassam at the
beginning of August. His first visit was relatively short: nine months
later, on 5 May 1894, he set sail for France again, pleading ill health,
and went to spend his leave on his property at Chennevières. Despite
the fact that during the three years of his posting he was very often
resident in France, Binger was nevertheless considered a 'good
administrator' who promoted the growth of resources in the territory.
In particular he increased customs revenue, supported economic
imperialism and broke with his former comrades in the army. He
was very soon regarded as the promoter of economic interests,
opposed to the military occupation which, in his view, was damaging
to commerce. At the end of 1895, he was back at Chennevières and
everyone wondered if he would take up his post again. Indeed, he
tried to stay on in France, attempting to make contacts and win
support, but on encountering a certain amount of hostility he
decided at the beginning of 1896 to ask for retirement.

By now he was forty years old and no doubt envisaged a new
career for himself in business: he had solid connections and, in
regard to Africa, undeniable expertise. By staying in France, he knew
that whoever replaced him in Bassam would maintain the civil
tradition that he himself had defended, which would make his task
easier were he to leave public office to enter business.

However, there was a change of government, and on 29 April
1896 André Lebon became Minister for Colonial Affairs. One of his
first decisions was to appoint Binger Director of African Affairs. This
meant that among the members of the Cabinet, those who favoured
commercial exploitation of the Ivory Coast outnumbered the
supporters of military occupation: the arms trade would no longer
be threatened.

Binger remained in his post longer than the Minister who
appointed him. Lebon left office in June 1898, after elections in
which the question of the review of the Dreyfus trial played a major

part. Esterhazy had been acquitted in January, and France was divided over the affair. But henceforth Binger's position remained unshakeable and he ensured that there was no change in policy. Henriette Binger was six years old.

On his father's side

It is time to go back sixteen years, to 28 February 1883, when Louis Barthes was born in Marmande, in the Lot-et-Garonne. His ancestry was much less marked by exoticism than that of his future wife, Henriette Binger. His father, Léon Joseph Barthes, was an inspector for the Midi regional railway company. Léon's mother, Berthe de Lapalu, Roland's paternal grandmother, was completely different from his maternal grandmother, Noémie Binger. As Barthes was to comment later, 'One was good-looking, a Parisienne. The other was good, a provincial: steeped in bourgeoisie – not in nobility, from which she was nevertheless descended.'[4]

Born in Tarbes, Berthe followed her husband to the various towns in the south-west of France where his work took him. If Noémie was the star of the salons, Berthe, in contrast, was the star of the kitchen: she shone at making pickles, preserves and pastries. Later, looking back, Barthes provided the following description of his grand-parents:

> My class origins are, I think, bourgeois. I have provided the following list of my four grandparents' origins so that you can judge for yourselves (which is what the Vichy authorities did during the Nazi occupation to determine how much Jewish blood an individual had). My paternal grandfather, who worked as an inspector for the Midi railway company, was descended from a line of notaries who had settled in a small town in the Tarn (Mazamet, I believe). My paternal grandmother's family were the impoverished descendants of provincial nobility (from the region of Tarbes). My maternal grandfather came from the Alsace, from a family of master glassmakers. As for my maternal grandmother, the only wealthy member of this constellation, her parents were from the Lorraine and they owned a small smelting works in Paris.[5]

Léon (Barthes), Berthe (de Lapalu), Louis (Binger) and Noémie (Lepet): they are all there. Léon and Berthe had a son called Louis, Roland's father, a child of the south-west and a Catholic, as one would expect. Louis and Noémie had a daughter called Henriette,

Roland's mother, who was born near Paris but nevertheless brought up in the Protestant faith of her Alsace ancestors.

Louis Barthes had hardly any schooling and began his naval career at a very early age. At first it seemed as if piecing together his career would be an impossible task, since the central office of the military archives in Pau replied to my request by stating that they were not allowed to release any information of the kind I was looking for. Then by chance, several days later, the naval archive department (which I had written to simultaneously) sent me what the military archives in Pau had refused to release: an extract from Louis Barthes's enrolment certificate. On this certificate the various stages of his career had been carefully noted. An additional help was the report on Louis's death, which a rear-admiral had enclosed. Contradictory responses from the different military authorities can sometimes be of use to the researcher.

On 10 January 1903, at the age of twenty, Louis embarked on the steamship *Amiral Courbet* as an apprentice seaman for a long cruise of two months and twenty-four days. Then he spent twelve months in the port of Toulon as an ordinary seaman. On 26 May he set sail again, but this time he served before the mast on the steamship *Cordillère*, which took him, after a month and a half's voyage, to Bordeaux. From 9 October 1905 to 22 September 1906, he was out of work again. Then he served for ten days as lieutenant on the *Vendée*. When he was mobilized the military authorities discounted both this voyage and the following five months he spent on the same boat, which took him to Dunkirk, as 'coastal navigation'. His career continued its erratic course: from 10 January 1903 to 13 February 1913, a period of ten years and thirty-three days, he spent just over seven years at sea on different steamships (the *Bretagne*, *Montréal*, *Québec*, *Ferdinand de Lesseps*, *Mexico* . . .).

In 1909 he was in Fort-de-France but the rest of the time he was laid up in Le Havre. In 1913, according to his naval enrolment record, he was a 'captain of ocean-going ship first class' and was recruited as a 'reserve lieutenant'. During these four years, he had crossed the Atlantic to Quebec as lieutenant on a steamship, and during the crossing had met a young passenger, Henriette Binger. She was on her way to visit her brother Philippe, who had emigrated to Canada to make his fortune. Henriette and Louis fell in love at first sight and were married very soon afterwards, despite Noémie's disapproval. She regarded the marriage as a mismatch: her new son-in-law's family was not wealthy and the position he held was lowly.

Thus on 12 November 1915 at 107, Rue de la Bucaille in

Cherbourg, Roland Gérard Barthes was born. Roland was not even a year old when his father, in command of the patrol boat *Montaigne*, died in combat in the North Sea. According to naval records, the patrol boat was in fact a small converted trawler armed with a 57 gun. On 27 October 1916, in open sea off Cape Gris-Nez, the *Montaigne* was attacked by five German destroyers. Its single gun was put out of action almost as soon as the attack began and, according to the report, 'its firepower was destroyed by enemy fire at point blank range.' Louis Barthes was mortally wounded during the first few minutes of the attack. According to the survivors, 'he used his last reserves of strength to command the manoeuvres the situation demanded.' He was posthumously commended for bravery and made a Chevalier de la Légion d'Honneur. Thus Henriette found herself a war widow and Roland found himself a ward of the nation – or almost. He was not officially 'adopted by the state' until 30 November 1925, after a decision had been made by the civil court in Bayonne.

Of course, it is a truism to say that for a very young boy the death of his father is an event which is bound to leave its mark. But Barthes hardly ever alluded to his father's disappearance, and on the rare occasions when he did it was always in passing. For example, he recounts how embarrassed he felt when, in the fourth form at Louis-Le-Grand Lycée, his French teacher ('a little old man, a socialist, a nationalist'[6]) decided to list on the blackboard all the relatives of his pupils who had 'fallen on the field of honour'. There were uncles and cousins, but the only one who could lay claim to a dead father was the young Barthes: 'Yet once the blackboard was erased, nothing was left of this proclaimed mourning – except, in real life, which proclaims nothing, which is always silent, the figure of a home socially adrift: no father to kill, no family to hate, no milieu to reject: great Oedipal frustration!'[7]

Thus if we are to believe Barthes, the absence of his father turned his home into a place without conflict, hate or struggle. As we shall see, as an adolescent he planned to write a novel in which, in contrast to reality, his family was transformed into the centre of a violent conflict.

Bayonne

After Louis's death, Henriette moved back down south to live with his family. The fact that she did not go back to live with her own mother may indicate that, even at this stage, they were not close. She settled in Bayonne, where Roland's paternal grandmother, Berthe Barthes, and his aunt Alice lived. Their house on the corner of the Allées Paulmy and the Avenue de la Légion-Tchèque was 'a large house with a garden that had formally been a rope factory'.[8] Nowadays 'La Maison Lanne', as it was called, no longer exists. As Barthes was to write, with partly justified scorn, the house was 'swept away by the housing projects of Bayonne'[9] and replaced by a six-storey block, the 'Résidence Longchamp', which is indistinguishable from dozens of others of its kind.

The town of Bayonne grew up where the Adour and the Nive rivers meet. In the Middle Ages it was an important port. Wine, honey and leather were exported to Flanders and to England in return for imports of cloth, tin and oils. Then it became a fortified town, with walls designed by the architect Vauban. By the beginning of this century, it had still not outgrown this fortified enclosure. Indeed, from 27,416 inhabitants in 1876, by 1911 the population had grown by only around 400 to 27,886 inhabitants. Nevertheless, the new railway line put Paris only a fifteen-hour journey away and gave new impetus to local industry. After 1881, ironworks were set up to produce railway tracks using coal imported from Wales and ore from Biscaye. However, local financiers were unwilling to support these new ventures, preferring to invest their money where they were assured of a return, in the pine forests of the Landes or in property. When the Barthes family settled in Bayonne, the port was in full decline.

The Allées Paulmy, a magnificent esplanade which ran alongside the fortified walls down to the quayside, dated from the eighteenth century. On the other side of the embankment, behind Vauban's ramparts, lay the cobbled streets of the old town. These streets around the Cathedral of Sainte Marie – the Rue de la Salie, the Rue de la Vieille-Boucherie, the Rue Tour-de-Sault, the Rue du Port-Neuf – formed the heart of the town and they fascinated the young Roland Barthes, a fascination they were to exercise on him throughout his life: 'Bayonne, Bayonne, the perfect city: riverain, aerated with sonorous suburbs (Mouserolles, Marrac, Lachepaillet, Beyris), yet immured, fictive: Proust, Balzac, Plassans. Primordial image-hoard of childhood: the province-as-spectacle, History-as-odour, the bourgeoisie-as-discourse.'[10] If we ignore here the concepts which have been added retrospectively by Barthes the adult (province, history, bourgeoisie) and focus on the primary perceptions (spectacle, smells, discourse), these remarks can be read as summarizing the sensory impressions of Barthes the child: Bayonne is a something which moves, smells, chatters.

He went to primary school in the Arènes district behind the Allées Paulmy, an area full of the villas of the well-to-do. In the evenings he would often walk the long way home along the Allées Marines, by the banks of the river Adour. During these long walks, as he daydreamed among the trees, he was aware that there lurked what he later described as 'the sexuality of public gardens, of parks'.[11] He was drawn to the river and always remained faithful to his memory of it.

Henriette and Roland lived in the Marrac district, which was a new district quite a distance from the centre. The building sites of the numerous houses under construction provided wonderful playgrounds for the children of the area. Nevertheless, the young Roland spent a great deal more of his time at his grandmother's house, and it was this house on the Allées Paulmy that he was to remember most. His aunt Alice was a piano teacher and she gave him his first piano lessons. The house echoed to the sound of scales, as one pupil followed another. Between lessons, Roland used to clamber up on to the piano stool and try to decipher the music. According to him, he was producing little compositions for the piano long before he learnt how to write. But the thing he remembered most about the house where he spent his childhood – and later most of his school holidays – was the garden:

> That house was something of an ecological wonder: anything but large, set on one side of a considerable garden, it looked like a toy model (the folded grey of its shutters merely reinforced this impression). With the modesty of a chalet, yet there was one door after another, and French windows, and outside staircases, like a castle in a story. The garden, though continuous, was arranged in three symbolically different spaces (and to cross the boundary of each space was a significant action). You crossed the first garden to reach the house: this was the 'worldly' garden, down which, taking tiny steps, pausing often, you accompanied the ladies of Bayonne to the gate. The garden in front of the house itself consisted of narrow paths curving around twin lawns; in it grew roses, hydrangeas (that awkward flower of the southwest of France), carpet grass, rhubarb, kitchen herbs in old crates, a big magnolia whose white flowers bloomed on a level with the upstairs bedrooms; here in this garden, undaunted under their mosquito netting, the B[arthes] ladies, each summer, settled into canvas chairs with their elaborate knitting. At the far end, the third garden, except for a tiny orchard of peach trees and raspberry bushes, was undefined, sometimes fallow, sometimes planted with vegetables that

needed no tending; you didn't go there much, and only down the centre
path.[12]

However, the strongest feeling he experienced as a child was not,
if we are to believe him, these sensations, these secret emotions, but
something else: boredom, a feeling which was always ready to
surface. 'As a child I was often and intensely bored,' he was later to
write, adding the following remark which, from a man who was
always so aware of etymology, may seem rather strange: 'Might
boredom be my form of hysteria?'[13] *Hysteria*, from the Greek word
Hustera, or uterus: it was a word which often came up in his speech
or in his writing, but more often than not it was applied to other
people, to aspects of their behaviour he did not approve of. Why
would he liken his childhood fits of boredom – which resurfaced not
only during the various official meetings, panel discussions and
committees that his position obliged him to attend, but also when he
was among strangers at parties and during group amusements[14] – to
what in psychoanalytic terms is considered a neurosis and in lay
terms a typically feminine affliction?

It is very difficult – or rather only too easy – to say what he meant
by hysteria, but we must take this man of words at his word: the use
of the word *hysteria* can hardly be accidental. In fact, both the town
of Bayonne and the house 'La Maison Lanne', where he spent his
childhood and his holidays as an adolescent, were a feminine
universe. His mother, his aunt and his grandmother all kept a careful
watch on the young Roland, and he was surrounded by female
affection. One day, for example, while he was playing with his
school friends on a building site in the Marrac district, he got
trapped in a hole. His friends, who had all managed to get out of the
hole, made fun of his plight. His mother, alerted by their cries,
rushed over and rescued him. Then she carried him off in her arms
'far away from the other children – against them'.[15]

When the fine weather began he would be taken to the beach in
the 'baladeuse', an open carriage attached to the white tram which
travelled between Bayonne and Biarritz: 'Today both tramway and
open carriage have ceased to exist, and the journey from Biarritz is
anything but a pleasure.' These are memories of a happy childhood,
a childhood that left him with a strong sense of belonging to the
south-west of France. He always felt that he was Basque or Gascon,
never Parisian, and still less, of course, Norman. This sense of
belonging was a matter of choice not chance. It was not something
imposed on him by an accident of birth, a family move or by the

war: throughout his life the accent of the south-west was to act as a
kind of catalyst for his childhood memories. As he wrote:

> Most probably because it was the intonation model of my early
> childhood. For me, the gascon accent (in its broadest sense) has a very
> different resonance to the other southern accent – the accent of the
> eastern, Mediterranean coast. The accent of the south-east has become
> well established in the France of today, promoted by a whole folklore: the
> cinema (Raimu, Fernandel), advertising (oil, lemons) and tourism. The
> accent of the south-west, which is heavier, not so lilting, does not have the
> same connotations of modernity. Its only claim to fame is that it is always
> heard in interviews with rugby players.[16]

These lines have an almost nationalistic ring to them. They were
written in July 1977 for the Communist daily *L'Humanité*, which
was publishing work by writers from different regions.

But this feeling of belonging to the south-west was not strictly
restricted to an accent – which, in any case, Barthes did not have.
There were other images engraved in his memory, for instance of the
streets of Bayonne, of the Sunday mornings after Mass when the
ladies of the town would go to buy cakes in a shop in the town
centre. But what he remembered most about this region in the
foothills of the Pyrenees was the quality of its light. It was a misty,
rain-filled light with a strangely green quality to it, considering it lies
on the same latitude as the Var. In other words, there was a certain
quality of life in the south-west that made it very different from life
in the north.

It is interesting to compare Barthes's somewhat idealized accounts
of this 'ideal town' with those of a professional writer. Barthes
finished his last year at school in Bayonne in June 1924, and it was
about the same period, just before Barthes left the town, that two
famous travellers, John Dos Passos and Ernest Hemingway, stopped
in the town en route to the Pamplona fiestas. In *The Sun Also Rises*
Hemingway gives the following description of Bayonne:

> Bayonne is a nice town. It is like a very clean Spanish town and it is on a
> big river. Already, so early in the morning, it was very hot on the bridge
> across the river. We worked out on the bridge and then took a walk
> through the town . . . We went into the street again and took a look at the
> cathedral. Cohn made some remark about it being a very good example of
> something or other, I forgot what. It seemed like a nice cathedral, nice and
> dim, like Spanish churches . . . There were pigeons out in the square and

the horses were a yellow, sunbaked colour, and I did not want to leave the café.[17]

Was it Hemingway's passion for Spain that made him see Bayonne, even before he had reached the border, as a Spanish town? Why did Barthes never mention the town's Iberian character? Just as he seems to have forgotten the death of his father, when for other sons – for instance Jean-Paul Sartre in *Les Mots* (*Words*) – it was a significant event, he seems to have forgotten that the cultural make-up of his favourite region is determined by the fact that it straddles a frontier. It is neither French nor Spanish but Basque, and it is Basque culture which gives the region its predominant characteristics. However, it is also true that the women who brought him up were not Basque and not all of them were from the south-west. His grandmother and aunt were from the Occitan and his mother from the east. The young Roland was only 'Bayonnais' by virtue of living there at the time. Later in his life he regarded himself as such out of choice and nostalgia.

Nevertheless, up to the age of nine he was a hundred per cent 'Bayonnais', though perhaps a little shyer and more withdrawn than the other boys. He was, after all, a 'ward of the nation', with all the connotations of poverty and wretchedness that this expression carried with it: during the postwar period it was virtually a social category. But even though he was shy and withdrawn, he still played the same games in the same places as other children his age. The capital, Paris, which was later to become the centre of his professional life, the starting point for the reputation he would later build, was at that time a completely foreign universe to him. Once a year during the summer holidays Henriette would take her son to Paris, where his other grandmother, Noémie, lived. A horse-drawn cab would collect the travellers and take them to Bayonne station, where they would take the night train to Paris. From 1924 onwards, Paris, the place they went for holidays, was to become their place of residence. Their journeys were reversed, and at Christmas, Easter and in the summer – indeed, whenever they could – they would travel down to the South.

Barthes's childhood was drawing to an end. Much later, in an interview with Jacques Chancel for the radio station France-Inter[18] he drew up the following balance sheet of his childhood:

I was happy because I was surrounded by affection and in this extremely important respect I had, in a sense, everything I could wish for. But at the same time my childhood and my youth were not easy. This is not a privilege, or a mark of distinction or specialness, but as you know I came from what would be called the liberal bourgeoisie, but from a bourgeois family which was poor, which had fallen on hard times ... My mother brought me up in material, in financial, circumstances which, to be perfectly frank, were extremely difficult. I think this also marked my childhood.

Then he went on to talk about the boredom and loneliness he had experienced as a child: 'Actually, I had no real social context in my childhood and adolescence, in the sense that the only person I was really attached to was my mother. She was my home and I did not have any social milieu. As a result, I experienced a certain degree of loneliness.'

His childhood was about to end and this break, this rupture, corresponded to the fundamental geographical change which took place when he moved from the provinces to Paris. Although he was to come to love Paris and to feel very much at home there, Bayonne would remain the trigger for his childhood memories and the south-west the symbol of a kind of paradise lost.

2

A Little Gentleman

Henriette had decided to leave Bayonne. Roland's days at the primary school in Arènes and his daily walks along the banks of the Adour were over. In 1924, he moved to Paris, and started school at the Lycée Montaigne, in the sixth arrondissement behind the Luxembourg Gardens. Eventually this park came to be one of the centres of his life. He crossed it four times a day, in the morning and the evening, and it also served as a playground for him and his friends. Their favourite game was prisoner's base, a team game which remained one of his favourites. Looking back on this game as an adult, he was also, as was often the case, to give this memory a theoretical gloss:

> When I used to play prisoner's base in the Luxembourg, what I liked best was not provoking the other team and boldly exposing myself to their right to take me prisoner; what I liked best was to free the prisoners – the effect of which was to put both teams back into circulation: the game started all over again. In the great game of the powers of speech, we also play prisoner's base [on joue aussi aux barres]: one language has only temporary rights over another [un langage n'a barre sur les autres que temporairement]; all it takes is for a third language to appear from the ranks for the assailant to be forced to retreat.[1]

'Jouer aux barres, avoir barre sur quelqu'un', play prisoner's base, have a hold over someone – here, as always, Barthes's taste for etymologies comes into play, etymologies which are sometimes, as in this case, rough approximations. A predisposition which meant he always looked in the origins of words for an underlying meaning, a superimposition, and which made him see his childhood game as the prefiguration of an analysis of discourse. One may suspect such an analogical mode of thinking of being essentially more literary than theoretical.

Schooldays

Barthes stayed at the Lycée Montaigne until he finished the third form in 1930, and he lived successively in the Rue Jacob, Rue Bonaparte, Rue Mazarine, Rue Jacques-Callot, and Rue de Seine. The family never moved outside St-Germain-des-Près which, at the time, as Barthes was later to comment, was like a neighbourhood in a small town. During the school holidays, he went back to Bayonne to visit his grandmother and aunt Alice in the house on the Allées Paulmy. All traces of the years Barthes spent at the lycée have disappeared. During the Second World War, the school was commandeered by the German army to serve as its staff head-quarters and all its archives appear to have been removed in order to make more space. The only thing we know about this period is that, in the third form, his French teacher was the highly distinguished Grandsaignes d'Hauterive, who would later publish a *Dictionnaire d'ancien français* and a *Pessimisme de la Rochefoucauld*. However, the things the young Barthes most remembered him for were his elegance, his horn-rimmed pince-nez and his division of the class into clans, each with its own chief. He would organize competitions between the clans about the Greek aorists, and later Barthes would ask himself, 'Why are old teachers such good *conductors* of memory?'[2]

When Roland was fourteen, he left the Lycée Montaigne. A few years previously, Henriette had met an artist and ceramist, André Salzedo, who lived in the Landes near Bayonne at Saint-Martin-de-Hinx. On 11 April 1927, at the age of 34, she gave birth to her second child, Michel Salzedo, Roland's half-brother, at Capbreton (which was then a small fishing village seventeen kilometres north of Bayonne). When André went to register the birth of the child at the town hall, he got the place and date of birth of the mother wrong (Paris instead of Chennevières and 8 July 1894 rather than 18 July 1893). Were his errors the result of haste or did they reveal a lack of interest? After the birth of her baby, Henriette returned to the Rue Jacques-Callot, in Paris.

Here we come up against our first problem of interpretation. Faced with several different interpretations, the only course open to the biographer is to include them all, particularly since they are all of equal interest and significance. On the one hand, we have Barthes's own version of events, as pieced together from the accounts of his friends at the time. In this version, Henriette's 'misdemeanour', the fact that she had 'stepped out of line' and gone against the conventions of bourgeois respectability, was taken very badly by the family, above all by her own family. Noémie, Barthes's grand-mother, refused to accept such an infringement of respectable moral standards and decided to forbid her daughter ever to set foot in her house again.

This reaction seems all the more surprising given that Noémie herself had led a life which, by the standards of her time, could hardly be called conventional. Her marriage to Louis Binger had been shortlived and had ended in divorce. She had then remarried; her new husband was a philosophy teacher at the Lycée Saint-Barbe, a socialist and a follower of Jean Jaurès.

Noémie Binger, now Noémie Révelin, was rich and she lived in a magnificent set of apartments in the Place de Panthéon, where she presided over a glamorous and renowned salon: the poet Paul Valéry, the politician Léon Blum, the nuclear physicist Paul Langevin, Valéry's great friend, the philosopher Léon Brunschvicg, Charles Seignobos, and the art historian Charles Focillon were all frequent visitors. But Madame Révelin refused to give her daughter any form of help. While she lived in luxury in the Place du Panthéon, several hundred metres away Henriette struggled to survive in the direst of financial straits.

Henriette took up bookbinding and with great difficulty made just enough money to supplement the meagre war widow's pension she received. This period was to leave the young Roland bitter, and his feelings of bitterness remained with him throughout his life. All his friends could sense a kind of aggression, resentment or bitterness in the ironic way he would always refer to his grandmother:[3] he never forgave her for abandoning Henriette to such destitution. He also never forgot these experiences of hardship and shame and they led him to develop a deep sense of solidarity with the poor. It is this sense of solidarity which in part explains the political positions he was later to adopt.

This is the first scenario, the story according to Barthes, the one he told various friends. The convergences between their different accounts validates Barthes's story on at least one count: even if it is impossible to assert that his is the 'true' version of events – or at least that it has a certain truth – then at the very least, since all his friends give the same version, this must be the version he believed or wanted to believe.

But there is another, perhaps less bourgeois scenario told by Michel Salzedo, Roland's half-brother. In his version, Noémie Révelin could not bear her daughter quite simply because she was jealous of her. Henriette's very presence, her youth and beauty, reminded Noémie of her age, and she did not want to grow old. She wanted to shine as the eternally youthful star of her salon in the Place du Panthéon. In addition, Noémie had had another son by her second marriage, who was thus Henriette's half-brother, but the same age as Roland. Since he was not as bright or as academically successful as Roland, her son came off very badly in comparison with her grandson. This would explain why Noémie showed so little liking for her grandson, who was only allowed to visit her once a year, and why she preferred his half-brother, Michel Salzedo, who was allowed to visit her much more often. According to this 'story', which is very different from the first, it was not Noémie Révelin but the Barthes family in Bayonne who took such exception to the birth of Roland's half-brother and spurned their daughter-in-law. This second version is supported by Philippe Rebeyrol, Barthes's lifelong friend. Rebeyrol points out that it was after Michel was born that Henriette began renting a house for the summer in the Landes close to Bayonne, at Capbreton or Biscarosse, so that Roland could spend a few weeks with his grandmother and aunt before rejoining her and Michel for the rest of the holidays. But she herself never visited the Allées Paulmy again, as if she had been forbidden to do so.

Thus we have two scenarios on which it is difficult to pronounce judgement, even if the second one does seem more plausible. As has been seen, well before her 'transgression' Henriette and her mother did not appear to be on very close terms. But why opt for either one version or the other? In these two different versions of the same situation all the ambiguity of the relationships between different members of a family which has been divided, turned upside down by divorces, deaths, half-brothers and second marriages is played out. Above all, they show how the child, the young Roland, must have imagined the situation as he was pulled this way and that between his 'women': his mother, his two grandmothers, his aunt. No doubt he was more emotionally attached to Bayonne, to the garden, to the piano, to his earlier childhood memories than to the salon in the Place du Panthéon. So perhaps he constructed for himself a version of events that fitted his emotional preferences. Besides, in terms of their consequences, the two accounts can hardly be said to differ much. Between these two versions of the same events there lies, in some sense, part of Roland's apprenticeship, his initiation into the taboos of the bourgeoisie.

In the same year of 1930 Roland began to develop a taste for the theatre. 'I used to go to regularly to the Mathurins and the Atelier to see shows by Pitoëff and Dullin.'[4] This sounds like a typical reminiscence from a comfortable childhood, since at the time the theatre was even less accessible to most people than it is now. Nevertheless, according to him during this same period he was living in a state of near misery:

> Simply this, that my childhood and adolescence were spent in poverty. That there was often no food in the home. That we had to go and buy a bit of pâté or a few potatoes at a little grocery on the rue de Seine, and this would be all we'd have to eat. Life was actually lived to the rhythm of the first of the month, when the rent was due. And I had before me the daily spectacle of my mother working hard at bookbinding, a job for which she was absolutely unsuited . . . I remember for example, the small crisis at the start of each school year. I didn't have the proper clothes. No money for school supplies. No money to pay for schoolbooks. It's the small things, you see, that mark you for a long time, that make you extravagant later on.[5]

He also discusses this in *Roland Barthes by Roland Barthes*, where he relates how problematic shoes, schoolbooks and even food were.[6] There was a marked contrast between the Barthes's standard of living and that of their grandmother, Noémie Révelin, in her home in the Place du Panthéon. The first scenario, Roland's version, resurfaces here as if he still harboured a grudge.

For several years to follow, however, the calm life of the Barthes household was interrrupted only by the stormy relationship between Henriette and André Salzedo: Salzedo was already married and was never to live with Henriette. The two brothers went to school, while their mother rebound old books. They had a cat at home (and always would), and on Sundays they went to Isle-Adam, where their grandfather Louis Binger lived until his death in 1936. They would spend the summer holidays in the Landes, and Roland would go to stay for part of the time with his grandmother and aunt in Bayonne. In the summer, practically the whole family was to be found in this small corner of the south-west: grandmother and aunt at Bayonne, of course, Henriette and her children at their holiday home nearby, but also their grandmother Noémie at Hendaye, where she had a villa on the coast. She only lent this villa to her daughter once, during the war, fearing that an empty house might be requisitioned. Roland was twelve years older than his brother Michel. Although this gap was to become less significant as they grew older, when he was fourteen or fifteen it seemed immense. Michel was almost completely absent from Roland's adolescence. Roland had his own games, his own friends and his own intellectual concerns.

From 1930 to 1934, from the fourth form to his sixth-form philosophy class, Roland attended the Lycée Louis-le-Grand, which had its entrance in the Rue Saint-Jacques, just behind the Sorbonne and three hundred metres away from his grandmother's home. The Lycée was a school for the children of the privileged classes, the future elite. With him went his classmate Philippe Rebeyrol, who had also been a pupil at the Lycée Montaigne the year before. The two soon became friends, and Rebeyrol remembers Barthes at the time as a shy and reserved boy, prone to long silences, someone whose genuine poverty – of which Rebeyrol only gradually became aware, since his friend was extremely reticent about it – was to have a lifelong effect on him.

In order to feed her children Madame Barthes worked as a bookbinder, as we have seen, but the end of the month was always a struggle. For many years Roland would remember the days when his mother used to send him shopping with only a little money, or none at all, and he would have to mutter somewhat shamefacedly to the shopkeepers, 'Mother will pay later.' However, the family had more than financial problems; they also, as Philippe Rebeyrol recalls, had moral ones. Henriette Barthes and André Salzedo would never live together, and relations between them were always strained, at least according to Philippe Rebeyrol. He remembers remarks made by his mother, who had become friends with Henriette. For her, Henriette's attraction to Salzedo seemed to be something 'completely negative'. One can imagine what Roland's adolescence must have been like.

At least his academic progress was unproblematic. He did not have to repeat any classes and each year he collected a reasonable share of the prizes. Thus on 12 July 1931, at a solemn prize-giving ceremony presided over by His Excellency Dinu Cesiano, 'special envoy and Minister Plenipotentiary of His Majesty the King of Romania', the name of Roland Barthes, form 4A1, was mentioned on the roll of honour. He won the first prize in history and geography, plus six certificates of merit: first place in French composition, fourth in Latin prose, first in Latin unseen translation, third in Greek prose, first in recitation and fifth place in physical education. Only two pupils in his class were placed higher: Paul Faure, who won the prize for excellence, eight prizes and one merit, and Philippe Rebeyrol, cited on the roll of honour, and winning four prizes and four merits. The fact that Barthes received a merit for recitation totally contradicts what he himself was to claim years later: 'When I was at school we had exams in recitation . . . they were a terrible ordeal for me, I was always terrified and only just scraped through.'[7] As for the certificate of merit in physical education, the mind boggles given Barthes's dislike for sports: a dislike which was later to be compounded by his illness.

The following year, on 12 July 1932, at the end of the fifth form, he collected more prizes. He was cited on the roll of honour and got three merits (French composition, Latin prose, and Latin unseen translation). In all these subjects he was outshone by Philippe Rebeyrol. They had agreed that once they had taken their bacca-lauréat they would both prepare for the entrance exam to the prestigious École Normale Supérieure in the Rue d'Ulm.[8]

Just like every other summer, Barthes went down to the south-west, where he wrote many letters to his school-friends, Sadia Oualid, Jean Huerre and, above all, Philippe Rebeyrol. It was the beginning of a correspondence which was to last for forty-eight years. He also read Mallarmé and Valéry and began to study harmony with his aunt, a subject which, like maths, he found difficult. But although maths was to remain a closed book to him, he was to become a more than passably good pianist. The sixteen-year-old Barthes was an ardent socialist and he regretted not having anyone in Bayonne with whom he could discuss politics. He attempted to convert his grandmother, who was a loyal *Figaro* reader, to socialism. He was overjoyed when one day she finally admitted, after being bombarded with questions, that she would prefer a revolution to a war. Nevertheless, he still hid from her the fact that he was reading whatever texts by Jean Jaurès he could lay his hands on. There were indeed limits to insolence – in the etymological sense of the word – which the children of the bourgeoisie were duty-bound to respect.

During the course of the summer of 1932, he discussed his favourite writers with Philippe Rebeyrol: these were still Valéry and, to a lesser extent, Mallarmé. Barthes was a proselyte, in literature as in politics, so on his return to Paris he attempted to convert his school friends to Valéry, to get them to share his own enthusiasm for the poet.

However, during the summer of 1932, his greatest enthusiasm was for the writings of Jaurès. Before discovering Jaurès, he had converted to socialism out of a spirit of rebellion against reactionary and nationalistic trends. But his reading of Jaurès made him realize, so he said, the impossibility of maintaining the liberal, lukewarm, happy medium which was so dear to the French. He discussed his ideas in passionate, emphatic terms, a kind of language which today might seem slightly ridiculous. He felt the ideas of Jaurès to be so wide reaching, so powerful and so true (in fact, almost holy) that he could not understand how anyone could resist them. But what impressed him most was Jaurès' dialectics: Barthes thought that his works provided the answers to all those pathetic objections which, eighteen years after his death (indeed, because of his death), were raised by wretched and venomous journalists desperately seeking to counteract the sincerity, the probity and the nobility of Jaurès' concept of socialism, almost as if he had foreseen them.

Léon Blum's brand of socialism, on the other hand, he found far less impressive and considerably different from that of Jaurès. For him, Blum was the man of ministerial machinations, whereas Jaurès seemed more concerned with humanity in general than with political scheming. But perhaps his mistrust of Blum is linked more to the fact that the politician was a regular visitor at Noémie Revelin's salon.

It was during the same holiday period that he discovered a writer whose work was to play a vital role in his life – Marcel Proust. The young Barthes could not understand why some people found Proust boring and were put off by his prolix sentences. For him, the author of *Remembrance of Things Past* was, at heart, a poet who wrote prose, who used the concrete details of everyday life to analyse the emotions and the memories that these objects and facts aroused in him. Philippe Rebeyrol remembers an image Barthes used when referring to Proust: he was like someone who observes the concentric circles caused by throwing a stone into water.

Writing projects

In September 1932, the family returned to Paris. Roland entered the lower sixth form at Louis-le-Grand. Once again, he resumed his old routine of school and daily conversations with Philippe Rebeyrol. Barthes lived in the Rue Jacques-Callot, Rebeyrol in the Rue Littré, and after school the two boys would spend hours strolling along the Rue de Rennes discussing literature and poetry. Philippe, who was two years younger than Roland, was fascinated by his talent. He was convinced that Roland would one day become a great French writer, not the critic and theoretician he was eventually to become but 'a contemporary Victor Hugo'. Sometimes, in the Barthes's small apartment, Roland would play their old piano and teach Philippe about classical music. Since his departure from Bayonne and his early piano lessons with his aunt, there had been no money to pay for lessons, and Roland had worked at improving his technique on his own. The one thing his mother had managed to do, despite her money problems, was to hire a piano. He much preferred reading a score and then playing it to listening to someone else play. Despite being self-taught, he made steady progress. His aunt was able to verify this on his Christmas and Easter visits to Bayonne, when she could give him lessons again.

In fact it was in Bayonne, in April 1933, that he first conceived the idea of writing a novel. Just before they had broken up from school his friend Philippe had told him about his plans to write a novel, and Barthes did not want to be outdone. So he invented the story of a sensitive and intense young man from the provinces called Aurélien Page, who rebels against his family and its hypocrisy. The latter is symbolized by his maternal grandmother, who forces him to obey her wishes. Explaining the plot to Rebeyrol, Roland insisted that Page did not represent himself. When pressed, he admitted that many of the details in the story were in fact to be taken from his own life – or at least from the life he would have had if he had remained in Bayonne, the provincial life he recognized in the writing of Proust. Thus Aurélien longs to escape, but is held back by his mother, whom he can neither abandon nor take with him. As he grows older, he sees his imagination, interests and revolutionary aspirations bring him into conflict with the narrow, provincial attitudes of those around him. As these conflicts become more and more frequent, and his arguments with his grandmother more and more violent, this young man (who seems to have everything one could possibly need to be happy, coming as he does from a well-to-do and apparently united family) gradually rebels. He becomes increasingly bitter and finds himself confronted by the incomprehension of his own social class.

Then he falls in love with Hélène Manory, a young girl whom his grandmother will not accept because she does not have a dowry. His grandmother's continual repetition of this phrase, 'no dowry' – which our young author probably borrowed from Molière – only increases the hero's sense of bitterness. Nevertheless, he gives in and

accepts that he must exist in a state of constant antagonism to the
society in which he is forced to live. On the day his grandmother
tries to make him agree to a marriage of convenience with another
young girl who has expectations of an inheritance, he tries to escape.
However, his fear of scandal quickly makes him submit to the family
law, to order.

Although the 'literary' value of this project can obviously be
criticized (the plot is not exactly impressively original), its interest
lies more in what it reveals about Roland's relationships with his
own family. He spelled out the moral of the story to his friend
Philippe during one of their daily seminars on the Rue de Rennes:
Aurélien's only fault is to belong to a bourgeois family. This Aurélien
was fated never to be anything more than a creature of Barthes's
imagination. Since there is no trace of a first draft of this novel, there
is nothing to suggest that his project ever came to fruition.
Nevertheless, is it really true that this character had nothing in
common with our budding novelist? The similarities between them
are obvious, as is the desire (of the author) to shield the mother (of
the protagonist) from the conflicts and ideological struggles which
are the novel's subject matter. It all seems as if the revolt expressed in
these few pages, the violent conflict, had jumped a generation, so as
to fall not on the blameless and innocent mother, but on the
grandmother, the source of all evil.

But with the Easter holidays at an end, Barthes's writing projects
had to be consigned to memory. He had to go back to Paris for the
final push towards the first part of his baccalauréat in June 1933. On
30 January 1933, Hitler became Chancellor of the German Reich.
On 23 February, a certain Van der Lubbe, who may have been half-
mad but who was almost certainly used as a tool by the Nazis, set
fire to the Reichstag. Across the Rhine events snowballed: in March
the Communist party was dissolved, and in April the Gestapo was
set up. In May, Goering proclaimed self-confidently that 'Hitler is
now the law.' In June, the Nazi party became the only legal political
party. Such events were bound to have an impact on the schoolboy
Roland Barthes, with his passion for Jaurès' brand of socialism and
his hatred of nationalism and bourgeois principles, and a year later
he was to help set up a small anti-fascist group. A photograph from
this period shows him on the Boulevard Saint-Michel with two
friends. He is standing in the middle, wearing a sober dark suit with
a white collar and dark tie. He also looks very thin – although later
he would be embarrassed by his tendency to put on weight. Forty
years later, Roland Barthes was to write the following caption

for this photograph: 'In those days, lycée students were little gentlemen.'[9]

At the time the little gentleman was studying for his baccalauréat. For one thing, he loved his studies, and for another (more importantly), he was all too aware of the sacrifices his mother had made to risk letting her down. His French teacher, M. Dupouey, struck terror into the hearts of all the boys at the lycée. From the thirty or so members of the class, he had a habit of singling out the four or five boys whom he considered to be the best students, and he would only address himself to them, and in a very aggressive manner. Barthes and Rebeyrol were among the 'chosen few', even though they would have preferred to remain anonymous.

A document from his sixth-form studies, reproduced in *Roland Barthes by Roland Barthes*, tells us something about this period. On a piece of graph paper, the staple of all schoolwork, Barthes has written the following:

Barthes   Saturday 13 May 1933
1A1
                     French Homework

His writing still looks somewhat childish. Barthes the pupil evidently had no first name, just a surname, Barthes, with '1A1' below it, like a regimental number (it was of course the number of his year and his form). We have no indication of the subject of the essay – judging from the teacher's comments it must have been something like, 'Tell, or invent, the story of the difficulties and setbacks of a famous man.' The composition begins thus:

> I once read in a book that one is only taught how to live once one's life is over. Having lived the first part of my youth in the illusory belief that my education had made me invincible this has been a cruel lesson for me to learn. Today, thanks to the changing tides of political fortune, I find myself reduced to playing a minor and most disappointing role.
>   Born into a family of the honourable bourgeoisie of old, which certainly did not foresee that its days were numbered, I was raised by an old-style tutor, who taught me many things. He believed that . . .[10]

The text comes to an abrupt end here, although of course it would have continued on the other side of the page, which was not reproduced. The reader is therefore left to imagine for himself or herself what this old style tutor's beliefs were. There are only the

comments of the terrifying M. Dupouey, who has written at the top
of the page:

> A lucid and extremely interesting treatment of the subject, written with
> taste and personality. Your style is a little clumsy on occasions, but
> nevertheless always gratifying. The 'difficulty' you imagine is fairly
> intriguing, but not convincing enough. Do you really believe that it is
> necessary to have a social revolution before the superiority of a well-
> trained mind over one crammed full of facts becomes apparent?[11]

In the margin he has conscientiously marked the following corrections:

> What or who is this mysterious 'they' [on]? Your first sentence is far from
> clear.
>
> Impr. It is not the role itself which causes disappointment but the hope of
> playing a more important one.[12]

Lower down the page, the word which I have transcribed as *perte* is
underlined and in the margin next to it there is the abbreviated
comment 'illis.' meaning 'illisible' (illegible). Here again, Barthes
adds a subtitle or caption to these photos from a bygone era: 'Any
law which oppresses a discourse is not well founded.'[13]

But this is the judgement of a fifty-year-old man. Most probably at
the time the little gentleman took a much more respectful view of his
teacher's knowledge. As has been seen, he did well in literature and
history but showed a complete lack of interest in the sciences. He
imagined himself becoming a French or classics teacher. With
Rebeyrol and some other friends, he established the 'abbaye de
Thélème', a discussion group whose members met in a café in the
Place de la Sorbonne or, if the weather was fine, in the Luxembourg
Gardens. Several of his school-friends took part in the discussions –
Genthon, Huerre, Oualid – but from the very beginning there were
serious differences of opinion. The group's two founders wanted it to
be a free space for the discussion of subjects as diverse as politics, sex
and the arts. As Rebeyrol comments wryly today, theirs was a
somewhat '68ish' vision. The others did not agree, and 'l'abbaye de
Thélème' limited the scope of its discussions to literature.

Barthes was seventeen and a few days away from taking his exams
for the first part of the baccalauréat. He passed these exams and
obtained good marks. In his French composition paper he was
offered the inspiring choice between a commentary on a La Bruyère
judgement of Corneille and Racine, an analysis of a passage from

L'Art poétique on the sonnet and a portrait of 'the Romantic hero as represented in the novels, poetry and drama of the 1840s'. For his Latin translation paper he had one of Cicero's letters, and in Greek he was given an untitled piece beginning 'the Athenians and Lacedaemonians must act in concert'. He passed without any problems and was overjoyed. On 13 July 1933, at the end of 1A1, he was awarded three merits (French composition, recitation, history).

The school year was over and our model pupil left for Bayonne to spend the summer holiday at his grandmother's house. During the holidays he wrote his first text, a pastiche of Plato's *Crito*. In prison, Socrates is offered a bowl of delicious Corinthian figs. Tempted, he reaches out his hand but then draws back. 'What is the point,' he says to himself, 'since I have to die and I won't even have time to digest them?' His friends try to persuade him to follow Crito's advice and flee. Socrates resists all their attempts, but he is still tempted by the bowl of figs. Finally he reaches out, takes a fig and eats it. By this simple gesture he signifies his agreement with the escape plans and his refusal to submit to the laws of the city. That evening, aboard the boat which is taking them to Epidaurus, one of his followers asks, 'But what about history?' 'History?' retorts Socrates, 'Bah, Plato will take care of that!' In these few pages, then, the young Barthes amused himself by changing the course of events.

Forty years later, introducing this piece 'En marge du Criton' in the journal *L'Arc*,[14] Barthes sees it as containing three different interlocking cultures. Firstly, the culture of a seventeen-year-old lycée pupil who, according to him, knew nothing about contemporary literature apart from Gide. Secondly, the academic culture of a good student who had been trained in the classics, Latin and Greek, and then, finally, culture in its broad sense. Then he turns his attention to the dish of figs that occupies the central position in the text. Why figs? He admits that he hated the figs that grew in the family garden, which were 'shrunken, violet – always unripe or overripe' and that he only discovered a taste for this fruit much later, in Morocco, 'and also more recently, at the restaurant Voltaire, where they are served with huge bowls of fresh cream'. The fig, he explains, only existed for him at the time he wrote this piece as a literary, biblical fruit. Then, alluding precisely to the culture of the schoolboy crammed full of Latin, he adds, 'Unless, hidden behind the fig, there is the sex, the *fica*?' However, it is in vulgar, not classical, Latin that *fica* means vulva and it is doubtful whether the young Barthes would have possessed such a detailed knowledge of etymology. Whatever the case, the text was written for a review which 'l'abbaye de Thélème' was planning to produce and it was the project Barthes devoted most of his energies to during these summer holidays of 1933.

He also wrote numerous letters to his school-friends Genthon, Huerre, Rebeyrol, Oualid, Brissaud and Pichon, urging them to send him the articles they had promised. He also gave a few lessons to earn some pocket money and, of course, he practised the piano. His mother Henriette and his half-brother Michel Salzedo were at Biscarosse and he spent several days with them at the end of August. He then spent a week at Bagnères-de-Bigorre with his aunt. Finally at the beginning of September, Rebeyrol, who was staying with his parents in St Jean-de-Luz, paid him a visit. Then the holidays came to an end and the members of 'l'abbaye de Thélème' returned to Paris to continue studying for the second part of their baccalauréat.

Barthes and Rebeyrol once again resumed their interminable discussions in Rue de Rennes, and talked about their respective plans to write a novel. But Roland was about to abandon Aurélien Page to his mediocre fate and in January 1934 he informed Philippe of his decision. The gist of his explanation was that during the Christmas holidays in Bayonne he had led such a pampered existence (like one of Anatole France's canons) that he felt it would not be possible for him to write a really convincing novel about the bitterness of youth faced with the hypocrisies of the bourgeoisie. His friend tried to dissuade him from giving up the idea, but Roland replied that one had to get used to the idea of changing and growing older. He added that he now found his grandmother's prattle and her tales, which only a few months before had appalled him, merely amusing and he could not get angry about them.

This proves that Aurélien's grandmother in the novel really was a direct transposition of Barthes's grandmother. Having tried unsuccessfully to convert her to socialism, he had then considered getting his revenge on her by writing what was intended to be a bitingly satirical novel. But finally he had found his hatred for his grandmother softened by his enjoyment of the New Year celebrations and had decided instead to treat his previously unbearable conversations with her as a source of amusement. Perhaps he meant to treat them, long before he began to use the term, as 'minor mythologies'. He was eighteen and his life was filled with school, friends and music. There was still no trace – at least no discernible trace – of any love affairs or romantic experiences.

In 1934, France was the scene of an important rising of the extreme right. On 6 February, in the Place de la Concorde, a demonstration was organized by three right-wing groups: L'Action Française, Les Camelots du Roi and Les Jeunesses Patriotiques. The 'leagues' tried to take over the Assemblée Nationale and, although the attempt failed, the casualties amounted to seventeen dead and 2,329 injured. As a result, the Daladier government was forced to stand down. The same group, Jeunesses Patriotiques, were a strong presence at Louis-le-Grand, and its members were in the majority in the philosophy class. Barthes was one of the founding members of a small anti-fascist group called the Défence Républicaine Anti-fasciste, or DRAF, which met regularly in a café in the Rue Bonaparte. The group had only a handful of members: Philippe Rebeyrol, Jean Heurre (whose dream at the time was to become a cadet at St Cyr and who would eventually become a Benedictine abbot), two or three others and, of course, Barthes. Later he was to say that for a boy of his generation he was extremely conscious of the dangers of fascism. Nevertheless, despite his awareness of the contemporary political turmoil, he still devoted a great deal of his time to his school-work: French, Latin and above all Greek, which was his favourite subject. His exams were looming on the horizon and he was studying as hard as he could. After his success in July 1933, he hoped to finish the lycée that year and, with Rebeyrol, to devote his time to preparing for the competitive entrance exams to the École Normale Supérieure, and later for the agrégation.[15]

This was their common project, their goal, and the only future they could imagine: they would both go to the École Normale, both take the agrégation and both become teachers. But an adolescent proposes and life disposes.

The onset of illness

On 10 May 1934, a catastrophe struck which interrupted Barthes's smooth progress from one academic success to another. He suffered a haemoptosis with a lesion of the left lung, and the illness which ensued was seriously to affect the next ten years of his life. The first doctor to examine him was the father of his school-friend Jean Brissaud. Barthes was coughing up blood, a sympton of pulmonary tuberculosis which, at the time, was an extremely serious disease. He was immediately sent to Bayonne to rest. He was devastated by this enforced separation from his friends, his philosophy class and his studies. For a while he contemplated taking his baccalauréat exam in July in Bordeaux, but his doctors advised against it and he was forced to put it off until the autumn. He was treated with injections of gold salts and spent his days resting in bed. He read – a little Balzac, Mauriac, Giraudoux and a lot of Arsène Lupin – and also thought up an idea for another novel. Mostly, however, he spent his time moping over the fact that he would not be able to take his baccalauréat with the rest of his friends on Thursday, 28 June in Paris.

Since his condition did not improve, the idea of spending a year in the mountains was mooted. He did not object, and even seemed to resign himself gradually to being a consumptive, entering into the spirit of the illness and assuming his condition almost as if it were a religion. It was as if he suddenly developed the typical psychological characteristics of a sick person: the slightest little thing was enough to terrify or reassure him. He spent his days thinking about his illness, speculating on the links between his symptoms and external events. Tuberculosis, as he told Rebeyrol, was a serious illness which either in reality or in the imagination brought one face to face with death. In particular he felt as if other people, healthy people, imputed mysterious powers to the illness – and it was indeed contagious. This fostered an atmosphere of panic which communicated itself to the patient and made him panic too.

Despite his strong desire to return to Paris, to resume his studies and see his friends again, Barthes's health showed no signs of improvement. Finally it was decided to send him to Bedous, a small village in the Pyrenees, to see if the mountain air would cure him, and his mother subsequently rented a house in the village. The air cannot have done him any harm, of course, but it was his brother Michel who seemed to derive most benefit from this year spent in the mountains. During the summer Roland carried on studying for his baccalauréat. He also wrote letters to his friends telling them how disappointed he was that they had not written and explaining that he felt abandoned and forgotten. However, in September he saw Rebeyrol at the Brissauds' house in Saint-Jean-de-Luz and then took the train to Paris, where he sat the second part of his baccalauréat: the exams in natural and physical sciences and the philosophy dissertation. For the dissertation he was given a choice between two questions, either 'Characterize the following psychological states: belief, doubt, certainty' or 'What does it mean to forget? What is the significance of forgetting in psychological processes?' Naturally he passed, but he was aware that he had to go back to Bedous and remain there indefinitely, while his friends continued their studies in Paris.

Thus began a long period of isolation and loneliness for him. He toyed with the idea of taking a degree by correspondence, and he asked Rebeyrol to find out about the cost and how to enrol. He reminded him that since his mother was a war widow, he might be exempt from having to pay fees. Mostly, however, he withdrew into himself and he fell into a state of depression, dreaming about Paris, longing to be back there carrying on with his studies and seeing his friends. The days passed and he went for walks in the mountains, picked wild strawberries and began to develop a love of nature. But he still felt that real life was not here in Bedous but elsewhere, in Paris, and that he was connected to it only by the slim threads of his friends' letters. He came up with ideas for two new novels, 'L'histoire de Judith' ('Judith's story'), which he described as an objective, realist novel, and 'L'île joyeuse' ('The joyful island'), a fictional narrative about 'the pagan'. This notion of 'paganism' was his way of justifying intellectually his somewhat uneasy relationship with official religion. He devoted a great deal of thought to it, and discussed it with Rebeyrol. Occasionally he worried that as an idea it was too vague, too aesthetic, and that he had built his theories on a flimsy foundation.

Time passed slowly. When the snow began to fall, he went out less, spending his time instead practising Bach's preludes and reading the books Rebeyrol sent him. Rebeyrol's weekly letters were like a breath of metropolitan air for Barthes. During the Christmas holidays, to prevent himself from feeling bored, he wrote a draft of a short play called 'Le voyage d'Arion', a text which was littered with references to ancient Greece. Arion is a musician and poet mentioned by Herodotus. In his play Barthes also makes him immortal: his immortality is a gift from Apollo, a reward for his music, which has moved the god to tears of joy. In the play Arion delivers Barthes's greetings and news to Rebeyrol and other school-friends who are holidaying in the Alps, at the Hôtel des Trois-Dauphins.

'Is he feeling sad?' asks Reyberol.

'He's feeling much better after receiving a fifty-franc postal order. This modest sum has enabled him to go shopping in Oloron and get a change of scene.' (Reyberol had sent Barthes some money.)

'And what about his health?' asks Rebeyrol.

'Slightly improved,' replies Arion. 'His greatest afflictions are boredom and loneliness.'

The play ends with the departure of Arion and with a voice (Barthes's) calling from the wings: 'And this is how I amuse myself!'

Leaving aside the private jokes about the character and idiosyncrasies of each of the protagonists, Rebeyrol, Brissaud, Monod, De Brunhoff, all former classmates, the play echoes once again Barthes's boredom and his current preoccupation with the notion of 'the pagan', the focal point of his discussions about religion with Rebeyrol. But he also manages to slip several individual messages to friends into the dialogue. It is not so much a case of killing two birds with one stone as turning one short sketch into four or five letters.

Several days later, on 17 January 1935, he composed a 'divertimento in F major' for the piano and transcribed it with a dedication to Philippe Rebeyrol. It consists of three pages, composed in double time and *moderato*, and having signed and dated the piece the budding musician has added the following comment: 'an extremely rare handwritten copy by the composer for his friend Philippe Rebeyrol.'

The days continued to pass. If Rebeyrol's letters were late in arriving, Barthes would feel restless and upset: why hadn't he written? He was only too aware, however, that in his current state of exile Rebeyrol was his only source of intellectual exchange. He needed his letters: they were a kind of window on to a world from which he was excluded, his only connection with Paris and the life he wanted to be leading.

Barthes managed to enrol for a law degree by correspondence and got hold of some textbooks, but he found it extremely difficult to drum up any enthusiasm for the subject. He found law an extremely dry subject and preferred to read Racine or Gide or think about ideas of The Beautiful or The Good, or write letters to Rebeyrol in which he would discuss their different notions of morality or religion. In Barthes's view, Rebeyrol was a dangerous Christian – because he was intelligent – whereas after reading Nietzsche, he himself had become a pagan. To explain his ideas, he wrote another text, an 'apologue' this time, which he called 'Les aventures d'un jeune Crétois', dedicated to his friends by the subtitle 'apologue ad usum amici'. One day a young Cretan is day-dreaming on the shores of his island. He cannot believe his teacher's stories about the existence of a distant country ruled over by an old king who is the master of all human destinies. How can he actually find this country? By searching for it with his eyes? Its distance means that it is forever out of sight. By placing his trust in those who claim to have seen it? This could never be a sufficient basis for belief and for justifying the sacrifices such a belief would entail. Through a process of reasoning? This last option seems more acceptable to the young Cretan, but since feelings can never be dictated by reason, it would require the revelation of the object of those feelings at the very least. And if this sovereign has never revealed himself to the young man, then how is he to revere him?

He falls asleep on a plank of wood and when he wakes up he finds that the waves have carried him out to sea. The following day he sights a coastline; he lands and meets an old man who says he is the country's ruler. The young man throws himself at the old man's feet. The old man says to him, 'So, you didn't believe I existed?' Ashamed of his error and his lack of belief, the young man admits that he did not, but the sovereign forgives him because he says that he knows the young man has an honest soul and that, despite his scepticism, he has always been true to himself. The moral of the tale? Obviously that if God does in fact exist and one has not believed in him but has been true to one's own beliefs, then God will forgive.

It seems that Rebeyrol was angered by his friend's tone, finding it both aggressive and flippant. Barthes begged him not to take offence, since it was not Christ he was attacking but the Christian world-view, which he believed could lead easily to intolerance and sectarianism.

However, none of these literary distractions could alleviate his boredom, which became increasingly difficult for him to bear as time went on. In Paris, Rebeyrol had begun hypokhâgne, the special class to prepare for the entrance exams to the École Normale Supérieure. One of his classmates was Raymond Picard, whose name will crop up again later in relation to the Racine polemic. As for Roland, 'after this bout of illness, naturally there was no question of my returning to school, attending the hypokhâgne class, getting up early and studying hard.'[16] Thus the theme of his illness, the millstone which prevented him from studying and leading the kind of life he wanted, makes its appearance in his discourse and was to remain a constant theme there throughout his life. He felt lonely and bored, hemmed in by the high mountains. He was unaware at the time that he would have to endure many more such years of loneliness and enforced idleness in the sanatorium. From time to time Madame Rebeyrol, aware that the Barthes's financial situation meant they had to perpetually economize, would send him parcels of newspapers; he would immediately pounce on them and devour the news sections. Around the end of March he went to Pau to have some X-rays taken. The results were encouraging: the disease had been checked, and there had even been a slight improvement in his condition (there were some spots of calcification). Despite the fact that from now on he would have to keep a careful watch on his health, his hopes rose:

perhaps he would be able to return to Paris and start school again the following October.

Meanwhile, distance and the fact that their only means of communication was by letter had led to several minor misunderstandings between Barthes and Rebeyrol. A more serious breach had also occurred – not over Christianity this time, but over their different approaches to discussing writers and literature. Roland had reproached Philippe for adopting the institutionalized language of academe, accusing him of no longer really thinking for himself. Since he himself was prevented by illness from being in an academic context, he reacted by condemning the tics of academic critical discourse. His early reaction against this kind of discourse contained the seeds of a revolt which he was to cultivate throughout his life. This revolt stemmed partly from his sharply critical outlook and partly from a certain amount of bad faith. Because he felt he had been cheated out of a university education by his illness, that it was out of reach, he turned his feelings of bitterness into sarcasm. He expressed astonishment at the way in which Rebeyrol now discussed authors such as Rousseau or Racine, at his adoption of the tone required to get into the École Normale. He attacked the idea that all writers must be given a label, reduced to a stereotype: for instance Bossuet and the art of oratory, La Fontaine and the fables, Montaigne and scepticism, Rousseau and pride, Racine and passion, Corneille and duty, Chateaubriand and imagination, Vigny and moral solitude, etc. He could not accept that anyone with an enquiring and open mind should waste time and effort trotting out such clichés.

However, spring finally arrived and with it the sun returned to Bedous. Roland quite happily lent a hand with the turning of the hay, and he wrote a composition for four hands for the piano. His love of music intensified: he developed a passion for Ravel's *sonatina*, and the fact that the composer was too refined for some people's tastes filled him with indignation. He believed Ravel to be the greatest musical genius of modern times. Alone in Bedous he ranted and raved, declaring imperiously that life should be lived in adoration of Ravel and mistrust of Wagner.

In the summer, Rebeyrol went on holiday to Germany, while Barthes remained in Bedous as usual. One day while he was at the grocer's, he met a young girl called Mima. This meeting transformed his life – or at least he felt it had at the time. He fell head-over-heels in love – or thought he had – and spent all his time dreaming about her. Unfortunately for him, however, Mima had an unbearable cousin who acted as her chaperone, and another, even more unbearable one whose pomposity and pretentiousness – plus the fact that he was a member of the militant Catholic organization the Croix de Feu – made Roland want to hit him as soon as he laid eyes on him. One Saturday evening during a public debate on fascism in the village, which was being chaired by a communist teacher, Mima's whole family began hurling abuse at the audience, calling them idiots and imbeciles. Roland began to think it was a sad fate indeed to have fallen in love with someone from such a terrible family: almost as tragic as the third act of a Corneille drama. On the one hand, he regarded Mima as the embodiment of poetic delicacy, on the other, he found her family oppressively ugly. In short, the young Roland was in love. However, a week later everything had changed: Mima was forgotten and a veil was drawn over this major event.

Several weeks later, he told Rebeyrol about his passion of a week, making fun of the way his imagination had a tendency to run away with him. For the time being, with Mima a thing of the past, he returned to his books and his music. Besides, summer was almost over, and with it his stifling period of martyrdom in Bedous. At the beginning of October he left the village for Bayonne, where he took the train for Paris. Once back in the capital, he enrolled for a classics degree at the Sorbonne, where he was to remain until 1939. For the first time in his academic career he had fallen behind and missed a year. He had also lost his chance of going to the École Normale and following the path he had always dreamed of. As for Rebeyrol, he would pass the entrance exams to the École Normale in 1936, rapidly complete a literature degree and then change direction to study history.

Towards the sanatorium

Roland's first year at university was to be overshadowed by events on the political scene. In order to resist rising right-wing extremism of the kind which had been behind the violent demonstrations of 1934, the left had united. On 14 July 1934, while Roland was still languishing in exile in the mountains, the Popular Front had been formed, close on the heels of the 'unity pact' between the socialists and the communists. The Front brought together communists, socialists, radicals and the various unions, as well as intellectual organizations such as the League of Human Rights and the anti-fascist committees. In January 1936 the Popular Front was presenting its political programme and was the main topic of conversation, both among the political class, as was to be expected, but also at the Sorbonne and in academic circles. Apart from his studies, Roland took a keen interest in the political events of the day. At the same time, he began working on a project which was to have a profound and lasting impact on him. With one of his fellow students, Jacques Veil, he set up the Ancient Theatre Group of the Sorbonne – along the lines of the Medieval Theatre Group created by Gustave Cohen, a lecturer in literary history, a few years previously.

Veil was an old acquaintance of Barthes. He was terribly shortsighted and always gave the impression of being lost and somewhat helpless. At Louis-le-Grand he had been picked on by almost all the other boys except Barthes and Rebeyrol. They, shocked by the anti-Semitic undertones of the jokes played on Veil, had defended him. Later he would be tortured and murdered by the Nazis.

The idea of the Ancient Theatre Group was to stage productions of the Greek tragedies and Latin comedies. Their first performance took place in the main courtyard at the Sorbonne on Sunday, 4 May 1936, the very same day that the Popular Front was elected to power. Rebeyrol, who was extremely busy working for the École Normale entrance exams and who had hardly seen anything of his friend since the beginning of the year, for once made an exception to his rigid timetable and came to see the performance. The play was *The Persae* by Aeschylus, and there is no way of knowing whether the audience perceived the (unintended) parallels between the events on stage and the events of this highly important election day.

In front of the royal palace at Susa, a crowd waits anxiously for news of the outcome of the battle of Salamis. A messenger arrives and announces disaster: The Greeks have destroyed Xerxes' fleet. In the midst of the general lamentation, the father of the defeated Xerxes, Darios, emerges from his tomb and curses his son's folly. Darios was played by Barthes, who had to stand at the top of the steps of the Sorbonne chapel. Later, he remembered how nervous he had been while delivering his lines:

> Darios, a part that always gave me terrible stage fright, had two long declamations in which I was likely to forget my lines: I was fascinated by the temptation of *thinking about something else*. Through the tiny holes

in the mask, I could see only very high up, and very far away; while I
delivered the dead king's prophecies, my eyes came to rest on inert – free –
objects and books, a window, a cornice, a piece of sky: they, at least,
weren't afraid.[17]

After Barthes's death the Ancient Theatre Group, the creation of
enthusiastic students, was to gain official recognition. On 15
October 1987 there was another performance of *The Persae* to mark
the group's fiftieth (actually, its fifty-first) anniversary. This time the
performance was held in the Sorbonne's huge amphitheatre.

Barthes devoted a great deal of time to theatre, more than he did
to his studies. He tried to justify what he was doing by telling himself
that it was a good way of preparing for his degree examinations. As
fate would have it, in his Greek oral in June 1936 he was questioned
precisely on the *The Persae*, and he 'dried up' miserably.

At the end of June, Rebeyrol was accepted at the École Normale in
the Rue d'Ulm. Over the moon, he rushed round to the Rue Jacques-
Callot to tell his friend the good news. Barthes congratulated him
warmly, telling him he had a bright future ahead of him and would
accomplish many things. Once Rebeyrol had left, however, he broke
down in tears. Philippe's success was too great a blow to his ego for
him to bear. For years Roland had dreamt of becoming a pupil at the
prestigious École Normale himself. As he later told his friend
Romaric Sulger-Büel, this was the most painful day of his life. He
knew he was just as capable of passing the entrance exam as
Philippe, and he cursed the illness that had prevented him from
doing so.

The summer holidays arrived. For millions of working people, the
summer of 1936 meant the advent of something previously unima-
gined: for the first time ever they received holiday pay, and this novel
and exciting experience was to remain forever associated in their
minds with the melodies of Charles Trenet's first songs. Roland went
to Bayonne, but despite being delighted at seeing his aunt again and
at being able to practise his music, he missed Paris. He practised the
piano every day, working on a Bach fugue, Schumann's *In der Nacht*
or Schubert's 'Theme and variations'. He thought nothing could be
more beautiful than music and it was always with him, during both
the significant and the trivial events of his life. But apart from music
he found his life pretty joyless.

When he returned to Paris in September, he found the city equally
charmless. His grandfather, Louis Binger – 'the explorer', as Barthes
always referred to him – had been taken into hospital in Val-de-

Grâce under medical observation. On visiting him, Roland found he was greatly changed and he died only a few weeks later. Back in Bayonne for a short time before the start of the new term, Roland fell into a state of depression. From now on, this was to be his most typical mood. Once more, he began to rethink the problematic question of the existence of God. This time he came to a somewhat original (and extremely comfortable) conclusion. He decided that nothing in his behaviour could possibly offend God, and that his actions were the only way he had of showing his love for Him. In short, God loved him and did not judge him.

Exempted from military service in 1937 because of his tuberculosis, Barthes made several trips abroad. During the summer he took part in a student visit to the University of Debrecen in Hungary. In all likelihood, the French students gave their Hungarian counterparts some conversation lessons: in the brief biography of himself Barthes gives at the end of *Roland Barthes by Roland Barthes* he somewhat glorifies this activity by calling himself a 'Lecteur at Debrecen during the summer'.[18] To a young man brought up by a Protestant mother, the town must have felt almost like a home from home: Debrecen (which was to become the seat of the first Hungarian government after the Liberation in 1944) had always been the centre of Protestantism in Hungary, and because of this it had been baptised the 'Calvinist Rome' or the 'Hungarian Geneva'. On the other hand, he was bowled over by a scene he witnessed in the streets of Budapest: two men who showed quite openly by their behaviour that they were homosexual. He only told Philippe Rebeyrol about this much later, but said he had been 'thrown into raptures' by this proof of freedom.

After three months spent in an unfamiliar environment, he began the new academic year in Paris. He resumed his studies in Greek and Latin and he spent a great deal of time on the theatre group. But the rumblings of history were about to shatter this tranquil life. At Easter he read Victor Hugo's *La Légende des siècles* and found his verses to be strikingly relevant to contemporary events. The world of big-time brigandry and violence described by Hugo, the dark, sinister figures of murderous counts and aggressive kings, brought him straight back to the terrifying reality of a world dominated by Hitler or Mussolini. The world was on the brink of war.

In July 1938 he went to Greece with the other members of the Ancient Theatre Group. Naturally they visited Athens, where they immersed themselves in the treasures of the National Museum and the Acropolis. When Barthes saw the white marble statues he remembered that they had originally been painted and regretted the fact that they had lost their flesh-like appearance. They then visited the Peloponnese, Mycenae, Argos and the islands of Delos, Ægina and Santorini. To get to Salamis, the group took a little boat which reminded Barthes of the little ferry which ran between Saint-Malo and Dinard. On Santorini they hired a boat and sailed around the volcanic cliffs, picking up the pumice stones which floated on the surface of the sea. While out walking on Ægina, Roland met a young blond shepherd with a perfect profile and finally felt he had caught a glimpse of the beauty of the ancient Greeks. Before this meeting, the modern Greeks had struck him as the exact opposite of their past splendour as regards their physical appearance: to Barthes they seemed small, swarthy, with bad teeth and weather-beaten skin. The students discovered the places which up until then had been only exotic names encountered in Greek translations. As they travelled through the land trodden by Ajax and Agamemnon, they saw the real backdrop to the plays they had performed at the Sorbonne. Nevertheless, what impressed them most were things that had not been mentioned in the Greek texts they had read: the piles of honeydew and water melons on sale in the streets, the warmth of the sea, the heavy retsina served with fried squid.

They returned to Paris via Italy, stopping briefly in Milan and Rome, whose flower markets Barthes thought enchanting. It was also a return to reality: in September Barthes had to spend more time in the Haute Savoie because of his health. He felt far from happy about this enforced holiday. Once more he had to put up with the sound of the neighbouring stream, the silence of the mountain pastures which was broken only by the tinkling of cow bells, and the feeling of nostalgia which came over him at dusk, when the sun had disappeared below the mountain peaks. All these details of daily life reminded him of his time in Bedous, and of how slowly those days of enforced idleness had passed. It made no difference to him whether it was the Pyrenees or the Alps. He decided he did not like being in the mountains and he complained about having no books or piano, about feeling bored. After a few weeks he returned to Paris, feeling as if he had just been released from prison.

In September, while the French were returning to work delighted with their new paid holidays, Daladier, Hitler, Mussolini and Chamberlain signed the Munich agreement, which allowed the German Reich to annex the Sudetenland and effectively gave the green light to Hitler's policy of expansion. Europe was on the brink of war, but at the time it did not appear so. On the contrary, in

France and Britain public opinion regarded the Munich agreement as bringing Europe a step closer to peace.

Meanwhile, Barthes returned to the Sorbonne and continued his slow progress towards obtaining his literature degree. In March 1939 Hitler broke the Munich agreement and invaded Czechoslovakia. In April, Mussolini's Italy invaded Albania. The Western powers made not the slightest move to prevent these invasions. In June, Barthes passed the fourth part of his degree exams: he had now passed in Greek, Latin, French literature and the history of philosophy. But even if this effectively meant that he had a degree and, for instance, would have been able to enrol for a postgraduate diploma, it did not constitute a teaching qualification. To teach, he needed to pass exams in grammar and philology. In August, Hitler and Stalin signed the German–Soviet pact. This threw a handful of militants in the French Communist party into despair, since they could not understand how 'the country of socialism' could enter into a pact with the Nazis. The vast majority approved, however, and most people still wanted desperately to believe that there would not be a war. On 1 September the German army invaded Poland. Two days later, on 3 September 1939, Britain (which had signed a treaty with Poland) and France (which had decided to support its ally) finally declared war on Germany. It was less than a year since the signing of the Munich agreement.

When war was declared, Roland was in Paris waiting to find out from the military authorities whether he was to be declared unfit for service or, as he feared, to be assigned to the auxiliary services. In fact, he was declared permanently unfit for service and immediately applied for a post as a literature teacher. On 21 October 1939 he was appointed by the Bordeaux education authority to a lycée in Biarritz 'on a temporary and provisional basis'. The contract stated that Barthes would be paid the salary of a teacher without a university degree since he did not have any teaching qualifications. Biarritz was downstream from Bayonne, so he would be close to his grandmother and his aunt Alice. His grandmother's health was getting worse (she was eighty-five and was to die in 1941) and his aunt Alice was still working as a piano teacher.

Henriette was not about to let her son go off to Biarritz alone, and so the whole family rented a small flat on the Rue du Cardinal-Lavigerie from an American. Michel went to the same school where his brother was teaching, and Henriette found work in a military hospital on the site of what is now the Hotel Régina.

Nothing of great significance happened during the next year. In

Biarritz the Barthes were far removed from the problems created by the war. Roland loved his job, especially the contact with the pupils, but found the mediocrity of his colleagues difficult to put up with. He did not like his fellow teachers, who made a fuss if asked to put in an extra hour, or even an extra minute, of work. He could not stand their moaning, and their mean-spirited adherence to petty rules and regulations. With all the enthusiasm of youth, he thought teaching should be a vocation, a sacred task which should never be entrusted to mediocre minds. He enthused over his students, whom he found charming.

In the evenings he would sometimes go for a stroll to the lighthouse, where from the terrace he would watch the reflection of the moon on the water down below. He thought of writing an essay called 'L'amour, la musique et la mort' ('Love, music and death'), but in his current circumstances he found it difficult to write: he was too worried about the war.

Nevertheless, he began to write a 'méditation sur un portrait du Greco' ('Meditation on a portrait by El Greco') and was planning to send it to Rebeyrol once it was finished. However, his friend never received it. With the end of the school year came the end of the war, at least as far as the French state was concerned: Pétain asked for an armistice in June 1940 and in July the government moved to Vichy. France began its period of collaboration.

The Barthes returned to Paris after the defeat. Roland, who had effectively been only a supply teacher in Biarritz, was unable to obtain a similar post and so he became a study and recreation supervisor at two schools, the Lycée Voltaire and the Lycée Carnot. He was studying for the final part of his degree, the philology exam. At the same time he was working towards a postgraduate diploma in Greek tragedy, which involved studying passages from texts by Aeschylus, Sophocles and Euripedes. Because of his illness he was still trying, six years after his baccalauréat, to finish a diploma which normally took four years. Together with his friend Michel Delacroix, the sensitive and frail son of a university lecturer, he had also decided to take singing lessons. They were both mad about music, but how were they to go about finding lessons? They wrote to Charles Panzera, the famous singer of French songs, to ask for the address of a singing coach. He generously offered to take them on as pupils himself, and for nothing. Barthes studied singing with Panzera until illness prevented him from continuing and he would always remain a fervent admirer of the singer. Later he wrote, 'Since then, I have not stopped listening to his voice, on the rare, technically imperfect records he has made.'[19] Thirty-five years later, in his seminar on the voice, he would sometimes play a tape of Panzera to his students. While everyone agreed that this tape was inaudible, Barthes nevertheless presented it with a great deal of emotion.

The deep admiration which both Barthes and Delacroix felt for Panzera did not, however, exclude irreverence. Panzera, whose wife was his accompanist at recitals, always made her go on stage before him. He would follow close behind, his arms thrown wide to acknowledge the audience's applause, his left hand raised and his right pointing down to the ground. The two friends used to find it very funny when, by a trick of perspective, it looked as if Panzera was, as Barthes put it, 'touching his wife's behind'.

Philippe Rebeyrol, who had been conscripted, taken prisoner and then finally escaped, was in Lyons, where he was studying for the agrégation. At the time communication between Paris, Bayonne and Lyons was difficult. Only state-issued postcards could be used for correspondence and they came with the following stipulations: 'Only correspondence of a familial nature not exceeding seven lines is permitted. It is strictly forbidden to write between the lines or to give any other kind of information. It is essential to write clearly so as to facilitate the task of the German authorities.' Once again, Barthes felt isolated, and his work was his source of consolation. In May 1941 he was studying for his philology exam but with little hope of passing it, since the amount of work on the syllabus seemed overwhelming. In fact, he had to study for the final part of his degree and for his diploma at the same time. Eventually, overloaded with work and with only a limited amount of time for studying, he decided that he would take his final degree exam on its own in June and would put off the diploma exams until October. However, his grandmother Barthes died, and he left for Bayonne on the very day he should have been sitting his philology exam. He spent the summer with his aunt, keeping her company and studying for both his diploma and the final degree exam he had been unable to sit.

In Lyons, at the end of September, Rebeyrol sat the exams for the agrégation (which had been put off until this date because of the war). He passed the written part of his examination easily and began to study for the orals. The thought of his friend's continuing academic success plunged Roland into depression. In addition, he had fallen ill again, having suffered a pulmonary relapse. Doctor Brissaud, the family doctor, had decided to perform a pneumothorax and, while his friend was on his way to yet another academic success, Roland was in bed, where he had already spent the last eight days. In November, when Rebeyrol passed the final part of the agrégation, Barthes was still ill. The pneumothorax had not been entirely successful: some adhesions had remained, and Brissaud had severed them. It had been a long and painful operation, but finally it appeared to have been successful.

However, the long saga of Barthes's illness had only just begun. At the end of November he set about applying for a place in the students' sanatorium at Saint-Hilaire-du-Touvet in the Isère. Since a reply was not to be expected until January, Barthes bided his time and observed his symptoms. He kept a careful watch on himself, like a seasoned invalid used to this cycle of improvements and relapses. For the moment he believed his health to be improving: he had put on a little weight and was able to get up for meals.

A new year, 1942, began. Rebeyrol left Lyons for Barcelona, where he had obtained a post as a French teacher. As for Roland, he had just received the reply he had been both expecting and fearing. His application had been successful and he was to leave Paris for Saint-Hilaire-du-Touvet.

3

In Limbo

The village of Touvet is situated on a plain and above it, eleven kilometres away, is the student sanatorium of Saint-Hilaire-du-Touvet. It is a magnificent setting: a series of immense terraces overlook the Grésivaudan valley, which is bordered by the Belledonne mountains on one side and the mountains of the Grande-Chartreuse range on the other. The view from the terraces is breathtaking: down below in the valley the geometric patterns of the cultivated fields can be made out, their colours varying according to the season. The slope is so steep that you feel as if you are about to dive off into the valley below, and the fields do actually look like little landing strips. It seems almost inevitable that Saint Hilaire should have become what it is today – a centre for aerial wind sports, mainly hang-gliding and paragliding. However, at the beginning of the Second World War, the village bore not the slightest resemblance to a holiday resort. The cable-car which today carries ramblers and skiers up to the slopes was built principally to take patients (and, if need be, the locals) up to the sanatorium. It was also used to bring down corpses, since tuberculosis was often fatal.

From its position at the foot of a depressing-looking grey-coloured cliff called La Dent des Crolles, which at its highest point reaches over two hundred metres, facing the Belledonne mountains, the sanatorium dominates the whole village. Although to the visiting tourist the view seems magnificent, it can rapidly take on a more sinister aspect. In the evening, when the sun has disappeared behind the mountains and the sky is still light, the ring of mountain peaks seems to form a sombre and oppressive barrier, like a prison wall around the village. Moreover, even on the most beautiful evenings, menacing clouds seep out from the cracks and gullies in the mountains and slowly invade the valley. At other times they rise from the plain and seem to settle right at the very foot of La Dent des Crolles, above the sanatorium. In winter, the whole place is snowbound for three months. Life here is muted, tucked away, slowed down.

Thus at the beginning of the winter of 1942, Barthes found himself once again confined to the mountains. At the time, the treatment of tuberculosis could involve drastic operations (of which more will be heard later). During the intervals between operations, the patient was prescribed only two things: silence and rest. As Barthes was to recall later, 'at the time, tuberculosis was truly a way of life, I would almost say an election.'[1] Indeed, it is true that despite his continual moaning and his moroseness, Barthes was in some ways quite suited to this enforced solitude, this confined, protected life.

The days passed slowly, punctuated by regular lung X-rays (in Barthes's case these took place every three months, whereas for some patients they were twice weekly). There would be an X-ray, an insufflation, another X-ray and then the doctor would examine the negative while the patient awaited the verdict. 'Well doctor?', he would ask anxiously. 'That's fine, that's better', the doctor would reply. Then the patient would go away to wait for the next X-ray. In the meantime, the patients kept a close watch on their temperatures. 'Have you taken your temperature?' was one of the stock phrases of their daily conversations: 36.9°C, 37.5°C, 37.8°C, they paid minute attention to these variations, discussing them endlessly. Their illness was at the heart of every discussion.

Since the discovery of streptomycin did not take place until several years later, at the time the prime objective of institutions such as Saint-Hilaire was to isolate the patients and to prevent the disease from spreading (while, naturally, trying to cure them). They all lived under the tyranny of Koch's Bacillus (or KB, as the patients called it) and they were all 'positive'. It was a weighty term, heavy with menace and was subsequently to disappear from the medical lexis for many years. When it resurfaced, it was in a context which, although undoubtedly very different, was just as gloomy: the onset of that other epidemic, AIDS. Barthes was later to comment that a 'person with tuberculosis might seriously consider, as I did, the possibility of living all his life in a sanatorium.'[2]

At least his year in Bedous had prepared him for this kind of life and this pace. It had also prepared him psychologically: he had already adopted the frame of mind of the tuberculosis sufferer. None the less, the shock of his confinement was severe. In order to bear it he had to erase his memories, banish from his mind every image of the past, of his house, of his mother, his friends, the streets of Paris. He had to draw a veil over his past and concentrate solely on the present, on the other patients, knowing he was going to have to live with them for a long time – quite how long he dared not even imagine – and that they had nothing in common apart from their disrupted studies and their illness. Then there were the others who were in an even worse condition, those who had undergone a thoracoplasty (referred to as 'thoracos' in the slang of the sanatorium). Behind the scientific term 'thoracoplasty' was a painful, and sometimes visible, reality: these patients had had one or more ribs removed to help the collapse of the infected lung. Some them did not wear a protective cover and in the summertime, under their open-necked shirts, the effort of breathing created a kind of rippling effect on their skin. Others, with a macabre form of vanity, would tie four or five of their ribs to the foot of their beds on a piece of string as if they were trophies.

But this 'cure' left ample time for leisure, especially at Saint-Hilaire, which was attached to the University of Grenoble. The students were encouraged to continue their studies and teachers came regularly from the university to give lectures. The doctors, who attached a great deal of importance to their patients' morale, approved of any form of cultural activity, whether initiated by the patients themselves or by people from outside. Thus Saint-Hilaire had its own theatre group, 'The Pedal' – this was an allusion to the fact that cycling was forbidden at the sanatorium, but this does not exclude the *double entendre*,[3] of course – a fine auditorium, which also served as a theatre, cinema and lecture theatre, and *Existences*, a quarterly magazine produced by the sanatorium's student union. The magazine's title had nothing to do with Sartrean existentialism (at the time virtually unknown) but was a reference to the lives which had been saved by the sanatorium. There was also a very good library and choral society.

In fact, conditions at the sanatorium were so good that the students from Grenoble who came to visit their friends thought them really lucky to live in such a place. To show them that their luck was not really so great, the patients had perfected a joke which involved taking them to see the operating theatre.

However, even if the living conditions at the sanatorium were far

from terrible, Barthes was still afraid they would appear so to
someone visiting from outside. His friend Rebeyrol was planning to
come to see him and Barthes was worried that he would find the
place terribly depressing. In 1940 he had spent three days at a
sanatorium on the Assy plateau visiting Michel Delacroix, and he
remembered the overwhelming sense of fear and sadness it had
inspired in him, despite his great love for his friend. He did not want
his friend Philippe to have a similar experience.

Rebeyrol had been teaching at the French lycée in Barcelona. He
made the trip to Saint-Hilaire, bringing Roland the everyday things it
was impossible to get hold of at the sanatorium, the things which
made up the inventory of daily needs: soap, brown shoe polish,
brown shoelaces, white cotton thread, a teaspoon, an electric torch
with batteries, a sun visor and manuscript paper. They met at
Grenoble station and then travelled to Saint-Hilaire together.
Philippe stayed overnight in a hostel near the sanatorium. But it was
only a short visit, and afterwards Barthes was alone again.

Like angels

The patients' opinions on the lively atmosphere at Saint-Hilaire
varied. Some found it pleasant and others thought it childish, even
vulgar. Roland was among the latter group: at twenty-seven he was
older then most of the other patients and was very critical of the
whole proceedings. It was true that the atmosphere in the canteen,
where the students sang a lot, resembled that of a mess hall. The staff
let the students get on with it, their only concern being that such
boisterous and enthusiastic singing would strain their lungs. In
addition, the atmosphere was extremely 'macho' and the neighbouring sanatorium for women students often came under attack – and
not just verbally – from the male patients. One evening in the
auditorium there was a change of style: a choir of girl guides and boy
scouts had come to give a concert – probably their good deed for the
day. Naturally the programme consisted of boy scout songs. This
caused a huge and not very friendly uproar: only Barthes came to the
scouts' defence, but without much success. 'They sang like angels,'
he said the next morning. But being angelic was not really in fashion
at Saint-Hilaire and Barthes found himself very much in the minority
on this occasion.

However, this was not always the case. As will be seen, he had a
great deal of influence over his fellow students. Some of them

thought him a poseur. Once when his room-mate wanted to sleep with the window open, Barthes protested: 'I'm a sick old man.' This expression got around, and Barthes acquired something of a reputation for moaning. Most of the students, however, respected him and often asked for his advice. The fact that he was rumoured to be having an affair with the director's wife, Madame Lardanchet, may have had something to do with his prestige. But this was not the only reason, since above all he was regarded as an avant-garde intellectual who was interested in Camus (whose philosophy of the Absurd was scandalizing right-thinking circles at the time) and in Sartre. He was also obviously keen on poetry since he had given some talks on Baudelaire[4] and Walt Whitman.

Barthes also published several articles in the student magazine *Existences*. It had a white cover and red title, and looked like a serious journal. He published an account of his trip to Greece, a 'Note on André Gide and his journal', a review of Bresson's film *Les Anges du péché*, and finally a review of Camus's *L'Étranger* (*The Outsider*).[5] His style, which was already dense and complex, provoked admiration in some and incomprehension in others. As one doctor put it, Barthes 'didn't make one want to read the book he was discussing'. Critics writing on Barthes, beginning with Barthes himself, have often said that this review of Camus was the first draft of what would eventually become *Writing Degree Zero*, his first reflection on 'l'écriture blanche ('colourless writing'), but less has been said about his article on Greece.

The piece on Greece consists of fragments called 'Islands', 'Athens', 'Museums and statues', and this fragmentary style is one Barthes was to adopt in his *Michelet*, his *Roland Barthes by Roland Barthes* and, finally, in the column he wrote in 1978 and 1979 for the *Nouvel Observateur*. It was a style he particularly liked, because he loved beginnings, he loved the first steps of writing a text. By multiplying brief forms, he multiplied what for him were highly privileged moments. This would seem to indicate that much of the future Roland Barthes was already present in this young contributor to the student magazine: the Camus texts and the fragmentary style, of course, but also the way he would immediately put to use theories he had only just discovered. In this case it was Bachelard, later it would be Sartre, Marx, Brecht, Ferdinand de Saussure, Roman Jakobson, and Mikhail Bakhtin.

The library at Saint-Hilaire was well stocked. Barthes read Sartre's *La Nausée* and *Le Mur*, and later *L'Être et le néant*. But his favourite writer was Jules Michelet, and as he read his texts he took notes on small index cards, perfecting a technique he was to use throughout his life. He also revealed another, less well-known aspect of his personality during this period: he took charge of the library and demonstrated his considerable practical and organizational skills. Noting that some of the books were hardly ever borrowed, while others were in constant demand, he organized what he called a 'circulating' system. The most popular books were listed and marked so that they could only be borrowed for a fortnight whereas all the other books could be borrowed for an indefinite period.

The students often discussed the books they had read, comparing their impressions and debating their ideas. Barthes spent a lot of time with a Lithuanian, Ralys, who was doing research on Dostoevsky. Ralys was a strange character and a violent anti-communist. Later, when he realized the United States was not about to declare war on the Soviet Union, he abandoned his intellectual interests and emigrated to Canada, where he worked as a lumberjack before finally committing suicide. Another patient at Saint-Hilaire was Georges Canetti, the brother of the future Nobel Prize winner Elias Canetti. Later Georges himself became a specialist in the treatment of tuberculosis. Oddly enough, considering the rumour that Barthes was having an affair with the director's wife, Canetti remembers a notoriously homosexual Barthes. What is certain, however, is that it was during Philippe Rebeyrol's visit to Saint-Hilaire that Barthes first told him that he was attracted to young men, and, at the time, Rebeyrol was extremely shocked. The story about the director's wife was only a myth: she may well have been attracted to Barthes, if we believe certain accounts, but her feelings certainly can't have been reciprocated.

However, the main thing in Barthes's life was his illness. In April 1942 he suffered a relapse, a pleural effusion that was not reabsorbed. He felt feverish, exhausted, but most of all absolutely furious. He had felt better on admission to the sanatorium four months previously than he did now, and he was obviously getting worse in the very place he was supposed to be getting better.

Of course, it was a matter of the internal evolution of the disease and his temporary relapse had nothing to do with conditions at the sanatorium – or at least so the doctors assured him. All the same, he tended to regard the cure as a fake, and claimed that he had been shut up in Saint-Hilaire for no good reason. What he really needed was to rest, but two things made this impossible: the altitude and the communal life. Firstly, the high altitude meant he was woken up every morning by the bright sunlight which streamed through the curtainless windows, and in winter this intensely bright light was reflected – and thus intensified – by the snow. Secondly, he complained bitterly about the noise of boys shouting on their way to the shower, the constant blaring of radios in neighbouring rooms, the days spent without a moment's silence or shade. His chronic bad mood made him think that he was ruining his health and that in fact he had felt much better in Paris.

Soon, however, he felt better and was able to participate in the communal life again. He resumed his reading and began taking part in discussions. Sometimes he would overhear a few bars of music on the radio and a feeling of melancholy would grip him. He analysed his emotional state in very similar terms to those he would use thirty-five years later in *Fragments d'un discours amoureux* (*A Lover's Discourse*). He felt extremely sensitive to everything that occurred around him: music, friendship, memories, they all aroused unbearable emotions in him. Once again his thoughts turned to Christianity. Catholicism seemed far less Christian than the more respectful sobriety of Protestantism. At times he thought the reformed religion – or rather the Protestant culture he had inherited from his mother – could be summed up by one principle: the rejection of pride. He considered pride to be a kind of poison, as if he himself had caught the virus of humility. Then, rejecting metaphysical explanations, he told himself the real reason he hated pride was that it stood in the way of love. Love was as necessary to him as food. If he did not have enough love, he felt hungry, and if he was starved of it, he would perish.

Popularity

In July he had to spend another month confined to bed. His morbid thoughts returned: the sanatorium was a waste of time, the treatment was a fake, he might never get well again . . . After four weeks he felt better and was able to join in the communal activities. His hopes rose. He observed with pleasure that he was becoming increasingly popular and influential among his fellow patients. He admitted to Rebeyrol quite openly the pleasure this gave him – even if it seemed rather like pride – explaining that he was beginning to exercise a certain fascination over the others which he found exciting. He told him he felt respected and admired, and that these moments of conquest were wonderful. Not being loved – or rather feeling he wasn't – made him unhappy, and he was revelling in his new-found popularity.

He had, in fact, just been elected by a considerable majority and, as he told Rebeyrol, 'with practically no campaigning' to the committee of the student association. As it happened, things had not been quite so straightforward. Barthes had been opposed by a list put forward by 'The Pedal' (the theatre group). It was a somewhat 'colourful' list which he found vulgar and so he had decided to do everything he could to ensure its defeat. However, he had acted through intermediaries, pulling strings from behind the scenes like a cardinal in the Roman curia, staying in his room and never coming out into the light of day. He may not have campaigned in the eyes of most of the students, but some of them were well aware of the role he had played in his own election. 'The Pedal' lost, and Barthes felt proud of his strategic abilities, yet at the same time he felt trapped, imprisoned by other people's expectations. It seemed to him that the way social recognition then turned into a form of dependence was similar to the way love affairs developed. He had become involved with several young men at Saint-Hilaire, and after having conquered them he had suddenly felt enslaved by them. But he needed these conquests, and he was well aware that almost all his friendships had begun as love affairs.

Rebeyrol had sent him some of his impressions of Spain, which Roland found both admirable and fascinating. He thought his friend highly talented and, by the same token, began to doubt his own intellectual abilities, his capacity to bring to fruition the projects he dreamed about. He wondered if he really had a clear grasp of books and ideas. In his own estimation, he lacked a dialectical training: he was a lazy reader, a ditherer, over-inclined to take refuge in the ineffable and in day-dreams. Above all, he did not believe he could write well. On rereading his texts, he found them 'stupid'.

His moods alternated between optimism and pessimism. When he was feeling better he would tell himself that all this self-doubt was simply the result of depression, but then he immediately felt depressed again, and wondered if he were not in fact at his most lucid during his moments of depression. Robert David and François Ricci, people I have been able to interview who knew Barthes during this period, remember him being respected and admired by the other patients, who at times regarded him as something of an 'aristrocrat'. It is true that he enjoyed certain privileges. For example, he was the only person to be given permission by Dr Douady to use the grand piano which had pride of place in the auditorium. Even when Douady (who was Jewish) had to leave Saint-Hilaire, it was as if, in the eyes of all the patients, Barthes remained under his protection.

But, as David and Ricci remember him, privileged or not, respected or not, he was still anxious, gloomy and unhappy. As will be seen, this is a trait which was to resurface often during his life.

The year 1942 ended on a tragic note. Michel Delacroix, the friend Roland had taken singing lessons with before the war and the first young man he had ever loved and been loved by in return, died of tuberculosis on 28 October. Roland was deeply upset by his death. Even the prospect of his imminent return to Paris did little to cheer him up. He returned in January to a newly opened convalescence home in the Rue de Quatrefages, near the Jardin des Plantes. He took this opportunity to sit the exams in grammar and philology which he should have taken in June 1941 and which he needed to finish his teaching degree. He rediscovered his love of books, of studying and also the streets of Paris, especially the Latin Quarter where he loved to wander around. Most importantly, he was reunited with his mother and brother. But this pleasant interlude was not to last long. Just when he thought he was on the way to recovery, he fell ill again. In July 1943 he had a serious relapse, and the doctors decided to send him back to Saint-Hilaire. His morbid thoughts, his depression and his furious resistance returned. Nevertheless, he went back to the sanatorium and resumed his old routines and his old friendships. He also made some new acquaintances. Among them was Robert David, a young student with whom Barthes was to form a lasting friendship.

The first time David heard Barthes's voice in conversation was to remain engraved in his memory. It was during an introductory music course which Barthes had decided to organize. The first lecture took place in a small classroom which could only seat about thirty people: the room was filled to capacity, there were people sitting on every available surface and some people had to stand outside in the corridor. The audience had been expecting a somewhat sentimental talk about music in the style of certain popularizing radio programmes. However, Barthes's style was completely different. The lecture was extremely theoretical and he discussed pitch, scales and tonality, while a friend illustrated what he meant by playing examples on the violin. The audience were particularly impressed by a Chinese scale he played.

The first talk was such a success that the following lectures were moved to the large auditorium, where Barthes was able to use the piano. The number of people who attended gradually decreased, probably because of the difficulty of the course. At the end of the first lecture someone had commented to David that Roland was 'the most intelligent bloke here'. David did not need to be persuaded of this. When he learned that Roland's room-mate was leaving, he quickly put his name forward as a replacement. The first discussions they had were extremely lively. David explained that previously he had shared a room with someone half-crazy who spent the whole night endlessly repeating 'tonight I will sleep deeply and wake up refreshed,' then with another weirdo, a homosexual. Actually he had referred to him as 'a queer', leaving Barthes in no doubt as to his negative attitude towards homosexuality. He still remembers the nightly conversations which followed, as Barthes explained to him how hurtful he found this term and the contempt it expressed. He would talk to him about his attraction to young men, his feelings, his concept of love. He remembers Barthes talking about the sun, Gide, Greece and metaphysics. He also mentioned the Greek heroes, who were allowed to cry openly over the death of a male friend. There followed a series of discussions which were to last many months.

In October 1943, Barthes finally took his obsession with illness to its logical conclusion and enrolled for the first year of a degree in medicine. He later said that his idea was eventually to study psychiatry. He read several textbooks in preparation for the June exam, but soon came back to his original idea of becoming a writer. The few weeks he had spent studying the sciences made him realize that he had only found the idea appealing because they were outside his own experience. Ultimately, the sciences were no more important or liberating than the arts. This brief excursion into the so-called exact sciences reaffirmed him in his earlier vocation: reading, writing, reading and writing. He told David that he loved to write under pressure, to a deadline. For example, when he promised to contribute an article to the student magazine on the pleasure of reading the classics, he derived enormous pleasure from writing under obligation, from having to stick to a strict schedule: so many pages per day, completion by a certain date. His previous belief that what he was producing was meaningless and stupid vanished.

In March he went to Paris for ten days' 'leave' (as it was known in the paramilitary jargon of the sanatorium). This visit left him feeling tired and, moreover, reminded him that the same old problems continued to dog him. He saw his mother again and was reminded of her monthly struggle to make ends meet. While he was away, far removed from this spectacle, he tended to forget it. He knew he had to get better and set about earning a living for himself and Henriette, and he longed to free her from her money worries. But in the face of his continuing illness his desire to get better did not count for much.

There was still a hole in his right lung, which treatment had failed to reduce. An operation was suggested, but the idea was dropped in favour of a different kind of treatment. He was to stay in bed for three months with his feet up in order to give his lung a complete rest. Once again, he had to endure a period of enforced leisure, without music and also without writing, since it was impossible for him to write lying down. Reading became his only distraction. He waited impatiently for the results of this strict course of treatment and longed for it to be successful so that he could lead a full life again. At least the other patients, who were given regular insufflations and X-rays, felt that something was being done for them. Barthes felt he had been abandoned to his fate. The threat of a thoracoplasty or an extrapleural operation was constantly hanging over him like a sword of Damocles.

Nevertheless, he was once again enjoying his previous high status among the patients at Saint-Hilaire and things were looking up for him socially. He was much talked about and was both admired for his intellect and trusted by everyone. One day in July 1944, Émile Ripert, a former lecturer at Aix-en-Provence and an arch-conservative, gave a talk at the sanatorium in which he attacked 'anarchism and hermeticism in poetry', an attack which, in fact, was aimed at modern poetry. Like Barthes, Ripert had been admitted to the sanatorium even though he was no longer a student – and it was years since he had been one. In his lecture he accused the hermetic poets of being fakes and their readers of being snobs. In his opinion it was not only poetry that had 'opted out' but also contemporary morality and social values.

For once, despite the fact that the atmosphere at lectures was usually one of gentlemanly civility, things turned decidedly sour. The normally nonchalant and reserved Barthes, whom Ricci describes as resembling 'a large, sensitive cat', decided to launch a counter-attack. Several weeks later the sanatorium's literary circle organized a collective response in the form of a series of lectures on various modern poets. Pélissier, a fine arts student who did indeed claim to be an anarchist, designed a poster for the occasion. In the weeks that followed, various students gave talks on their favourite poets. Barthes spoke on Michaux, Valéry, Whitman and Baudelaire. François Ricci gave a somewhat esoteric lecture on Patrice de la Tour du Pin, after which Barthes took him aside and told him 'you were inscrutable, well done.' Forty years later Ricci commented, 'I always like his inscrutability myself, even if it made him difficult to approach. But it was because it was about poetry that he opened up.'

A distant liberation

Barthes was not the only person who was talked about at the sanatorium. A trivial incident was about to shake up this closed society. Among the students were three Vietnamese – or 'Indochinese', as they were then known – students. One of them, Nguyen Khac Vien, who was deeply interested in Eastern philosophy, especially Mencius and Confucius, gave a talk one day about his country. Naturally, everyone was expecting plenty of picturesque detail and at first, speaking in soft and measured tones, he fulfilled their expectations by painting a picture of the Indochinese peninsula that was full of 'local colour'. Then he spoke of the French image of Asians. François Ricci, who later became a lecturer in philosophy at Nice University, remembers his speech almost word for word: 'You think the Asiatic races are cold and silent. However, as one of our proverbs says, all the devils unleashed in the world could not make as much noise as students when they are enjoying themselves.' He glanced around the room and then continued: 'But there you have it; you have been under occupation for less than four years and you are already more subdued. In our case, the occupation has lasted for more than fifty years.'

These words, spoken calmly and without aggression, made an enormous impression on the audience. It was 1944 and colonial guilt was practically unheard of. Later, Vien was to become head of the colonial section of the foreign office in Hanoi and the author of a history of Vietnam for Éditions Sociales. At the time, however, he was only an insignificant student suffering from tuberculosis. But he had upset some conventional prejudices and dealt a blow to the idyllic image most people had of the French colonies. Did Barthes have this incident in mind when, later, he attacked colonialist images in *Mythologies*? He may well have, but he never referred to it directly, just as he omitted any mention of the eminent role his grandfather Louis Binger had played in the colonialization of West Africa.

According to Ricci, everyone thought Vien had taken a courageous – even dangerous – stand, since he could easily have suffered disciplinary reprisals. Nothing of the kind happened, even though France was under the Vichy government and Saint-Hilaire's director was said to be a Pétain supporter. But the German occupation was nearing its end, and according to Ricci most of the students were 'wet liberal'. However, there was also a maths student, André

Régnier, who was a communist, plus several students who were known sympathisers of the Vichy government or of the Resistance. Saint-Hilaire-du-Touvet was not far from Vercors, where in June and July 1944 3,500 resistance fighters attempted to hold up German troops on their way to reinforce the Normandy front. The partisans were completely crushed, and their defeat may explain why the region was not liberated until very late in the war (the summer of 1945).

But for the students, the war was still a distant and rather alien event and someone like Barthes, who had made his anti-fascist feelings perfectly plain to Rebeyrol, could appear apparently unconcerned by an event which, in fact, was hardly mentioned in the sheltered environment of the sanatorium. Ten years previously, he had studied the texts of Jaurès in depth and then campaigned against fascism at Louis-le-Grand; if those friends, like Maurice Nadeau, who saw the most of him after the liberation are to be believed, his views remained unchanged. But he was by nature so reserved that he never imposed his views on other people. He had his political convictions, convictions which were often firmly held, but he was not – and never would be – a militant. Militancy always upset him. He considered it a form of exhibitionism, even hysteria. He used the term 'hysteria' so often that it seemed almost obsessional, as most of his friends have remarked. His childhood boredom was his own form of 'hysteria', the over-emphatic affirmation of feelings or emotions was 'hysterical' and militancy was 'hysteria'.

However, the Liberation was about to reach even the isolated region around Saint-Hilaire. Shots were heard and they were aware that fighting was going on in the valley. Some of the students felt ashamed to be in the sanatorium, sheltered from events. Then news reached them that the Germans had hung resistance fighters on meathooks at Grenoble. At Saint-Hilaire, however, the Liberation took place without any violence and not a single armed man was seen. Notices simply appeared one day announcing that the new regime had been established in Grenoble. The director, supposedly a Vichy supporter, discreetly vanished, to be replaced by a Jewish doctor who had returned from the United States.

Political passions were suddenly aroused and came into the open, setting the pro-Vichy students against supporters of the Resistance. One of the latter group decided to denounce the Vichy sympathizers but was persuaded by Barthes to give up the idea, which would seem to indicate that he had not openly declared his support for either group. This incident is significant on two counts. Firstly, it shows what could be termed Barthes's 'moral centrism', and secondly, it shows the high status he had among his fellow students, and his intellectual influence. His friends at the sanatorium do not remember him as being particularly politicized, but then he was hardly alone in this. According to François Ricci the students 'were not well informed and were not in touch with what was happening. However, among the students there were several supporters of the Resistance and several militiamen too. But most of us were apathetic. I must admit that this was my own position, and probably Barthes's too. But even those students who have taken sides were not really sectarian.'

Switzerland and Marxism

France had been liberated, but the students in the sanatorium were still prisoners of their illness. Barthes was still dogged by the same health problems, unable to control his own body. After October he had felt more hopeful again and thought he could feel himself getting better. The three months he had spent in bed had produced good results. He was now on his feet again, and there was no further talk of an operation. He had been confined to bed during the liberation of Paris and regretted missing those final days which, at Saint-Hilaire, had taken on the appearance of a village holiday.

Although he was up and about, he was told that he would probably have to stay at the sanatorium for at least another year, followed by a long period of convalescence. He accepted that this was a possibility and got used to the idea that he might take a long time to recover fully. He began to regard his illness as a kind of permanent, official status. But he was twenty-nine, still without a career, and he felt as if his youth had vanished during the war. Even if he had gained a certain amount of maturity and had grown older, he had still not achieved any kind of social recognition. He was about to turn thirty and, in social terms, he did not yet exist. He had not lived through the experience of the war, now in its final stages, since only its echoes had reached the sanatorium. In reality he had experienced it as a parenthesis or a hiatus between two periods of peace.

On 8 February 1945 Barthes and a group of his fellow patients, including Robert David, were transferred to Switzerland, to the sanatorium at Leysin, above Aigle. A group of bankers from Berne had decided to finance the transfer and to provide the students with a small monthly allowance. In addition, they would receive frequent invitations to the homes of Swiss families in Lausanne and Berne. This act of charity made Barthes indignant, since he felt it turned them all into 'grateful little poor boys'. However, this was not to prevent him from taking advantage of the situation.

From the lakeside a sharply twisting road climbed steeply up through vineyards, then pine woods. The village of Leysin was full of clinics, and indeed illness was its sole source of income. There were also a few cake shops and tearooms where the rich patients could go to gorge themselves. The other patients had to wait for Friday evenings, the highlight of their week, when they were served the 'Swiss menu': as many potatoes and as much butter and gruyère cheese as they wanted. A train connected Leysin to Aigle. The local peasants believed it was used to transport corpses down to the valley, and even today the old people of the Vaud still remember Leysin as place where people went to die, a place they avoided for fear of contagion.

Leysin, with its wooden chalets with slate roofs set in the gentle landscape of the Vaudois Alps, was the perfect place for relaxation and for day-dreaming. The Alexander Clinic, where Barthes was staying, would have made a charming setting for a weekend visit. He felt rejuvenated and his health improved in leaps and bounds. Such improvements were perceived not from his X-rays or his doctors' reports (which in any case he had learned not to trust) but from how he felt in himself, from his renewed appetite for life, his increased energy and vitality. The state of intellectual apathy he thought he had been living in for the previous three years vanished, and as soon as he began to feel better he started work again.

He was now engrossed in reading Michelet, the only writer whose works he would claim later to have read in their entirety. Usually he tended to skim-read a text, gleaning what he could as he went along, stopping to look more closely at a particular passage, then skipping the next few pages. With Michelet, he read each page carefully, making notes as he went, and reading aloud to David whatever notes he was in the process of writing. He made his notes on index cards, which he completed and filed with meticulous, almost obsessive care. According to him, they had to be the international format (7.5 × 12.5 cm), and must be used horizontally. The notes must be legible and contain all the relevant references: edition, chapter, page number, etc.

In fact, he had initially used them vertically, but realizing they were easier to look up if they were filed the other way, he spent a ridiculous amount of time copying out the contents of the nine hundred or so cards he had already written on to new cards. He had perfected a complex system based on pieces of wood and string which meant that he could pick out from the pile all the cards referring to a certain theme or idea. He hoarded these traces of his systematic reading of Michelet's texts as if they were precious stones. This kind of diligence sounds like drudgery, but Barthes denied it was anything of the sort. When David, who was studying law, asked his advice on his university work, he replied somewhat pompously that one had to adopt a relaxed approach, learn how to distinguish what was essential and forget the rest. Above all, one should not summarize the whole of a text but simply jot down the main points on a few index cards.

The students' new way of life hardly differed at all from life at Saint-Hilaire. The Alexander Clinic was part of the university sanatorium and the same kind of treatment was used as at Saint-Hilaire. The basis of this was 'fresh air'. Patients' beds were placed on the terrace facing the jagged peaks of the Midi mountains, but only their legs could be exposed to the sunlight. In addition there was the 'silence treatment', which basically meant taking lots of naps. This kind of therapy was used right up until the 1960s. The doctor in charge of the clinic, an Austrian called Klein, was an amateur violinist and Barthes used to play duets with him, a pastime he found extremely enjoyable. He also made some new friends: André Mosser, a young medical student who loved the theatre and Roselène Hartzfeld, who was staying with her husband, a young pastor, who was one of the patients. He also took Italian lessons with a former priest from Milan, called Cavalleri.

As usual, he wrote numerous letters, although he sometimes complained that he did not get as many back. But most importantly, his health continued to improve. He hoped he might be able to return to Paris in the autumn, and at last felt he could see the light at the end of the tunnel. He was very popular, both with the staff and patients at the sanatorium and with the Swiss families who often invited this 'grateful little poor boy' to their homes. In Berne, at the home of the Sigg family, he made quite an impression on their daughter Heidi. In Leysin, Roselène Hartzfeld, the pastor's wife, dazzled by Barthes's intelligence, declared one day to all and sundry that he would end up at the Collège de France.

At the beginning of September, Henriette Barthes came from Paris to visit Roland. The penniless Barthes collected together an enormous sum of money by borrowing from various friends and took his mother to Lugano, where they stayed in a luxury hotel on the lakeside. This anecdote is characteristic of Barthes's attitude towards money, as will become evident later. Meanwhile, his relationship with David had blossomed, but in a rather one-sided way. Barthes was in love with David, but although the latter cared very much for him, and respected him even more, he was definitely not attracted by the idea of a homosexual relationship. He told Barthes so more than once and they agreed that although they were very close to one another intellectually and emotionally, their relationship was not a love affair, and it was definitely not going to become sexual. Thus things fell into place. They had frequent and fruitful discussions about Michelet, literature, music and law.

David's health was improving and on 19 September 1945 he left Leysin for a convalescence home in Paris, in the Rue de Quatrefages. Barthes found himself alone again. The absence of his loved one plunged him into a state of great nervous excitement and he wrote to David every day for the next six months, sometimes even twice a day. His letters ran to at least eight pages, often resembling small books. They can be seen as a prefiguration of *A Lover's Discourse*, which he was to write thirty years later and which was published in 1977. All the themes explored in the book are present in the letters he wrote to David over the months that followed.

Most obviously there is the theme of absence, with the already implicit idea that the one who has left is not as much in love as the one who stays behind: 'I am loved less than I love,'[6] he was to write in 1977. There is also a musical metaphor: I am like a *do*, a note which of course exists on its own, and you are like a *fa*, which also exists independently, but *do* has infinitely more value, intelligence and sensitivity if it is part of a *do-fa* couple, if it is a function of *fa* . . .

There are also the constant reproaches: your letters are not frequent enough, not long enough. In 1977 he wrote, 'like desire, the love letter waits for an answer; it implicitly enjoins the other to reply.'[7] The theme of jealousy also surfaces. Before entering the sanatorium David had met a young woman, Françoise, and he started seeing her again when he returned to Paris. Barthes, knowing David was in love with her, suffered a great deal because of it, yet he allowed scarcely a hint of his jealousy to appear in his letters. On the contrary, reproaching himself for feeling this way, he advised David to follow through his feelings for her and he regarded this action as proof of his nobility of spirit. In 1977 he wrote: 'As a jealous man, I suffer four times over: because I am jealous, because I blame myself for being so, because I fear that my jealousy will wound the other, because I allow myself to be subject to a banality.'[8]

At times, of course, with thirty years' experience behind him, the strategies of the lover's discourse are adjusted. Thus in October 1945 Barthes sent David a telegram saying 'BIT BORED'. Then immediately he wrote to him explaining that this meant, 'I feel terribly bored without you, I miss you immensely,' but he had not wanted to put this in a telegram which could be seen by the postmistress. In 1977, evoking an absent lover from whom he has heard nothing, he rehearses in his mind everything he could say to him on his return – 'That wasn't at all nice,' or 'Do you know how much worry you caused me?' – and he concludes: 'Or, let this distress of mine be delicately, discreetly understood, so that it will be discovered without having to pester the other ("I was rather concerned . . .").'[9] It is the same figure of style, give or take a few nuances, but in 1945 the litotes is immediately translated, emphasized, while in the second it floats, remaining unspoken.

During this period, Barthes offers further evidence of the manic attention he often gave to detail (such as how to make notes on index cards). There were two postal services between Switzerland and France, airmail and surface mail. Naturally, airmail was more expensive. Barthes therefore decided to carry out an experiment by sending two letters at the same time, one via airmail and the other surface mail, to find out if the difference in price reflected the difference in the speed of service.

A relapse momentarily interrupted his correspondence with David. Without the slightest warning, his health suddenly worsened, and it was decided to operate on him urgently. He had an extrapleural pneumothorax operation, which was known as the 'Schmidt method'. This consisted of the attachment of the parietal pleura, and involved the removal of a piece of his rib. After the operation the Swiss doctors presented him with the section of rib wrapped in a piece of gauze. For many years he was to keep this relic in a bottom drawer along with old keys, a mother-of-pearl dance-card belonging to his grandmother, and a school-report book. One night he threw the rib out of the window, 'as if I were romantically scattering my own ashes, into the Rue Servandoni, where some dog would come and sniff them out,' he wrote in *Roland Barthes by Roland Barthes*.[10] Technically, the operation was a success and once more he began the wait for his imminent release.

He had in the meantime made some new friends. In particular, there was his room-mate, Georges Fournié. He was three years younger than Barthes, and his social background and subsequent life had been completely different from his. An orphan, Fournié had to earn his own living from the age of twelve or thirteen. He had also taken evening classes and eventually become a proofreader. At the age of seventeen, with the outbreak of the Spanish civil war, he had joined the republicans and had fought with the POUM[11] on the Aragonese front, where he had been injured. He had then returned to Paris, where he met his future wife Jacqueline and worked with militant anti-fascist groups. Through such groups he had met David Rousset and Maurice Nadeau.

Fournié had been a Trotskyist, an anti-fascist and a member of the Resistance. His code name in the Resistance had been 'Philippe' and his friends continued to call him this after the war. On 19 October 1943 he had been arrested by the Gestapo along with Rousset and other comrades and imprisoned at Fresnes and Compiègne before being deported to Buchenwald. Finally, he had been transferred to Porta Westfalica, a concentration camp near Hanover. For a year and a half his wife had had no news of him and it was only in the spring of 1945 that he returned, on a stretcher, exhausted and suffering from tuberculosis. At Bichat hospital he was given a pneumothorax and then sent to Leysin. His wife tried to make arrangements to rejoin him there. In October he met Roland Barthes.

However different their backgrounds and temperaments, both men had in common their aloofness from the general atmosphere of the place. Roland, at thirty, was a somewhat distant intellectual, while Georges had survived both the Spanish civil war and deportation. Both men were more mature than the average patient at Leysin. Neither of them liked the adolescent atmosphere and barrack-room humour, which were supposed to take one's mind off the illness and the constant threat of death. In the canteen, where the atmosphere was rather childish (glasses of water and spoonfuls of mashed potato were frequently thrown across the room), both men kept very much to themselves.

After several attempts, Jacqueline Fournié had finally found work in a luxury sanatorium for rich tuberculosis patients, The Belvédère, which is now a Club Méditerranée hotel. She visited her husband every evening and ate with him in the canteen every Sunday. She remembers Barthes as being extremely reserved in the expression of his thoughts and feelings. The only indication of how he felt was the expression in his eyes or the movement of his lips, and his somewhat mocking sense of irony. He never really laughed out loud, uninhibitedly, as if it would be indecent to let himself go. He seemed to be someone without strong passions, always self-controlled, completely a creature of nuance. In this he was the complete opposite of Fournié, the militant, who was about to initiate him into the previously unknown universe of Marxist theory and the reality of the class struggle.

The two would talk together for hours. Barthes discussed theatre, literature, and of course Michelet. Fournié talked about Marx, Trotsky and Spain. They had a mutual admiration for each other, and each taught the other things which had previously been foreign to them. Barthes was extremely lucky that at a time when initiation into Marxism usually came through the Communist party – and more often than not required unconditional support for the political positions of the Soviet Union – Fournié's Marxism was Trotskyist, anti-Stalinist and non-dogmatic.

Apart from his discussions with Fournié, Barthes continued to work enthusiastically on Michelet, getting through his works at an astonishing rate. Sometimes he read and made notes on as many as three hundred pages in one day. He raced through Michelet's *History of France* and his index cards piled up. By November he had nine hundred and at the end of December a thousand. He displayed them proudly to his visitors, laying them out on the table like a pack of playing cards, pairing them up and contrasting them, pursuing in a manual, physical way that investigation of structure which would later govern the organization of the book.

Final months at the sanatorium

At the beginning of December 1945 a sense of imminent departure hung in the air at Leysin. Numerous patients left the sanatorium for periods of convalescence or post-cure treatment closer to their homes. Barthes waited for his turn, and while doing so read the first edition of a new journal called *Les Temps modernes*. He found the introduction by Jean-Paul Sartre exciting and he discussed it with his friends, first with Fournié, and then with David. He explained that the analytical, bourgeois spirit of 1789 was doomed and must give way to a revolutionary spirit grounded in a more 'totalitarian' concept of man. The adjective is a direct quotation from Sartre, who wrote, 'We situate ourselves on the side of those who want to change both the social condition of Man, and his own self-conception.' He went on to clarify this conception in the following manner: 'I will call this conception totalitarian.'[12]

Of course this term sounds bizarre to us today, even if Sartre made a distinction from its fascist sense by explaining that the sense in which he was using it meant an approach which would take into account the totality of elements in a given situation. For Barthes, on the other hand, it fitted almost exactly with what he was learning about Marxism from his discussions with Fournié, and the enthusiasm he showed for this manifesto in favour of commitment in literature is interesting given that his companions thought his politics were centrist (as has already been seen). Sartre's violence, which Barthes supported, was in fact a purely literary violence. Barthes never made the move Sartre eventually did, from a critical theory of society to a critical, militant praxis. He was never to take to the streets, never to lend his support publicly to a particular cause.

Towards the middle of December Dr Klein was replaced by a Dr Van Rolleghem. He looked over the case notes of all the patients, visited Barthes and advised him to begin eating all his meals in the canteen, to go out as much as possible and to take walks. Barthes refused to follow the first part of his advice and continued to eat his meals alone in his room. The fact that he had been advised to spend time outdoors raised his hopes, since it showed the doctor thought he was on the mend. However, as 1945 came to a close, he was still at the sanatorium, still reading and making notes on Michelet, and writing to David every day. He spent Christmas at Leysin, which was an unbearable ordeal for him since he had to join in the Christmas festivities with people he regarded as mediocre. However, a brief visit from Philippe Rebeyrol from 28 to 31 of December cheered him up a great deal. Rebeyrol was now working at the Foreign Office, as head of the Cultural Affairs section, and Barthes was fascinated by what he called his friend's 'social power'. In particular, he realized that his friend could help him get a job abroad when he left the sanatorium. He dreamt of going to the United States, even though he worried about his poor English.

Rebeyrol told him about the new postwar France, which Roland knew little about. On 15 August 1945 Marshall Pétain had been sentenced to death, and then on 17 August pardoned by General de Gaulle, who commuted his sentence to life imprisonment. On 15 October Pierre Laval had been executed by firing squad and in November the Nuremberg trials had begun. Jean-Louis Bory had won the Prix Goncourt with his *Mon village à l'heure allemande* and Romain Gary the Prix des Critiques with *Éducation européene*. These echoes from the outside world made Barthes uneasy. What point could there possibly be in a study of Michelet – and indeed literary studies as a whole – in the new world outside the sanatorium which he was about to enter? Of course, he tried to find a way of justifying his work, explaining that 'old Michelet' still had an audience but that it was a highly specialized audience made up of 'old academics, autodidacts who read the history of France in libraries, 1848-style democrats and anti-clericals – and', he added, 'lonely, isolated types like me'. He was indeed isolated, his intellectual activity cut off from the new France which he glimpsed in Rebeyrol's descriptions.

At the beginning of 1946 an episode occurred which highlights the anxiety and the lack of self-confidence which characterized Barthes during this period. On 5 January he wrote to Robert David to tell him that an Italian, Russo, had asked him to contribute an article to the literary section of a Milan newspaper. He told David that he had nothing interesting to write about, except perhaps Michelet, which would in any case be of no interest to the newspaper. 'Besides,' he said, 'I can't write. I've got agraphia; I'm not very articulate.' It has already been mentioned that the act of writing threw him into a panic, and that he was genuinely convinced that his texts were 'stupid'. Two days later, however, on 7 January, he had produced five different drafts of an article on Camus, and he sent his final version to David, still insisting it was nonsense. In the space of forty-eight hours he had swung from being convinced he was incapable of writing an article he had rashly promised, to producing it. This kind of episode was to occur throughout his life.

Periods of hope alternated with periods of hopelessness. He stayed at Leysin during January 1946, feeling desperate about his continued incarceration. In his daily letters to David he outlined everything he hoped for, everything he expected from their reunion: a new life, a special relationship and an exemplary friendship. Sometimes David, who only wrote occasional letters to Barthes, would phone him. Barthes's love for him was intensified by the distance between them, and he was delighted by these telephone calls. Gradually their relationship changed and a new kind of relationship took its place. David, who visited Madame Barthes regularly and was very fond of her, was becoming 'one of the family'.

Finally, on 26 January, Barthes received a letter from his mother which changed his life: Dr Brissaud had agreed that he could return to Paris and was going to write to the director of the Alexander Clinic informing him of his decision. He made feverish preparations for his departure. He had to pack his trunks and sort out his books and his Michelet filing system. He also had to say good-bye to his friends and acquaintances: the Berne bankers who had arranged for the French students to come to Leysin had not only provided them with a monthly allowance, but had also arranged for them to stay with Swiss families from time to time. Barthes undertook a kind of 'tour of Switzerland' to say good-bye to all the people who had invited him to stay – the Siggs in Berne, the Chessex and Milhit households in Lausanne – with the ulterior motive of borrowing a little money to buy some things he needed before returning to France. He decided to sound out Heidi Sigg, who was a little in love with him. As they strolled through the streets of Berne he wondered how to ask her, and did not dare to. After some hesitation, he decided he would tackle the subject of his financial problems before they reached a certain street-corner. Telling David the story later, he apparently compared himself to Julien Sorel in *Scarlet and Black* when he swears to take Madame de Rénal's hand before the clock strikes ten.

But this is not the only similarity between the two. As Barthes saw it, the students had been assigned the role of 'grateful little poor boys' by the Swiss bankers, and he found this demeaning. He may have been comparing his own social status with Julien Sorel's, remembering Sorel's tirade at the end of the book (chapter 41) in front of the tribunal which was about to sentence him to death: 'I see before me men who . . . will wish to punish in my person and forever discourage that body of young men who, born in an inferior station, and to some degree oppressed by poverty, have the good fortune to secure for themselves a good education, and the audacity to mingle with what the pride of rich men calls society.'[13] Is there an echo of the revolt of Stendhal's sawmill owner's son in the revolt of this ward of the nation? When, as in this case, their knowledge of literature is so clearly interwoven with the most trivial events of someone's daily life, then drawing such parallels seems justified.

Barthes was not released from the sanatorium until February. He was almost completely cured of his tuberculosis, and he had become a Marxist. Before setting off for Paris, he went to Lausanne and bought some clothes with the money he had borrowed from Heidi Sigg: a loden coat, a pair of trousers, a tie and some shoes. He also bought presents for his mother and friends, aware of the hardships and suffering they were going through in postwar France. On 27 February, after spending the day in Lausanne, he took the night train to Paris, where he was reunited with his mother and brother in their flat in the Rue Servandoni (their home from now on). He returned to the Rue de Seine, where as a child he had gone shopping for his mother, to the shops he knew so well and the streets where he loved to wander. He was also delighted to be reunited with his friends, especially Robert David. That summer the two spent several months together in post-cure therapy at the students' sanatorium in Neufmoutiers-en-Brie, in the Seine-et-Marne region, and afterwards Barthes returned to Paris for good, or so he hoped.

But from now on, illness would always be a part of his world. Not just in a concrete form, in his body, in the difficulty he had breathing or getting his breath back after the slightest exertion during the first few years following his recovery, like every tuberculosis sufferer, but also in his imagination. In an interview in 1975, looking back over his life, he spoke about his illness; according to him, the modern attitude to tuberculosis and its treatment bore no relation to how it had been in the past:

> I became ill at a time when tuberculosis was a disease which made the patient the object of a taboo: the taboo of contagion. Besides this, it was a very long, very slow illness. You did not know yourself how it was progressing since you felt no pain. Except in the most serious cases, you felt perfectly fine and it was only the doctors who decreed you were ill. So you had to live with this kind of superior medical decision hanging over you for years.

And the sanatorium?

> The sanatorium gave you two fundamental experiences. The first was friendship: for years you lived with people of the same age, often sharing a room with two or three others. What kept you going were the close bonds of affection which developed in that kind of environment . . . The second thing, of course, was reading. What else did you have to do except read? I read a great deal during my time there, above all the classics, French and foreign. I also started to do a little writing, short pieces for the student magazine *Existences*. It was while I was at the sanatorium that I read the collected works of Michelet, whom I later worked on. So you see it was a very important experience for me.[14]

In fact, he tended to play down greatly the importance of this period in his intellectual development. His work on Michelet and the method he developed of making notes on index cards, the fragmentary style he experimented with in his article on Greece, his piece on Camus and 'colourless writing'. He sketched out his area of research, perfected a good number of his working techniques and outlined in draft form a good number of the ideas he was later to develop. This was one of his fundamental characteristics: he was a man of precocious intellect, but his ideas took a long time to reach fruition, developing only gradually. When he left the sanatorium he took with him the outline of at least two books: *Michelet*, of course, but also *Writing Degree Zero*. In addition, as has been seen, his prolific correspondence with Robert David (not to mention other, later letters about which we know nothing) contained some of what was to become *A Lover's Discourse*.

In fact, the disruption of his university education, which meant that he was unable to follow Rebeyrol's path of going to the École Normale, taking the agrégation and eventually becoming a teacher or a diplomat can be viewed, paradoxically, as a stroke of luck. Barred from taking this path, he was forced to seek an alternative route, one which eventually allowed him, after much struggle, to become Roland Barthes.

He had no way of knowing, of course, that his tuberculosis had saved him from what might have been a mediocre fate and that his time in the sanatorium had given him an invaluable stock of knowledge. He preferred to retain from this period only his deep sense of bitterness. In his own mind, he remained a 'sick old man', and throughout his life he would often cite tiredness as his reason for rejecting an offer of work or justifying a delay in finishing a promised piece of work. For the time being, however, he was free of his illness, even if the names Bedous, Saint-Hilaire, Leysin, the Rue des Quatrefages and Neufmoutiers had the same resonance for him as the names of the different prisons in which he had served time might have for a 'jailbird'.

Taulard (jailbird) and *tubard* (someone suffering from tuberculosis): they have more than their rhyme in common.

4

Paris–Bucharest

It was not until 1946 that Barthes finally left the sanatorium and began 'productive life', as he put it[1] – his life as a writer. This assertion is doubly false. To begin with because, as we have seen, he began writing before his final release from the sanatorium. Philippe Roger has pointed out that the seven or eight articles Barthes wrote in the sanatorium contained the seeds of his future writing: 'Gide, of course, Camus and Michelet but also Racine ... Loyola, La Rochefoucauld ... and Edgar Allan Poe. Nietzsche again and the parallels between Goethe and Montaigne.'[2] Curiously enough, it seems that Barthes himself never wished to acknowledge these articles. He told Maurice Nadeau that he had written nothing, 'not even a single article'.[3] Later, in an interview with Bernard-Henri Lévy, he replied to his question about whether he had written anything while he was in the sanatorium as follows: 'Just two pieces: one on Gide's *Journals* and the other on Camus's [*The Outsider*], which was the seed for *Writing Degree Zero*.'[4]

Why should Barthes be so reticent when, in the micro-society of the sanatorium, he had read the latest novelists and poets and had created around him a sort of cultural ferment, a permanent discussion about subjects which today would be regarded as the very substance of 'modernity'? Above all, why should he hide the fact that he had published his first texts during this period? Can this be seen as symptomatic of his rejection of this period of his life – a rejection so total that, in his mind, nothing worthwhile could possibly have come of it?

Furthermore, the idea that his 'productive life' began after he left the sanatorium is questionable in itself. Whenever he (reluctantly) agreed to supply biographical details, Barthes would always include, along with several important dates (his date of birth, his father's death, his baccalauréat, etc.), information about his 'career' and his illness, thereby emphasizing the important role it had played in his life. Every time he had occasion to talk about his adolescence and the formative years of his education, he would refer to tuberculosis as a particular way of life, often giving the impression that it could only be understood by the initiated, a kind of 'club' of tuberculosis sufferers. The 'biography' he includes at the end of *Roland Barthes by Roland Barthes* consists of a list of dates which finishes in 1962 with his appointment as *directeur d'études* at the École Pratique des Hautes Études, even though the book was published in 1975. Moreover, his illness accounts for more than a third of the entries, even though the dates cover forty-seven years of his life and his illness robbed him of at the very most, a sixth of that: from May 1934 to the beginning of the academic year 1935, then from October 1941 to mid-1947, according to the information he supplies. In addition, he comments below: 'A life: studies, diseases, appointments.' He continues with a strange opposition: 'the rest is in the text but not in the work.[5] Another example of his persistent attempts to get people to accept that in some way 'je est un autre,' to believe that it was pointless to keep searching, that there was nothing to be found in a life . . .

Reintegration

Back in Paris after his long years of absence, Barthes felt bitter and uncertain. Added together, his time at Bedous in 1934–5, his two periods of treatment at Saint-Hilaire and then his time at Leysin meant he had had almost eight years of treatment, shut away in an illusory state of freedom, far removed from what was happening on the cultural scene, or so he thought. In fact, he had read a great deal – all of Michelet, Proust and the early texts of Sartre and Camus. He had also discussed a great many issues, particularly with Fournié, and had acquired a rudimentary knowledge of Marxism. But what did he feel these years had given him? 'What did I gain? A form of culture, surely. An experience of "living together" characterized by an intensification of friendships, the assurance of having one's friends constantly close by, of never being separated from them. And also, much later, the strange feeling of being always five or six years younger than I really am.'[6]

This last phrase implies years spent in a kind of vacuum, time suspended. Suddenly he had to think about his future, about reintegrating himself into society, like a prisoner just released from jail. Should he look for another teaching job? He decided this was out of the question since the education authorities would never entrust children to the care of a former tuberculosis patient, even if according to medical opinion he was now completely cured.

In fact, someone who had suffered from tuberculosis could quite easily become a teacher, providing he or she agreed to have regular check-ups, and at least two of his fellow patients at the sanatorium, François Ricci and Robert David, took this path. But it seems Barthes never made the slightest move in this direction and it could be suggested that he had decided to look on his illness as a constraint, a check. There may, however, be another explanation, one borne out by the experiences of other tuberculosis sufferers during the same period. These regular check-ups took place every three months at first, then twice yearly. They caused such anguish to those who underwent them (who were already obsessed by fears of a relapse) that they sometimes triggered psychosomatic outbreaks of tuberculosis, complete with fevers, pains and coughing fits. In the light of this, any way of avoiding such an ordeal seems justified.

Barthes also had to finish his research on Michelet, but he was unsure exactly what form it should take. At the time he was preoccupied by questions of method: he wanted an approach that would be fresh and resolutely descriptive. During his reading he had been struck by certain recurring ideas and expressions in Michelet's work, and had painstakingly noted these down on cards. He believed that by drawing up a table of Michelet's thematic concerns, he could produce a profound and innovative study of his work. While he was at Neufmoutiers he had read Michelet's last work, the three-volume history of the nineteenth-century, and also Marx's *The Holy Family*, a text he found heavy-going and dull. Remembering his discussions with Fournié, he often compared the arguments between Marxist commentators over different tendencies and parochial issues to disputes among Protestant sects. He nevertheless told Rebeyrol and David that, in political terms, he thought Marxism an invaluable instrument of description of the real world. He hoped there would eventually be a new kind of society where everything would be spiritually and intellectually possible, and he thought that there could only be genuine inner freedom in a genuinely socialist society.

He returned to the flat in the Rue Servandoni where his mother and his brother Michel had been living for over ten years, since their return from Bedous. He had come back to the same old family habits, or at least some of them, and the usual money problems and worries about his future. One day in the autumn of 1946 while he was strolling round the streets of the capital, he met François Ricci, another ex-patient from Saint-Hilaire. Barthes confided his worries to him and asked if Ricci had any way of helping him get a job. Ricci, who was studying philosophy, was unable to do anything for him. He still remembers how distraught Barthes was: the same Barthes whom everyone at Saint-Hilaire had perceived as some kind of mysterious star, as an intellectual *au fait* with the main trends of the avant-garde, seemed worn down, almost pitiful.

As for Philippe Rebeyrol, he had left France to take up his appointment as cultural attaché in Romania. From Bucharest he let Roland know that there might be an opening for him in his department. Roland immediately bombarded him with questions, on the pretext they were details that Dr Brissaud, who had treated him for the past ten years (and was the father of their mutual friend), insisted on knowing before he would allow his patient to leave the country. What would his working conditions be like? How would he be paid? Would his mother be able to come with him? Where would they live? And so on. In his reply, Rebeyrol reassured him on all these counts. He explained that the vacant post was that of librarian at the French Institute, that the library was large and well stocked, and that the current librarian would be leaving in about ten months' time. Accommodation would be provided and his mother could come with him. He also sent him some money, and Roland felt liberated and reassured. The money Rebeyrol had sent would allow him to ditch the humble editing jobs and various tiresome tasks he had been forced to take on in order to get by and concentrate on his research on Michelet, which was going nowhere. His hopes rose: in ten months' time he would have a job and until then he was going to be able to make full use of his time and return to his work on Michelet, neglected for several months. It was December 1946 and his immediate future seemed secure. He would go to Bucharest the following autumn, which meant the end of their most pressing money worries, peace for Henriette and a pleasant job working among books for him.

So he began to work in earnest on his Michelet project, which he had decided to try and turn into a doctoral thesis. However, serious difficulties soon arose. Once he had finished reading and classifying the thousand or more index cards, arranged thematically, he tried to stand back and consider Michelet's writing and his own work critically. At once his whole project collapsed like a house of cards. Up to this point he had thought he had found the right approach to Michelet, an original reading of his work, yet as soon as he had to sit down and write it his doubts and uncertainties overwhelmed him. He suddenly felt as if a large part of what he thought he had discovered lacked any real interest: in fact, his project was quite dubious. Did he really have anything to say?

However, in February, despite his fears, he found someone who was willing to listen to him. René Pintard, a lecturer at the Sorbonne, thought his project worthwhile and even seemed quite enthusiastic about it. Pintard was a literature teacher, a specialist on the seventeenth and eigthteenth centuries, and the author of a thesis on 'erudite libertinage' in the first half of the seventeenth century. There was no reason why he should back a thesis on Michelet. None the less, he found Barthes's ideas interesting, and Barthes's spirits rose. With renewed hope, he began 'productive work' again, even though he never registered the subject of his thesis. Further evidence of the almost manic-depressive mood swings from euphoria to despair that were to remain one of Barthes's main characteristics.

During this period he also began to immerse himself in the Parisian intellectual scene, which at the time was vibrant and exciting. Numerous new magazines and newspapers such as L'Arche, Combat, Les Lettres françaises, Les Temps modernes had appeared, and a lively political and philosophical debate was being conducted, especially about existentialism and Sartre's theory of commitment. Drawing on his reading of Husserl's phenomenology and of Hegel, Sartre was developing his theory of man as a free subject, a subject, in fact, condemned to being free, who had to make choices every instant of his life and who was responsible for the choices he made. 'Existence precedes essence' was the soon-to-be famous phrase which encapsulated the idea that nothing is a given of existence except existence itself. Essence remains to be constructed.

Barthes was bound to find such an atmosphere exciting, since he considered himself both a Sartrean and a Marxist. He decided that his project was to combine these two philosophies in his approach to literature: to develop a 'committed' literature, and to justify Sartre in Marxist terms. But he was thirty-two and had just left the sanatorium. Even if there was a chance of a job in Romania – which in any case would take him away from the Parisian scene – he still needed to find a way of earning some money now. Rebeyrol's advance had disappeared much faster than he had anticipated.

He had in the meantime made contact again with Georges Fournié, who had initiated him into Marxism and Trotskyism at Leysin. Before the war, Fournié had been a militant in the International Workers' Party and one of his fellow militants had been a young man called Maurice Nadeau, who was passionately keen on politics and literature. In July 1947 Nadeau – who was now editor of the cultural section of *Combat* – and his family were spending their holidays with Georges and Jacqueline Fournié at Soisy-sous-Montmorency. Fournié had rented a large villa with its own grounds near the forest, since his doctors had advised him not to live in Paris. It was a beautiful setting and the villa, which belonged to the Comte de Las Cases, was spacious and pleasant, even if quite a distance from Paris, where Jacqueline commuted every day. It was here that Fournié first mentioned Barthes to Nadeau, who still has a vivid memory of the occasion:

> One day Fournié (whom his wife and friends still called Philippe, his code name when he was in the Resistance) said to me: 'At Leysin I shared a room with a really nice chap, a teacher or something like that who had been at the sanatorium before. When we weren't having treatment we used to spend our time either discussing the books we were reading or talking about politics. He was a middle-class intellectual, you know the type. No idea about the USSR, Stalin or Trotsky but really interested in what I had to tell him about Marx and historical materialism.'
>
> Jacqueline added: 'a really charming man, very sensitive and very refined. I wasn't always there during their discussions but if Philippe hadn't had Roland around . . . At least there was someone among all those patients he could discuss things with.'
>
> 'Anyway,' Philippe, interrupted, 'he's back in Paris and I'd like you to meet him.'[7]

Nadeau had no real desire to disturb the peace and quiet of his holiday, but Fournié managed to persuade him and finally the friends arranged a meeting. By this time Nadeau was already a figure of some importance on the literary scene. It was he who, at the end of October 1945, had reported on Sartre's famous lecture 'L'existential-isme est un humanisme' ('Existentialism is a humanism') in *Combat*, the newspaper created by Camus. He had also (again in *Combat*) hailed Sartre's *L'Âge de raison* (*The Age of Reason*) as 'the masterpiece of contemporary fiction'. Sartre and Camus were two of Barthes's main points of reference, and one fine summer's morning he took the train with Fournié from the Gare du Nord to Enghien. Here they took a local train to Soisy, then climbed a fairly steep track to the villa. The guest, out of breath after the climb and also feeling rather intimidated, was introduced to his hosts and shown round the house. Nadeau remembers Barthes as shy and reserved on this occasion: 'Roland was not demonstrative. He spoke quite slowly, in measured tones and emphasized the inflections in his voice with a smile. You sensed he was sparing in his gestures. Light eyes with a lovely expression. Nice but secretive.'

Barthes told Nadeau that he had read his articles, as well as those of Sartre and Camus. A literary conversation followed, in which Barthes said how much he admired Raymond Queneau, Jacques Prévert and Gaston Bachelard. He also said that he had raced through *Being and Nothingness*, that he knew nothing about the surrealists and then went on to talk about his thesis on Michelet, whom he had read and reread and found fascinating. They spent the afternoon on the lawn. The two convalescents seated themselves in the shade, where they rested and reminisced about their days at Leysin. When the time came for Roland to leave, Nadeau, who was always on the lookout for young talent, asked him if he would like to contribute some articles to his page in *Combat*, perhaps on Michelet.

At the time, *Combat* was a paper of considerable prestige. It had begun as an organ of the resistance in 1941, and at the time of its launch the editorial team consisted of Georges Bidault, Claude Bourdet, Jacqueline Bernard, Pascal Pia and Henri Frenay, who was editor in chief. When Frenay left for London in 1943 he was replaced by Pia. In the autumn of the same year, Pia brought Camus into the team. Written in Paris, printed in Lyons, and distributed with enormous difficulty, *Combat* ran to fifty-eight numbers produced in secret. Gradually Camus took on greater responsibilities. By 1944 he was in charge of recruiting new writers (he brought Sartre into the team) and of maintaining contact with the printers. He also put the finishing touches to the paste-ups in his flat in the Rue Vaneau and organized the paper's distribution.

When the Liberation finally came, the newspaper's headlines kept pace with all the important events as they occurred. On 21 August the headline ran 'The Battle Continues', on 23 August 'They Will Not Pass', on 24 August 'The Blood of Liberty' and on 25 August 'The Night of Truth'. The editorials were unsigned but were usually the work of Camus, or sometimes Pierre Herbart or Albert Ollivier.

Every kind of subject and controversial issue was touched on, from the death penalty and purges to De Gaulle's political intentions.

Then the paper came out of its clandestine phase and entered the public phase of its existence. The editorial team believed that it was necessary to create a press which, like *Combat*, was as free thinking as it was financially independent, a press which would not pander to sensationalism but would aim to provide the public with a critical reading of events, with 'selective information'. In short, they wanted a paper that would continue the work of the Resistance. Camus proposed that the paper should carry the subtitle 'From Resistance to Revolution', and this suggestion was immediately adopted. The editorial team's desire for honesty and clarity ensured that *Combat* became very popular among intellectuals. An important factor in its success was its impressive range of contributors, including André Malraux and Jean-Paul Sartre (who in 1944 had published eye-witness reports of the Liberation of Paris), André Gide, Raymond Aron and André Breton. It was in *Combat* that Camus in November 1946, broke in spectacular fashion with Stalinist communism ('Neither victims nor executioners'). At the time, the paper was selling over a hundred thousand copies and had a very good reputation. In the eyes of the general public *Combat* meant Camus – even if it was Pascal Pia who was actually in charge and Camus merely turned up now and again to write an editorial.

But its image as a prestigious, widely respected and successful newspaper was belied by a certain number of financial problems which were soon to have a significant effect on the managerial team. Claude Bourdet, one of the paper's original founders, had been arrested and then deported because of his activities in the Resistance. After the Liberation he had not returned to *Combat* but had begun working in radio. The editor, Pascal Pia, was trying to find a solution to the newspaper's financial crisis: a takeover by the *Voix du Nord* was considered and even De Gaulle showed an interest, but nothing came of these options and Pia, exhausted, resigned. On 2 June 1947 the paper's founding members sold their shares to Claude Bourdet, who was to guarantee the political continuity of the paper and who sold half the shares to a businessman, Albert Smadja, who owned a daily paper in Tunis. *Combat* had been bailed out of its financial crisis and continued on its way, but without Pia or Camus. At a meeting with the editorial team, Smadja assured them that he would not interfere in the commissioning of articles and would only concern himself with the paper's management. For the first few months, he remained true to his word.

The *Degree Zero*: inception

'Would you like to write some articles for my page in *Combat*, on Michelet for example?'

This, then, was the newspaper Nadeau had asked Barthes to contribute to. Barthes must have felt honoured and eager to take him up on his offer, to add his name to the paper's long list of prestigious contributors. However, he was rather intimidated and neither accepted nor refused the offer at first. He explained that he was trying to sort out his future and find a job, and that he would think it over. Several weeks later, however, a manuscript arrived on Nadeau's desk. He found it rather hard-going, 'beyond the level of most *Combat* readers, even though it was a paper for intellectuals'. He put it to one side to think about it and then mislaid it: even today he cannot remember what it said. Then a second text arrived with the strange title 'Le Degré zéro de l'écriture'. Nadeau was embarrassed at having lost the first text, so he read this one immediately. Despite finding it just as difficult, he decided to publish it together with an introductory foreword written by himself:

> Roland Barthes is a young, unknown writer. He has never published any work, not even an article. Yet, after several conversations with him, we decided that his young man, this fanatic about language (who has thought of nothing else for two years), had something new to say. He has sent us the following article, which is not, by any stretch of the imagination, a piece of journalism: its dense style and its seriousness make no concessions to the reader. We hope the readers of *Combat* will not take us to task for having published it, despite its difficulty.[8]

Was Nadeau exaggerating when he said that Barthes was exclusively interested in language? Can Barthes only have told him about this one aspect of his work? Whatever the case, for the previous two years Barthes had been almost exclusively interested in Michelet. However, it is also true that he was indeed to become 'fanatical' about language, and that Nadeau's remark exemplifies his considerable powers of intuition.

Many readers did indeed find Barthes's first article difficult and obscure, and also those which followed it: 'Responsabilité de la grammaire' ('The responsibility of grammar') on 26 September 1947, and then, three years later (from 9 November to 16 December

1950), 'Triomphe et rupture de l'écriture bourgeoise' ('The triumph and break-up of bourgeois writing'), 'L'artisanat du style' ('Style as craftsmanship'), 'L'écriture et le silence' ('Writing and silence'), 'L'écriture et la parole' ('Writing and speech'), 'Le sentiment tragique de l'écriture' ('Writing's tragic sense').

Paradoxically, the style of the final version of *Writing Degree Zero* is of an extreme simplicity, clearly illustrating its author's ideas, while at the same time revealing his sense of humour. The novel, he explains, has two basic characteristics: first, the use of the past historic tense, and second, the use of the third person (he/she). Thus a phrase like 'the Marchioness went out at five o'clock'[9] is the archetypal form of the novel, and it characterizes the narrator's distance from the story he or she is narrating. This is why, Barthes continues, Agatha Christie was able to deceive her readers in her famous detective story *The Murder of Roger Ackroyd*, where the reader finally discovers at the end of the story that the murderer is the narrator, the chronicler of Poirot's actions and gestures. The reader looks for the murderer among the characters the narrator describes, behind the 'he' or 'she' which are the very form of the novel itself, whereas the murderer in fact conceals himself behind the 'I' of the narrator. The novel's mystery stems from the way it breaks the code.

As in most of Barthes's texts, his ideas are clear, even if they are masked by his style of writing and idiosyncratic vocabulary. Writing, he explains, involves a choice for the writer, a choice which is doubly determined. First, by the social language he inherits, and second, by his own style, which comes from his body, his drives. Writing is 'an act of historical solidarity',[10] a formula which, translated into Sartrean terms, means writing is 'a form of commitment'. Thus there are different types of writing which correspond to different social positionings. One adopts a certain style of writing as one adopts a certain mode of dress, to show which group one belongs to. Barthes looks at different possibilities: at the style of writing in detective novels, at bourgeois writing, writing as work. He privileges two of them: the *conversational writing* (*L'écriture parlée*) of Raymond Queneau and the *colourless writing* (*L'écriture blanche*) of Camus's *The Outsider*.

The first type of writing, conversational writing, speaks for itself, as it were, and anyone who had read Queneau's *Zazie dans le métro* will understand what the term refers to – except, of course, that *Zazie* was not written until 1959. Barthes's text, written twelve years earlier, analyses Queneau's first novels, such as *Pierrot mon ami* or *Loin de Rueil* and his *Exercices de style*. It is astonishing that he intuited in these texts the Queneau in the making, the Queneau who was finally to make his explosive appearance in *Zazie*. As for colourless writing, it is a 'style of absence which is almost an ideal absence of style'.[11] The prime example is Camus's novel *The Outsider*, about which Barthes had already published an article at Saint-Hilaire and which concludes with exactly the same image as *Writing Degree Zero*: 'a style of silence, a silence of style . . . a white voice'.

However, here we come up against a problem. This article, 'Réflexions sur le style de *L'Étranger*' ('Reflections on the style of *The Outsider*'), the starting point for *Writing Degree Zero*, was published in June 1944. But in February 1943 Sartre had written a long article on *The Outsider* entitled 'Explication de *L'Étranger*'[12] and Barthes's ideas may well have been influenced by this article. Of course, Camus's novel is written in the perfect tense, and this choice, along with the idea of the writing of silence, a neutral white writing, forms the cornerstone of Barthes's analysis. As regards these two points, a comparison between Barthes's article and Sartre's is highly revealing. It should be pointed out, however, that where Barthes uses 'passé simple' (preterite), Sartre uses the term 'passé défini' (simple past):[13]

SARTRE	BARTHES
'The first part of *The Outsider* could have been given the same title as a recent book, *Translated from Silence*.'	'Writing and silence.'
'The sentences in *The Outsider* are islands. We bounce from sentence to sentence, from void to void. It was in order to emphasize the isolation of each sentence unit that M. Camus chose to tell his	'finally, the preterite is the expression of an order.' 'To create a colourless writing, freed from all bondage to a preordained state of language.'

story in the present perfect
tense [parfait composé].
The simple past is the tense
of continuity.'

'This is what enables
M. Camus to think that in
writing *The Outsider*, he
remains silent. His sentence
does not belong to the
universe of discourse.'

'a sort of basic speech
equally far from living
languages and from literary
language proper.'

The comparison between this same article of Sartre's and Barthes's own writing can be taken further, in relation to another article he was to publish in 1954, to which we shall return later. In effect, Sartre notes in his article that night has no place in *The Outsider*'s universe since '*The Outsider* gives us a succession of luminously clear views' and the book's season 'is Algiers' eternal summer'.[14] The article Barthes published in 1954 was called '*L'Étranger*, roman solaire' ('*The Outsider*, a solar novel'). Sartre's text continues: 'The man who wrote these lines is as far removed as possible from the anguish of a Kafka. He is very much at peace within disorder . . . The absurd man is a humanist; he knows only the good things of this world.'[15] Barthes had begun to explore the theme of the sun in Camus's work in an article he wrote for a Milan magazine in January 1946. In this text he said that the sun gave man a deep sense of calm and a necessary lucidity. Can the similarity between these passages really be a matter of coincidence? It would seem not. So is it a case of plagiarism? Perhaps not so much of plagiarism as of echoes or influences, one of the first signs of a tendency which can be seen in most of Barthes's work: his tendency to pick up ideas or scraps of theory from all over the place and to put them together in his own way to construct his own theories.

In his first book, *Writing Degree Zero* (which was published several years later), we can find an example of this mode of operation. The text begins:

Hébert, the revolutionary, never began a number of his news-sheet *Le Père Duchêne* without introducing a sprinkling of obscenities. These improprieties had no real meaning, but they had a significance [Ces grossièretés ne signifiaient rien mais elles signalaient]. In what way? In that they expressed a whole revolutionary situation. Now here is an example of a mode of writing whose function is no longer only communication or expression, but the imposition of something beyond language, which is both History and the stand we take in it.[16]

Of course *signifier*, *signaler* (to signify, to signal) are not being used here in any specific technical, theoretical or linguistic sense, but they herald a pair of concepts Barthes was to use in his later works (from *Mythologies* onwards): the oppositional pair of denotation and connotation. Denotation and connotation, taken from scholastic logic, became famous in their modern sense through the work of the Danish linguist Louis Hjelmslev, whose work Barthes could not have known at the time he wrote *Writing Degree Zero*. Hjelmslev's *Omkring sprogteoriens grundlaeggelse*, first published in 1943, was not translated into English until 1953,[17] and the French translation, *Prolégomènes à une théorie du langage* dates from 1968. Although a detailed review of the work by André Martinet was published in the *Bulletin de la Société de linguistique de Paris* in 1946, it is unlikely that Barthes would have read such a specialized journal. Since he did not have the necessary concepts, Barthes used the common verbs *signifier* and *signaler* in an almost intuitive fashion and much later replaced them with the formalized distinction between denotation and connotation, just as one borrows someone else's clothes.

It is time to return for a moment to his meeting with Maurice Nadeau, the starting point for his first articles. The two had since become friends, and one day Barthes invited Nadeau and his wife to his mother's flat. Nadeau remembers the Barthes's quaint, old living room. 'His mother welcomed us. She was a real "lady", simple, cultured, friendly. She paid us a visit in return. She was worried about Roland's future: Would he eventually settle down and get married? She felt he was so very close to her, so fragile, so different from his brother.'

This theme – when would Roland find a job, when would Roland get married – came up time after time in her conversations with Madame Nadeau. A few months later her mind was set at rest on at least one count. The job of librarian at the French Institute in Bucharest which Philippe had mentioned several months earlier finally came up, and Roland's application was successful. He spent November obtaining the visas he needed: one for Bulgaria, one for Yugoslavia, an inter-Allied visa for Trieste, a visa for Switzerland. His doctors advised him not to travel by plane for fear that the cabin pressure, which was not as reliable as it is nowadays, might trigger a spontaneous pneumothorax, so he had to take the train. He set off with his mother for Romania, to take up his first job since leaving the sanatorium. The Barthes's flat in the Rue Servandoni was sublet to Robert David, who lived there for the whole time they were abroad.

A small town in Romania

In 1940, on the accession of King Michael I to the throne of Romania, Marshal Ion Antonescu had declared himself Conducator. This was the Romanian equivalent of the German Führer or Italian Duce, and with the support of his openly fascistic Iron Guard he had maintained a firm grip on the country, aligning it with Hitler's Germany. Throughout this period of totalitarian rule, the French Institute in Bucharest (which was linked to the University of Paris) had provided a forum for lively and brilliant intellectual exchange. The institute arranged lecture series and concerts – one of which brought together the violinist George Enesco and the pianist Dinu Lipatti – and above all, it provided a breath of fresh air: Rebeyrol's predecessor Jean Mouton recalls that 'both the Romanians and the French went to the institute to have a sense of freedom.'[18] Because of its links with the universities of Bucharest and Paris, the institute was able to provide a more exciting intellectual fare than other, more traditional French institutes, which more often than not resembled shops selling French culture. At a time of rampant fascism, it seemed a bastion of freedom. Among the numerous French teachers in Bucharest was Pierre Guiraud, who worked at the Lycée Français; he later became a famous linguist, but at the time he was mainly involved in gathering information for the British. There was also Charles Singevin, who was to play an important role in Barthes's intellectual development later, when they were both in Egypt.

The political balance in Romania was about to change. After the battle of Stalingrad, the king once again took control of the reins of power, and had the dictator Antonescu arrested. Romania was realigned with the allies: a government of national unity (a coalition of socialists and communists) prepared the ground for Romania's passage into the Soviet sphere of influence. When Barthes arrived in 1947, King Michael was still on the throne and had even been made a Hero of the Soviet Union. A large room had been fixed up for Roland and Henriette on the first floor of the French Institute (above the library and the offices), where Rebeyrol and his wife were already living. Partitions were installed, and Roland and his mother settled in as best they could.

They began the life of 'the French abroad', receiving invitations and doing the social round. In the evenings, in their little flat, frequent discussions took place over impromptu dinners. Philippe Rebeyrol took part, of course, but also other new friends, among them Charles Singevin and Jean Sirinelli, a young Hellenist who was both director of studies at the institute and also temporarily teaching at the university (standing in for the holder of the chair in French). Barthes showed him his boxes of index cards on Michelet, and Sirinelli was impressed by his detailed knowledge of the author of the *Histoire de France*. Barthes spoke about Michelet as if from within, with a detailed knowledge of his passions, his moods and his tempers, interspersing sociological observations with details of his taste in coffee and tobacco or even his illnesses, as for instance when he described how Michelet took his own pulse. Later he would write, 'I have always wanted to remonstrate [argumenter] with my moods.'[19] Perhaps he was sensitive to Michelet's moods for similar reasons, because he regarded these minor details of daily life as the starting point for an analysis. Sometimes he made ad hoc theorizations: what he meant by 'moods' had nothing to do with the notion of 'good' or 'bad' moods; there was nothing social about it – it had to do with one's entire inner being, one's viscera and brain. What he was outlining during these discussions – which earned him a reputation as a brilliant conversationalist – was a kind of *ontology* of moods, which was to remain one of his favourite themes. According to Sirinelli he had the kind of intelligence which 'had nothing sharp-edged about it. It embraced the forms of things rather than slicing them up,' and above all, he had a generosity of spirit and an openness to others which were quite rare.

Very soon the institute's new boarder began to give lectures. He began with a series of four talks on French songs, accompanied by extracts from songs. The title of one of them, 'La môme Paif et Yves Montand' ('The Piaf kid and Yves Montand'), was a bit cryptic for its Romanian audience and at first his talk caused some astonishment. However, it went on to be a big success: it was on an aspect of French popular music which, quite understandably, was unheard of at the time in Romania, where hardly anyone knew who 'la môme Piaf' was. Later, in another talk, he spoke about Charles Trenet, and then, with a radical change of subject, gave a talk on Voltaire. He explained that although he was a historian, Voltaire had come before the century of history, the nineteenth century. His lecture style was a combination of erudition and popularization: his tone was that of an expert, yet his talks were still accessible to the general public.

In fact, he was trying out the style he would later use in *Mythologies*. It was a style which developed because of the place where he was speaking. If he had taught in a university, he would have adopted a different tone, moulded his discourse into the forms of classical academic discourse. At the institute, however, speaking to a cultured but non-specialist audience, he perfected in oral form what was later to become his style of writing. In a sense it was here, in his lectures, that he began to explore a route which was an alternative to the first path he had imagined himself taking (the Rue d'Ulm, the agrégation, etc.) and which he had been barred from. He was to follow this second path for the rest of his life.

He also explored Bucharest which, despite being a capital city, was really only a town compared with the capital he was used to. He used to spend his free time buying the traditional embroidered clothes and sending them to his friends in France (especially Jacqueline Fournié, who had just given birth to a baby boy). He also met boys through the French classes he gave at the institute. His colleagues, seeing him tirelessly carrying on discussions with his students after class, admired his conscientiousness and considered him, as one of them put it, 'an apostle of pedagogy'. But above all he devoted his energies to organizing the institute's library, which held over thirty thousand books and was very popular among Romanian intellectuals.

The political situation remained unclear. Events could have taken any of several different turns, but were finally precipitated by the introduction of the Marshall Plan in 1947. The Iron Curtain fell between Eastern and Western Europe. After hesitating for a few days, Stalin decided to refuse American aid and imposed the same decision on his satellites. It was almost inevitable that Romania would topple: posters of the Workers' party appeared on the walls of the capital demanding King Michael's abdication, while one demonstration followed another. Feeling powerless to resist this movement, the king bowed to these pressures and abdicated in December 1947. At the beginning of 1948, the People's Republic of Romania was founded.[20]

Thus the new French Institute librarian found himself in a country where Marxism was the official ideology. This did not bother him unduly since, as he had confided to Philippe, he was a Marxist, in the sense that when it came to politics he could only think in Marxist terms. In his view it was the only theory which could produce an effective analysis of social situations. In Charles Singevin's view, Barthes was a Trotskyist who passed for a communist. As for Rebeyrol, he wondered how Barthes could continue to hold his convictions living as he was under a dictatorship, and one which, among other things, was extremely intolerant of homosexuality.

Indeed, the situation soon became very uncomfortable. France was considered an imperialist country, an ally of the United States, and the authorities tried to impose a kind of quarantine around the institute. The cultured, francophile Romanians who had previously gone there regularly, gradually started staying away, fearing reprisals. They also asked their French friends not to telephone them any more. As Rebeyrol says, 'If I had wanted to compromise someone or have them imprisoned, all I would have needed to do was to telephone him and speak to him warmly. The phone taps and the police would have done the rest.' It became almost impossible to hold any kind of cultural event: a lecture on Alfred de Musset had to be cancelled and another on Pierre Emmanuel was banned, since both, in the view of the authorities, were products of 'Atlantic culture'. On the other hand, they had no problems when they invited Dominique Desanti, a journalist working for L'Humanité.

One last French initiative was approved by the authorities and proved to be an enormous success: a visit by Louis Aragon and Elsa Triolet. In front of a stadium packed with Romanian workers who could not understand a word of French and who applauded at regular intervals as ordered, Aragon spoke for two hours on 'Elsa and I'. He concluded his speech by declaring grandly, 'Elsa is my wife and I love her.' Two days later he gave a lecture at the French Institute which caused Philippe Rebeyrol some problems, since the authorities insisted on carefully inspecting the guest list.

The institute's scope for organizing any form of cultural activity grew narrower every day. While King Michael had been on the throne, before the Marshall Plan was announced, there had been some room for manoeuvre. Thus one day the former secretary-general of the Communist party, Patrascanu, who had become Minister of Justice, had organized a breakfast meeting between Philippe Rebeyrol and Anna Pauker, the Minister for Foreign Affairs, where the young cultural attaché had been able to plead the cause of French culture. But since the sovereign's abdication, the situation had become untenable. At the time there were around two hundred French teachers in Romania as compared to a handful of English and Spanish teachers. The authorities regarded their presence as a form of imperialism. Rebeyrol, who knew about Barthes's sexual preferences, did not, however, know all the details of his private life during this period. He only found out from Barthes later, and when he thought back to the risks Roland had run it made him break out in a cold sweat. Secrecy was essential if he was to meet his friends and Roland's behaviour could have jeopardized the position of the institute at any moment had he not acted in his usual extremely prudent and discreet fashion.

The tension mounted to such a point that Madame Rebeyrol returned to Paris at the end of 1948, where she gave birth to her first child. In January 1949 hostilities broke out. Initially, there was a campaign of insults in the press, denouncing the 'brackish water of Atlantic culture' which flowed through the French Institute. The institute was accused of being the stronghold of 'puppets of Marshall' who were trying to spread 'colonial culture'. All the French nationals were accused of spying, but the police files were, in fact, empty. All the campaign reflected was the authorities' desire to break off relations. Rebeyrol thinks that 'if they had had anything on Roland's private life, it would have been emblazoned all over the press.' The authorities forced the Lycée Français to close, followed by the institute. In addition, they intended to take over the institute's building.

This move provoked an immediate and strong response from the Quai d'Orsay, which decided to treat the Romanian consulate in Paris as the equivalent of the French Institute in Bucharest. If the Romanians tried to seize their building, the French would do the same to the consulate. This firm reaction saved the building, but all the teachers were expelled. In February, Rebeyrol returned to Paris, leaving Barthes behind as the rearguard along with a few administrative staff. For three months he worked in the deserted building, organizing and classifying the files and dealing with day-to-day matters. He tried to give away the library books to francophile Romanians, but they did not trust him. He then tried to find some way of bequeathing them to a university library, but all his attempts were met with a wall of indifference.

Besides all this, there was his own fate to think about. What would happen to him once he returned to France? As he was only on a contract, there was a strong chance that he would find himself out of a job. For a time he considered staying on in Bucharest. Even if the institute was forced to close, the embassy would remain open and he could take on the job of cultural attaché, since he was already, in effect, performing such a role. Then the possibility of a job in Rome was mentioned, but this came to nothing. It was a difficult time for him. His hopes were raised only to be dashed. To his career problems were added health problems, in the form of an attack of jaundice. In his regular reports to Philippe Rebeyrol (called 'The Institute News') he gave minute accounts of the day-to-day problems (should the staff's holiday pay be paid in francs or in local currency? What was to be done with the records, the projector, the car?) and of the larger political questions (what was to be the future of French culture in Romania?). The final outcome of all this was the abrupt decision by the Romanian authorities to expel the staff of the 'imperialist' French Institute at the end of July 1949. For no apparent reason, Barthes's name was not on the list. This was not at all convenient for him since, in Paris, Rebeyrol and Sirinelli had worked out a way of finding new jobs in Egypt for all their Bucharest colleagues. If Barthes stayed in Romania too long, he risked missing out on this redeployment.

It was not until two months later that his name was finally added to the list of undesirables. On 22 September he organized a final concert, and before they listened to Glück's *Orpheus* he addressed a few words to the still faithful audience. He explained that no one would be replacing him and that there would no longer be a cultural attaché in Romania, which also meant the French university would no longer have a presence alongside the Romanian one. Then, having reminded the audience in what might seem a rather demagogic fashion (though doubtlessly sincerely meant, since he had nothing to lose) that he himself was a firm believer in the 'the critical methods of dialectical materialism', he launched into a curious attempt to defend French culture in Marxist terms. Philippe Rebeyrol has kept the following copy of his speech:

> The critical function of French science, scholarship and thought has been carried out through the centuries by millions of French teachers and intellectuals, from Montaigne to Valery, Gerson to Marc Bloch. It constitutes a solid historical fact in comparison with which the closure of a library or the departure of a cultural attaché are laughable, in historical terms. Thus it is with absolute peace of mind that I reflect upon the future of this institute. What matters is the spirit it conveys and this has already been borne out and championed by history itself. History could never deny its own march.

Was this experience of life in a socialist country, of daily life behind the Iron Curtain, a bitter one for Barthes the Marxist? It is difficult to tell. He would later tell friends that his days in Bucharest had been the happiest of his life, but here he was referring to his love life. On the eve of his departure, for example, he wrote to Sirinelli: 'I am desperately unhappy at the thought of leaving the country where I am in love.' Of course, Sirinelli thought he was referring to a woman, further proof not only of how discreet Barthes was about his private life, but also of how ambiguous he could be. He was not hiding anything or lying (he did not mention a woman), yet he was not revealing anything either.

No matter how he felt, he left Romania and arrived back in Paris in September 1949. Despite his worries, his immediate future was secure. At the Quai d'Orsay, Rebeyrol and Sirinelli had sorted out the problem of the 'deportees', as they were referred to. Most of them had been reassigned to Egypt. Some, like Louis Delamare, the former secretary-general of the institute (who was murdered in 1981 while serving as ambassador in Beirut) and Paule Priet, the headmistress of the primary school, were to leave for Cairo at a later date. For the time being Barthes and Charles Singevin were assigned to Alexandria, where Roland would go without his mother. She was to stay behind in Paris with Michel, for the first year at any rate, and would perhaps join him later.

5

From Alexandria to
Writing Degree Zero

In 1949, Alexandria was a bizarre Franco-British trading post whose doubly colonial situation can be summed up by saying that the English represented the police and the French represented culture. There was absolutely no point in foreigners learning Arabic, since one could easily get by with French or English. Educated Egyptians all spoke perfect French and sent their sons and daughters to French lycées or convent schools respectively. All the shops, restaurants and cinema signs were in Arabic, naturally, but with French 'subtitles'. Since the mid-nineteenth century, French had replaced Italian as the daily *lingua franca*, as it had throughout the Middle East. This was compounded by a certain anti-English sentiment which was beginning to surface among the members of this cosmopolitan society. The well-to-do Greeks, the sons of oil merchants, learnt philosophy and mathematics in French, preferring, through a form of anti-imperialism, the language of Descartes to the language of Shakespeare. Sympathy for Egyptian nationalism was shown to by a preference for French culture and it was also a way of emphasizing one's opposition to British officialdom. The British were characterized as cold and haughty and the francophone world was considered infinitely more attractive. The singer Georges Moustaki, whose father owned a French bookshop, remembers the atmosphere at the time:

> After the war, we started getting the first French films and songs, which
> we found really exciting. We lived in a state of constant antagonism with

the English-speaking community. During the war, the pupils at English schools had American films and music and we'd had nothing comparable. This gave them a kind of unbearable superiority over us. That's why, after the war, we were thrilled to have an equivalent, to have our own 'anti-culture'. It didn't matter whether it was *The Count of Monte Christo* or Cocteau, Piaf or Félix Marten, Trenet or Jean Drejac.

The bourgeoisie listen to the piano with their eyes closed

In the autumn of 1949, when the deportees from Romania arrived in Al Iskandariyah, to give it its Arabic name, the city seemed more like Bordeaux or Marseilles than a Middle Eastern city. Among the new arrivals were Roland Barthes and Charles Singevin, who had already spent ten years in Poland before his ten years in Romania and who would never return to live in France: after his time in Egypt, he went to Italy. In Alexandria the two found Algirdas Julien Greimas, who had arrived a few weeks earlier. Greimas was a Lithuanian who had studied in Grenoble before the war and who did not become a French national until 1951. He would also become the great French expert on structural semantics and semiology. The three men were all French 'lecteurs' at the university, which meant quite simply that they gave language – and sometimes literature – classes.

Barthes had, in fact, had problems getting into the country. The Egyptian authorities, having seen his medical records, particularly the record of his pneumothorax, had expressed reservations, fearing that he might still be contagious. Greimas had intervened to make sure he was allowed in, but Barthes had to agree to undergo a monthly check-up to see if his illness was under control. Such a humiliation was bound to reawaken his sharp sense of being handicapped by his illness.

His difficulties with the Egyptian authorities were soon compounded by difficulties with members of the official French colony in the city, which still had its supporters of the Vichy regime (after the 1940 armistice the French fleet had been confined to Alexandria for a large part of the war and several traces still remained). During his first public lecture, Roland Barthes committed an error of 'taste'. He was talking about music when he used the following expression: 'In the eighteenth century the aristocracy listened to music with their eyes open, whereas today the bourgeoisie close their eyes when they listen to the piano.' This expression, typical of the style he would use in the future, hit home. This mention of the 'bourgeoisie', which would later become the centre of his theoretical reflections but which at this stage was a convenient catch-all concept (half-Flaubertian, half-Marxist), made his audience shudder. There were mutterings in the drawing rooms and he was classified from then on as a dangerous revolutionary. Tubercular in the eyes of some and a communist in the eyes of others, Barthes found himself trapped between two kinds of intolerance. His isolation meant that he spent a great deal of time with Algirdas Greimas (who soon changed his strange first name to Guy) and his wife Anna, and to the Singevins, whom he had known in Bucharest but who now became his close friends.

With the Greimases he did not talk a great deal about himself. A couple of times he mentioned sadly the 'fiancée' he had left in Romania (this is the term Greimas remembers, but Barthes probably did not specify the person's sex). On discovering that Greimas, who had studied at Grenoble before the war, knew Saint-Hilaire-du-Touvet and had visited one of his friends who was at the sanatorium (another Lithuanian called Ralys who was a patient at the same time as Barthes), he also talked a little about the sanatorium. But nothing else. For a short time Barthes lived in the residential seaside suburb of Sidi Bishr, then he moved into a place near the Singevins' apartment. From then on he had lunch and dinner with them every day. Their mealtime conversations were usually about fairly trivial topics. Madame Singevin remembers Barthes's endless complaints about his living conditions, his lack of money, the brother he had to support and the endless bureaucratic hassles he had to endure. Because his room was too small for the piano he had rented, he kept it at the Singevins' and in the evenings he would sometimes give their daughters lessons. Thus Barthes became part of the university teachers' clique, one of the many cliques in the town. There were also the secondary school teachers, the doctors, the business people (the Crédit Lyonnais, the Société Générale and the Comptoir d'Escompte all had busy and prosperous branches in Alexandria). These different groups of French nationals did not mix, and more often than not regarded one another with suspicion.

After dinner, Roland often went out with his new friends to a café, where they joked and talked. They were known as 'the Romanian mafia' or 'Singevin's gang'. According to Greimas, Singevin was their intellectual guru. He describes him as 'the group leader', an 'eloquent speaker', 'a humanist', 'enthusiastic', and says Singevin had a considerable influence on them all. For his part, Philippe Rebeyrol does not think Singevin was a mentor for Barthes: 'If Roland ever had one, it was Greimas.' Nevertheless, it is true that Singevin, who was ten years older than the rest of them, was the most highly educated and experienced. He was the organizer of a 'philosophy group' which met on Wednesdays at the house of André Salama, a young doctor who had studied with Heidegger in Fribourg for three months. During these weekly meetings, Singevin shared with the others his knowledge of the Polish school of logic and of Husserl.

Barthes had read Sartre and Nietzsche, while Greimas was more familiar with Maurice Merleau-Ponty, whom he thought had a better understanding of the problems of language. They would discuss such topics for hours on end. Singevin and Barthes were both 'language assistants' in the French department at the university. Greimas had a more presentable title, he was a 'senior lecturer' and taught the history of the French language. In fact, the students often went on strike in protest against the corrupt regime of King Farouk. On average, the teachers worked for three out of twelve months in the year, seven or eight hours a week. Moreover, since the low standard of the students meant they did not have to do much preparation, they had plenty of leisure time and plenty of time for philosophy. Some of them went to the beach or played tennis. There was also another distraction: the young bourgeois girls who had just left their convent schools or the Lycée Français, and the dance parties. Barthes, who was both extremely charming and an excellent dancer, shone on such occasions. He would croon a song to his partner while dancing, usually Prévert and Kosma's recent hit *Autumn Leaves*, and he would also play the piano – music 'of the heart' by Debussy, Ravel and Bartok, and 'music of the mind' by Bach and Scarlatti. 'Music and songs were interspersed with philosophy and great epistemological debates,' Greimas recalls.

Music continued to play an important role in Barthes's life, and sometimes he revealed a certain dogmatism as far as his tastes went. For example, he hated Sviatoslav Richter, whom he said played Beethoven's sonatas with unbearable variations in tempo, thumping away at the piano as if he were deaf. He adored Schumann, but hated Chopin, because only virtuosos could play his music. More often than not, however, while the others were going to the beach or playing bridge, Barthes went out on the prowl. 'He was obsessed,' according to Madame Singevin. One evening, when Charles was feeling tired, she went to the cinema with Roland. 'Everything was fine until a young man came in and sat down behind us. Roland kept turning round all the time to look at him. At midnight, as we left the cinema, he just dumped me there in the street and went off, saying he had something to do.'

But very few people knew anything about his private life. He was renowned, above all, for his eloquence and for the condensed formulations he used. This earned him the reputation of a man of brilliant intelligence, even if sometimes a little difficult to understand. He was known as an excellent lecturer, even if some people criticized his somewhat solemn tone. The truth of the matter was that he hated speaking in public, but nobody seems to have noticed. Apart from the weekly philosophical debates presided over by Singevin, Barthes and Greimas spent hours lost in discussion. Barthes, who had just turned thirty-four, talked about his publication of 'Le Degré zéro de l'écriture' in *Combat*, which, forty years later, Greimas remembers as 'an article on the *passé simple*'. Two years Barthes's junior, Greimas was a specialist in Old French and was also very interested in lexicology. In turn, he told Barthes about his doctoral thesis on the vocabulary of fashion. As with Maurice Nadeau two years before, Barthes mentioned his idea for a thesis on Michelet, showed Greimas his notes and got him to read the hundred-and-fifty or so pages which were later to become the *Michelet*.

'It's very good,' Greimas commented, 'but you could use Saussure.' 'Who's Saussure?' Barthes asked. 'He's essential reading,' Greimas replied peremptorily. Barthes, who was already very receptive to the new linguistics which was beginning to develop in France, set aside Michelet and began to read Saussure, the founder of modern linguistics. Then, again on Greimas's recommendation, he immediately went on to read Roman Jakobson, the Russian linguist who had emigrated to the United States, and then the Danish linguist Brøndal. In this way he initiated himself into the nascent structuralist movement. For someone who was so 'fanatical' about the question of language and who, as Nadeau put it, 'thought of nothing else', his ignorance of Saussure seems a little surprising. However, it should be understood that Barthes was primarily interested in literature, in style, and it was Greimas who showed him that he would need to use linguistics in his analysis.

Greimas's influence was such that Charles Singevin made the analogy that Greimas was for Barthes what the road to Damascus was for Saint Paul. But there is some contradiction in the accounts of when Barthes first discovered Saussure: Greimas and Singevin are both certain that it was while he was in Alexandria, between 1949

and 1950, whereas Barthes himself says he first came across the
Swiss linguist in 1951.[1]

During their long discussions, his friend told him about 'metaphor' and 'metonymy', and he made a mental note of them, though
it was not until 1963, while he was working on La Bruyère that he
thought again about their discussions and 'worked up a great
enthusiasm for the *metaphor/metonymy* opposition'.[2]

Despite this intense and stimulating intellectual life and his
productive discussions with Greimas, Barthes was not very happy in
Alexandria. At first he had been very keen on the climate, which
reminded him of Biarritz, and he was also interested in the history of
a place on which so many civilizations had left their mark. He had
made a trip to Upper Egypt, to Aswan, which he found fascinating.
But he quickly became disillusioned. He considered his new milieu
'second-rate, conformist, snobbish and suspicious of any form of
intelligence and sensitivity' and, according to him, it was impossible
to envisage living in such a wretched country in the long term.
Nevertheless, he wanted to stay for another year, and even this was
not guaranteed. The business over his tuberculosis had still not been
cleared up and in December he had been called before an Egyptian
government commission, which had refused to grant him the official
status of 'lecteur'. Since then, the matter had dragged on and on and
although he had been paid, he still had not been officially appointed
nor had any definite answer about the following year, despite his
efforts. He thought the whole affair absurdly nit-picking, especially
given that Egypt would not even have to bear the cost of any health
care he might need. This was the French government's responsibility,
but it made no difference and he grew increasingly irritable.

It was a strange life in a strange town. The 'expatriates' regarded
themselves as being only 'temporarily' in Alexandria while waiting
for a post elsewhere, preferably in France, and if possible in a
university. Barthes was not getting anywhere with his work on
Michelet. He felt desperate at the thought that he was producing
only a kind of essay, something which was not sufficiently
theoretically grounded to be a piece of research. He knew he had to
make it look like a coherent piece of academic research, but had no
access to any books or to a proper library. He was afraid he would
soon be unable to progress any further for lack of sources and
reference books and, as a result, he hardly worked on it at all.
Talking about it with friends, he explained that his problems had to do
with the relationship between the historical method and the structural method of analysis. As far as he was concerned, the structural

analysis which he had already carried out by making notes and classifying his index cards was nothing more than a necessary but insufficient prelude to a historical analysis. The problem was how to put the two together.

Once again he became extremely depressed and lost all interest in the country in which he was living. He did not learn a single word of Arabic: despite his interest in linguistics, he was never really interested in learning modern languages and a basic reading ability in English was the limit of his ambitions. He did not show the slightest interest in Egypt's vast archaeological treasures. In this, however, he was not alone. According to Greimas, 'One didn't bother about that sort of thing. We discussed philosophy and mathematics. We were there without really being there and it wasn't until later, after the Suez affair in 1956, that Singevin and I started to mix with Egyptians as a mark of our anti-imperialism. But Roland had left a long time before that.'[3] Financial considerations also played their part in their indifference. They were badly paid and spent a lot of time doing extra teaching in order to supplement their incomes. For instance, Barthes taught in a girls' boarding school (the 'Pensionnat de la Mère de Dieu'), a sinecure he passed on to Greimas when he left Alexandria.

Besides, their first real contact with a Third World country was extremely disillusioning for these young intellectuals who may have flirted with Marxism but were still, when it came down to it, fairly naive. Singevin, their intellectual leader at the time, summed it up as follows: 'When we arrived we thought we needed to teach our students French language and culture. We were wrong: the only thing we could do for them was to give them a sense of historicity.' They felt as if, as far as their students were concerned, nothing ever changed, things had always been the same and 'history' was a useless concept. They were all amazed that the inhabitants of the city did not even know who Alexander the Great was, when the city had been named after him.

Greimas and Singevin stayed in Alexandria until 1958, as there were no posts available elsewhere. As for Barthes, he found life there increasingly intolerable and was relying on his connections in Paris to help him get back to France. He was the only one in the group to have such connections, the only one who might have his application 'supported'. After Romania, Philippe Rebeyrol had been sent to the French Institute in London, but he still had his contacts in the Foreign Office, and he managed to get Barthes a job in the Cultural Affairs section. Barthes was therefore able to return to Paris.

The day of his departure was the first time Greimas heard anything about his homosexuality:

> He was always so discreet about his private life. The Singevins, who had known him in Romania, knew about it, but they had never said a word. On the morning of his departure, I offered to help him pack. So I went over to his place – I'd never been there before – and we started packing. At about the same time, Madame Singevin dropped in on my wife. She said to her, 'You don't know about Roland, do you? . . .' My wife, knowing that I was at his place, flew into a panic: 'Oh God, what's going to happen to my darling husband!' When I got home I was greeted by all sorts of questions which, naturally, I couldn't make head nor tail of.[4]

This anecdote exemplifies the ridiculous way homosexuality was generally perceived at the time, and the kinds of imaginings it could trigger off. It no doubt explains why Barthes was so discreet about his private life and why such a large number of his friends had no idea about his sexual preferences until much later.

The years as a bureaucrat

Barthes left Egypt quite happily at the end of the academic year 1949–50, even though he may have felt a slight tinge of regret for the carefree life he was leaving behind. He left all his music scores with Anna Greimas, since he did not think he would be able to afford a piano in France.

He began his new job in the Cultural Affairs section of the Foreign Office, where he dealt with missions and the teaching of 'French as a foreign language'. He lived with his mother in their fifth-floor flat in the Rue Servandoni, a stone's throw from Saint-Sulpice. He fixed up a study above the flat, in what had formerly been a maid's room. Later he was able to build a trapdoor in the ceiling of the flat with a ladder to link it with his study, but at the beginning he had to go down five flights of stairs to get to the service entrance and then climb up to the sixth floor again. Eventually, much later, he even rented a second-floor flat so as not to disturb his mother.

His grandmother Noémie Révelin was still living in the Place du Panthéon and from time to time he paid her a visit. There was still a slight touch of irony in his voice whenever he mentioned her to his friends, most probably masking his resentment. She had a first edition of the lexicographer and philosopher Littré which Barthes coveted. When Greimas came to Paris on holiday, Barthes laughingly asked him how to persuade her to lend or give him the Littré. But in his heart he felt the same: bitterly resentful of the fact that she had not used her wealth to help her daughter Henriette.

Roland was bored with his new job almost as soon as he started it. For a while he thought about going abroad again, then looked for another job in Paris, feeling as if he were going round in circles, looking for a way to escape, like a fish in a net. In particular, after a day's work at the office he found it difficult to do any of his own research. He jotted down some notes on his cards and wrote a few pages from time to time, but it hardly seemed earth-shattering. In addition, he now found Paris – the city he had loved so much, the city he had been so happy to return to after Bucharest and had missed so much in Alexandria – deeply boring. On the evenings when he felt too tired to think of ideas and write them down, which occurred all too often, he found himself at a loss as to what to do, who to see. In fact, he felt he was reverting to being the 'moaning minnie' of his childhood.

In July 1951 he went through what he called his 'annual crisis of indecision or re-decision'. There had been talk of a possible job as a language assistant in Cambridge; on the other hand, Greimas had sent him to the lexicologist Georges Matoré, and Matoré had suggested another option, painting a glowing picture of a project for a new dictionary Barthes might be able to work on. But he felt the British option would suit him better. Of course it would not be very well paid, but it would be enough to support Henriette, and its intellectual advantages appealed to him. He would have free time, interesting work, comfortable surroundings, the opportunity and time to learn English, long holidays. There was also the status of the university and its proximity to Paris.

In October, however, Roland was still in Paris, working in the same ministry. In the end, he had decided to turn down the job at Cambridge. At Christmas he was still there, and told friends he longed to take off, to go to a hot country to do a job he loved and which would leave him some free time. Despite having been so bored in Alexandria, he was now dreaming of somewhere identical. However, when he was offered a post as a lecteur in Bologna, he turned it down just as he had the offer from Cambridge. When he was asked why, since he did nothing but complain about his life in Paris, he replied by quoting Lucretius: 'Those who travel change horizons, not their souls.'

He was about to turn thirty-six, and he still did not have a secure job, but he had decided that his future lay in Paris. It was here that he would have to find a solution before it was too late. He took on a number of small jobs. Under Georges Gougenheim, whom he had met through Matoré, he collaborated on the initial stages of what was to become the *Dictionnaire du français fondamental*. This consisted of a making a tape-recorded survey to establish which were the one thousand, then the two thousand words most frequently used by French speakers. This would then lead to the creation of a basic French dictionary which could be used by foreign students, and also as a vocabulary book for teaching French as a foreign language. Of course, Barthes's work on the dictionary was a way of supplementing his salary, but he also seemed to take a genuine interest in the project. Having discovered theoretical linguistics through his friendship with Greimas, he was now getting to grips with the concrete task of carrying out a project of description. He thought the survey was a first-rate idea which would considerably extend the field of linguistics. He was enthusiastic about the various different directions in which the project could develop, and how it opened up the prospect of finding out about *multiple* French languages, different social discourses. In fact, during this period his interests seemed to lie in the direction of sociolinguistics, a branch of linguistics which had only just begun to be developed, but which would become increasingly important.

In addition, he had a vague idea about producing a book on contemporary France for Hachette, but this eventually came to nothing. Finally, he was thinking of putting together the articles he had written for *Combat* and publishing them as a small book. His involvement with these different projects meant that the famous thesis on Michelet was put on the back burner and the fact that he had to give up his own work, even if only temporarily, was more than a little to blame for his bad mood. He was also getting more and more fed up with his job in the Cultural Affairs section. He dealt with the awarding of honorary doctorates, the organization of teachers' conferences, and even the sending out of the 'portable kits' – a kind of 'portfolio for the perfect teacher' dreamt up by the cultural services which consisted of textbooks and charts. Even if his job did mean he had some free time, he would have preferred something a bit different, since he had no energy left to do his own work.

In May 1952, despite his wish to remain in Paris, what seemed like an interesting opportunity came up: the possibility of sending him on a Unesco educational project to the Lebanon was mooted. At first it was only a vague suggestion, but then the project became more concrete. He was his department's first choice, and could already picture himself living in Beirut, being paid a high salary and doing what was in fact, at the end of the day, an interesting job. Unfortunately, it all fell through at the last moment when the Lebanese delegate to Unesco, who had the final say and whom Barthes was to describe as a 'hypocritical priest', chose another candidate for the job, probably for reasons of internal politics. Once again Barthes was stuck in the same job.

Meanwhile, he was in contact with Maurice Nadeau again. Nadeau had left *Combat* after the dismissal of Claude Bourdet by Smadja in February 1950. Together with Gilles Martinet and Roger Stéphane, he had founded *L'Observateur Politique, Économique et Littéraire* which had soon become *France-Observateur*. Nadeau had been put in charge of its literary supplement, whose contributors included Georges Limbour on painting and, of course, Roland Barthes. In January 1953, the magazine published the results of a survey on 'literature and the left'. One of the people who responded to the survey was Edgar Morin, with whom Barthes struck up a friendship which was later to lead to a professional collaboration. When, in 1953, Nadeau set up *Les Lettres nouvelles* with Maurice Saillet, it was natural that Barthes would be a contributor. He was asked to write a regular column on whatever subject he chose – linguistics, his research, anything. The only problem was his health. He was not sure if he would have the strength to write articles regularly and to a fixed deadline. He had just published a piece on wrestling in *Esprit* in October 1952, an ironic glance at that peculiar Olympus of the gods of the ring in which he had explained that wrestling was not merely a sport but a spectacle in which everything was a sign, a signifier. He decided to continue to write in this vein.

Month after month, Nadeau would telephone him to remind him about printing deadlines. Barthes complied and, somehow or other, his little 'mythologies of the month' were produced. It was when these were published together in a single volume, *Mythologies*, in 1957 that Barthes's fame was ensured. They were both a kind of chronicle of the 1950s and an insight into Barthes himself. They dealt with the Dominici affair, (a case of unsolved murder in the French countryside), Joseph Mankiewicz's film of *Julius Caesar*, Elia Kazan's *On the Waterfront*, the world of advertising (washing-powder ads for Omo and Persil), the Abbé Pierre, Poujade, Billy Graham, wrestling, the Tour de France, the Citröen DS19, the *Blue*

Guide, etc. In short, *Mythologies* captures the whole decade, as if photographed by a critical lens. 'The purpose of *Mythologies*', he was later to explain in a television interview, 'is to tackle systematically, as a block, a kind of monster which I have called the "petite bourgeoisie" (even if this does tend to mythify it) and to tirelessly chip away at it.'

In fact, there is a very clear evolution through these texts. Barthes begins by describing the allegories which society uses to talk about itself, and then gradually moves on to describe its lies. According to him 'myths' attempt to impose a distorted interpretation of the real. Thus when the right-wing politician Pierre Poujade violently attacked intellectuals, Barthes regarded it as a means of 'Accusing one's adversary of the effects of one's own faults. Of calling one's own blindness obscurity and one's own deafness verbal disorder.'[5] Semiology, or at least 'his' version of semiology, which some linguists were later to criticize, gradually became a weapon for him, a means of social critique.

Nadeau remembers how difficult it was for him to 'get Barthes established', to get him recognized. Some people, like Maurice Saillet, one of Nadeau's contributors, resented his jargon, while others, like Georges Limbour, loved his language and his 'Voltairean' style. Whatever the case, at the centre of all his targets of criticism, all his interventions and within the different media he attacks (*Elle*, *Paris-Match*) can be found that *bourgeoisie* which in Alexandria he accused of listening to the piano with their eyes closed. Another aspect of his project is the idea of using semiology as a critical tool. He and Greimas had begun to discuss this idea in Alexandria, and they continued doing so. Every summer the Greimases came over from Egypt for their holidays and stayed in a hotel in the Rue Servandoni and the two men would resume their discussions enthusiastically. They were in a state of permanent excitement, completely won over by the idea of this nascent discipline of semiology, with its demands for a rigorously scientific approach and its ideological justifications.

Barthes was to recall their mood in his inaugural lecture at the Collège du France: 'It seemed to me (around 1954) that the science of signs might stimulate social criticism, and Sartre, Brecht, and Saussure could concur in this project.'[6] Although the term 'semiology' had been coined at the beginning of the century by Saussure in his *Cours de linguistique générale*, and defined by him programmatically as 'the science which studies the existence of the signs at the heart of social life', such a science had still not been invented. In the mid-1960s Barthes was to find himself at the centre of a huge theoretical debate which would pit him against the advocates of orthodox linguistics.

At the time, it was the concept of 'connotation', taken from Hjelmslev, which enabled him to move between the realms of the scientific and the political. In his essay 'Le mythe aujourd'hui' ('Myth today') in *Mythologies*, Barthes located ideology on the level of connotation, in what is not said explicitly but is implied and thus carries even greater force. It was during this period, when he was beginning to elaborate his theoretical framework, that he became increasingly preoccupied by political issues. His 'Marxism' was pushing him inevitably towards the Communist party, in the classic role of 'fellow traveller', but as usual he felt faint-hearted and unsure. He discussed his doubts with Philippe Rebeyrol, now working in Cairo, but temporarily back in Paris. He explained his worries about 'the party', how he was tired of seeing intellectuals paralysed, unable to decide where they stood in relation to communism. Above all, he was depressed by the impotence of left-wing intellectuals, and faced with so many contradictory opinions from people he respected, he had the feeling of drifting.

The *Degree Zero*: completion

Despite his political doubts and the difficulties he was having in getting his interpretations accepted, Barthes was gradually moving from the private phase of his life into the phase of public recognition. His articles were beginning to be noticed and discussed. If he wanted to leave the Foreign Office and get a grant from the CNRS,[7] it was not simply because he was bored with office life but because he had more and more ideas for writing projects and needed more free time. The previous summer, Greimas had organized a trip to the country retreat of Charles Bruneau, famous author of a history of the French language, in order to 'sell Roland Barthes'. Bruneau, who was extremely kind and helpful, promised to do all he could to get Roland a job as a trainee researcher in lexicology at the CNRS, where he could begin work on a new research project, since he had temporarily abandoned his research on Michelet. It was yet another promise and yet another period of waiting.

Despite this, things were looking up for him. He was writing pieces for *Esprit*, *Les Lettres nouvelles* and had also been commissioned to produce a text on Michelet for a publisher's series on 'écrivains de toujours'. *Writing Degree Zero* was due to be published by Seuil in February or March 1953. In fact, Raymond Queneau had tried without success to get Gallimard to publish it a few months earlier. Jean Cayrol and Albert Béguin had taken over his efforts and got the book accepted by Seuil. Only the title was taken from the 1947 article published in *Combat*, and it consisted of a combination of his 1950 articles plus several more unpublished pieces. Seuil was a small publishing firm which had been set up during the Resistance. It had a catholic list, publishing both the review *Esprit*, founded by Emmanuel Mounier and edited by Jean-Marie Domenach, and *The Little World of Don Camillo*, which had sold over a million copies and thus ensured the firm's financial survival. The team at Seuil included Francis Jeanson, who later became famous for his work with the support network for the FLN (the Algerian Front de la Libération Nationale), Jean Cayrol himself, and Chris Marker, the film-maker, director of *Lettre de Sibérie*, who was responsible for the Petite Planète series.

They formed a small, close-knit team which, although unable to compete with the big publishing houses like Gallimard, was much more in touch with what was happening on the ground in political terms. Thus it was Seuil which published Frantz Fanon's *Black Skin, White Masks* and the texts of Léopold Sédar Senghor, future president of Senegal, the bard of negritude and the author of a book against torture. Such choices meant it was unpopular in certain quarters and more than once the OAS, the illegal organization bitterly opposed to Algerian independence, carried out bomb attacks on the firm's offices. Seuil also published the first French translations of *A Hundred Years of Solitude* by Gabriel Garcia Marquez and Solzhenitsyn's *Gulag Archipelago*.

At the end of November, having finally been awarded a grant by the CNRS, Barthes left his job at the Foreign Ministry. He was to devote his energies to lexicology, scouring the National Library for texts on commerce in 1830 and filling up index cards for a new Ph.D. project on the vocabulary of the social question. His personal life also underwent a change. Thanks to Jean Cayrol he began to meet a new circle of people, all of whom were in some way associated with Seuil. He was still preoccupied with political questions. In February 1953, after attending a conference organized by *Esprit*, he told Rebeyrol that there were still many battles to be fought, and that he thought obscurantism was on the increase in their times. He referred to the Slansky and Rosenberg trials, and denounced Eisenhower and Franco. He also told his friend of his clashes with Jean Sirinelli, who had become a Catholic and who, according to Barthes, saw nothing objectionable in the fact that Franco was also a Catholic.

It was at this time that he received the proofs of *Writing Degree Zero*. Rereading his own text, he found it 'weak', an adjective he often applied to his own work, and he feared that he was laying himself open to criticism – and severe criticism at that. This first publication marked the beginning of a lifelong collaboration with Seuil. Indeed, loyalty was one of Barthes's most enduring character-istics, and he did not forget his publishing debut with *Combat*. In the copy of *Writing Degree Zero* he dedicated to Nadeau, Barthes wrote that it 'rightfully belonged' to him and signed it 'in loyal friendship from your old friend'. Nor did he forget his debt to Greimas and their conversations in Alexandria. He sent him a copy with an almost identical dedication: 'My dear friend, these few shared concerns rightfully belong to you, along with my loyal and deep affection.' When it comes to dedications it is indeed difficult to be original.

Despite his fears, this first publication by an unknown young writer was quite well received by the press. Maurice Nadeau, loyal as ever to his 'discovery', wrote an eight-page review of the book in *Les Lettres nouvelles*, which concluded: 'We must congratulate the author on what is a remarkable debut. It heralds an essayist who stands head and shoulders above his contemporaries.'[8] *France-Observateur* also gave the book a favourable three-page review,[9] while in *Médecine de France*, Guy Dumur sang its praises. However, not all the reactions were so favourable. In *Le Monde* Dominique Arban's review, while full of praise for the book, was none the less somewhat bizarre. Her account of *Writing Degree Zero* makes one wonder what her understanding of it was:

> This little book has come at exactly the right time; in fact, it is astonishing that it has not appeared sooner. It may help to foster a greater understanding between authors and readers since it is incomprehension which prevents many readers today from engaging with the profound poetic experience that is pursued by a lonely and heroic few.[10]

Barthes as a way of approaching modern poetry? Whatever the case, it was *Le Monde* and it was a favourable review. In *Carrefour*, Roger Nimier referred to the book as 'M. Barthes's remarkable essay' and, reviewing it together with Bernard Frank's first book *Géographie universelle*, he used *Writing Degree Zero* in a subtle way to analyse the latter.[11] But most significant of all was J.-B. Pontalis's seven-page review in Sartre's magazine *Les Temps modernes*. His treatment of the book was serious, intelligent and severe. 'The rigidness of Barthes's distinctions and his often irritatingly self-confident tone seem to be an attempt to mask a certain amount of confusion in his ideas,' he wrote. He went on to ask whether it was enough 'to limit one's criticisms to the schematic nature of Barthes's views and to accept the method he is advocating'. He concluded by saying that 'the presence of a great writer is felt among us in a different way from that of a piece of period furniture, an economic structure or even an ideology.'[12] However, he failed to make any links between Barthes's notion of writing and Sartre's notion of commitment, or mention any ways in which they might converge philosophically. Nevertheless, on the whole Barthes's first book got extremely good reviews.

This did not make its author feel any happier, however. In his letters and in his remarks to friends, he tended to feel bitter. He complained about his salary, which had hardly risen at all and was practically on a par with a student grant. His mother was earning very little from her bookbinding and Michel was still living at home, without any clear future plans, changing from painting to studying Hebrew. To make ends meet, Barthes had to give French lessons to foreign students at the Sorbonne. He felt uncomfortable, spurned by the established university teachers, and once again blamed the illness which had prevented him from taking the entrance exams for the École Normale and then the agrégation. In addition, he was not getting anywhere with his new research project on the vocabulary of the social question in France around 1830 and he felt he was being taken advantage of, made to pay a social price for his entrance, however tentative, into the literary world, that he was being swallowed up. It was a world which fascinated him, but he felt disconcerted by its rituals and unsure of himself.

However, certain people he met were to have a lasting effect on him. One of these was Violette Morin, Edgar Morin's wife and, like her husband, a sociologist. Later they would work together on the review *Communications*, but for the time being they saw a lot of each other socially – at dinner parties or shows. Roland sometimes took Violette to Alfred Cortot's public classes in musical interpretation at the Salle Wagram. Equipped with a score and a pencil, he would scribble away, taking notes, underlining and later he would try to play the piece according to the Master's suggestions. Thus, at the age of thirty-eight, he was making a timid entrance into this new world, constructing for himself a character, a psychology to which he would remain faithful. The accounts of those who knew him all agree on one point: he always promised too much – to write an article here, give a lecture there – as if he had to devour, bulimically, anything that was offered to him, even though it meant he was never able to keep his promises. When this happened, he would always complain about everything: his work, his health, the 'pains-in-the-neck', the climate. At thirty-eight, he had doubtlessly decided to remain true to his moods, or at least not to fight them, to remain the 'moaning minnie' he had been as a child. He was also about to revive one of his youthful passions – his love of the theatre.

6

The Theatre Years

In 1953, Noémie Révelin, Barthes's grandmother, died. Roland, who was on holiday in Holland at the time, rushed back to Paris and found himself faced with the task of sorting out the various bureaucratic formalities, so as to relieve the burden on his mother. There was, of course, an inheritance, but how much? A little or a lot? He discussed his political scruples as a left-winger with Greimas, imagining himself soon becoming a millionaire. Talking it over with Philippe Rebeyrol, he said he could not assess how much the inheritance was going to affect the family situation since its value was difficult to assess, and it would be even more difficult to convert it into money in order to make the changes in their lives he dreamed of. The kinds of changes he wanted to make required money rather than the property and industrial wealth he thought they were going to inherit. Naturally, his priority was to make sure that Henriette had a comfortable and peaceful life and his prime concern was to find them a bigger place to live. Then there was the matter of the flat in the Place du Panthéon: although it did not belong to Noémie, she had left them the lease. What was to be done with it? They had absolutely no desire to live there, but Roland wanted to move in so it could be used as a bargaining counter in the negotiations he anticipated would take place. Then there was the smelting works. Obviously he had no intention of taking over their running and his aim was eventually to sell, but he knew that would take time.

As usual, he tended to focus on the problematic or annoying aspects of whatever good fortune came his way. He confided to his friends that the whole family found these changes to their financial situation distressing. As usual, he complained about the difficulties he was having with his work. He wasn't progressing fast enough for his liking on the Michelet book he had promised Seuil. He had thought the project would be easy and fun to do, but in fact it was proving extremely difficult and he was not enjoying it. In the meantime, and despite his frequent declarations to the contrary, he moved into the flat in the Place du Panthéon, whose windows overlooked the grounds of the Lycée Henri-IV. It was gloomy, too large, and luxurious in a stuffy bourgeois manner. Neither he nor his mother felt comfortable there. He tried in vain to persuade Greimas to come and stay there on his regular summer visit to Paris. In the end, his slightly vengeful occupation of the flat, where the presence of Noémie could still be felt, only lasted a few months. He invited the Greimases, the Singevins, the Fourniés, the Nadeaus, Bernard Dort and others to the flat and they all remember its rather stuffy bourgeois décor. A more pleasing windfall was his grandmother's old-fashioned but sumptuous Panhard car, which he used in the evenings to go out on the town.

The settling of Noémie's estate took a long time and was a conflictual and complex process. Her inheritance was to be shared between Henriette and Philippe Binger, her children by her first marriage, and her son by her second marriage to their uncle Révelin. First of all, her assets had to be assessed, and this was followed by negotiations with the other heirs. Their occupation of the flat in the Place du Panthéon was part of their negotiating strategy, since although they did not actually own the flat, a lease on a flat in this part of Paris was worth a fortune. However, the owner quickly decided to recover the lease, and in the spring of 1954 Barthes and his mother returned to the Rue Servandoni, where Michel was still living. When the time came to get rid of his grandmother's furniture, Roland sold a large wooden bookcase to Jean Sirinelli and gave the Fourniés two magnificent armchairs, which still have pride of place in Jacqueline's holiday home.

Théâtre populaire

During the same period, in 1953, the review *Théâtre populaire* was founded. The idea originally came from Robert Voisin who, at the publishers Arche, brought out the plays Vilar put on at the Théâtre National Populaire (TNP). He had read several of Barthes's articles on the theatre in *Les Lettres nouvelles*, contacted him and, together with Guy Dumur, Jean Duvignaud, Morvan-Lebesque and later Bernard Dort, they got the project under way. The idea was to create a review which would champion a certain vision of theatre. Dort, who was finishing his studies at the École Nationale d'Administration, was mad about the theatre, went around with Arthur Adamov and wrote reviews for *Les Temps modernes* and *L'Express*. He also did book reviews for *Les Cahiers du Sud*, a magazine set up in Marseilles in 1923 by Jean Ballard.

Dort and Barthes soon became friends, discussed ideas and went out together. For a time they were very close to one another intellectually, and their ideas developed in similar directions. They would go and see new plays almost every evening. Both smoked cigars, although Dort preferred Toscanis, a popular brand, and Barthes, when he could afford it, smoked Havanas. To justify this luxury, he would allude to Brecht's habit of smoking Havanas. For a long time, he smoked Punch Culebras, strange, spiral-shaped cigars, and it was not until much later, in the mid-1970s, that he changed his brand, joking that Lacan had begun to smoke the same brand and he did not want it to look as if he were trying to imitate him. But perhaps there was another reason: Barthes had gone to Lacan for psychoanalysis but Lacan had refused to take him on as an analysand.

The two men's tastes in food were also very different. Dort loved offal ('like a Greek athlete,' Barthes told him), while Barthes himself preferred blanquette of veal, anything that was smothered in a sauce or cream. Barthes's comment about Dort's taste for offal seems reminiscent of a fragment called 'Acrocôlia' which he wrote at Saint-Hilaire in 1944 for the students' review *Existences*:

> In the Grand-Alexander restaurant an ancient Greek tradition has survived: the eating of acrocôlia or offal, any part of the animal which trembles, turns red (and then green) inside it. The ancient Greeks loved these complicated and decadent meat dishes. They preferred brains, livers, foetuses, pancreases and udders to roasts. Any kind of meat that was soft, pulpy and ephemeral – no sooner had it made your mouth water than it began to go off.[1]

Once again it seems as if Barthes's later style is already wholly present in this early text – not to mention his relationship to food. Later, when he was able to afford it, he would have deliveries of Bordeaux and Lalande de Pomerol wines and would eat in good restaurants like the Falstaff and the Bofinger. He did not like the Lipp, where he said the food was as bad as at La Coupole. In fact, he was greedy in quite a matter-of-fact sort of way, yet at the same time was afraid of getting fat. He sometimes went on savagely strict diets, calculating in minute detail the number of calories in each bit of food. He thought that being thin made one look intelligent.

> I have had the kinds of problems many people suffer from, I think. When I was an adolescent, I was the thin type ... Then at a certain point my body's morphology changed, I began to get fatter and I had to get used to a new body, a body which had to struggle with its tendency to put on weight. It is fascinating, there's nothing more exciting than going on a diet, everyone knows this because there are detailed discussions of dieting practically every week in all the magazines ... Women want to be beautiful, so perhaps do young men. There may be an element of vanity in this, but it also involves a desire to be intelligent. Emaciated, busy people are, in the end, thought to be more intelligent than well-padded ones.[2]

Robert David, who remembers Barthes's voracious appetite, tells the story of one evening when his wife had made couscous for dinner. Roland had eaten up almost all his helping of couscous before the sauce and vegetables had even been put on the table. Edgar Morin also found Barthes's eating habits at home, where his mother served him like a child, somewhat unusual. He would gobble down his food 'in an elemental, animal-like fashion. There was something intense, all-consuming about it.' As for Violette Morin, she describes the way he ate as follows: 'At the table he was like a lizard with its darting tongue. During a dinner party with eight or ten people he did not know, he would help himself with his fork, jabbing at a dish three or four times with the speed of a lizard's tongue.' But she also recounts how Barthes – who loved to have slices of bread spread thickly with butter and jam for breakfast – sometimes found he had to weigh the thin slice of bread and the tiny amount of butter he had allowed himself, calculating the number of calories with an air of intense suffering.

Bernard Dort found these cycles of dieting and bingeing amusing. He was fascinated (and sometimes exasperated) by Barthes's love of life, of comfort, which did not, however, seem in any way bourgeois. He found Barthes's tastes in food and clothes slightly irritating. Barthes wore cashmere or alpaca sweaters in shades of green or yellow, and there were often holes in them from cigar burns. But he could not bear to be criticized; he liked his relationships to be as 'smooth' as his food, and he reproached Dort for his aggression. Aggression was what he hated most, because of his enormous fear of hysteria.

The two also talked a great deal about music, mainly about Schumann. Dort remembers the records Roland bought for him – Debussy, Schumann, and also a record of German choral music. Nevertheless, he rarely heard him play the piano, and only knew that he sometimes played duets, in particular with Vladimir Jankélévitch, the philosopher.

In fact, this happened only once, when Barthes was introduced by Violette Morin to the philosopher, who was a friend. Vladimir had two pianos in his flat and suggested they should play a duet. He immediately began improvising on a piece by Fauré, forcing Barthes to follow him. Barthes complied, yet although he liked nothing better than to decipher a score, he said to Violette afterwards, 'I hope he won't touch the piano straight away – I sweated so much the keyboard is completely wet.'

But, above all, Barthes and Dort shared a love of the theatre. One day, Dort took Roland to Lyons to see a performance of two Adamov plays which were being put on by Roger Planchon. At the end of May 1954, they saw the Berliner Ensemble's production of *Mother Courage* at the Paris international festival. It was a revelation to Barthes, who with astonishing speed came up with the following phrase to describe its impact: 'Brecht is a Marxist who has thought about the sign,' a phrase he was to use many times. As far as the two friends were concerned, Brecht provided Marxism with the aesthetics it lacked. Barthes regarded Brecht's theatre as 'anti-hysterical', since there was no identification between the audience and the characters, and this provided the audience with a means of critique. He wrote that in *Mother Courage* 'the audience is never totally involved in the performance.' He had hated Maria Casares' performance in *Phèdre*, because she had acted as if she were personally involved, and he was captivated by the method of acting Brechtian theatre involved, by what he called the 'Brechtian social gestus'.

Barthes encouraged Dort to read Marx, particularly his *Critique of the Gotha Programme*, and in return Dort introduced him to the work of Alain Robbe-Grillet. He had already read *Les Gommes* on its publication in 1953, now he read *Le Voyeur* in 1955 and *La Jalousie* in 1957. Robbe-Grillet soon became their principal literary argument against Camus, as the advocate of the 'objective' novel. Robbe-Grillet, this 'objective novelist' later wrote with a great deal of humour that Barthes, 'who does not need lessons in guile from anyone,' was simply using him as a means of elaborating his own thesis:

> Grappling with his personal demons, he did his best to outwit them by searching for a 'writing degree zero' in which he's never believed. My so-called neutrality [blancheur] – mere protective clothing – came at just the right moment to fuel his discourse. And so I was dubbed 'objective novelist' or, worse still, one who was attempting to be objective but who, without an ounce of talent, merely succeeded in being dull.[3]

So Barthes never believed in 'the degree zero of writing'. Obviously this assertion is surprising and calls for further analysis, but today Alain Robbe-Grillet refuses to say anything more about it: 'I have already written or said everything I want to about Roland. I do not like discussing confidential matters lightly, and it upsets me to see them later in print.'[4]

Barthes's passion for the theatre and the *nouveau roman* left little time for his research project on the vocabulary of the social question in 1830. In January 1954 he became panic-stricken about the report he had to write for the CNRS detailing how his research was progressing. What could he say? As usual, he confided his doubts and problems to Philippe Rebeyrol: there was no one to help him, he explained: Georges Matoré had disappeared from sight, for over a year he had been unavailable. He also felt an extreme lack of confidence and was close to believing that his lexicology was a bit of an illusion – that it could never be used to analyse his research topic in depth. His doctoral thesis – that perennial burden – seemed once more to be at a standstill. In the circumstances he was almost tempted to fall back on a more traditional kind of research topic, but after the success of *Writing Degree Zero* and the reaction to some of his articles, he was aware that such a step would be thought an aberration. He was known as an innovator and he had to go on innovating.

Moreover, he felt that with the passing of time his vulnerability only got worse and that it was not a source of creativity because it had no literary outlet; he thought he had a writer's sensibility while he claimed to be a theoretician. 'Intellectually I feel strong but existentially I feel completely vulnerable,' he told Rebeyrol.

However, he cobbled together a research report (which in his own opinion was dreadful), hoping his teachers would ask him to give up the project, a step he dared not take himself. He had finished the

Michelet at the beginning of the winter, and it was due for publication in the spring. He was becoming more interested in the sociology of the theatre, and in addition was still writing articles and trying to sort out the continuing disputes over his grandmother's will.

Michelet, the fruit of his reading at the sanatorium, was published by Seuil and created far less of a stir than the *Writing Degree Zero*. Once again his friends rallied round, especially those who worked on *Théâtre populaire*: Jean Duvignaud, who wrote in *La Nouvelle NRF* and Bernard Dort in *Critique*. Dort's review carried the somewhat bizarre title, 'Vers une critique totalitaire' ('Towards a totalitarian criticism') and this adjective was in fact taken from Sartre's 'presentation' to *Les Temps modernes*, which made such an impression on Barthes in the autumn of 1945. But *Le Monde*, which had looked favourably on *Writing Degree Zero*, gave *Michelet* the cold shoulder. With a title that is a clear indication of its tone, 'Un Michelet extravagant', the unsigned review is an ironic imitation of Barthes's style and formulaic expressions ('Water as fish', 'The smooth', 'Death as sleep' and 'Woman as wild strawberry'),[5] a prefiguration of the quarrel which, ten years later, would pit him against Raymond Picard. The review concluded by pleading with him to say what he wanted, 'but please, sir, say it in French! Then you will see that your discoveries are commonplaces given a falsely scientific air by their comical labels.'[6]

However, the *Michelet*, which is the least talked about of Barthes's texts, is in fact one of the most important – both in terms of the method he employs in it and its form. It will be remembered that by January 1945 Barthes had already filled over a thousand index cards with notes on Michelet. He took them with him to Romania, Egypt, everywhere, and tried out different combinations of cards, as in playing a game of patience, in order to work out a way of organizing them and to find correspondences between them. He worked for twelve years (from 1942 to 1954) on a book that was just over a hundred pages in length! These years were not wasted, however, since it was through his research on Michelet that Barthes discovered a style and method which suited him. This consisted of writing out his cards every day, making notes on every possible subject, then classifying and combining them in different ways until he found a structure or a set of themes.

Michelet is a typical product of this process. On a first reading, it is a disconcerting text. It begins with an evocation of Michelet's 'migraines'[7] and moves quickly on to surprising themes such as 'The victim of history', 'Michelet the walker', 'Michelet the swimmer', 'Michelet the predator.'[8] In fact the ironic review in *Le Monde* seems quite justified. If one looks at it more closely, the text seems to consist of an explosion of index cards, with quotes by Michelet on one side and comments by Barthes on the other. The *Michelet* is not a coherent text but a succession of fragments, hardly begun when they are finished, fragments which could fit on to the back of an index card, as a commentary on quotations.

Thus a short piece by Barthes, 'Water as fish', is followed a few pages further on by extracts from Michelet with the title 'Water or fish' which echo his comments,[9] and the same duality is found with regard to different themes, for instance: 'History stops: narcotics', 'Marat as toad', 'Rose and bull', 'The woman as wild strawberry'.[10] In fact, Barthes's procedure highlights Michelet's different themes, and in addition the opening half-page of the book and the four concluding pages are a kind of instruction manual or 'directions for use'. At the beginning Barthes points out that his book is not an account of Michelet's ideas or of his life but an attempt to 'recover the structure of an existence (if not of a life), a thematics, if you like, or better still: an organised network of obsessions.'[11] At the end of the book he comes back to this mode of reading: 'Michelet's history is covered by a network of themes . . . Michelet's discourse is a kind of cryptogram, we must make it into a grid, and this grid is the very structure of the work.'[12]

When this long journey has finally come to an end, when what was very nearly a doctoral thesis has ended up as a small book, it is legitimate to ask what lay behind this long passion: what was it in Michelet that attracted Barthes? The thematics which are dealt with in the book? Certainly. Michelet's ethnological approach to the history of France, as Barthes was to comment later, pointing out that he himself had 'ethnographed' France?[13] No doubt. But in addition, there is something more unexpected and less obvious: the duality of a face. At the end of the book he includes the following note: 'Michelet wrote nothing about anyone without consulting as many portraits and engravings as he could. All his life, he conducted a systematic interrogation of the faces he passed.'[14]

What this note does not say is that Barthes had scrupulously imitated this habit of Michelet's. He had got hold of all the available portraits of him, the reproductions of canvases by Couture, Belloc, Flameng, a lithograph by Lafosse, and finally a photograph, and had spent a long time studying them, looking for the man behind the images. He had been fascinated by Couture's portrait of Michelet sitting at his desk with a slightly disdainful, superior air. He told his friends about the dark flame in Michelet's eyes, his sorcerer's face and his demoniacal air, and explained that he had decided to work on Michelet because, from the pictures of him, he seemed to be the complete opposite of Barthes himself. It was Michelet's apparent wickedness that attracted him. Then in December 1945, while he was at Leysin, he had received a postcard from Robert David – a photograph of Michelet. In the photo, he was older, his face more rounded and his eyes softer than in the portraits. First of all, Barthes was embarrassed by this apparent goodness, which contradicted the wickedness of the portraits, and he commented on this disparity to his friends. Which was the true Michelet – the good one or the demoniacal one? He went back and forth from the portrait to the photo as he was sorting his index cards in search of an organizing principle, and tried to make sense of it. There is an echo of these two opposing images of the same man in Barthes's 1959 preface to an edition of Michelet's *La Sorcière* when he recalled that, for Michelet, Satan was one aspect of God.[15]

In the meantime, Barthes had lost his post as a trainee researcher at the CNRS. His two year contract was not renewed and the difficulties he had experienced in putting together a coherent report of his research had been a contributory factor. Even though he had expressed a desire to leave the CNRS, he was deeply affected by the decision. Once again, he saw any prospect of a teaching career fade into the distance. The incident reopened that narcissistic wound which was to take such a long time to heal and redoubled his feelings of being frustrated by institutional structures. In addition, he was having money problems again. He thought of applying for another post at the CNRS, in the sociology department this time, and with the backing of Georges Friedmann, but he would have to wait at least a year for this.

This time it was Voisin who came to his rescue by taking him on at Arche as a literary adviser. He went on to become an editor, and also the kingpin of *Théâtre populaire*. The review's Brechtian stance hardened in this period, leading to the departure of some of its founding members, including Duvignaud and Morvan-Levesque. In addition, Barthes persuaded Voisin to take on Jacqueline Fournié, who was unemployed at the time, as executive secretary, and for several months they both worked at the same offices in the rue Saint-André-des-Arts. Roland worked at Arche in the afternoons and in the mornings stayed at home in the Rue Servandoni and began work on what he called 'a sociology of daily life'. The analyses he wrote at this time would later became *Mythologies*. He had planned to go and see Rebeyrol in Egypt at the beginning of the winter of 1954, but he had not been able to afford it. In the autumn of 1954 he rescheduled his visit for February 1955, but again was unable to go for the same reasons. He promised Rebeyrol that he would visit him the following year, provided he got a grant from the CNRS.

In the spring of 1955, almost two years after his grand-mother's death, her will was finally settled. Throughout this period, Rebeyrol's uncle, Pierre Davy, had been advising the Barthes on how to invest their inheritance. Roland was full of praises for 'Uncle Pierre', whom he regarded as an invaluable help, and without whom he would have felt lost. Davy was a broker and his knowledge of the world of finance seemed miraculous to Henriette and her two sons. They entrusted their assets to him and followed his advice to the letter: part of Henriette's inheritance was invested according to 'Uncle Pierre's' instructions. Several years later, however, he was involved in some bad deals and the Barthes lost a great deal of money.

The rest of the inheritance enabled them to buy their flat in the Rue Servandoni, and to have a ladder and trapdoor installed in the ceiling linking the flat to Roland's study upstairs. Whenever Roland chose not to come down from his study, he had what he needed (food, mail) hoisted up to him in a basket. In this way he managed both to maintain the distance he needed from his mother, yet still remain in close proximity, since she was the centre of their family life. When Nadeau or Jacqueline came to visit them, Roland would put in an appearance then disappear back to his work, and his brother Michel would be busy with his painting. So it was left to Henriette to offer the guests tea and to make conversation. However, the question of who was to have the villa 'Etchetoa' in Hendaye was not settled until July 1957, when Henriette finally bought back the house (which was much coveted by her half-brother) at auction.

At the time, Barthes and Dort were effectively in charge at *Théâtre populaire*. Their 'discovery of the year' was *The Caucasian Chalk Circle* which the Berliner Ensemble had brought to the Sarah-Bernhardt theatre in Paris. For them, the work of Brecht and Adamov represented a sort of non-dogmatic realism which they found completely fulfilling. But 1955 was remarkable for two major confrontations: the controversy caused by Jean-Paul Sartre's play *Nekrassov* and Barthes's polemic with Camus.

Nekrassov caused a huge scandal. Its stance was overtly in favour of the Communist party, and it violently attacked the right-wing press and its anti-communist propaganda. In particular, the character of Jules Palotin, director of *Soir à Paris*, was an obvious caricature of Pierre Lazareff and *France-Soir*. As a result, Sartre brought down on himself the wrath of most of the press. *Paris-Match*, *L'Aurore* and *Le Figaro* were quick to condemn him. The reaction of *L'Express*, however, was more surprising. Their review, which was strongly critical of the play, was written by Françoise Giroud. She did not normally write the theatre reviews, but she was a friend of Lazareff. So, according to Simone de Beauvoir in her book, *The Force of Circumstance*, she got herself invited to the dress rehearsal, beating Renée Saurel, the weekly's regular theatre critic, to it. Saurel promptly resigned, while Giroud gleefully panned *Nekrassov*. All the papers, or almost all of them, followed suit. It was Dort who was actually in charge of theatre reviews at *L'Express*, and it was he who had taken on Renée Saurel. They both resigned in protest over Giroud's aggressive tactics. As for Françoise Giroud herself, she remembers it as a relatively minor incident:

> I remember very little about the matter. I only remember that I went to one of the first performances and I thought it was a really bad play. The caricature of Pierre Lazareff was beside the point and the famous phrase about Billancourt's despair absolutely comical. But at that time you didn't dare question anything Sartre did unless you wanted to bring the heavens down upon you. Sartre was sacred, and only pearls of wisdom could drop from his pen. If one disagreed, one was immediately classed as a right-wing bastard who had sold out to imperialism. Despite this, I published that small piece in *L'Express*, which caused a bit of a stir. That's all I can tell you.[16]

Back to Simone de Beauvoir, faithful chronicler of Sartre's good and bad fortunes:

> A play can weather the attacks of the critics when it can command the favours of the [theatre-going public]; this was the case with Anouilh: he appeals to the rich, but *Nekrassov* was an attack on precisely those people who assure the box office its receipts; the ones who came found the play amusing but made sure to tell their friends they had been bored stiff. In the name of culture, the bourgeoisie will swallow a great many affronts; this particular bone stuck in its throat. *Nekrassov* lasted for only 60 performances.[17]

Only Jean Cocteau, Gilles Sandier and Roland Barthes made their voices heard in support of the play. Barthes's review in *Théâtre populaire*[18] follows on directly from his previous attacks on that somewhat mythical enemy, the bourgeoisie, a theme which will be looked at later. In the review he wrote: 'Every evening, for as long as possible, *Nekrassov* will liberate those French people who like me, are in danger of being suffocated by the prevalence of the bourgeois sickness. Michelet once said *France hurts me,* and this is why I found *Nekrassov* such a breath of fresh air.'

Today the play's qualities are far from obvious: did Barthes really like it or did he merely want to come to the aid of a writer he had admired for a long time, someone he thought was being attacked by the bourgeoisie? Bernard Dort says he and Barthes really did think *Nekrassov* was a good play, 'the birth of a French form of satirical comedy along Brechtian lines'. However, it may be more accurate to say that Barthes was on the lookout for targets. At the time Pierre Poujade, who in 1953 had founded the UDCA (The Tradesmen's and Artisans' Defence Union), was on his way to electoral success in 1956. In *Les Lettres nouvelles*, Barthes published a vitriolic piece entitled 'Poujade and the intellectual' (which was later republished in *Mythologies*), and both this attack on Poujade and his defence of *Nekrassov* were his way of making plain his resolutely 'anti-bourgeois' stance.

Am I a Marxist?

Barthes certainly did not look for the polemic with Camus. He had often said he only wrote if commissioned, and after the publication of *Writing Degree Zero* he was asked to write two reviews of Camus for two magazines of a similar sort, the *Bulletin du club du livre français*, and the *Bulletin du club du meilleur livre*. Both were aimed at members of mail-order book clubs. '*L'Étranger*, roman solaire?' was published in 1954[19] and '*La Peste*: annales d'une épidémie ou roman de la solitude?' ('*The Plague*: the annals of an epidemic or a novel of isolation?') in 1955.[20] Camus, who read the second article before it was published, replied in the same edition of the magazine and Barthes responded to him in a letter published two months later, in April 1955.[21] The subject of their polemic is interesting since Camus, perhaps unwittingly, pushed Barthes into defining his philosophical position. Barthes had criticized *The Plague*'s lack of 'solidarity' and its ethical perspective. Camus had replied with considerable skill to these points. He explained that, firstly, from *The Outsider* to *The Plague* there was precisely a movement from individual to collective revolt. Barthes's criticism was therefore wide of the mark. Secondly, if one were going to accuse him of rejecting history, one should define one's own idea of 'history', and if criticizing his ethics, one should clearly define one's own.

This question obviously goes back to 1952, to the polemic between Camus and Sartre which had led to the public rupture between them and which had its roots in their differing views of Stalinism and the Soviet Union. In May 1952, in *Les Temps modernes*, Francis Jeanson had strongly criticized Camus's *The Rebel*. In August Camus had replied: 'I am getting a little tired of being criticized by people who have only ever participated in the march of history from their armchairs.' In the same edition Sartre dealt the final blow: 'First of all your moral principles became moralism, today they are nothing more than literature, tomorrow perhaps they may become immoral.' Camus was therefore exasperated by the way he was regularly put on trial, and at the same time he had developed a certain skill at this kind of debate. The substance of his response to Barthes was, to translate it into the language of contemporary discourse, 'What position are you speaking from?' and 'Are you for realism in literature?'

Barthes, forced into a corner by Camus's skill at polemics and forced to make a choice by this formal demand, chose to take the plunge and declare his commitment (but what else could he do?). He replied that he was speaking from the position of a historical materialist. Doubtlessly such an affirmation, which was partly strategic, was the only choice open to him, but it naturally had repercussions. In the *Nouvelle NRF*, Jean Guérin wondered whether the author of the 'little mythologies of the month' was a Marxist and Barthes replied in *Lettres nouvelles* – in an article provocatively entitled 'Suis-je marxiste?' ('Am I a Marxist?') – that such a question had overtones of McCarthyism.[22] But he had nailed his theoretical colours to the mast. Added to his championship of Brecht, and his defence of the *nouveau roman* – which was considered 'realist', 'objective', and later 'object' [*objectale*] literature – it gave him an image which he might have found it difficult to live up to. Previously he had been perceived as being 'on the left' because of the newspapers he had chosen to contribute to: now he had openly declared himself to be so.

Was Barthes a Marxist? According to him he had been a Marxist for a long time: when he had left the sanatorium at the end of the war he had deemed himself as a 'Marxist and a Sartrean'; in Bucharest he had told Rebeyrol that as far as politics went, he could only think in Marxist terms. However, both his Marxist formation and his Sartrean positions can be questioned. First of all, as his articles in *Combat* show, at the beginning of the 1950s he was part of a group which was considered anti-communist by supporters of Stalinism. Moreover, he was writing for a paper in which, in February 1948, Claude Bourdet had called for the union of left-wing forces, of 'non-Stalinist revolutionaries and progressive spirits of all tendencies'.

Of course, one could be a Marxist without being a fan of the Communist party, but Barthes's polemics had never situated themselves within the closed sphere of Marxist rhetoric, and never would. Thus, in *Writing Degree Zero*, when he savagely attacked Roger Garaudy and André Stil, two particularly orthodox pillars of the Communist party, it was not on the grounds of their interpretations of Marxism but their conception of literature: 'Of course, we must allow for mediocrity; in the case of Garaudy, it is impressive.'[23] He concluded that Stalinist ideology had instilled a holy terror of discussing any formal problems in writing and thus the tendency was to choose a bourgeois form of writing, which was less dangerous than any questioning of it. None of which would have earned him a reputation as an expert in the science of Marxism. Edgar Morin, who had been expelled from the Communist party in 1951, and who did possess a genuine Marxist culture, considered that Barthes's Marxism was the vulgar Marxism of intellectuals who had perhaps read a few pages of Marx or, more likely, of Sartre.

But in claiming to be a Marxist – as he had once before in another very different context, during his farewell speech at the French Institute in Bucharest – Barthes for once overcame the reserve which characterized all areas of his life. As has been seen, what he hated most was exhibitionism. As he often told his friends, he hated aggression and hysteria, which he regarded as underlying any form of over-assertively militant discourse. While he was fascinated by the Sartrean notion of commitment, he was appalled by the translation of this theory into practice and he avoided meetings, demonstrations and crowds. Camus had succeeded in making him publicly state his position, which was one of the rare occasions in his life when he was forced to drop his habitual reserve.

In July 1955, in the foothills of the Alps near Barcelonette, he met Philippe Rebeyrol who was taking an enforced holiday because of health problems. He did not mention a word of the polemic with Camus or of the text he had just written in which he openly affirmed his Marxism. On the other hand, he dragged Philippe off to see a stage of the Tour de France. 'But what has it got to do with you?' his friend asked. 'I think it's exciting, it's extraordinary, sociologically it's very interesting,' Barthes replied. In fact he was researching one of his 'mythologies': 'The Tour de France'.

For his part, Greimas was still in Egypt but trying to come back to Europe. In 1955 a teaching post in French became available at the University of Uppsala in Sweden. It was a post which had previously been held by Georges Dumezil. Greimas applied for the job but was turned down in favour of a twenty-nine-year-old philosophy student who had passed the agrégation and was an assistant teacher in the literature faculty at Lille University. His name was Michel Foucault and several months later, at Christmas 1955, Barthes was introduced to him through a mutual friend Robert Mauzi. Barthes and Foucault had many things in common – their ideas, their critical position in relation to the dominant ideology, and, of course, their homosexuality. Yet there were perhaps more things which divided them. Barthes was reserved, hating any form of outburst or exhibitionism, whereas Foucault was the exact opposite. Nevertheless, the two became friends. They would have dinner together when Foucault was in Paris, then go out to a Saint-Germain-des-Prés nightclub. They often met up on holiday, usually in Morocco, until the quarrel which led to their estrangement.

Mythologies

Barthes began 1956 with an act of self-defiance. From now on, he would refuse to allow himself to be ruled by the weakness of his lungs, what he scornfully referred to as his 'softness'. He decided his pulmonary problems were over and that he could take up classical singing lessons again. He contacted Charles Panzera (who had taught him in 1941) and at the end of January started having lessons again. However, this arrangement was not to last long. Barthes's voice did not improve and he blamed his illness again, and also his age (he had just turned forty). In April he decided, somewhat sadly, to give up his lessons. At least, as he explained to Panzera, he would always have a thorough understanding of music and singing, but he knew he would never be able to sing in a way that would satisfy him.

It was around this time that he began to relinquish his links with *Théâtre populaire*. He had got another research assistant's post at the CNRS, this time in the sociology department, but most of all he was preoccupied with the book he was in the process of producing for Seuil: a collection of the 'little mythologies of the month' he was still contributing to Nadeau's review. Out of the fifty-four texts in the book, only two had not been previously published in *Les Lettres nouvelles*, the opening essay about wrestling (published in *Critique* in 1952) and the one about 'The writer on holiday', which was published in *France-Observateur* in September 1954.

Apart from collecting together the mythologies themselves, he also had to write a new text – a preface or a postscript – which would give the book unity and direction. During the summer of 1956 he discussed the matter with Bernard Dort while the two were on holiday at his grandmother's villa (which now belonged to Henriette) at Hendaye. The house was by the sea, on the road to Saint-Jean-de-Luz. Bernard loved to go swimming every day, and after his swim Madame Barthes would mix him a kir while Roland, who did not like the sun and the sea, wrote his postscript. Initially he had thought of writing about himself: after all, his own family were members of the bourgeoisie, his own patterns of behaviour had been formed by it, and he smiled ironically to himself at the thought of ending the book with a 'mythology of Roland Barthes'.

Dort encouraged this idea, to provoke Roland a little. He had always believed Roland was not the theoretical writer he claimed to be and was more cut out to be a great bourgeois novelist, 'but the novel he could have written had already been written: Proust's *Remembrance of Things Past*'. Finally, Barthes decided that the postscript would be a theoretical essay, 'Myth today', a kind of continuation of his discussions with Greimas in Alexandria. This essay marks his entrance into the semiological order, just as one would enter a religious order. The tone of the fifty-four mythologies which precede this postscript is very different from the tone of the essay itself. In the events he was reacting to, Barthes was seeking out – and denouncing – ideological distortions, the attempt to make what is thoroughly cultural seem natural and what is acquired seem innate. In other words, he was hunting for what is falsely self-evident, what he himself referred to as the 'what-goes-without-saying':

> The starting point of these reflections was usually a feeling of impatience at the sight of the 'naturalness' with which newspapers, art, and common sense constantly dress up a reality which, even though it is the one we live in, is undoubtedly determined by history. In short, in the account given of our contemporary circumstances, I resented seeing Nature and History confused at every turn, and I wanted to track down, in the decorative

display of *what-goes-without-saying*, the ideological abuse which, in my view, is hidden there.[24]

So myth is to be understood as having two meanings. Firstly it is, as its Greek etymology suggests, a legend, a symbolic account of the human condition. Secondly it is a lie, a mystification. In these monthly articles Barthes revealed the ideological misrepresentation, the social 'lie' in a film, an advert, or a discourse. Nevertheless, during the summer of 1956, while he was writing his essay, he came up against a problem. What was the link between these different descriptive pieces, all of them written separately and now to be collected together in a single volume? The first thing that connects them is, quite simply, repetition, accumulation. The repetition of the myths described in each piece, of course, and also the repetition of their meanings. As one moves from text to text, the favourite target of this myth chronicler becomes apparent: the bourgeoisie, or more specifically, the petite-bourgeoisie: 'The petit-bourgeois myth of the negro' (p. 170, 'Bichon chez les Nègres'); 'What the petite-bourgeoisie respects most in the world is immanence' (p. 96, 'Quelque paroles de M. Poujade'); 'I have already signalled the petite-bourgeoisie's predilection for tautological arguments' (p. 109, 'Racine est Racine'); 'This bourgeois promoting of the mountains' (p. 136, 'Le guide bleu'); 'Since from now on there will be bourgeois trips to Russia' (p. 147, 'La croisière du Batory').[25]

It was in this very superfluity that Barthes found his solution. In fact, the repetitions make sense. In his view, the myth-allegories and the myth-lies form part of a code – the code through which the bourgeoisie disseminates its ideology. What is more, neither Sartrean nor Brechtian, nor even Marxist theory provides sufficient tools for describing this code. This is why he wrote 'Myth today' and why he became interested in semiology. In order to move from the accumulation of these short, sharply critical pieces on current events to a more general discourse, to move from being a 'mythologue' to a 'semiologue', he was to make use of concepts taken from Saussure and Hjelmslev (whom he had discovered through Greimas). The concepts he would use were 'sign', 'denotation' and 'connotation'.

In myths the sign is turned aside from its proper function (its primary denotative function), since in myth, connotation is parasitic on denotation. Thus the Latin phrase 'quia ego nominor leo', on the level of denotation, had a signified (or, to put it more simply, a meaning): 'For I am called a lion.' But this phrase is often used in school textbooks as an example of the agreement of the complement and thus, on the level of connotation, it has another meaning: 'I am a grammar example.' Another example is that of the literary critic who is generally regarded as competent (at least by the readers of his paper) and who writes of a so-called *nouveau roman* novel: 'I don't understand any of it.' On the level of denotation he seems to be admitting his incompetence, but since his competence is already recognized, his declaration must be understood on the level of connotation as meaning: 'there is nothing to understand.' One final, more everyday example: the picture on the cover of the magazine *Paris-Match* of a young black soldier proudly saluting the French flag.

> All this is the meaning of the picture. But, whether naively or not, I see very well what it signifies to me: that France is a great Empire, that all her sons, without any colour discrimination, faithfully serve under her flag, and that there is no better answer to the detractors of an alleged colonialism than the zeal shown by this Negro, in serving his so-called oppressors.[26]

The same goes for all the myths through which petite-bourgeoisie ideology reveals itself and this is the essence of the mythologue's task: to elaborate a semiology of this bourgeois world. But even if here Barthes mobilizes several new concepts, he was in fact simply giving a more theoretical gloss to the approach he had already been using, an approach which can be seen to be at work in the opening lines of *Writing Degree Zero*, quoted previously: 'Hébert, the revolutionary, never began a number of his news-sheet *Le Père Duchêne* without introducing a sprinkling of obscenities. These improprieties had no real meaning, but they had a significance [Ces grossièretés ne signifiaient rien mais elles signalaient]. In what way? In that they expressed a whole revolutionary situation.' Signify (*signifier*), signal (*signaler*); denote, connote. There is an almost perfect parallelism between these two pairs of concepts. What this exemplifies is something that was to become a constant feature of Barthes's approach: the use of other people's concepts to theorize his own practice. Here he was beginning to take the concepts of others and develop them in his own direction, a practice he continued throughout his life.

Collected together, these small pieces represent an exciting account of the first half of the 1950s. They are both an echo of a particular historical period and at the same time reveal a particular vision, Barthes's vision, and an analytical instinct. Umberto Eco and

Isabella Pezzini have said of Barthes's *Mythologies* that it is 'pages apparently put together at random but which in fact are governed by a superb instinct for systematic organization'.[27] There is nothing to add to this, except to say that instinct can sometimes be proved wrong.

The year 1954 began with a severe winter. In Paris, temperatures fell to $-20°$ (and in some regions $-30°$). During the night of 4 January a baby died from the cold, yet the Minister for Reconstruction and Housing, Maurice Lemaire, had just rejected the project for emergency shelters put forward by the Mouvement Républicain Populaire senator Léo Hamon. A strange character then appeared on the scene: Henri Grouès, a former Capuchin monk who had become a curate and who, during his days in the Resistance, had used the name 'l'abbé Pierre'. Incensed by the misery which was increasing around him, the creator of the Chiffoniers d' Emmaüs launched an appeal for solidarity and charity, which was quickly taken up by the media. A year after this campaign had begun, in January 1955, Barthes published 'The iconography of the Abbé Pierre', in which he describes the Abbé Pierre as covered by 'a forest of *signs*'.[28] Reading this text much later, in 1990, when the Abbé Pierre came into the news again because there was a book and then a film about his life, one was struck by the continuing relevance of Barthes's concluding remarks: 'I then start to wonder whether the fine and touching iconography of the Abbé Pierre is not the alibi which a sizeable part of the nation uses in order, once more, to substitute with impunity the signs of charity for the reality of justice.'[29]

On the other hand, his analysis in January 1954 of Joseph Mankiewicz's film *of Julius Caesar* is less convincing. In the film, the director made a series of choices which ought to have interested the editor of *Théâtre populaire*. In basing his script almost entirely on Shakespeare's text, opting to shoot in black and white when colour was all the rage and having the battles narrated rather than showing them, Mankiewicz had offered one possible solution to the problem of how to translate a play on to the screen. However, all Barthes noticed was the actors' fringes, a sign of 'romanness', and he remarks that all signs of baldness have been hidden and that all the characters' faces sweat constantly: 'Labourers, soldiers, conspirators, all have their austere and tense features streaming (with Vaseline). And close-ups are so frequent that evidently sweat here is an attribute with a purpose. Like the Roman fringe, or the nocturnal plait, sweat is a sign. Of what? Of moral feeling.'[30]

It seems surprising that this reader of Brecht, this theoretician of the theatre, did not reflect on the theatricality of the film. Even more so when one cannot help noticing on seeing the film itself that although it does indeed contain a few fringes, it also contains a lot of bald heads. Moreover, one is not immediately struck by the sweating faces: Barthes seems largely to have invented the film to be able to fit it into what is in the main an *a priori* interpretation. There are further examples of this kind of distortion in all the mythologies if one compares them with the original event which produced them: it is often at this price that systems are constructed.

Mythologies came out at the beginning of 1957. The author typed his own 'blurb' for his editor to send out to the press. On the draft copy he used the abbreviation R.B. three times and this acronym was later adopted by Philippe Sollers: 'Arbee' ('Erbé') was to become the most common way of referring to him among his closest friends. But, at the time, acronyms were not very fashionable, with the exception of B.B. for Brigitte Bardot. Speaking about himself in the third person, Barthes wrote the following:

> For the past three years, R.B. has been trying to carry out a 'committed' form of criticism in several different fields. Firstly, that of literature, in his essays and in his features on the novels of Cayrol (in *Esprit*) and Robbe-Grillet (in *Critique*) and then in the field of theatre, with the founding of the review *Théâtre populaire* and finally his articles in *France-Observateur* on daily life in France today, from which these *Mythologies* are drawn.

As was to become his habit, he then observed the reactions of the press to his book closely. In *Le Monde* Jean Lacroix, who was in charge of the philosophy section, reacted belatedly but with a fairly benevolent review.[31] The right, however, reacted as if it considered Barthes its enemy. *Rivarol* denounced his 'progressive idiocies',[32] and Pol Vandromme in *L'Écho du centre* described *Mythologies* as 'part interpretive delirium and part pedantic jargon'.[33] Jargon? At the beginning of July, *Mythologies* was chosen by *L'Express* for its 'holiday book choice', and the jury for the Sainte-Beuve essay prize awarded it seven votes, only two less than the nine votes awarded to Cioran's *La Tentation d'exister* ('The temptation to exist'). If in this period Barthes's style, his analyses seemed difficult, they were soon to become the shared property of a certain intelligentsia, and today seem quite self-evident. Of course, the book did not sell in great numbers, but it continued to sell, and it still does today. If it is *Writing Degree Zero* which is often quoted and which has achieved almost cult status, it is *Mythologies* which is most widely read. Intellectual life in France was entering into the era of models, and *Mythologies* was very soon to form part of a new 'myth', that of structuralism.

Écrivain, écrivant

The theatre was playing a smaller and smaller role in Barthes's life, or rather Barthes was distancing himself more and more from the theatre. He would only make one brief return to it, much later, after his trip to Japan. Was this a matter of choice or of necessity? In fact, this way of distancing himself is a common feature of his life, as if he were afraid of becoming tied down by what he was doing or trapped by his choices, and felt the need to 'unhook' himself and move on to something new. In 1960 he wrote his last article for *Théâtre populaire*, on Brecht's *Mother Courage*, which was published in the summer edition. A month later, in *Arguments* he put his name to an article called 'Écrivains et écrivants',[34] which revealed the new direction his thought and his interests had taken.

In 1956, Edgar Morin had launched the review *Arguments* for the publisher Minuit. It was modelled on the Italian review *Raggionamenti* which his friend Franco Fortini was involved with. Its regular contributors included Colette Audry, Kostas Axelos, François Fetjö, Pierre Fougeyrollas and Serge Mallet.[35] The idea was to create a non-dogmatic space in which, for example, both socialists and communists could write, without anyone regarding it as their exclusive territory. Barthes was a member of the editorial team right from the beginning. In the years that followed he was to contribute to a large number of reviews, and sit on numerous editorial boards, since he was incapable of refusing any request, for fear of appearing aggressive. He tended to say yes to everything, then practise a form of conscientious objection, pulling back sharply from his responsibilities. This inability to say no landed him in some tricky situations. He wrote endless letters of apology for not being able to attend certain symposiums or debates as he had promised.

However, his involvement with *Arguments* was very different. Barthes felt comfortable with its flexible brand of Marxism, which was free of any hint of Stalinism. He had agreed to participate principally out of friendship for Edgar Morin, but he soon discovered in it a form of political involvement which suited him. In fact, *Arguments* was to be his second 'site' of theoretical development, after *Théâtre populaire* and before *Communications* and *Tel Quel*. In the first edition of the review he had published an article on Brecht,[36] then one on Robbe-Grillet[37] but 'Écrivains et écrivants' is of a completely different order of importance in the development of his ideas. First of all, the distinction referred to in the title had a grammatical reality for him. *Écrivain* for 'writer' is a noun and the *écrivain* fulfils a function: for him or her the verb to write [*écrire*] is intransitive. *Écrivant* for 'writer' is the nominalization of a transitive verb and in this case the writer carries out an activity. The first *writes* whereas the second *writes something*. Above all, they have different places in the social order. The *écrivain* makes one think of a priest whereas the *écrivant* makes one think of a clerk. The *écrivant* justifies his writing by writing what he thinks, whereas the *écrivain*'s justification for writing is that he works on language. Once again, at the time Barthes's ideas may have seemed obscure, but today they are a matter of common sense, as if Barthes's talent lay in giving shape to ideas which, once made concrete, have come to seem self-evident.

It was during this period that he made his first trip to the United States and discovered New York. There are two traces of his reaction to this trip: one public and the other private. In private, with his mother and brother, he seemed thrilled to bits by New York's modernism, like a child who falls in love with a new toy. On his return to the Rue Servandoni he told them that they must change everything in the flat and replace their old domestic appliances with new sophisticated electric ones, since their toaster, tin-opener and cooker were medieval. However, this enthusiasm did not last long and the subsequent trips he made to attend conferences or symposiums left him feeling less euphoric – especially as the Americans became increasingly anti-smoking and he was incapable of giving a class or a lecture without smoking.

But he had loved New York, its streets, its crowds, and his public reaction to the city was expressed in the form of an article he wrote on an exhibition of paintings by Bernard Buffet.[38] He wrote that the painter had fallen victim to the myth that high buildings are inhumane, and to the prejudiced notion that one is happier living in Belleville than in Manhattan. He had wanted to see New York as a city of skyscrapers where it was impossible to be happy. Completely sold on this idea, he had foregrounded vertical shapes or, as Barthes put it, he 'geometrizes New York the better to depopulate it' since 'to paint New York from above, at the top, is to rely once again on the first spiritualist myth, i.e. that geometry kills man.'[39] This was not at all the town Barthes had seen, and he defended his vision fiercely. While it was true that he thought it would be awful to work there, it was not the city itself which was terrible, but work. The article's conclusion, which is a real demolition of the painter, is a confirmation of his private reactions and his passion for modernism and for gadgets: 'The intentional desolation of his New York – what can it mean except that it is bad for mankind to live in groups, that number kills the spirit, that too many bathrooms are harmful to the spiritual health of a nation? . . . Buffet once again diverts history into metaphysics.'[40] For Barthes, Buffet implicitly attributed the American malaise to technology, not to anything else. The central idea of Barthes's argument is that it is a bit easy to limit his analysis of the city to the commonplace that money doesn't make happiness: 'the most reactionary remark of human history, the alibi of all exploitations'.[41]

From a psychological point of view, this passage is extremely interesting. It reveals all the contradictory forces at work in Barthes during this period. On the one hand, there is his almost visceral support for the cause of the poor and oppressed, a feeling of solidarity which, as has been seen, stems from his adolescence. On the other hand, there is his longstanding and recently reaffirmed Marxism. Finally, there is his more recent passion for modernism. The Bernard Buffet exhibition is, of course, merely a pretext in the literal sense of the word: something, an event, which comes before the text and justifies it, allowing him to marshal his ideas. These may well be contradictory, but he was also to make them dialectical: behind Buffet's (false) vision of New York there was, once again, a little mythology to catch hold of. It was not the United States itself which was the devil, it was no good condemning the 'American way of life'; it was capitalism – even if this word does not actually appear in the article – which was to blame.

However, Barthes's American trip was merely a brief parenthesis. He had also started work on a new research project. After *Michelet* and his thesis on the 'vocabulary of the social question', he was now working on a third doctorate proposal, this time on the subject of fashion. As far as Greimas is aware, there were three drafts of Barthes's thesis on fashion and almost as many potential supervisors. In 1958 Barthes asked Lévi-Strauss to supervise him, but Lévi-Strauss refused to take him on since he considered him too literary. Later Lévi-Strauss was to tell Didier Eribon: 'I never felt close to him and my feelings were confirmed later by the direction his ideas took. The ideas of the late Barthes were diametrically opposed to those of the early Barthes, which I am certain were not those he would naturally have held.'[42]

Lévi-Strauss refused to supervise his thesis, but gave him the following advice. First of all to confine himself to 'written' fashion, or rather the way that fashion is written about in the press. Secondly, he advised him to read Propp's *Morphology of the Folktale*. Their meeting, which took place in the Avenue d'Iéna, had its amusing side. At the time Lévi-Strauss was sharing an office with four colleagues in what had formerly been a bathroom in an annex of the Guimet museum. He received his visitor on the landing, where they sat in rickety old garden chairs. Greimas, who had been waiting for Barthes in a café on the corner, saw him return frustrated ('he does not want anything to do with my thesis') but also excited by Lévi-Strauss's mention of Propp. Vladimir Propp, a Russian folklorist who was born in 1895 and who taught ethnology at Leningrad University was unknown in France at the time. Although Propp's text had been written in 1928, it was only with the advent of structuralism that it would be appreciated and understood. By analysing several hundred Russian folk-tales, Propp had developed an underlying basic model from which they were all derived. Barthes and Greimas eagerly set about reading *The Morphology of the Folktale* in its English translation by Roman Jakobson's second wife. Barthes later commented that the discovery of Propp 'made it possible to apply semiology with some rigour to a literary object, narrative.'[43] From this reading came the idea of 'narrativity' and the 'structural model of the actants' which Greimas later developed in his *Sémantique structurale*, which was published in 1966.

Barthes still did not have a supervisor for his doctoral proposal. Pierre Guiraud, who had been in Romania before Barthes and was now teaching linguistics in Groningen in the Netherlands, suggested he try the linguist André Martinet. So one summer evening in 1954, Barthes, Guiraud and Greimas were invited to dinner with Martinet in Sceaux. He had just returned from the United States, where he had lived for several years. During dinner, Barthes asked which item of women's clothing was the most important. Martinet, clearly focusing on the sexual connotations of his question, immediately replied, 'the legs, of course, that is, the stockings, the shoes'. 'Not at all,' Barthes replied, 'semiologically speaking, the legs don't stand up.' He explained that legs, with or without stockings, with or without seams, with or without high-heeled shoes, were not a very rich semiological system, whereas the shawl had at least thirty elementary categories.

He went on to improvise a long talk on the different kinds of shawl (bertha, cape, foot-warmer, stole, pelerine): the shawl differed from the scarf because it was worn around the shoulders and not the neck, and from the collar because it was not attached to the bodice. Barthes took his terms ('marked/unmarked', 'distinctive oppositions') largely from the field of phonology, where Martinet's own interests lay. Was the linguist impressed by Barthes's brilliant and paradoxical performance? Whatever the case, he agreed to supervise the thesis.

Barthes, however, was never to complete the necessary steps for registration of his proposal. His planned doctorate on Michelet had become a book, the *Michelet par lui-même*, and the same was to occur with his research project on fashion, which turned into *Système de la mode* (*The Fashion System*). It was as if the temptations of an academic qualification were really only the result of a nostalgia and not of any real desire. In fact, these vague desires to write a thesis also raised for him the problem of writing. In order to write a doctoral thesis, one had to adopt a certain academic language – the somewhat dull, instrumental language used by researchers in the human sciences to report the results of their work. Barthes's own tastes inclined him towards a different kind of style, one that was less conventional and more personal. Aware, perhaps, that he would never be able to complete this or any thesis, he had already theorized his practice, or his paralysis, in the famous distinction between the *écrivain* and the *écrivant*. On one hand there was *écrivance*, the kind of writing which he rejected, and on the other there was *écriture*, which at the same time as it communicated an idea called into question its own status as discourse.

This awareness that *language exists*, that it is everywhere and that the subject, man, is constituted by it, was to be the foundation of his subsequent theoretical positions. To be aware that one is speaking is already to be working upon writing. It was this awareness which for him constituted the main tenet of structuralism and it was also the basis for his famous assertion that, contrary to Saussure's belief that linguistics is part of a vast science of signs called semiology, semiology forms part of a more general science of linguistics. Language always exists prior to man, and he has to come to terms with it; this is the idea behind Barthes's somewhat strange-sounding assertion during his inaugural lecture at the Collège de France in 1976 that language is fascist, meaning that language forces one to speak. Against the scientist's or researcher's attitude to language, against *écrivance*, Barthes comes down on the side of *écriture*: once

his thesis is out of the way, he will become – or try to become –
a writer.

For the time being, Lévi-Strauss's piece of advice helped Barthes to
structure his approach to the fashion system around the written text.
He would not look at clothes as they are worn but as they are
written about, at fashion writing, or rather at the 'narrative of
fashion', and this was to become his central theme.

It was during the same period that Olivier Burgelin, the director of
the Maison des Lettres, came to see him to ask him to give a lecture.
Naturally he suggested a talk on theatre, since this was publicly
perceived to be his most obvious focus of interest. Barthes agreed,
but to Burgelin's surprise, he said that he would not be talking about
the theatre but about fashion. For Olivier Burgelin, the lecture was a
revelation. He heard, or thought he heard, the 'application of an
engineer's mode of thought to the human sciences, their extreme
formalization'. Looking back on it now, he thinks that this
formalized, scientistic approach was more in his perception of the
proceedings than in the proceedings themselves, and adds, 'Barthes
did not just stop there, and you might say he was never taken in by
such scientificity.' He notes that Barthes never rejected interpretations of his work so long as they could be justified, thus leaving
his listeners and readers free to take what they heard or read in
whatever way they wanted.

Nevertheless, the fact remains that the discourse Burgelin heard
that day seemed radically innovative and revolutionary. In this sense,
Lévi-Strauss had played an invaluable role in the development of
what was still, at this stage, only a research project. We can follow
its evolution through a series of articles that were published: 'The
history and sociology of clothing';[44] 'Language and clothing';[45]
'Knitting at home';[46] and 'Towards a sociology of clothing'.[47]

We must move from these few texts to *the* text, take the bull by
the horns and tackle the main work, the thesis itself. During the
summer of 1960, at Hendaye, Barthes tried, with difficulty, to write.
He had a lectern made, thinking he would find it easier to write
standing up. He worked each day, but found it a difficult task and
made very slow progress. He did not like the tone of the text: he was
worried it might be boring. Moreover, since it was taking a long time
to write, he was afraid it would turn out to be the work of an
écrivant. *The Fashion System* was under way, but it would take
several years for it to emerge.

It was in the same year, 1960, that he had his first difference of
opinion with Maurice Nadeau. Sartre's magazine *Les Temps*

modernes and Nadeau's *Les Lettres nouvelles* both had their offices in the buildings of the publishing firm Juillard. When the trials of those involved in channelling support to the Algerian revolution (in particular, the Jeanson network) were announced in September, the two editorial teams discussed the appropriate way to react. Nadeau, Jean Pouillon, Blanchot and several others produced a text which has since become famous as the Manifesto of the 121 (because it was signed by 121 people), but which was actually called 'The declaration of the right to insubordination in the Algerian war'. The signatories were all well known, but the list of those who had been asked to sign and refused was even longer. Among them, along with Edgar Morin and Claude Lévi-Strauss, was Roland Barthes.

His action represented a break with his old friend Nadeau (despite his pleas), with Jean-Paul Sartre, whose theory of commitment he had espoused in the 1940s, and with Bernard Dort, who had also signed the declaration. Nadeau now thinks that it was this refusal which perhaps signalled the parting of their ways, even if, as will be seen later, they would always support one another at important moments. For Bernard Dort, Barthes's refusal cast a shadow between them. None the less, they shared the same view of the Algerian war. When in 1956 Bernard had feared he was about to be called up and was agonizing over whether he should desert if it came to it, Roland gave him moral support. According to Dort, he even took part in a few demonstrations against the war, even though he had always hated such 'hysterical' forms of behaviour.

As for Nadeau, he does not recall ever seeing Roland on the streets: his was a literary approach to politics and his *Mythologies* seemed to him a more effective form of political intervention than a manifesto or a demonstration. 'He should have signed, but he refused to,' concludes Nadeau. But Nadeau resented Edgar Morin's refusal even more. Morin was an old friend whose *Autocritique* Nadeau had published and who, not content with simply refusing to sign, wrote an article criticizing the declaration in *France-Observateur*. 'I was ready to sign the first paragraph on insubordination,' Morin says today, 'but not the rest, which gave its implicit support to the FLN, because at the time Messali Hadj's partisans were being eliminated. The FLN's treatment of the Messalists resembled the communists' treatment of the Trotskyists ten years previously.' But Morin, who remembers discussing the matter with Barthes, no longer remembers if the latter shared his views and refused to sign for the same reasons.

It was the beginning of the 1960s and the colonial era was nearing its end. Algeria would soon become independent and the Manifesto of the 121 become a historical footnote. Henriette, Roland and Michel continued to spend their holidays in the Basque country. But the advantages of the villa 'Etchetoa' were also its drawbacks. Its splendid position overlooking the beach meant that it was constantly surrounded by tourists, by the noise of transistor radios and cars. So they started looking for a quieter place and decided on Urt, a little village on the left bank of the River Adour, upstream from Bayonne. In March 1961, Henriette bought the 'Maison Carboué', which from then on was to be their holiday home. It took them two years to sell the villa in Hendaye, their last link with Noémie Révelin.

7

The École, At Last

It was the beginning of the 1960s and a new life for Roland Barthes. In 1960 he was appointed *chef de travaux* in the sixth section of the École Pratique des Hautes Études, in the department of economics and social sciences, and then, two years later, *directeur d'études* in the 'sociology of signs, symbols and representations'. He was to remain in this post for eighteen years, until his election to the Collège de France. Olivier Burgelin was also at the Hautes Études. Burgelin had left the Maison des Lettres at Edgar Morin's request and had taken over at the editorial offices of the review *Communications*, which had just been set up by the 'Centre for the Study of Mass Communications'.

The editorial board included Georges Friedmann, Claude Brémond, Violette and Edgar Morin, and Barthes, but the review also attracted younger researchers such as Christian Metz, Tzvetan Todorov and Jean-Claude Milner, who were embarking on the 'semiological adventure'. Among the different members of this team and, more generally, among the staff at the school it was probably Barthes who took his administrative tasks most seriously. Burgelin was struck by this, since he had expected that the researchers would devote their time exclusively to their intellectual work and would react indignantly to matters of bureaucratic form-filling. For instance, he remembers one day coming across an overjoyed Barthes in the corridor. He had just been congratulated by the school's extremely serious head of administration, who had told him he was 'the best *directeur d'études* in the school'. Obviously, he was referring to

Barthes's conscientiousness and not to the content of his teaching. This largely unknown aspect of Barthes's character, which later Jacques Le Goff was to stress, is important given the number of people who have indicated that, on the contrary, he did not take his teaching work and his relationship with his students very seriously.

Also in 1960, another review called *Tel Quel* was launched by Seuil. The key figures involved were Philippe Sollers – a young novelist whose book *Une curieuse solitude* (1958) had received praise from both François Mauriac and Louis Aragon – and Jean-Edern Hallier. The only relation between these two events in 1960 seemed to be one of proximity in time and space. However, the respective paths of Barthes and Sollers were soon to converge and continue along parallel lines for a long time. The first meeting between the two men took place in 1963, rather by chance, in a small hall in the Latin Quarter where Francis Ponge was giving a lecture. Barthes was sitting at one end of the room, listening to Ponge, and Sollers was at the other. They had already seen one another from a distance in the corridors of Seuil's offices, and they recognized each other, but that was all. However, the fact that they had both come to listen to a poet whose every poem was a tiny philosophical meditation on language constituted in their eyes a guarantee of each other's worth. Henceforth, Barthes and Sollers were favourably disposed towards each other.

A few days later they met again at an informal cocktail party given by Seuil. Sollers had read Barthes's *Mythologies* and *Writing Degree Zero*, whereas Barthes had read nothing of Sollers's work. Barthes was forty-eight and Sollers was twenty-seven. The former was discreetly homosexual, while the latter flaunted his homosexuality. Barthes was suspicious of any kind of exhibitionism, whereas Sollers loved to be the centre of attention. Above all, one came from a Protestant (or rather, 'Ghibelline', according to Sollers) background and the other was a Catholic and considered himself a 'white Guelf'. Sollers's distinction was later taken up by Barthes:

> Michelet used to oppose the Guelf spirit (passion for the Law, for the code, for the Idea, the world of legists, scribes, Jesuits, Jacobins – I should add: of militants) to the Ghibelline spirit, resulting from an attention to the body, the ties of blood, based on a devotion of man, for man, according to a feudal pact. I feel I am more Ghibelline than Guelf.[1]

Thus there were many differences between them, but they were also drawn to one another. A few days later, Sollers sent Barthes a questionnaire on behalf of *Tel Quel*, to which he replied. This became 'Literature and signification', his first appearance in the review, which was republished in *Critical Essays* later that same year.[2] Thus they were brought into contact by their interest in literature, and it was once again through literature that their friendship developed, in relation to two publishing events. In 1965 Sollers published *Drame* which Barthes reviewed in *Critique*[3] and in 1966 Barthes's works, which until then had been published as part of the 'pierres vives' series, became part of the 'Tel Quel' series under the editorship of Sollers. First among them was *Critique et vérité* (*Criticism and Truth*), Barthes's intervention in a polemic about Racine, which will be discussed later.

During this period, while his ties at Seuil with François Wahl, Severo Sarduy and Sollers were strengthening, other ties were becoming weaker. Until now, Barthes and Michel Foucault had seen a lot of each other (they met almost every evening). When Foucault published the first version of *Madness and Civilization* in 1961, Roland wrote a highly favourable review of it for *Critique*,[4] which he then republished in 1964 in his *Critical Essays*. But their meetings suddenly grew more and more infrequent until finally they stopped altogether. Did they quarrel? Not according to Daniel Defert, who obviously had a privileged perspective on events since he was Foucault's partner until the latter's death. Defert thinks that Foucault simply distanced himself from the group of friends he used to see almost every evening in order to devote himself to his work, his research:

> It was more like a 'milieu', and without meaning to, I think I contributed to its break-up in 1963 and 1964, when I started living with Michel Foucault, since their almost daily meetings were incompatible with our hours of work. For us, the late evening was the best time for working so Michel Foucault, whose first love was his work, chose to go out less. This period of intense activity for him, when he wrote *The Order of Things*, coincided with his starting to distance himself from his friends.[5]

But Philippe Sollers offers another version of events. One day, during the same period, he was having dinner with Foucault when the latter made some critical remarks about Barthes. When Sollers defended him, Foucault said, 'One can't be friends with both of us.' On the other hand, according to Sollers, 'Barthes never said anything about Foucault. It was Foucault who fell out with Barthes, because he had an extremely jealous nature, and at the time Barthes was very famous, more so than Lacan, Foucault, Althusser.'

Violette Morin has a third version, which she says she got from Barthes himself. He went on holiday to Tangiers with Foucault and Jean-Paul Aron. Foucault kept complaining that his friend, who had stayed in Paris, hadn't written to him. One day, a letter arrived at the hotel. Barthes took it to Foucault, who was sitting on the terrace of a café with lots of other people, and handed it to him with a laugh, commenting somewhat ironically, 'At last he has written.' Was Foucault upset by his tone? Or by the public reference to his impatience? Whatever the case, 'things were never the same between them again.'

Nevertheless, according to Sollers the friendship that was slowly developing between him and Barthes was based on 'a certain organization of transcription', on a common 'devotion to writing' and approach to life. In some respects, Barthes found in Sollers an *alter ego*. In fact, he had numerous close friends, and central among them was his friendship with Violette Morin. They phoned each other at nine o'clock every morning and saw each other two or three evenings a week. Roland would go to dinner with Violette in the Rue Soufflot and help her daughters with their Latin translations, chatting about everything under the sun. Without fail for twenty-five years they would phone each other every day to say hello, to arrange to see each other that evening or for no particular reason. Of Barthes, Violette Morin says: 'I have never met anyone more concerned about other people than him. If, for instance, I was going off somewhere, he would say to me, "When you get to Rome, please phone me to let me know you've arrived safely." '

Sometimes he took Violette with him to the parties he was invited to, and she remembers his irony, the way, in a glance, he would censure what was ridiculous or highlight what was unexpectedly interesting.

> What was such fun about going to a party with Roland was that suddenly everyone appeared in a different light. The people who were supposed to be nice started to seem dubious, the nervous ones became witty, the dull ones brilliant and the people who looked intelligent and who talked a lot seemed like idiots . . .When you were at a party with Roland, the world seemed topsy-turvy.

She recounts how they would laugh so loudly as to seem almost rude. When, for example, some celebrity of the time launched into a long, pedantic speech, Roland only had to catch her eye and make a sign to her and both of them would start laughing.

This picture of a carefree, funny Barthes is not the usual picture painted of him. On the contrary, most people remember him as being rather sad, rather stuffy or, sometimes, as something of a moaner. However, whenever he came to dinner at Violette's with Raymond Queneau, the whole evening was spent telling jokes and making puns. Violette remembers one evening in particular when Roland told Queneau his favourite story: a crippled man arrives in Lourdes in his little wheelchair, goes to the edge of the swimming pool and, before jumping in the water, says, 'Dear God, when I get out again, please let things be better. Dear God, when I get out again, please let things be better.' He jumps in; then he and his wheelchair are pulled out again and, lo and behold, a miracle! God has answered his prayer: there are now new tyres on his wheelchair.

From *Mythologies* to Publicis

In order to have a better understanding of Barthes's growing notoriety, it is necessary to evoke the atmosphere of this period. In 1964, two years after the end of the Algerian war, the political scene on the left in France was being shaken by the explosive relations between the Communist party and its student wing. In *Génération* Hervé Hamon and Patrick Rotman write that the 'Italians' – the anti-establishment members of the Union of Communist Students (the UEC) – were thrilled by Barthes's assertion that in New Wave films meaning was 'suspended', since the works aimed at provoking answers, not providing them. In fact, Barthes was talking about suspended meaning in relation to different kinds of art forms, more particularly the theatre of Brecht.[6] But Hamon and Rotman's observations, even if not entirely accurate, are indicative of the status Barthes was on his way to achieving. After *Mythologies* and *On Racine*, he had just published *Critical Essays* and he seemed to be the spokesperson of a new kind of literary criticism, of 'modern' discourse. In *France-Observateur* Renaud Matignon asked him naïvely what criteria he used to decide whether a book was really literature or not.[7] Barthes replied that as far as literature was concerned he did not think in terms of good and evil, but certain books seemed 'dangerous' to him and this made him want to talk about them.

So the anti-establishment members of the UEC read Barthes. In March 1965, at their congress in Montreuil, a shock unit of Roland Leroy, Pierre Juquin, Guy Hermier and several other apparatchiks put a great deal of energy into excluding these annoying young people, and to do so they used some expeditious methods. In their view, the latter had no respect for anything, especially not for the dogma of democratic centralism. They continued to refer to Nikita Khrushchev, even though he had been sent into retirement by their Soviet comrades, and looked towards the Italian Communist party led by Togliatti for an alternative model. All these insolent students were therefore excluded, to Hermier's great satisfaction. He subsequently took control of the UEC and began to build his political career. An author is partly defined by his readers. Barthes, who was already regarded as one of the main reference points for modern literary criticism, also became in the collective imagination part of the 'good left', that is, the non-Stalinist left (to which the likes of Leroy, Juquin and Hermier did not belong).

Thus the public image of Roland Barthes gradually formed, like a little mythology, through the accumulation of defining characteristics. Barthes was a Marxist, a Brechtian, he was a member of the *Arguments* team, so he was not a Stalinist. He had a semiologist's critical vision of society and he offered an innovative reading of literary texts. What is paradoxical in all this is that at the centre of this mythology a much more fluid theoretical system is to be found. Barthes did not really like systems: he was above all a man of intuitions, of immediate reactions, of moods, and he would later turn them into theories by using whatever concepts he came across. Thus far he had, because of what he had happened to be reading at the time, drawn on Sartre, Marx, Hjelmslev and Saussure. Later he would use Jakobson, Benveniste, Bakhtin and Lacan. But he was to follow none of these theories as they stood: he took possession of whatever ideas he came across, adapting them to fit his own methods and purposes. By placing one building block on top of another, it is sometimes possible to construct a wall, given luck and the right cement. Nevertheless, his whole theoretical edifice could easily collapse at the first puff of wind. Barthes had managed to build a wall, an innovative wall, with 'bricks' borrowed from Sartre, Brecht, Saussure, Jakobson or Bakhtin because he had his own cement which made the whole thing cohere, but it would be rash to say this constituted a 'theory' — more like a certain perspective on things.

The view of society which Barthes inaugurated in *Mythologies* was slowly becoming part of public discourse. With the support of Sartre, *France-Observateur* had become *Le Nouvel Observateur*, the weekly magazine of the non-communist left. In his articles for the magazine, Jean-Francis Held translated the style and method of *Mythologies* into the field of newspaper journalism by applying Barthes's way of decoding connotations to cars. Already, in 1964, Jean-Luc Godard in his film *La Femme mariée* had created a montage of 'little mythologies' relating to feminine alienation. Even if he had not read Barthes, it is obvious that Godard excelled in capturing the mood of the times and Barthes was now part of that mood. In 1967, he produced a second 'Barthesian' film, *Deux ou trois choses que je sais d'elle* ('Two or three things I know about her').

But it was in literature that Barthes's influence is most apparent. Georges Perec's novel, *Les Choses* (*Things*), which won the Prix Renaudot in 1965, was a deeply Barthesian novel. Jérome, who is twenty-four, and Sylvie, who is twenty-two, give up their studies and get jobs as market researchers, researching into motivation in the, at the time, fashionable field of psychosociology. They love objects unearthed at antique dealers, English clothes, deep-pile carpets, leather sofas, they read *Le Monde* but, even if they sometimes deny it, it is *L'Express* which really represents their views – or rather *Madame Express*, to be more precise. Using the past-historic tense (a nod towards *Writing Degree Zero*?), Perec paints his identikit picture of the petit-bourgeois couple in the making:

> They leaped ecstatically into fashionable English clothes. They discovered knitwear, silk blouses, shirts by Doucet, cotton voile ties, silk scarves, tweed, lambswool, cashmere, vicuna, leather and jersey wool, flax, and, finally, the great staircase of footwear leading from Churches to Westons, from Westons to Buntings, from Buntings to Lobbs.[8]

In short, Jérome and Sylvie are characters from *Mythologies*, to the point where its obvious Perec had read Barthes's book, and had to some extent taken his inspiration from it.[9] Further proof that Barthes, or at least the public perception of him, really was part of the spirit of the times.

Even if *Mythologies* is widely perceived to be a sharp critique of advertising, and *Things* is regarded as a ruthless dissection of the 'consumer society', the advertising world itself was not to turn its back on the new science of semiology. In 1963, the *Cahiers de la publicité* asked Barthes to write an article. He gave them a text entitled 'Le Message publicitaire' ('The advertising message'), which was eventually published at the end of the summer under the title 'Rêve et poésie' ('Dreams and poetry'). The article, argued along classical theoretical lines – adverts are messages, because there is a transmitter (the firm which wants to promote a product), a means of transmission (the advertising medium) and a receiver (the public) – attracted the attention of Georges Péninou, the head of the research department at the largest advertising company, Publicis. Péninou was a singular character. He was in his late thirties, had studied philosophy and had been working in advertising for ten years. He was an avid reader of Bachelard, Lévi-Strauss and the review *Arguments*, through which he had discovered Jakobson and Barthes.

In November 1964, in *Communications*, Barthes returned to the attack with 'Rhétorique de l'image' ('Rhetoric of the image'), an intelligent and subtle analysis of a poster advertising Panzani pasta. The article deals with the relationship between the text and the image (the text's famous function of 'anchoring' the image to one of several possible meanings). It also explores the connotations of different colours: Barthes points out the 'Italianness' of the poster, since apart from the Italian-sounding name Panzani it contains the colours of the Italian flag). The advertisers, who until now had been influenced primarily by psychoanalysis, started to think that something interesting might be going on in the field of semiology. Péninou, who had never really believed in psychoanalysis, decided to go and see for himself. He enrolled in Barthes's seminar and was immediately won over by the intelligence of the proceedings, by Barthes's mode of expression, his parenthetical phrases, the tangents he explored. Analysing the highway code, Barthes took off in unexpected directions, came back to his original proposition, and finally invited Jean-Paul Aron to talk about 'nobility and blood'.

At first, their relationship was one of teacher and student, but Péninou and Barthes had a lot in common. Péninou had been born in the south-west, in Pau, and in addition he had had tuberculosis and been sent to the sanatorium at Saint-Hilaire-du-Touvet, a few years after Barthes's stay there. He loved literature and, above all, he had an analytical mind, a mind almost ideally suited to structural analysis. All of these points brought them closer together, but most important, in Péninou's view, was their shared experience of tuberculosis. In fact, Péninou thought that semiology might have its origins in the attempt to compensate through the sharpness of one's analysis for breathing difficulties, diminished respiratory capabilities and the impossibility of dilation.

He registered for a Ph.D. thesis on the 'semiology of advertising' and soon became the standard-bearer for this new science: first at Publicis and then throughout the advertising world. With his enthusiasm and his gift for popularization, he was a catalyst, an energizer; thanks to him, semiology, which had aroused the interest of the profession, was to become a mode of operation. One day he brought Barthes to the Publicis offices in the Place de l'Étoile to give a lecture to some executives. Later, he would offer him a contract to study the semiology of the state-owned Renault company; starting from images, a set of photos and posters he had been given, Barthes produced an analysis of the advertising strategies used to sell the car.

Gradually, the semioclastic aim of *Mythologies* was becoming endorsed by professional advertisers. In the offices of the research department at Publicis they did not limit themselves to thinking about Barthes's analysis of the Panzani poster and discussing his methods, as at the university. They analysed two, three, four hundred posters in the same way, in order to criticize the work of the people who had thought them up, to detect the errors in strategy, see what did not work. They studied production systems, the way shampoos, cars, washing powder, tinned food, politicians or TV sets were represented in advertising. This approach, which owed as much to the work of Jakobson as to that of Barthes, and which was later to borrow from the work of Greimas – but with very different aims in mind from those of these writers – must have left a strange taste in Barthes's mouth. Was it a case of recuperation? Of recognition? The fact that Barthes had accepted the Renault contract, that he had used his scientific or intuitive skills, albeit momentarily, to improve car sales might lead to the conclusion that he himself was fascinated by a world which elsewhere he criticized.

In this same period, Annette Lavers, a young Frenchwoman who had gone to live in England, sent him a book she had just published on the image of the psychoanalyst in literary texts, *L'Usurpateur et le Prétendant*. Barthes sent her an extremely kind letter in reply, telling her he had found her book 'very enjoyable and very useful'. Several months later she came to France, met Barthes and suggested to him that she should translate *Le Degré zéro de l'écriture* and 'Éléments de sémiologie' into English. Barthes was thrilled by the idea and the following year the two texts were published together in one volume in London by Cape, under the title *Writing Degree Zero*. The translations were published separately in the United States, the Hill and Wang edition of *Elements of Semiology* having a preface by Susan Sontag. A year later, it was the turn of *Mythologies*, which the publisher insisted should be edited in order to produce a smaller volume. On being consulted about this, the author made only one stipulation: that 'Le monde où l'on catche' ('The world of wrestling') not be cut.

At her first meeting with Barthes, which was followed by many others in Paris and London, Annette Lavers was struck by something of seemingly marginal importance. Barthes seemed fascinated by England – unlike the United States which, despite his initial passion for New York, he did not like much. Above all, he was very interested in what might be happening abroad, what was thought of the French human sciences, which authors were known and read. He went to London and was shown round by Lavers. It was then that she discovered what his characteristic approach to cities was (and there is an echo of it in his book on Japan, *The Empire of Signs*). He always asked her to take him to the centre of London, to Piccadilly Circus: 'it's only the centre of towns which interests me.'

Urt

In 1961, Henriette had sold the villa in Hendaye and bought a house in Urt, twenty kilometres from Bayonne. From now on Roland and his mother always spent their summer holidays in Urt. Roland would drive 'down south' whenever he could, through Orléans, Tours, Poitiers, Angoulême: 'When I'm driving from Paris (a journey I've done hundreds of times) and I get to the other side of Angoulême, then a sign tells me I've crossed the threshold of the house and I'm entering the land of my childhood.'[10]

Sunflowers lined the road to Libourne, and then gave way to vines. After Bordeaux, the road continued on through the pine forests of the Landes. Green oaks mingled with the pines and the ground was dotted with purple heather. Then he drove past fields of maize. At Bayonne, he took the minor road along the Adour, which had formerly been a towpath. He drove along with the river on his right and the maize fields on his left until he reached a little iron bridge, which made a deafening, rather disturbing noise as he crossed it, like a train crossing a viaduct. Once over the river, he turned left into Urt.

Urt was a typical southern village. In the streets people greeted each other, said hello and joked in their heavy Gascon accents. Such familiarity was, of course, completely foreign to the reserved Roland Barthes. But above all, there was the special light of the Adour valley, whose praises he sang to his friends regularly.

> The light of the south-west is both noble and subtle. It's never grey, never dull (even when the sun isn't shining). It's a space, as well as a light, defined less by the way it alters the colours of things (as in the south-east)

Roland Barthes in 1963. *(Photograph: Cartier-Bresson)*

The sanatorium at Saint-Hilaire-du-Touvet. *(Photograph: Robert David)*

Fancy dress party at the sanatorium. Roland Barthes is on the far right, dressed up as Barrès, member of the Academie Française. *(Photograph: Robert David)*

Above: With Robert David in Lausanne, 1944. *(Photograph: Robert David)*

Facing: In the train bound for Switzerland. Roland Barthes is in the last row but one, in the centre. *(Photograph: Robert David)*

Below: Arrival in Switzerland. *(Photograph: Robert David)*

The Institut Français des Hautes Études in Romania. *(Photograph: Philippe Rebeyrol)*

The administrative staff of the institute in January 1949. Roland Barthes is in the back row, second from the right. *(Photograph: Philippe Rebeyrol)*

LE DEGRÉ ZÉRO DE L'ÉCRITURE

Roland Barthes est inconnu. C'est un jeune ; il n'a jamais publié, même un article. Quelques conversations avec lui nous ont persuadé que cet essai du langage (depuis deux ans, il ne s'intéresse qu'à cette question) avait quelque chose de neuf à dire. Il nous a remis l'article ci-dessous, qui n'est pas, de loin, un article de journal, tant la pensée en est dense et sans pittoresque extérieur. Nous pensons que les lecteurs de Combat ne nous en voudront pas de l'avoir tout de même publié.

ON peut discerner chez certains écrivains d'aujourd'hui la recherche d'une écriture neutre, d'un style au degré zéro, d'une sorte d'état inerte de la forme. Une comparaison empruntée à la linguistique rendra peut-être assez bien compte de ce fait nouveau : on sait que certains linguistes, comme le Danois Viggo Brondal, établissent entre les deux termes d'une polarité (singulier-pluriel, prétérit - présent) l'existence d'un troisième terme, terme neutre ou terme zéro ; ainsi, entre les modes subjonctif et impératif, l'indicatif leur apparaît comme une forme amodale.

Toutes proportions gardées, le briste qui produit un pur repo

The beginning of Barthes's writing career. *Combat*, 1 August 1947. *(Photograph: D.R.)*

In Bucharest. Roland with his students. His mother is in the front row, second from the right. *(Photograph: Philippe Rebeyrol)*

"Le degré zéro de l'écriture"

Par DOMINIQUE ARBAN

C'est au vif de notre temps que se greffe l'intelligent essai de Roland Barthes, Le degré zéro de l'écriture (1). Il est une réponse à la question qu'un très vaste public se pose, ce public qui n'approche qu'avec malaise ou refuse d'approcher les plus significatifs de nos écrivains d'aujourd'hui. Car, reflet d'une époque de transition, la littérature suit des chemins nouveaux, des sentiers qu'elle se fraye à mesure et qui sont parfois abrupts ; et sa démarche est souvent propre à déconcerter le lecteur.

C'est un fait : nombre de nos auteurs refusent de se servir d'un style traditionnel, le seul où le public se sente à l'aise. C'est

une idéologie parmi d'autres. Selon que l'écrivain s'est senti solidaire ou non de sa classe sociale, selon qu'il est « allé au peuple » ou au contraire s'est réfugié dans « l'art pour l'art », on a vu naître des écritures populiste, travaillée ou parlée, et la pire de toutes parce que la moins authentique, l'écriture qu'affecta « le réalisme socialiste » d'un Garaudy, voire d'un Maupassant. Les exemples que cite Roland Barthes à ce propos amusent et convainquent. Et l'on ne peut que partager son avis lorsque, nommant Flaubert et Mal-

ment aujourd'hui, et les débutants poètes savent ce qu'il en coûte en 1953 de chanter comme Lamartine : aussitôt ils voient se fermer les portes des revues, même des moins sévères. C'est que la poésie d'aujourd'hui se propose de tout autres buts ; elle assume aussi des risques plus graves, et avant tout celui de n'être comprise que de fort peu de gens. Ceux de nos lecteurs qui se tiennent éloignés de l'expérience poétique actuelle liront avec fruit le chapitre que Roland Barthes intitule : « L'Ecriture poétique. » Oui, l'instrument poétique n'est plus cette phrase articulée, plus ou moins ornée, plus ou moins rythmée. L'instrument poétique est le mot. Le mot qui veut saisir l'absolu de l'objet qu'il nomme, en contenir

The first article on Roland Barthes. *Le Monde*, 3 October 1953. *(Photograph: D.R.)*

At the time of the publication of *Writing Degree Zero*. *(Photograph: Robert David)*

Opposite: Henriette Barthes. *(Photograph: Robert David)*

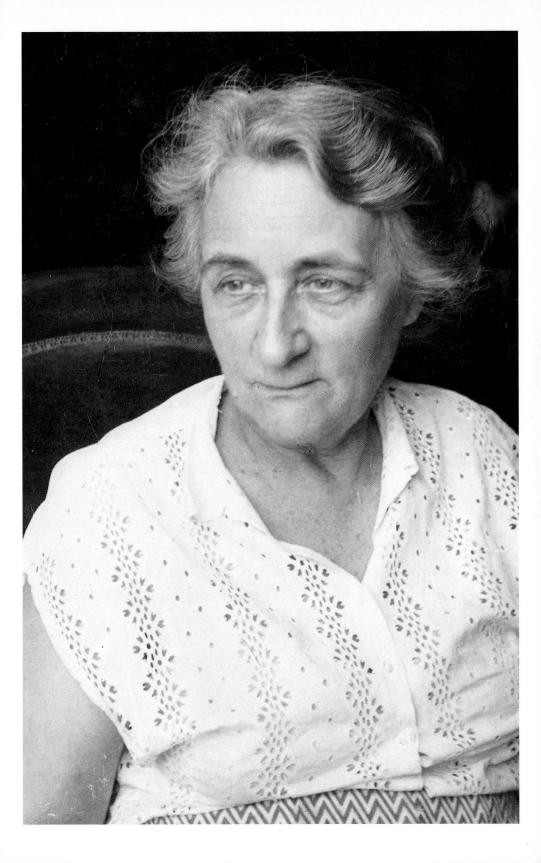

Mythologies

'Each sign in wrestling is therefore endowed with an absolute clarity, since one must always understand everything on the spot . . . not only is ugliness used here in order to signify baseness, but in addition ugliness is wholly gathered into a particularly repulsive quality of matter: the pallid collapse of dead flesh.' (*Mythologies*) (*Photograph: Laurent Maous/Gamma*)

'The bravado of the petit-bourgeois consists in setting the very statistics of egalitarianism against the forces of change . . . M. Poujade is well aware that the principal enemy of this system of tautologies is dialectical thought, which he dismisses as being more or less equivalent to a kind of sophistry.' (*Mythologies*) (*Photograph: A. Sas/Gamma*)

'In spite of its extreme beauty, this face, not drawn but sculpted in something smooth and friable.' (*Mythologies*, trans. A. Lavers) (*Photograph: Gamma*)

ロラン・バルト氏

From **Empire of the Signs**, . . .
(*Photograph: Skira*)

遺文化使節として来日した。二十
日まで滞在し、その間東大、京
大など数カ所で講演を行なう予定
である。

しかし、い
ティックな言
トはフランス

人文科学を駆使
バルトの名前は日本ではほとん
ど知られていない。〔処女作「文
体=エクリチュールの原点」が
森本和夫氏によって「零度の文
これまでの著

「問題の」批
るだろう。前
シュレ論〕一
ー文論」「批
論」「批評と

'This Western
Lecturer, as soon as
he is *cited* by the
Kobe Shinbun finds
himself *Japanned*,
eyes elongated,
pupils blackened by
Nipponese
typography.'
(*Empire of Signs*,
trans. R. Howard)

'Whereas the young
actor Teturo Tanba,
citing Anthony Perkins,
has lost his Asiatic eyes.
What then is our face, if
not a *citation?*'
(*Empire of Signs*,
trans. R. Howard)

. . . to **Camera Lucida**

'Is it possible that
Ernest is still alive
today: but where?
how? What a novel!'
(*Camera Lucida*,
trans. R. Howard)
(*Photograph: André
Kertész/Ministry of
Culture, France*)

At the École Pratique des Hautes Études, 1973. *(Photograph:* L'Express)

'Doodling.' *(Photograph: Romaric Sulger-Büel)*

MINISTÈRE DE L'ÉDUCATION NATIONALE

ÉCOLE PRATIQUE DES HAUTES ÉTUDES
VIᵉ SECTION - SCIENCES ÉCONOMIQUES ET SOCIALES
SORBONNE

54, RUE DE VARENNE, 75007 PARIS
TÉL. : 222.66.20

PARIS, LE   19

à RM
7·IV·76
RB

'As much flavour as possible . . .' seminar at the Hautes Études, 1973. *(Photograph:* L'Express)

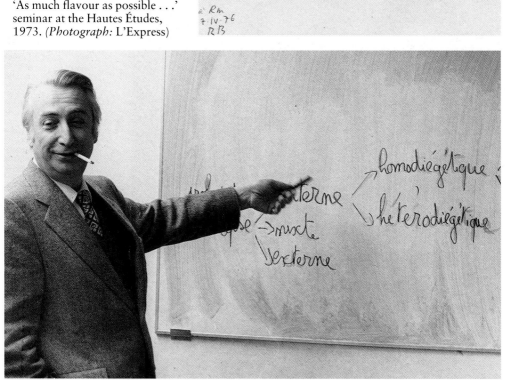

Round table:
Roland Barthes
with Michèle
Cotta.
(Photograph:
L'Express)

On the publication of *The Pleasure
of the Text*, from *Le Figaro*, 1973.
(Photograph: D.R.)

Roland Barthes is invited to lunch
with the President of the Republic,
1978. *(Photograph:
Pavlovsky/Sygma)*

At the Collège de France, 7 January 1978: Roland Barthes gives his inaugural lecture on his appointment to the Chair in Literary Semiology.
(Photographs: Pavlovsky/Sygma)

Le Monde, 14 February 1975. 'To type: nothing exists, and then all of a sudden the word is there: not approximation, no *production*, there is no birth of the letter, but the explosion of a little scrap of code.' ('Fautes de frappe/Typos', *Roland Barthes by Roland Barthes*, trans. R. Howard) *(Photograph: D.R.)*

Roland Barthes with Marie-France Pisier, playing the role of Thackeray in André Téchiné's film *Les Soeurs Brontë. (Photograph:* Les Cahiers du Cinéma)

In Tunis with Philippe Rebeyrol. *(Photograph: Philippe Rebeyrol)*

'The bourgeoisie listen to the piano with their eyes closed' *(Photograph: Bassouls/Sygma)*

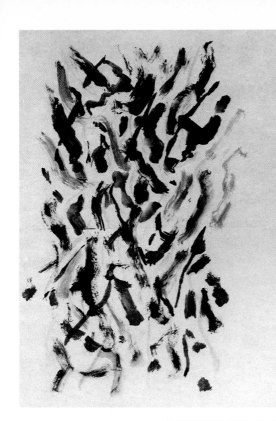

Le bleu de l'aigrette est
plus pur, le rose de l'aigrette est
plus allègre que le bleu et le rose
de mon encre. Mais l'aigrette,
parfois, s'envole et ses ailes
font alors un nuage tout gris.

Watercolour and ink by
Roland Barthes.
*(Photographs: Romaric
Sulger-Büel)*

(Photograph: Julien Guideau/L'Express)

than by the eminently *habitable* quality it gives to the land. The only way I can describe it is that it is a luminous light.[11]

Once he had passed the bakers, he crossed the village square with the chemists on his left and the bistro on his right, passed the church and finally turned into the Campas road, where their house was to be found. The house itself was solid, massive, with a flagstone floor that gave it a somewhat monastic air.

Within this country house, Barthes had recreated his Parisian surroundings, even going so far as to put his desk and piano in exactly the same positions. The days all had the same, or nearly the same, rhythm. Every morning, he got up at seven o'clock, made himself a cup of tea, fed the birds in the garden with breadcrumbs, dusted his desk, emptied the ashtrays, listened to the seven-thirty news on the radio, and generally started the day off slowly. At eight o'clock he had breakfast with his mother: two boiled eggs, toast, and black coffee without sugar. After breakfast, he went out to buy the local paper *Sud-Ouest* and then started work. He worked until half-past ten, when he had a break (a black coffee, his first cigar) and then continued working until one o'clock, lunchtime. After lunch he had an hour's nap, and then he spent a while pottering about, burning papers at the end of the garden or getting a box of index cards ready. He set to work again at four o'clock and worked through until seven, with a short tea-break. Then he watered the garden, played the piano, and had dinner. After dinner he watched TV or wrote notes on his index cards and listened to music. At ten o'clock he turned in, and read until he fell asleep. Accumulating such 'biographemes', Barthes said the only interesting thing about them was that they 'indicate your class allegiances'[12] and the narration of such details helped to construct the mythical image of the writer. Once again, this apparent rejection of biographical detail occurs at the very moment when he is describing his daily routine in minute detail.

Besides, he had always organized his days meticulously and, despite his constant complaints about feeling tired, he did a lot every day and was keen to stick to a certain structure. He would draw up timetables for himself on pieces of paper, using different colours, dividing his days into several segments – playing the piano, working, meetings, seeing friends. He set himself work programmes, deadlines, and tried to stick to them. In the daily slots in his timetable set aside for writing, he would first of all write a draft of a text by hand, then make deletions and correct this draft. Finally he would type it up, making changes as he went along. He kept a meticulous record of every book or article he published, noting the details down in a notebook, and numbering every text. Later, this practice was to lead François Wahl to assert that only texts which were in the notebook could be considered Barthes's work.

In the evening he sometimes had dinner at the Auberge de la Galupe, on the riverbank, or if he felt like a drive, went as far as Pamplona, in Spain. But more often than not he stayed at home watching television. These evenings spent in front of the television gave him food for thought. The colloquial language he heard made him think about the 'jargon' which, at the time, he was afraid of writing and at night, according to him, thoughts of his adjectives would wake him up.

Sometimes Violette Morin would go with him to Urt and spend a few weeks with him and Henriette. She remembers Roland sometimes had violent migraine attacks during the journey. He would have to stop at the first hotel they came to and have a few hours' sleep before setting off once again. Curiously enough, although Urt was his holiday home, a place to rest, and he should have relaxed there, he suffered more than usual from migraines when he was there. He preferred the word 'migraine' to 'headache', but he wondered what lay at the root of this semantic preference. It was a nice word but it wasn't exactly accurate in his case, since it wasn't half his head he suffered from: the word 'migraine' comes from the Latin *hemicrania*, a medieval term borrowed from the Greek *hêmikrania* or 'half-skull'. Unless it was accurate for a different reason: migraines were the characteristic affliction of society ladies and writers, and once again this was an indication of his social class. He reflected incessantly on words and preconceived ideas, commonplaces which he admitted to looking for first and foremost in his own discourse.

One day, for instance, while he was walking through the village he saw within a few hundred yards of each other three signs, all carrying the same message but in a different form: *vicious dog*, *dangerous dog*, *watchdog*. The third was simply informative, giving an objective piece of information (a dog is guarding the house), whereas the first was aggressive, and the second philanthropic and protective ('Be careful, you might be bitten'). All three notices conveyed the same message ('Do not enter'), but they each said it in different ways, revealing three different mentalities, three alibis of ownership, three image repertoires.[13]

Indeed linguistics, since it was only interested in messages, did not have very much to say about these divisions between languages. In a lecture given in 1973, Barthes referred to what he called this 'war of languages'. He explained that the example of the three notices came from the same social class, that of small landowners, whereas this 'war' was much more evident in society as a whole. Here, the languages which developed in the shadow or under the protection of power (the discourses of the state, institutional and ideological discourses), what he called *encratic languages*, were in conflict with the languages which developed outside power or in resistance to it, which he called *acratic languages*.[14] Barthes asked the question: what could, and should, the intellectual do when confronted with this 'war of languages'? On the one hand he had to commit himself, adopt one of these languages, but on the other he could not forego the ecstasy (*jouissance*) afforded by a language unmarked by any reference to power. The only practice which could escape such determination, which could mix these languages and to some extent blur the lines, was the production of *text*, which did not respect this law of the separation of discourses. The fact that this theoretical construct stems from Barthes's observation that there are different ways of saying a house is guarded by a dog – that is, from daily life – is completely in tune with the way he functioned. Fifteen years after *Mythologies*, we find that the same principle is in action, a kind of ethnography of society through an analysis of the signs that society produces.

Barthes's life was now definitely fixed around two geographical poles and two places – Paris, and this small corner of south-west France. The fact of belonging to two different places seemed to him characteristic of the French nation as a whole:

> My own situation maps on to that of most French people. My life, in terms of where I live, has two coordinates. As in the case of most French people, there's Paris, and then there's another, provincial origin. The lives of most French people are structured around these two points, Paris and everywhere else ... In this sense, I am totally representative of my countrymen, I am a good Frenchman.[15]

Even if his surname is not pronounced in the Gascon way ('Barthès') but the Parisian way ('Barthes', like 'Barthe', without sounding the 's'), he always retained a strong sense of attachment to the south-west. It was a corporal attachment: he loved its smells, especially after it had rained, and its colours. According to Julia Kristeva, he and Sollers would spend their time congratulating themselves on their common place of origin, on the refinement of people from this south-western part of France, on the coastal, slightly English side to their character which made them foreigners within France.

But even if Barthes felt 'at home' in Bayonne, he 'loved' Paris. For him, Paris was not the opposite of the provinces but the provinces plus something extra: the exhilaration of the new, the idea that the unexpected could occur at any moment, something that was impossible in the provinces. Besides, for him Paris meant the small area extending from the Sorbonne to Saint-Germain-des-Prés. Within this area he had his routines, in the etymological sense of the word, his 'little routes', and he said that whenever he left this quadrilateral he felt as disoriented as if he were in a strange town. His life was fixed around these two poles: Paris–Urt, flat–house, which were different in many ways but similar in one respect. He had made sure that in both places his workspace was fixed up in exactly the same way, with exactly the same layout: the desk he wrote on and the telephone, on the left, and on the right a table where he put his index cards, then further away, a work surface on which he could draw, and then the piano.

The Racine affair

It was from Urt in June 1965, on learning that *Les Lettres nouvelles* was in danger of folding after René Julliard's death, that Barthes wrote to Maurice Nadeau:

> I have not seen you for a long time, for the silly reasons of which you are aware, like work pressures and exhaustion and the usual Parisian problem of doing too many things at once. But I always think of you with affection, loyalty and solidarity. I hope you know that you can always turn to me and that, if you ever need me, for whatever reason, you have only to say so.[16]

Numerous other people have mentioned Barthes's affirmations of loyalty, his habit of writing letters saying how much he regretted no longer having the time to see his friends.

On this occasion, the threatened closure turned out to be a false alarm. Denoël took over the review and it survived for a further ten years. But Nadeau appreciated Barthes's gesture. Despite their difference of opinion over the Manifesto of the 121, they remained close. When at the beginning of the autumn of 1965 Raymond

Picard, a lecturer in French literature at the Sorbonne and a Racine specialist, published a pamphlet entitled *Nouvelle critique ou nouvelle imposture?* (*New Criticism or New Fraud?*),[17] Nadeau once again rallied round in support of Barthes. The origin of the quarrel was Barthes's book *Sur Racine* (*On Racine*), which had been published by Seuil in 1963. It was a collection of essays, all of which had been published elsewhere. The first had been the preface to a 1960 edition of Racine's collected works by the Club du Livre Français; the second was a review of a TNP production of *Phèdre* which had been published in *Théâtre populaire* in 1958; and the final essay had appeared in *Annales* in 1960.

In the blurb, the book is described as a series of reflections on literary criticism: 'Either in a direct sense, when the author says academic criticism should openly admit the psychological foundation of its judgements, or indirectly, when he brings one of the various theoretical languages available today to bear on the Racinian text.' A three-page foreword puts these essays into perspective and sets the tone of the book from the outset:

> the analysis presented here is not concerned with Racine at all, but only with the Racinian hero: it avoids inferring from the work to the author and from the author to the work; it is a deliberately closed analysis. I have put myself in Racine's tragic world and tried to describe its population (which may be readily abstracted under the concept *Homo racinianus*) without reference to any source in this world (to be found, for instance, in history or biography). What I have attempted to reconstruct is a kind of Racinian anthropology, both structural and psychoanalytic.[18]

In *Le Monde* of 12 June 1963, Pierre-Henri Simon voiced his scepticism regarding Barthes's 'dialectical virtuosity, which alternately ... dazzles and ... disturbs'. He found it difficult to believe that Racine had disguised the mythical sense of his texts so masterfully that 'until now no one, not even Racine himself, has been aware of it'. But other newspapers reacted more favourably. Roger-Louis Junod, writing in *La Tribune de Genève*, called the book 'A new perspective on the Racinian universe'. The title of Guy Dumur's piece in *France-Observateur* was 'How to get more out of Racine'. Then there was the article in *La Croix*, 'When new criticism attacks the classics', and finally Robert Kanters on 'Roland Barthes and the Racine myth' in *Le Figaro littéraire*.[19]

Several months later, from January 1964 onwards, it was the turn of the reviews. *Le Mercure de France* gave the book the thumbs up, as did *La Nouvelle NRF*. *La Pensée* did not entirely disapprove: 'Despite some questionable guesswork, the book contains a number of profound insights which bring a new perspective to bear on our vision of the Racinian world and thus shed light on previously unrecognized aspects of the œuvre.'[20] *Critique*, in an article over twenty pages long, which dealt not only with Barthes's book but also with another study of Racine, Lucien Goldmann's *The Hidden God*, asserted that 'today it is only Marxist and psychoanalytic criticism which can rediscover the meaning of Racinian tragedy . . . Humanist criticism will not explore anything outside poetic discourse itself.'[21]

Whether it was humanist or not, 'academic criticism', championed by Raymond Picard, was about to fight back. Picard had studied with Philippe Rebeyrol for the entrance exams to the École Normale Supérieure while Roland had been nursing his tuberculosis in Bedous. He was the author of *La Carrière de Jean Racine*, the editor of the prestigious Pléiade edition of Racine's works and a lecturer at the Sorbonne. As such, he could not stand by and see the institution he represented called into question. He replied with an article in *Le Monde*: 'Attacking the university is part of avant-garde orthodoxy, and M. Barthes is one of the avant-garde's principal representatives.'[22] Picard decided to tackle the structuralist monster head-on in his pamphlet on *New Criticism or New Fraud*, which was published in Jean-François Revel's 'Liberté' series in the autumn of 1965.

While 'avant-garde' intellectuals and students who read Barthes may have laughed at Picard, the popular press applauded his intervention. In *Le Monde*, Jacqueline Piatier gloatingly referred to 'Roland Barthes's astonishing interpretations of Racine's tragedies'. She went on: 'Picard's principal weapon is ridicule. The strength of his critique lies in the fact that he makes one laugh simply by recourse to rigour, coherence and logical thought.' She concluded by saying, 'I do not think it would be possible to define one's position and tell one's adversary what is what in a more rigorous and witty fashion.'[23] She was to return to the attack a few months later when she referred to Picard's pamphlet as 'a scathing and witty attack'.[24]

A month before Piatier's first intervention, Jean Duvignaud, Barthes's former colleague on *Théâtre Populaire*, had put his name to a far from enthusiastic review of *On Racine* which had appeared in *Le Nouvel Observateur*: 'Barthes could not have made a worse choice than Racine as the next step in his research. At any rate, his approach to the author of *Phèdre* diminishes not only the critic but the poet himself.'[25] Bernard Pingaud, for his part, came to Barthes's defence in *Le Monde*: 'Of course Barthes's book is questionable; it is written from a particular standpoint and its author has always been perfectly frank about this. At least it is an interpretation of Racine's work and not simply a dull commentary upon it.'[26]

It is true that, intellectually, Barthes had grown apart from his friends in theatrical circles, especially those who worked on *Théâtre Populaire*. His intellectual relations now centred on Philippe Sollers, Gérard Genette and Jacques Derrida. During the polemic over Racine he had felt extremely isolated, helpless, fragile and vulnerable to criticism. He remarked to Philippe Rebeyrol: 'You know, what I write is ludic. If people attack me, there's nothing left.' Alain Robbe-Grillet describes how at the time Barthes was 'excessively upset by Picard's reproaches ... the wrathful glare of the old Sorbonne paralysed him with a complex feeling of hate and terror.'[27] Philippe Sollers remembers him as feeling very hurt and bitter when confronted by the almost unanimous support for Picard. Once again he found himself defenceless, powerless in the face of a society which had revealed its hostility towards him.

A week later, *Le Monde* published a letter from a certain Édouard Guitton: 'What comforts and reassures me when I put down the works of Barthes, Mauron or Goldmann on Racine is the knowledge that Racine's theatre survives their exegeses.'[28] The previous year, the same Édouard Guitton had written another letter to *Le Monde* in which, with uncanny insight, he had asserted that 'M. Barthes's works will date more quickly than M. Picard's!'[29] *Le Journal de Genève* announced triumphantly: 'Roland Barthes knocked out in one hundred and fifty pages.'[30]

All this fuss upset Barthes. He had always paid a great deal of attention to how his books were received, to the reactions of the press. He took the 'after-sales service' which many authors loathed extremely seriously. He always drafted the blurb for the cover himself, and took a great deal of care over it. Then he would draw up a list of sympathetic journalists and suggest possible strategies to the press relations people. This was followed by the ceremony of the dedications. Barthes wrote numerous, highly personalized dedications. They were often long and always complimentary, containing references to friendship and loyalty but also to the theoretical perspicacity of the person to whom they were addressed. He would stress his indebtedness to whoever was involved, making many of those who received such a dedication believe that he valued their ideas.

If Picard's attack had caused a media stir, it also provoked three separate responses. In 1966, Barthes published *Criticism and Truth* (his first appearance in the 'Tel Quel' series), Jean-Paul Weber published *Néocritique et paléocritique*; and Serge Doubrovsky published *Pourquoi la nouvelle critique?* ('Why new criticism?'). The whole polemic erupted once again. *La Gazette de Lausanne* announced the outbreak of 'The war of the critics',[31] which was contradicted by *La Tribune de Genève*'s announcement that 'There will be no war of the critics',[32] itself in turn contradicted by *Notre République*'s confirmation that 'The critics' civil war' had broken out.[33] *Le Nouvel Observateur* opened its columns to Picard, who dispatched Barthes with the comment that 'he is plunging deeper and deeper into obscurity.'[34] Several weeks later, the same magazine carried the headline: 'Barthes v. Picard: third round'.[35] The 'war of the critics' had been transformed into a boxing match, but even if the metaphor was different, the bitterness of the conflict remained obvious to everyone.

Such an uproar and such verbal violence may seem perplexing today – what exactly was at stake in this debate? Most probably it was the culmination of a conflict which, as far as Barthes was concerned, had begun many years previously, when he was prevented by illness from sitting the École Normale entrance exam. In 1935 he had accused Philippe Rebeyrol, somewhat unfairly, of using a conventional, stereotyped kind of language to talk about literature, of talking in clichés. It was precisely a certain way of discussing literature, the discourse of academic criticism, that Barthes was putting in the dock, and Picard was right to regard the emerging 'New Criticism' as a challenge to the institutional discourse (or *encratic* discourse, to use Barthes's own neologism).

Later, in his global analysis of institutional discourse, the sociologist Pierre Bourdieu was to describe the unity of discourse at the Sorbonne and the École Pratique des Hautes Études as an example of 'the structural complicity between the different powers'.[36] But perhaps one would do better to concur with the judgement of that most serious organ of public opinion, the *Times Literary Supplement*, when in June 1966 it heralded this turbulence in the Parisian intellectual microcosm as the greatest crisis since the polemic between Sartre, Camus and David Rousset. The article in the TLS concluded, in French, with a quote from the poet Paul Valéry adapted for the occasion ('New Criticism' being substituted for 'Mankind'): 'La nouvelle critique est grande par ce qu'elle cherche et souvent absurde par ce qu'elle trouve.'[37]

For the present, once he had published his reply in *Criticism and Truth*, Barthes took refuge in work and travel. In May 1966 he went to Tokyo, at the invitation of Maurice Pinguet, director of the Franco-Japanese Institute, to give a seminar on 'The structural analysis of narrative'. 'Japan is one of the few countries I would still like to see,' he wrote to Pinguet. During his stay he seemed genuinely enthusiastic about the country. As Pinguet was to describe later: 'Every single day he was stimulated, bowled over by everything new there was to discover, to experience. His curiosity was insatiable, and he never tired of meeting people. He was an inexhaustible source of anecdotes, or rather of verbal snapshots.'[38]

In Japan, as elsewhere, Barthes showed absolutely no interest in the living language. He was, however, fascinated by the opacity which confronted him, and he explained why in his reply to a questionnaire produced by Guy Scarpetta for the magazine *Promesses*:

> To live in a country where one doesn't know the language, and to live audaciously, outside the tourist tracks, is the most dangerous of adventures ... If I had to imagine a new Robinson Crusoe, I would not place him on a desert island, but in a city of twelve million people where he could decipher neither speech nor writing: that, I think, would be the modern form of Defoe's tale [la forme moderne du mythe].[39]

And it is easy to discern Tokyo behind that city of twelve million inhabitants where you do not understand either what is said or, above all, what is written. Between 1966 and 1967 he went there three times, bringing back with him from the few weeks he spent there not only the material for the book on Japan he would eventually write, *L'Empire des signes* (*Empire of Signs*), but also a huge sense of nostalgia, almost of homesickness, for the country he had conceived an immediate passion for. He spoke to Robert David, for one, about the intensity of life there, the extraordinary kindness of the people, and of how difficult he had found it to leave what had seemed to him to be the land of his fantasies.

It was a country he had perhaps discovered too late in his life, when he was in his fifties, and he refused to return there for any further visits, replying to the invitations he received that it was 'too far away'. Nevertheless, Japan had given him a new way of looking at things. The visions he brought back with him, and which would later form the basis of his book, were fragmentary, like his *Mythologies*, but whereas the latter tended towards sarcasm, the tone of the Japanese fragments was more tender or indulgent. As if, contaminated by the land of Zen Buddism, he were in more meditative mood.

In October he travelled to Baltimore in the United States to attend a conference on criticism organized by the Johns Hopkins University. Also speaking at the conference were Derrida, Todorov and Georges Poulet. Barthes's lecture was on 'The languages of criticism and the sciences of man'. He continued to produce numerous articles, always 'on commission', claiming never to have written anything of his own accord. This is only partially true, but it is illustrative of an interesting trait of his character: he loved to give a good rhetorical performance on any topic whatsoever, one suggested by someone else, be it the Eiffel Tower, Bernard Buffet or Egyptian hieroglyphs. Sometimes, of course, he took on too many such commissions and, faced with a build-up of deadlines, he would 'bury his head in the sand', as he called it.

The seminar

When Nadeau and Erval founded *La Quinzaine littéraire* in 1966, Nadeau once again gave a boost to Barthes's career. Barthes contributed a few articles on Benveniste or Lacan but, above all, he recommended young writers or books which had just been published to Nadeau. He no longer had any time to write himself: 'Teaching at the École des Hautes Études has become a full-time job. My workload is very heavy and I have to struggle constantly to keep alive even the possibility of writing a book from time to time. However, even this seems doubtful.' It is true that since he had to keep changing the subject of his seminar, he felt as if he were under constant pressure. From 1962 to 1964 the seminar had been devoted to the study of 'Contemporary signifying systems', which had led to the publication of two articles by him in *Communications*, on 'The rhetoric of the image' and 'Elements of semiology'. At the beginning of the year he distributed the seminar programme and also a five-page list of terms (what he called 'an outline of basic terms') ranging from *amorphous* to *variation* via *commutation* and *signifier*. The definitions used were all taken from key authors: Martinet, Saussure, Hjelmslev. He also gave out an extremely sociologically oriented bibliography, which included Fourastié, Friedmann, Crozier, Touraine and Chombart de Lawe.

Those of his friends who attended his seminars, Christian Metz, Bernard Dort, Olivier Burgelin and Robert David, would meet up afterwards in a café in the Place de la Sorbonne. With work over, it was the turn of friendship. As more newcomers joined them, another Barthesian network gradually formed. As will be seen, there existed several such networks and they hardly ever overlapped.

Between 1964 and 1966, the subject of the seminar was 'Studies on Rhetoric', and Barthes's notes were later published in article-form as *'The old system of rhetoric: an aide-mémoire.'*[40] Once again, he handed out an outline of the seminar programme at the beginning of the year and it was meticulously set out in the American manner, arranged according to numbers: 1 'The rhetorical chain', followed by 1.1, 1.2, etc., then 2, 2.1, 2.2, up to 5.1 'The genres of discourse' and 5.2 'Meta-rhetoric as narrative'. He added a four-page document on 'Rhetoric', a chronological account dating from the eighth century BC (Corax, Gorgias, Hippias of Elea) to the nineteenth century (Gaillard and Fontanier).

In 1966–7, the seminar tackled 'The linguistics of discourse', and then, for the next two years 'The structural analysis of a narrative text: Balzac's *Sarrasine*'. The latter became *S/Z*,which was published in 1970. Thus Barthes developed a method of working. The seminar was the testing ground for his books and articles, the place where their initial problems were ironed out. It acted as a kind of laboratory, where he experimented verbally, in what was an essentially transient form, with the ideas that he would later cast in writing.

Apart from the inner circle of the faithful, his nearest and dearest who, year after year, assembled to perform the same acts of communion, the seminar was also attended by the university's drifters. These were students disaffected with the traditional academic system, and who were probably therefore precursors of May '68. As one of them commented, 'the seminar was a bit like a life-raft for the misfits, those who felt out of place everywhere else.' In fact, there was a whole generation of politicized students who had discovered Althusser, Lacan and Barthes at one fell swoop, coming to them in search of what they could not find elsewhere: an unconventional yet theoretically rigorous discourse. Barthes, because of his involvement with *Théâtre Populaire* and then *Arguments*, was regarded as part of the 'good left' – even if some of the students found such credentials a bit weak in comparison to the more radical positions of the journal *Socialisme et barbarie*, for example, and if others took a more Situationist stance and consigned all this 'high society' to the dustbins of history. May 1968 was fast approaching.

At the end of 1965, a young Bulgarian student called Julia

Kristeva turned up at Barthes's seminar. In Sofia she had read Sartre, Camus, Blanchot and a few of Barthes's books (*Writing Degree Zero*, *Mythologies*). Tzvetan Todorov, another Bulgarian who had settled in Paris and who knew Barthes, strongly recommended his seminar to her and told her where it was held. So she went to E-staircase in the Sorbonne, where the École Pratique des Hautes Études was located. She was primarily struck by Barthes's charm, and above all by his voice. Fifteen years later, she wrote an article about it: 'The fragile yet firm quality of his voice, despite his discreet way of talking and despite the distance, gave his calls all the immediacy of physical contact . . . These telephone calls were timid, ironic in tone, as if to underline the inanity of everyday language and of his own request.'[41]

Everyone who attended the seminar highlights this contradiction: although the public perception of Barthes was that he was a man of the written word, he was primarily a speaker, a man of the spoken word, in the great tradition of university teaching. Even to the extent that those who knew him could hear his voice whenever they read his texts.

At the time, in both France and Bulgaria, teachers tended to be quite starchy and formal in their relations with their students, and Kristeva was pleasantly surprised to find two teachers whose friendliness made them the exceptions to the rule. First there was Lucien Goldmann, who was the 'salt of the earth' type, and then there was Barthes, whose style was more refined. She asked Barthes if she could see him to discuss her work. At the time, she was working on a critique of structuralism using Bakhtin, a post-formalist critic whose work had just been published in Eastern Europe. She was stuck first of all by the fact that Barthes did not expect his students' ideas to echo his own, but always tried to bring out what was potentially original in their work. He was more attentive to the other person than to his own image. She discussed two of Bakhtin's texts with him, his study of Rabelais and his study of Dostoevsky. Barthes became very excited and suggested she give a paper at the seminar.

The seminar had moved to 44, Rue de Rennes. At the start of the 1966–7 academic year, Barthes was expounding a somewhat closed and narrow body of doctrines whose key concepts were taken from linguistics, in particular from Hjelmslev and Martinet (for example the notion of the corpus). At the same time, he was putting the finishing touches to *The Fashion System*, his former thesis project which had turned into a book. All the seminars followed the same

pattern. One of the regular seminar group or someone from outside
would talk about their research or present another topic. During the
1966–7 academic year, Kristeva spoke on Bakhtin, Gérard Genette
on 'the gap/deviation' ('l'écart'), Christian Metz on the semiology of
the cinema and Philippe Sollers on Mallarmé. Kristeva remembers
the day she had to give her paper:

> I can still see the polite yet amazed expression on Roland's face during my
> talk on the dialogic, principally in reference to Bakhtin, but also to
> Rabelais, Dostoevsky, Joyce and a few other modern writers he was not
> really familiar with (which is why he had kindly given me a platform at
> his seminar in the Rue de Rennes). Faced by these new tools for attacking
> the garden of great literature, he was as impressed as a watering-can faced
> by a bulldozer. But he knew how to adapt most of the semiological
> instruments to which he was introduced to his own style. By translating
> them, by softening them, by making them more flexible, he managed to
> publicize them and thus to impose the obscure, yet often extremely
> penetrating insights of linguists and ethnologists on a whole tradition of
> great literature which was proud of its conservatism.[42]

So Kristeva, Genette, Metz or Sollers spoke and then it was
Barthes's turn. He would base his comments on what the previous
speaker had been saying. He would stand almost totally still and
speak in a low, velvety, seductive voice, a cigarette or a cigar
between his lips. He smoked either English cigarettes (his cashmere
sweaters were also English) or the Havana cigars of which Brecht
was so fond. As Raphael Sorin says, 'he was an anglophile as far as
his tastes in clothes and cigarettes went,' like Jérome and Sylvie, the
characters in Perec's novel. Barthes's tone was conversational and he
was brilliant at improvising, even though in any other context he
hated having to improvise. From the broadly convergent accounts of
his different students, it becomes obvious why he regarded 'the
seminar' as a privileged space. Nevertheless, he claimed to be
mistrustful of the spoken word and of its potential for seduction: 'I
prefer writing to speaking. I find making speeches embarrassing
because I'm always afraid of self-dramatization – I'm afraid of
theatricality, of what might be termed hysteria. I'm afraid that while
I'm speaking I may get carried away and find myself giving
conspiratorial glances, winking at the audience . . . involved in more
or less willing seductions.'[43]

However, Olivier Burgelin, among others, insists that, on the
contrary, Barthes was a wonderful speaker: 'He never said anything
empty or pointless in his speeches. In fact, he never spoke unless he

had something to say, and this didn't just apply to the more elaborate, formal instances of his speech, but equally to his most trifling remarks, for example his meal-time conversations.'

The inner circle of the faithful, convinced by Barthes's theoretical references, set about immersing themselves with all the zeal of neophytes in the texts of Louis Hjelmslev (whose *Language: An Introduction* had just been translated and published by Minuit), André Martinet and Roman Jakobson. Gérard Genette's role was to ensure that nobody went overboard: he would intervene to set the record straight with three or four extremely succinct, if slightly dogmatic, formulae. Another more marginal group consisting of Raphael Sorin (who was working on Raymond Roussel), José Augusto Seabra (working on the Portuguese poet Fernando Pessoa) and Michel Giroud (who later became an expert on Dadaism) were more inclined towards the study of purely literary texts. They were sceptical of Barthes's more formalist aspirations and sometimes took issue, in a friendly way, with his scientistic approach. The seminar was conducted in an atmosphere of intellectual freedom and exchange. There was ample proof on many occasions and in many different ways of the extremely close nature of Barthes's relationship with his students. For example, at the end of the year he would take the seminar group out to dinner at the Chinese restaurant in the Rue de Tournon, opposite the Hautes Études.

At the beginning of each new academic year, the make-up of the seminar group was always slightly different. Some people had left, making way for others. But, like the ship of the Argonauts, the seminar as a whole remained unchanged, or at least there was a certain structural continuity. All those who took part, at whatever period, describe 'the seminar' in the same terms: it was part court, part Fourierist utopia, and part great brotherhood, and this was despite the existence of a number of smaller groups whose only common link was Barthes himself.

Apart from the seminar, Barthes also saw his students on a one-to-one basis in his flat in the Rue Servandoni, usually towards the end of the afternoon. He was rather a singular supervisor, since he would give them practically no advice or hints on methodology. He would listen to them carefully, punctuating what they said with remarks like 'that's fine, carry on', 'okay' or 'you're on the right tracks'. He replied similarly to those he was supervising by post. 'Just keep plugging away, it's amazing what you'll come up with', he wrote several years later to Michel Bouvard, who was doing research on photography while living in Rabat. To Gérard Miller, who wanted to work on Marshal Pétain, he gave the following piece of advice, which might seem strange coming from a supervisor: 'above all, don't try to be exhaustive.' In regard to his own work he was meticulous, almost maniacal, but he gave his students very little direction. He trusted them and did not try to impose his own theories or doctrines upon them (unlike many of his colleagues). He simply listened to them and, by doing so, he boosted their self-confidence. In this sense, perhaps, his style of teaching was profoundly Socratic.

On the dot of seven o'clock, Henriette would come up through the trapdoor from the flat below, bringing Barthes and the student who was with him a cup of tea and some little cakes. It was a regular, unchanging ceremony. If he was not having a meeting with a student, he would leave his study and come downstairs to have tea with his mother and Michel. The fourth member of the household was the dog, Lux, a mongrel which Michel had found abandoned one evening in the street, outside the Lux cinema. He had brought the dog home and Henriette had immediately adopted him. It was also when Barthes had no visitors that he worked or dealt with the enormous amount of correspondence he received. He was always scrupulous about replying to all the letters. While he was doing it, he listened to the radio: France Musique was his favourite choice for background music.

In parallel with his teaching, Barthes read a great deal, even if in a rather cursory fashion. During this period, he was reading the French linguist Benveniste, whose *Problems in General Linguistics* came out in 1966. He was also reading Jakobson, in the French translation of his work by Nicolas Ruwet, and Jacques Derrida, whose *Of Grammatology* was published in 1967. Then there was Greimas's *Structural Semantics*, published in 1966 along with Foucault's *The Order of Things*. He had also discovered Bakhtin (thanks to the paper Julia Kristeva had given at the seminar), and the Russian Formalists (Todorov's anthology *Theory of Literature* dates from 1966). This remarkable convergence was, in the space of a few years, to give rise to what came to be known to the public as 'structuralism', a perception that rapidly became a myth.

Just as Barthes tended to distance himself from each successive theory which he adopted and adapted, he would sometimes grow apart from friends (for example Greimas and Dort) and develop closer relationships with new friends. This did not, however, mean that he turned his back on his old friends. During this period, he grew very close to Sollers, and the two men saw each other frequently. It was a professional relationship, but also a friendship. At Seuil, Barthes had two circles of friends. The first centred around François Wahl and Severo Sarduy, and the second around Julia Kristeva and Philippe Sollers. Bernard Dort never felt very close to Sollers himself, and one day he said to Barthes: 'Come on, tell me what you really think of him.' Barthes replied, 'Sollers is family to me,' which cut short any further discussion. It is true that Sollers and the *Tel Quel* group annoyed a lot of people, and were often accused of constantly making radical shifts in their theoretical stance. Over the years, the members of the group were perceived successively as fellow travellers with the Communist party, then as Maoists, then as Paleochristians – even though Sollers would not have regarded himself as a fellow traveller of any kind, but as travelling his own path.

Nevertheless, the directions taken by *Tel Quel*, the review which Barthes's name was linked with from this point on, might be considered surprising by many people and, above all, they might be thought to jar with Barthes's constant anxiety, his need for discretion and his fear of 'hysteria'. Today, Sollers believes Barthes's involvement with *Tel Quel* was 'a coldly calculated hysteria'. According to Sollers, Barthes's support for the review reveals his great political sense: 'It was in the interests of both parties. It is a fact that *Tel Quel*'s brand of aggressive mobility helped him a great deal in the ten years that followed the Picard affair.'

During this period, for the first time in his life, he was wholly involved in academic life, and he had a proper role within it, even if the École Pratique des Hautes Études was a somewhat marginal institution in the university system. His involvement with this system culminated in the publication of *The Fashion System*, as academic a text as could be hoped for, a hefty tome which is an 'objective' piece of 'scientific' research and far less 'writerly' than his previous books. He had been working on this project for a long time and, as we have seen, it had almost been a doctoral thesis, supervised by Claude Lévi-Strauss, then by André Martinet. It ended up as a book, and Barthes himself defined it as follows in the dedication of the copy he sent to Greimas: 'For you, dear Guy, these first semiological scales, for having kept watch over me with such friendship while they were being practised.' Thus, if Barthes is to be believed, these 'first scales' heralded other future efforts. Five years earlier, he had dedicated a copy of *On Racine* to Greimas using a similar formula: 'For Guy, these faltering first attempts at a structural analysis.' There is obviously a sense of progression here from 'faltering first attempts' to 'first scales' to, presumably, mastery.

In fact, what the book primarily represents is a desire for systematization, a dream of scientific method: 'A method functions from the first word: now, this is a book of method; it must therefore stand on its own.'[44] Thus from the outset, the tone is given, and it is maintained throughout the book. *The Fashion System* combines both a *theory* and a *practice*. The theory derives from Saussurean linguistics (even if Barthes does invert Saussure's formula of the relationship between semiology and linguistics and maintains that semiology is a branch of linguistics) and from phonology, whose scientificity is considered archetypal. The book studies a very specific corpus, the 'written system of fashion', that is, texts from fashion magazines. Using these texts, he distinguishes 'commutative classes', analyses how they function, reveals different levels of signification, and finally proposes a model, that of the 'signifying matrix'. According to his analysis, every fashion utterance is composed of an object aimed at by signification (O), its support (S), and a variant (V). For example, in the two syntagms *cardigan with an open collar* and *cardigan with a closed collar* there is the same object (the cardigan), the same support (collar) and the element which receives the variation (open/closed being the two variants).

There may be some doubt as to why Barthes, apart from the development of a methodology, decided to study women's fashion, since he was not really interested in women. But the female body itself is absent from written fashion, it is merely a pretext, a prop. The way in which Barthes had already written about the painter Erté is a good illustration of his point of view. From 1913 onwards, Erté had worked for the great French couturier Paul Poiret, specializing in fashion design and costumes for the theatre and ballet. In 1915, he had designed the first front cover of the magazine *Harper's Bazaar* and he became famous for his drawings of sinuous, lanky, almost snake-like women. What Barthes picks up on in his piece on Erté is this reduction of the body to a mere silhouette, a 'clothes-horse':

> In Erté's work, it is not the feminine body which is dressed (gowns, furs, crinolines, trains, veils, jewels and a thousand baroque trinkets, whose pleasure is as inexhaustible as their invention); it is the garment which is extended as a body ... Woman entirely socialised by her adornment, adornment stubbornly 'corporeified' by woman's contour.[45]

In fact it is the social aspect of fashion discourse which interests Barthes. The body is absent from Barthes's 'commutative classes', just as it is from Erté's designs as analysed by Barthes. This was the era when texts in the human sciences were beginning to cause as great a stir as literary texts, and sometimes to sell as many copies. Claude Lévi-Strauss, then Jacques Monod and François Jacob were about to publish books which, although complex and difficult, sold like bestsellers. In 1967, Lacan's *Écrits* and Lévi-Strauss's *From Honey to Ashes* were the talk of the town, almost to the same extent as the winners of the Goncourt or Renaudot prizes. But even though these books were on the margins of science, even though they were definitely not fiction, they could be termed 'writerly'. This was not the case with *The Fashion System*, in which Barthes had conformed to all the laws of a serious, weighty genre, that of academic discourse. It was a technical book, the illustration of a method, like his *Elements of Semiology*. One might have imagined that it heralded more texts along similar lines and that it proved that Barthes's research had taken a resolutely 'scientific' direction (as indicated by the dedication he had written to Greimas). In fact, it meant nothing of the sort. As will become clear, in the books which followed he took a completely different path, as if his desire for systematization had been exhausted and satisfied.

8

Structures Do Not Take to the Streets

In May 1968, France woke up to the existence of what the Press dubbed 'the anti-establishment'. In Paris, the nights were shattered by the noise of grenades and slogan-shouting. One morning, the capital's inhabitants awoke to find barricades in the streets. The Latin Quarter was in a state of uproar. It was a spring when everything seemed to be teetering on the brink, a time that has been described or commemorated a thousand times over. The political class were overwhelmed by events, the political parties outflanked – even General de Gaulle, who went off on a jaunt to Germany, leaving people with the feeling that the seat of power was vacant. There were new faces and names (Geismar, Cohn-Bendit), people who seemed just as important and to carry just as much weight as the more traditional politicians. Hitherto unknown or little known movements also hit the headlines: the 22 March Movement, the Pro-Chinese Movement, the Trotskyites. The walls were plastered with posters (many of them printed at the École des Beaux-Arts) whose style and tone were new and different. A new press also sprang up, papers with ephemeral titles such as *Action* and *L'Enragé*.

However, what struck Barthes most was not the barricades, the units of CRS (state security police), the violence, the demonstrations, all the things he had always hated or feared, but that, in this symbolic clash between the forces of 'bourgeois order' and the 'anti-establishment' students, he felt rejected by the students, whose cause he supported almost instinctively. The courtyard of the Sorbonne had been invaded by stalls, streamers, portraits of Lenin, Mao,

Trotsky and Che Guevara; it was hung with Vietnamese, Breton and Occitan flags. But even though it was the same courtyard where, thirty-two years previously, the student Barthes had played Darios, it was now a place which felt singularly foreign to Barthes the lecturer.

Far from the barricades

Nothing was the same as it had been. Of course everyone lived May '68 in their own way. People went from the barricades to demonstrations, from demonstrations to frenetic meetings in which, discipline by discipline, academic knowledge was called into question. But Barthes kept his distance from all this unrest. One May evening, while he was having dinner in the Latin Quarter with François Wahl and Severo Sarduy, Wahl, having just found out that clashes were taking place between students and police near the Panthéon, suggested going along to see what was happening. Sarduy agreed, but Barthes refused and the others left on their own: but not before Barthes had made several bad-tempered remarks about the petit-bourgeois roots of the 'events' and the narcissism of the student generation. On another occasion, again with François Wahl, he went to the huge lecture theatre in the Sorbonne to listen to the numerous uncoordinated speeches, to watch a spectacle which had fascinated a good many observers. But Wahl remembers Barthes making absolutely no comment on the proceedings. According to Wahl:

> In fact, Roland did not like '68 at all, and the reason was precisely because it was all about the spoken word ... Because speeches were the main thing. For example, in the lecture rooms at the Sorbonne, it was speaking and not writing that mattered, and he regarded this as a kind of degradation of the written word, a disregard for the written text and, in this sense, a deficiency.[1]

It is true that Barthes never showed the slightest bit of enthusiasm for what was going on, and that he never gave any public sign of support for, or even acquiescence in, events. Barthes, who had always been part of the avant-garde, or at least in sympathy with it, saw nothing in the events of 1968 which merited his support. Indeed, his reaction seems to have been one of rejection or even defiance. No echo of such defiance can be found in his texts, except perhaps for a short passage in *Sade/Fourier/Loyola*, which was published three years later. In this passage, he explains that Fourier chose 'domestics'

over 'politics' because 'politics does not allow for desire, except in
the case of the *neurosis of politicizing*.'[2] He illustrates what he means
by way of an example: 'In May 1968, there was a proposal to one of
the groups that were spontaneously formed at the Sorbonne to study
Domestic Utopia – they were obviously thinking of Fourier [on
pensait évidemment à Fourier]; to which the reply was made that the
expression was "too studied", ergo "bourgeois".'[3]

Should the above be read as Barthes showing his claws? As proof
that he is ironically distancing himself from the events of May 1968?
Probably, but one point remains unclear: Who exactly is this 'on',
this 'they', whose proposal to study a particular topic was refused?
The skilful use of the indefinite pronoun allows this sentence to be
read as meaning either 'someone suggested' or 'I suggested' and,
given what has been related, one might well opt for the second
possibility.

So to Barthes the upheavals of 1968 seemed vulgar and pointless.
He was also physically afraid of the crowds, afraid things might get
out of hand. But one still had to get on with the tasks of daily life. At
the École des Hautes Études, Lucien Goldmann (the author of the
study of tragic vision in Pascal and Racine called *The Hidden God*)
had reacted immediately to events by setting up an 'action
committee', thus identifying himself from the outset with the broad
movement that was immediately baptized 'anti-establishment' by the
press. All the teachers at the École were approached by the students.
Some came to the students' meetings as curious observers, others as
militant supporters.

Barthes, on the other hand, committed a blunder. He announced
his willingness to conduct a seminar on the relationship between
'language and the student movement'. His offer was received with
scorn by the students, who did not think it was the time for
seminars. As for Goldmann, he was not displeased to see a
competitor in the field of Racinian studies disqualify himself in the
eyes of their student audience. Indeed, as in the 'domestic utopia'
incident, Barthes had obviously been trying to steer the student
movement in the direction of his own particular field of research, to
place his knowledge at the service of the common cause, and his
failure to do so doubtless played a major part in the negative verdict
he passed on the whole proceedings.

This was compounded by the fact that events did not stop there.
Gradually the number of committees grew, but the tendency was
towards setting up groups within the different disciplines in order to
engage in collective discussion. The students who attended Barthes's

and Greimas's seminars got together to form an action committee on language at the Sorbonne, which involved endless discussions on the underlying ideologies of semiological theories. The two friends, finding the pace a bit exhausting, decided to take the seminar on alternate days, Barthes one day, Greimas the next, a sort of part-time revolution. On one particular occasion, it was Greimas's turn to fulfil his revolutionary duties. The students' discussions touched on every subject under the sun, and the teacher was not allowed to intervene except to answer questions. Structuralism was often in the dock. On this occasion, after two hours of discussion at this rather erratic pace, Catherine Backès-Clément arrived. Along with philosophy classes she also attended Barthes's and Greimas's seminars. She announced to the students: 'I've come from the general assembly of the philosophy department. We have just passed a motion which concludes "it is obvious that structures do not take to the streets." '[4] Since structuralism was central to semiology, the students pounced on this formulation and started to discuss it. Barthes, who was having a day's break from the revolution, was not even present and thus had nothing to do with formulating the phrase. Nevertheless, the following day a huge poster appeared in the corridor of the fourth section of the Hautes Études on the first floor of the Sorbonne which read: 'Barthes says: Structures do not take to the streets. We say: Neither does Barthes.'

Greimas found this interesting abuse of authorship highly amusing, yet several months later he was surprised to see just how famous this phrase had become. In the autumn of 1968, he went to the United States to give a series of lectures. On his first day there, in San Diego, he was taken to a lecture theatre where he found the phrase, in French, written up on the blackboard. He found the same phrase written up on blackboards in every place he visited. It had travelled across the Atlantic and become a kind of slogan, an attempt to show that one particular illusion about structuralism had been shattered. Foucault, Lacan, Lévi-Strauss and Barthes, in the eyes of the public the founding fathers of structuralism, had often protested against such a superficial conception of their work, the way it was subsumed into one category. But equally problematical was the idea that the 'structuralist' model of analysis (which concentrated on the relations between elements rather than the elements themselves) was necessarily linked to the wave of anti-establishment protest that had swept across Europe and was now making its appearance in the United States.

'Structures do not take to the streets': it sounded like a divorce decree when there had never even been a marriage. The diverse research projects which were lumped together under the umbrella of 'structuralism' were not linked in any way to the political and social concerns of the generation of May '68. Only Barthes, particularly through his *Mythologies*, could give rise to such an impression, not by any stretch of the imagination Lévi-Strauss with his *Mythologiques*. Greimas could only regard this slogan as a somewhat ironic question: what are the links between structuralism, your structural semantics and the movement of May 1968?

As far as Barthes was concerned, however, there was nothing amusing in all of this. As has been said, Lucien Goldmann had tried to whip up anti-Barthes feeling by implying that Barthes was on the side of the establishment. Above and beyond these petty jealousies which sometimes flourish in academic life, Barthes reacted extremely badly to the fact that, for the first time in his life, his commitment was being called into question, or so he thought. In a television interview recorded in 1970,[5] he spoke about his friend Georges Fournié, who had first introduced him to Marxist ideas while they were at the sanatorium. The gist of his remarks was that the Trotskyism of those days 'bore no relation to present-day leftism and its ideological excesses'.

Barthes and Goldmann were brought together, however, in the middle of May 1968 when they both sat on the jury at Kristeva's M.A. thesis viva. Kristeva, worried she would be forced to return to Bulgaria, had asked for and been granted a special dispensation to take her viva despite the fact that there was a 'revolution' taking place. Goldmann was vehemently opposed to both structuralism and psychoanalysis, and he congratulated the candidate on having gone beyond both to consider history. He argued that there had been enough talk about sex and that psychoanalysis was not effective. It was an attack on Barthes, but an indirect and veiled attack, since he was criticizing Barthes's structuralism by praising Kristeva. In those days, it was not yet the done thing to settle scores openly during vivas.

Despite this interruption, which went unnoticed, the 'events' of 1968 continued to unfold, and not in a direction that was to Barthes's liking. What he found most hurtful was that he was not even regarded or recognized as a comrade, let alone a precursor. Here it is worth taking another look at the Picard affair. Barthes believed that the reason for Picard's attack was not just to warn Barthes off his own preserve, but because 'New Criticism' threatened the very foundations of the academic edifice. The very fact of labelling academic criticism as such, of singling it out and explicitly stating that 'there is an academic form of criticism' called into question the very foundation of the university system – the examination system – since the judgements of academic criticism were revealed to be subjective opinion, not objective truth. Barthes thought that from the moment one highlighted the historicist aspect of literature, it became difficult, even impossible, to question a student in order to pass judgement on him or her. In Barthes's eyes, it was precisely this system of controlling knowledge that was being challenged in May '68. So he may have thought that his seminar, his writings, were natural extensions of this movement and thus was unable to understand why he was being criticized, practically being lumped together with Picard and his like.

In addition, just before the events of May '68 proper had begun, he had taken a strong stand in defence of Henri Langlois, the director of the Cinémathèque, the French National Film Theatre, whom André Malraux had wanted to sack. On 14 February 1968, despite the fact that he was afraid of crowds and despite his lack of physical courage, he had taken part in a demonstration in front of the Palais de Chaillot along with other celebrities such as Jean-Luc Godard, François Truffaut, Claude Chabrol, Michel Piccoli, Jean-Paul Belmondo, Simone Signoret and Jean Marais. There were also other, less well-known people there, such as Daniel Cohn-Bendit. Of course, Barthes had not taken part in clashes with the CRS as some demonstrators had, but he had shouted for Malraux's resignation along with everyone else. Although Malraux did not resign, he did back down. Langlois kept his job and, in retrospect, this demonstration was considered in some quarters as heralding the May unrest. It was the first time during this period of French history that the state had appeared relatively weak, the first time it had been forced to back down by a street demonstration.

Lastly, for Barthes structuralism (if such a generic term has any meaning) was the space of ideological critique *par excellence*. According to him, *Tel Quel* represented 'the dialectical articulation of a revolutionary, Marxian political stance and an avant-garde cultural activity'.[6] Sartre, on the other hand, in an interview in *L'Arc* in 1966, rejected structuralism for being 'bourgeois'. The gist of his argument was that the human sciences studied structures, attempted to reduce mankind to structures, whereas, despite this attempt, mankind still continued to make history. On 20 May 1968, this same Sartre spoke in the main lecture theatre at the Sorbonne. The hall was jam-packed, and the audience spilled out into the surrounding corridors and courtyard, where they were able to hear his speech thanks to an improvised public address system. The students listened attentively and made hardly any objections at all. They saw his mere presence as a sign of the vital support of a thinker whose ideas had shaped them. As for Barthes, he felt marginalized: 'structures do not take to the streets'. He spent May '68 at *Tel Quel* meetings, far removed from the demonstrations and the lecture theatres.

In November, at the age of fifty, Georges Fournié died. Someone who had been one of Barthes's most formative intellectual influences, along with Singevin and Greimas, had therefore disappeared. He wrote to Jacqueline Fournié to say how sad he felt, but he never saw her again. According to her, he was caught up in a whirlwind of new relationships, but in his letters, sent from whichever country he happened to be travelling through, he always expressed his loyalty to past friendship and his regret at no longer being able to see her as often as he would have liked. In January 1969 he started teaching at the École Pratique des Hautes Études again, continuing the seminar which he had begun in 1968 and which had been interrupted by the student strikes. The subject of the seminar was Balzac's short story *Sarrasine* and he often discussed his ideas with Sollers and Kristeva over dinner in Montparnasse, at the Falstaff or the Rosebud. One of his main problems was what to call the book he was working on. He wanted a title that was not too ponderous, but which would convey the ambiguity of Sarrasine/Zambinella.

It was Sollers who suggested the idea of calling it *S/Z* and this episode is described in Kristeva's book *Les Samouraïs*, written as a novel but also as a chronicle of this period. In the book, Bréhal (Barthes) has given Sinteuil (Sollers) the manuscript of his analysis of Balzac's *Cousin Pons*. Sinteuil is full of praise for the manuscript and says, 'Le Cousin Pons, k + z + s. That's an anagram of Balzac, if you count the c as a k . . .' Then he asks Bréhal:

— Have you thought of a title?
— That's exactly the problem, I'm stuck.
— Why not *Balzac written out* [*Balzac en toutes lettres*]?
— Sinteuil wrote the letters on a match box: C/S/Z.
— It's abrupt, incomprehensible, hesitated Bréhal.
— It can be understood if one's willing to read your book.[7]

These meals, like others with other intellectual friends, often served as 'testing grounds' for ideas which later appeared in his books. For example, Kristeva believes he was working out, while they had a drink or dinner together, his ideas on Proust. Naturally, this meant that his friends were hardly ever surprised by his texts when they appeared. A large proportion of the ideas they contained had already been worked out in his seminar or in conversations with friends.

Nevertheless, even if by all external appearances his life seemed to be unchanged, if he carried on with his teaching duties or his writing just as he had in the past, in fact Barthes was a changed man. In the wake of the events of May 1968 his heart was no longer in his work. Something had snapped and he felt a confused need to take a step back from his life. When Zaghloul Morsy, a Moroccan academic he had met in the course of a short visit to Rabat in 1965, suggested he come and teach at the Mohamed V University in Rabat, Barthes jumped at the chance. Of course there were a few practical problems to sort out, in particular the question of what to do about his mother. But he was determined not to let this stand in his way – his mother would go to Morocco with him. Leaving Henriette in Paris, he left for Rabat to look for a flat for them both, a three-year contract as a 'volunteer teacher' in his pocket.[8]

Rabat

In June 1969, the literature department at Rabat University was in a state of turmoil. The staff had just found out that, unbeknown to them, Roland Barthes had been invited to come and teach in the department and would be joining them at the beginning of the next academic year. Reactions were mixed. Wouldn't their normal routine be upset by this new arrival? Wouldn't he overshadow all the other volunteer teachers who, up until now, had had absolutely no competition to contend with? Whatever the case, it was decided that an urgent refresher course was required, since they could not welcome such a celebrity without having read his books. However, they were nearing the end of the academic year, right in the middle of the exam period, and Barthes's texts were said to be difficult. Josette Pacaly, the head of the French department and one of the few people who had actually read his texts, was asked to undertake the theoretical initiation of her colleagues. This took place in the Council Hall of the university, and for once all her colleagues were present: the literature teachers of course, but also the philosophy and the history departments and even the Dean himself. She explained the 'elements of semiology' to them, and armed with this new science the teaching corps was ready at last to welcome the newcomer − or, as some would have it, the intruder.

For his part, the intruder was preparing for his departure. He was also involved in drafting a piece of writing which was atypical of his usual production. It was a piece for the annual congress of the French Catholic Bible Studies Association, which was being held in Chantilly on 6 September 1969. He had been invited to attend by Edgar Haulotte, and his acceptance was characteristic of his liking for commissions, his tendency to regard as a challenge the fact that he had to produce, like a good student, a serious analysis of a subject he had never thought about before. On this occasion, he rigorously applied the principles of structural analysis to a passage from the Acts of the Apostles, offering these bible students an approach to 'their' text with which they can hardly have been familiar.[9]

After this biblical interlude, he went to Morocco, arriving at the beginning of the autumn term. Rabat was the administrative capital of Morocco and, like all towns designed by Lyautey, was divided into two parts. There was the 'native' part, which was dominated by the Oudayas fortress on the edge of the Bou Regreg wadi, which separated it from Salé and the European part of the town, where the royal palace, the administrative buildings and the university were located. Barthes found a flat near the station, above a Chinese restaurant called 'The Pagoda'. It looked out on to a magnificent palace with ornate Moorish-style windows. These false windows, which he saw every morning when he opened his shutters, would set him daydreaming. He settled in and started hunting for furniture. He explained to his friends that he needed small pieces of furniture because his mother was coming and she was small.

Sometimes his few acquaintances at the university or members of the French community in Rabat would come to visit him. The latter group included the director of a large factory and a bookseller, both highly cultured and well-read. He also had to sort out his financial affairs. Although he had been employed as a lecturer, he did not in fact have the necessary qualifications for the post, and they wanted to pay him the salary of a teacher in a secondary school. It was the reopening of an old wound, that of the illness which had interrupted his studies, the agrégation he had not taken, the thesis he still had not submitted. It took several months, in fact the whole of the first term, to sort things out. At Christmas he drove back to Paris via Spain and after the holidays brought Henriette and Michel back to Rabat with him in his little red Volkswagen. Michel stayed a few weeks and Henriette two months.

Parallel to this private, family life there, he also had, of course, his public life at the university, where he soon felt that the perception of him was at cross-purposes, or rather 'upside-down'. In France, everyone knew who he was, but in Morocco they evidently had no image of him.[10] That is, he was seen as part of *Tel Quel*, which, at the time, was intensely Marxist, so he was perceived as being Marxist too. He was expected to provide them with an introduction to dialectical materialism. It is true that the situation in Rabat bore a strong resemblance to the one he had just left in Paris. The years 1969 and 1970 were the 1968 of the Moroccan students. On the left of the National Union of Moroccan Students was a grouping of socialists together with 'wet' communists, who rejected their French literature classes for being 'too bourgeois' and wanted theory and linguistics classes. Only one 'literary' text found favour with them: Sartre's preface to Frantz Fanon's *The Wretched of the Earth*. The rest were confined to the dustbin. Claudel was on the syllabus but he was boycotted since in his *The Satin Slipper* there is a scene which takes place on the seas off Essaouïra during the conquest of the New World by the Spanish and this was regarded as colonialist.

They also preferred Goldmann's Marxist analysis of Racine, in which he sees the plays as reflecting contemporary society, to Barthes's more literary study. In Morocco, in fact, Barthes found himself up against the same anti-establishment feelings as he had left behind in France. In addition, they all lived at such close quarters in the town that he found it difficult to maintain the discretion he had always striven to preserve as regarded his private life. In a somewhat provocative fashion, he decided to lecture on Edgar Allen Poe and also gave a course on Jules Verne's *The Mysterious Island*. To everyone's surprise, he showed a great interest in *bricolage*[11] and manual work, an interest which was not just literary (Abdallah Bounfour, one of his students, discovered on being invited to his flat one day that Barthes owned a complete toolkit). He also gave a course on Proust, and thus set himself completely against the dominant political mood of the times.

However, the students' rejection of 'neo-colonial' literature, itself proclaimed in the language of the colonizers, gave Barthes food for thought. Replying to Guy Scarpetta's questionnaire in *Promesses* a year later, he made a direct reference to his experience in Morocco: 'In certain countries still encumbered by a former colonial language (French), there currently prevails the *reactionary* idea that one can teach French (as a foreign language) and repudiate French literature (as "bourgeois"); unfortunately, language has no threshold; it cannot be stopped.'[12] In spite of everything, looking back twenty years later, some of his Moroccan students say that Barthes's lessons reconciled them to literature and that the time he spent in Rabat made teaching at the university respected again, since he created a bridge between linguistics and literary studies. But at the time the atmosphere was far from peaceful.

Of course, he was invited to various dinners and was 'received' into local society. One of his colleagues, Fernand Bentolila, remembers that when he invited him to dinner one evening Barthes arrived with a present of lemons he had picked himself in the country. Everyone who met him at one of these parties among 'dear colleagues' was sure that he found them extremely boring. One day, when the conversation had turned to structuralism, yet again, Josette Pacaly's husband suddenly began to talk about a subject that obsessed him: his Crested Cardinal bird, the pride and joy of his aviary. This beautiful red bird had injured itself and, because it was temporarily blind, could not feed itself. Its only food was *tenebrio molitor*, a worm bred in a barrel from which it bores its own food. Until it had recovered its sight, it had to be fed using a pipette. Suddenly Barthes perked up, fascinated by this story, and began to ask questions. 'That was the only time', says Josette Pacaly, 'that I saw his eyes sparkle, and I said to myself that he must really be bored here if he finds a little story like that, at once idiotic and poetic, so fascinating.' Every time the French department held one of these get-togethers (where there would be a few Moroccan teachers, terrified by the presence of the Master and the French volunteer teachers), Barthes felt bored.

Of course, he was too urbane not to play the social game and enter into the rhetoric of polite conversation. So he would talk about Paris, how it was impossible to live there any more. He would describe what he referred to as his afternoon 'dental surgery', the series of half-hourly appointments in which he dealt with the large number of students who wanted him to supervise their M.A. dissertations, and with any other requests. His story was that he had come to Morocco to escape the pressures of his working life in Paris. While it was true that he had been overwhelmed by the amount of correspondence he had had to deal with and by the meetings he had had to attend, the main factor in his decision to leave Paris had been the anti-establishment student movement of 1968. In this sense, his trip to Rabat could not be considered a success. The highly charged atmosphere at the university was impossible for the French volunteer teachers, who were baited by the students and confronted by demands they considered to be unacceptable. Some of their Moroccan colleagues gave behind-the-scenes support to the students, believing the unrest in the university to be the forerunner of more significant political upheavals. Other colleagues, French nationals, supported their Moroccan colleagues in siding with the students.

By inclination, Barthes would have liked to do the same. But he also had some key ideas on which he was not prepared to compromise and which he defended with obvious courage. One of these was literature, which he continued to teach against all odds. He also rejected the idea of a dictatorial general assembly in which every vote would carry equal weight, and where staff and students would make decisions together. In the face of such calls for direct democracy, he claimed the right to vote by secret ballot, and to separate colleges. In addition, every time his students asked him for his views on the political situation in Morocco, he expressed opinions which were much closer to those of the Istiqlal party than to the Maoist positions espoused by his student interlocutors.

Despite all this, he had nothing really to complain about, and his colleagues envied what, in retrospect, they called his 'powers of seduction'. During their own lessons, they suffered endless interruptions and were bombarded with aggressive questions, whereas Barthes managed to impose a quite different system on his students. They would be allowed to ask their questions in one special session at the end of the academic year. Barthes's kindness, his ability to listen and his moderate replies disarmed the hardliners, the most anti-establishment section of his audience. During the same period, Michel Foucault was having his classes at the new university of Vincennes interrupted by Maoist militants led by André Glucksmann and Jean-Claude Milner, who wanted to 'destroy the class-based university system'. Lacan, whom Foucault had invited to give a series of lectures, had to abandon the idea after his first lecture ended in uproar.

Barthes's situation seemed almost enviable in contrast. But to Barthes himself it seemed intolerable. According to Josette Pacaly, 'Barthes, who had such a deep need to be liked, rather bravely chose a path which meant that, because people did not understand, he was mistakenly seen as being right-wing'. Of course, he was not the right target, and neither French literature nor the French volunteer teachers were responsible for the oppression (real or imagined) which the Moroccan students felt. But to attack any other target, a target closer to home, would have been extremely dangerous. The regime of King Hassan II did not take kindly to protests of any sort. Many intellectuals had already been imprisoned or had disappeared, and it was safer for the students to limit their attack to symbolic targets.

In addition, Barthes had no intellectual contact with his colleagues, and had nothing in common with them. He was considered too literary by the other linguists, too impressionistic. As for the literature teachers, they did not understand his work: his texts still had a reputation for being difficult. The only people at the university with whom he had any kind of intellectual relationship were a few of his students (Abdallah Bounfour, Abdeljib Zeggaf and Joël Lévy-Corcos) and a small group of the younger volunteer teachers (Michel Bouvard, Jean-Claude Bonnet). Every Tuesday they would have dinner, either at one of their houses or at a restaurant if it was Barthes's turn to play host. The first time Barthes came to dinner at the Bouvards' house, he declared that he did not want anything to eat, or only very little, because he was on a diet. He informed them that he had weight problems. Nevertheless, they got through two bottles of champage before sitting down at the table, where Barthes tucked in greedily. 'I eat by colour,' he said one day, admiring the greenness of the peppers, the redness of the tomatoes and the granules of Kamoun on the Moroccan kebabs.

His greediness was evident to Hervé Landry even before he actually met Barthes. At the time, Landry was living in Tours, where he read *Writing Degree Zero*. Greatly impressed by Barthes's book, he sent him a copy of the draft of a novel he had written. Barthes replied to his letter, and the two began to correspond. However, Landry thinks today that it was perhaps not so much his talent Barthes was taken with as the boxes of stuffed prunes from Poireau, the great Tours patisserie, Landry used to send him. In Bayonne, too, they remember Barthes's passion for Cazenave's hot chocolate, which was thick and frothy and served with a little bowl of fresh cream (the best hot chocolate in the world, according to Barthes).

Sometimes, after morning classes, he would go to the Bouvards' house for lunch. He would ask Bouvard what he was doing for lunch and when the latter replied that he had no plans, would suggest they went to a restaurant. Then Bouvard would invite him to have lunch at his place instead. It was during one of these meals that Michel Bouvard told Barthes that, since his son's birth, he had taken over six thousand photographs of him. Barthes was amazed and replied, 'there you go, that's the thesis subject you've been looking for for so long: ask yourself why you took these photos.' A glimpse here of something his readers were to discover ten years later, his interest in photography. In fact, what interested Barthes was not so much the photographs themselves as what they represented in emotional terms. Remembering this conversation (and of course Bouvard's thesis on the semiology of photography, which he himself had supervised), he wrote in *La Chambre claire* (*Camera Lucida*): 'I was like that friend who had turned to photography only because it had allowed him to photograph his son.[13]

In a context where the volunteer teachers socialized with one another a great deal, often inviting one another round, Barthes remained something of an outsider. Some of the teachers were afraid they would be disturbing him, thinking he had work to do. He was, in fact, writing up his 1968–9 seminar notes on 'Balzac's *Sarrasine*', which was to become *S/Z*. He was also putting the final touches to *Empire of Signs*, his book on Japan. A designer was even sent by his publishers, Skira, to Rabat to sort out with him some difficulties with the illustrations.

But he confided to some of his friends that he found his colleagues rather distant, and that he would have appreciated a few more invitations. The first time that Michel Bouvard, feeling somewhat intimidated, inquired whether Barthes might have an evening free at some point to come and have dinner, Barthes replied, 'but of course, whenever you like, I'm always free.' So the various accounts of his behaviour contradict each other on this point. According to some versions, he is seen as a bored guest on the occasions when he was invited to dinner, whereas others give the impression that, on the contrary, he was delighted to be invited. Is there a contradiction here or not? Perhaps not, if one remembers how moody he was, and how his behaviour changed depending on his mood, on whether he felt grumpy or sociable, attentive or absentminded. Talking with the same people in the same place would alternately amuse and bore him, depending on what mood he was in. It is easy to imagine him at home on his own after work, feeling bored and wishing someone would invite him out somewhere; however then, once the desired invitation had materialized, feeling equally bored in the company of the very people he had wanted to see.

In fact, he did not really enjoy living abroad at all. He always felt out of place, and would often remark to his friends, 'I'm like a bottle of Cahors wine – I don't travel well.' The only thing he enjoyed about the experience was being surrounded by a barrage of incomprehensible language. For Barthes, a foreign language acted like blotting paper, absorbing people's usual everyday vulgarity and allowing only what was essential, their bodies, their gestures, to be grasped. However, in Morocco, this rarely occurred, since all the intellectuals spoke fluent French. Morocco was not foreign enough to live there for long.

Nevertheless, whether he felt bored or not, as far as his love life (or rather his sex life) went, Morocco did have its compensations, like the nights on the town he occasionally allowed himself. What he found in Morocco is discussed with almost complete frankness, even with a certain audacity, in a passage in his book *Sade/Fourier/ Loyola*. The Sadean novel, he explains, is more real than the realistic novel, and he goes on to say that if the improbable Sadean practices appear implausible: 'we need only travel in any underdeveloped country (analogous, all in all, to eighteenth-century France) to understand that they are still operable there; the same social division, the same opportunities for recruitment, the same availability of subjects, the same conditions for seclusion, and the same impunity, so to speak.'[14]

As far as sex went, a volunteer French teacher in Morocco could indulge himself as much and in whatever way he liked, just like an aristocrat of the ancien régime, and Barthes felt a certain amount of guilt about the fact. This feeling of guilt was increased by the precautions necessary to prevent 'Maman' from finding out, since she must not be upset. One person who accompanied him on these nights on the town, Georges Lapassade, found the contradiction between Barthes's apparent respectability and the fact of his sexual encounters with Moroccan youths hard to stomach. Lapassade was someone Barthes had met about ten years previously through his collaboration with the review *Arguments*. Lapassade, who had become a kind of official theorist of the trance in Morocco, had at the time an extremely bad reputation, so much so that he was having problems with the Moroccan authorities. He even had to lie low in a friend's flat for a while, believing the police were after him. Barthes's refinement, and his celebrity status, really got on Lapassade's nerves. He preferred the grandiose provocations of a Jean Genet (who was also living in Morocco at the time). He did not care for the way that Barthes, following his sex sessions with young boys, could resume his pose of respectability. So Lapassade, who loved scandal, decided, as he told his friends, to 'drop Barthes in it'.

To be fair, it should be said that, according to some people, Barthes was never open about his homosexuality. Throughout the whole of their friendship, which lasted thirty-three years, Maurice Nadeau had no idea about it until just before Barthes's death. When he did find out, it made him consider in a new light many details of Barthes's behaviour he had hardly noticed before. For example, in the mid-fifties, the great Italian revolutionary writer Ignazio Silone had organized a meeting of representatives from all the various European left-wing journals in Zurich. Nadeau and Barthes had attended, and Nadeau remembers that Barthes always left the others every evening at around seven o'clock to go for a stroll in town alone. He did not even discuss his homosexuality with his brother Michel, although Michel was of course aware of it, until after their mother's death. However, he did discuss it with other friends, Sollers in particular.

His discretion can partly be explained by historical reasons. At the time, homosexuality was almost totally rejected by all conventional members of the bourgeoisie. Another reason is Barthes's own rejection of any form of hysteria, his refusal to 'militate' for any cause. However, many of his friends think that the principal reason for his discretion was that he did not want to upset his mother. Some are even prepared to bet that she never had the slightest inkling about it. This seems rather hard to believe, but on the other hand, nothing was ever said. Whatever the case, the fact remains that he never gave any explicit sign of being homosexual. Perhaps he thought it was part of his private life and had nothing to do with anyone else. Edgar Morin remembers him making only one direct reference to it, when he explained why he was wearing a huge pair of sunglasses: they were hiding a black eye which he had got the night before on the beach at Biarritz, where he had been beaten up and robbed. Much later, he would frequent the gay bars of Paris, and in Morocco he also went to brothels, but he never publicly admitted that he was homosexual. He never, for instance, campaigned with the militant homosexual revolutionary organization, the FHAR. André Téchiné wonders what use it would have been: 'he wanted to avoid two related traps, shame and triumph.' By contrast, the way Lapassade behaved was, in Barthes's view, hysterical. According to François Wahl,[15] when Barthes died he was about to publish a notebook of his days in Morocco. This text, which was published in 1987, is somewhat surprising. Usually the language Barthes used was discreet and extremely restrained in tone, but in this text his vocabulary is extremely crude:

> The art of living in Marrakesh: a conversation between a moving horse-drawn carriage and a bicycle; the cigarette is handed over and a rendezvous arranged, the bicycle veers sharply and speeds off.

A little Marrakesh schoolteacher who says, 'I'll do whatever you want,' his eyes full of enthusiasm, compliance and complicity. Which means *I'll fuck you over* and nothing more.

Gérard, French father and native mother, wants to show me the way to the Gazelle d'Or. He leans back in the car, as if to tempt me with his attractions, then offers, like a rare titbit, a final, irresistible argument: 'You know, my thingy hasn't been cut.'[16]

Retrospectively, these posthumously published passages, along with others, reveal many of Barthes's other texts like *Empire of Signs*, *Sade/Fourier/Loyola* or *A Lover's Discourse* in a different light. What is explicitly present in the former is also found in a veiled form elsewhere, in the form of a half-suggestion, a hint. Even if Barthes really did intend to publish this text (which is impossible to prove), it is highly significant that he only contemplated doing so after his mother's death. Without denying the part played by changing sexual behaviour and attitudes towards sexual behaviour, and the fact that gradually homophobia had become less wide-spread, this proves that the main motive for his discretion was his desire to spare 'Maman' any distress. It was only her death which, while not making him completely throw off his former reserve, made him less secretive.

Nevertheless, if he was reserved, he never pretended to be anything he was not. It would be wrong to suggest that during his stay in Morocco he attempted to conceal something. On one occasion when he had just been on a trip to the south of the country, he had shown his friends some photographs he had taken of the camel market in Goulimine. 'They're not very good,' a friend commented. Barthes replied with a smile, 'You know I was more interested in the camel drivers than the camels.' On another occasion, the Bouvards told him that their four-year-old son had said: 'When I'm grown up I'm going to kill Daddy and marriage Mummy.' Barthes had discussed this with them, talked about the Oedipus complex of course, and then gone on to tell them how close he was to his mother and to confide that he was homosexual.

But it is more interesting to consider the fact that there is no link between Barthes's own sexuality and the content of his texts. Or so it would seem. In the case of Michel Foucault, for instance, one can see that his interest in minorities, in madness, in prison or in whatever is marginal might be connected to his homosexuality. This is not the case with Barthes. The only direct but discreet allusion to his homosexuality in the texts published during his lifetime is a few lines in *Roland Barthes by Roland Barthes* under the heading 'The goddess H':

> The pleasure potential of a perversion (in this case that of the two H's: homosexuality and hashish) is always underestimated. Law, Science, the *Doxa* refuse to understand that perversion, quite simply *makes happy*, or to be more specific, it produces a *more*: I am more sensitive, more perceptive, more loquacious, more amused, etc. – and in this *more* is where we find the difference (and consequently, the Text of Life – life-as-text). Henceforth, it is a goddess, a figure that can be invoked, a means of intercession.[17]

Of course, the use of the term 'perversion' in this context has been criticized, but this is the only place in any of Barthes's texts published during his lifetime where the term 'homosexuality' is linked to the first person pronoun 'I'.

At the end of the summer term, Barthes drove back to Urt through Spain, via Salamanca and Valladolid. There he resumed his old habits. In the normal course of events he should have returned to Rabat after the holidays and begun his second year of teaching at the university. But his escape from the upheavals of May '68, his withdrawal to what he had hoped would be a safe haven, had not been a success. He decided to stay in France, and his Moroccan interlude came to an abrupt end with a breach of contract.

Paris revisited

Barthes returned to Paris and began teaching at the École Pratique des Hautes Études again. In 1970–1 the subject of his seminar was 'The notion of the idiolect' and the following academic year it changed to 'Ten years of semiology'. He also taught a course in rhetoric at the University of Geneva. The seminar had moved again, first to a theatre and then to the buildings in the Rue de Tournon. It was also beginning to take on the atmosphere and appearance of a fashionable first night. Because of the huge crowd it attracted, the École had had to hire the hall belonging to the Société Française de la Théosophie. Barthes would now speak from the stage, under the spotlights, to an audience of hundreds of anonymous listeners. One day the exasperation and dissatisfaction many felt with such abnormal working conditions, with the way the seminar had been transformed into a media event, surfaced in the form of a student protest.

The seminar was moved back to the Rue de Tournon, where it was decided that only those who were properly enrolled would be allowed to attend. Barthes divided the students into three groups, and ran three separate seminars in conjunction. Ideally, he had hoped to restrict the numbers in each group to around ten people. With access restricted, the seminar would thus become a closed, eroticized, protected space. But it was no use. Sometimes students arrived up to three hours before the seminar was due to start in order to get a seat. There were people everywhere, even on the stairs. It regularly took at least half an hour to get those who had no business being there to leave. Barthes, annoyed by all the fuss, had to play the policeman, explaining that it was a research seminar, not a circus. But it made no difference: the seminar was famous, it was in fashion, and this had transformed it into a 'show'. None the less, Barthes himself hardly said a word until the very end of the proceedings. The students would present their research papers or report on their progress while he listened, and it was only when they had finished that he took up where they had left off, summarizing what they had said, expanding on it, always trying to valorize what they had said, to bring out the best. Even if the paper had not been wonderful, his synthesis was always brilliant and fascinating.

In 1970, he published two books which marked an important turning point in his writing. His most recent publication, *The Fashion System*, had been a weighty tome, for once perhaps more the work of an *écrivant* than an *écrivain*. But both *Empire of Signs* and *S/Z* were in a completely different mould. During his visit to Japan, which had provided him with the subject matter of *Empire of Signs*, he had experienced an 'intense feeling of pleasure' – and more than intense:

> The pleasure I experienced not just in travelling around Japan but also in writing this text, was intense, total, both raw and subtle at the same time. And since I believe desire to be the essential thing in writing, I can say that in writing Japan I carried out the mission of writing, which was the fulfilment of a desire.

He goes on to explain this further:

> This text represents a rupture with my previous writing since here, perhaps for the first time . . . I entered fully into the play of the signifier. I shook things up, I lifted the constraints placed upon me by my super-ego; even those of the ideological super-ego, since I did not force myself to talk about Japanese capitalism.

As for the other text, *S/Z*, it was a kind of rewriting of a Balzac short story and was the fruit of the seminar he had given just before going to Rabat. It was heavily influenced by the work of Kristeva, from whom Barthes took the notion of *intertextuality*. Kristeva's work was just becoming known to a wider audience (her first book, *Desire in Language: A Semiotic Approach to Literature and Art*, had been published by Seuil in 1969). However, behind this strange new term lay a concept that was more familiar, at least to readers of Barthes's previous work. The notion of intertextuality rendered the author of a text anonymous, cut him or her out of the text, since a text was regarded as the projection of other, earlier texts: as both a derivation and a transformation, and even, in fact, as a parody and a plagiarism of earlier texts. But *S/Z* also contained traces of Claude Lévi-Strauss, the same Lévi-Strauss who later confessed to never having liked the book.

This is yet another example of Barthes's practice of using concepts from other people's theories to flesh out his own intuitions. *Connotation* as an idea is present in Barthes's writing right from the opening lines of *Writing Degree Zero*, necessarily so. But it only appears in conceptual form later, when he borrows the term from Hjelmslev. Similarly, Barthes's rejection of the biographical approach to texts, seen earlier, which informs the whole of *On Racine* and can already be found in the *Michelet*, does not find theoretical expression until *S/Z*. Of course, a text has its origins, but these were to be found in the text itself and not in the author's life. Rather than produce a structural analysis of Balzac's story along the lines of Propp's analyses, Barthes tries to follow what he calls the 'threads of meaning' present in the text. He chops up the text into successive fragments or 'lexias', which are reading units of varying lengths. The first unit, for example, is composed of a single word, the title, whereas the twenty-first unit is eighteen lines long. Thus Balzac's story is divided up into 561 lexias and the whole of Barthes's text is organized into ninety-three sections or chapters. 'Why ninety-three?' a friend once asked him. 'Because that's the year my mother was born,' he replied with a smile.

Barthes had thus produced two decidedly non-academic texts. On his return from Morocco, he found that the French cultural scene had shifted. New reviews like *Actuel, La Cause du peuple* (whose editorship Sartre had taken over after the arrest of Jean-Pierre le Dantec) and *Charlie Hebdo* had appeared, and new groups dedicated to ideological intervention had been formed (Le Secours Rouge, the Mouvement de Libération de la Femme, Pour l'Année

1970, d'Autres Suivront, etc.). The universities had also undergone a change. The human sciences had arrived in force, and Barthes's own works had begun to be recognized. From now on he would find himself able to teach in a less embattled, less marginal space. However, it was precisely around this time, towards the end of 1970, that he made the following remarks:

> I recommend my students to play the game of the academic institutions at which they are studying. To do this means, on the one hand . . . respecting their desire to write, a desire every student should have, but, on the other, covering themselves as far as the institution is concerned. By this I mean that they should cast their research, their work, their writing in forms which will not offend the stylistic sensibilities of their teachers and examiners.[18]

Thus, at the very same moment as he himself was publishing *Empire of Signs* and *S/Z*, he was encouraging his students to write in the style of *The Fashion System*. That is, to mask or re-channel the impulse to write, to cheat, if need be, in order to please the institution. He was certainly entering a period of contradictions, firstly as concerns his own theories, and secondly between his own ideas and those theoretical groupings he was associated with, most notably *Tel Quel*. Finally, there were contradictions between his own political positions and actions and those of friends or former friends. It was not just the cultural landscape that had changed, but also the political landscape.

In 1971, the Groupe d'Information sur les Prisons and the Front Homosexuel d'Action Révolutionnaire were set up. While some of his friends got involved in these groups, they left Barthes himself cold. He regarded such groups as expressions of 'hysteria', a hysteria which reached its peak in 1972 with the Bruay-en-Artois affair and the setting up of 'popular tribunals'. For his part, he refused to join a minority group of any kind. He did not want to be classified or labelled by the outside world either as a homosexual or a militant in any group. When Michel Foucault and Gilles Deleuze involved themselves in the Toul prison uprising, Barthes merely observed events from a distance. He was struck by the way homosexuals behaved differently from in the past, particularly by the fact that they no longer felt ashamed. But he did not personally care for what, in his eyes, amounted to a form of collective indoctrination, the moment when liberated individuals formed new groups and regimented their behaviour. He thought that by virtue of their 'liberated' behaviour homosexuals were conforming to another stereotype. In effect, by distancing himself from what was happening, he widened the gulf which for several years had existed between him and Michel Foucault.

Excommunication by the linguists

The contradiction between the author of *The Fashion System* and the author of *S/Z*, between the advocate of a pure and rigid form of structural analysis derived from phonology and the advocate of intertextuality, was soon to be resolved. This was partly due to the way his personal preferences had evolved, as he gradually moved away from ideas which he had previously upheld passionately. But there was another factor involved, a theoretical exclusion. Previous attacks on him, such as Picard's, or criticism, like that in the press, had all come from the same direction, from the advocates of traditional literary criticism. Now, however, he was about to come under attack from quite a different quarter, in fact from the very theoretical grouping he had so often invoked in his seminars, articles and interviews over the past ten years: the field of structural linguistics.

Structural linguistics had been founded by Saussure fifty years earlier, and it had come to be dominated by the figure of André Martinet. When Martinet had returned to France from the United States in the mid-1950s, linguistics was practically unrepresented in French universities. Martinet was appointed to the first chair in 'structural linguistics', held jointly at the Sorbonne and the École Pratique des Hautes Études. Gradually his students got their doctorates and started teaching in the universities: Jean Dubois was appointed at Nanterre and Georges Mounin at Aix-en-Provence. After 1968 the floodgates opened and new posts were created throughout the French university system. Numerous young doctors of philosophy became lecturers and senior lecturers. At the time, linguistics was a new science, and it was in fashion.

But now Martinet, who for fifteen years had been the undisputed leading light of French linguistics, suddenly found his position challenged by other, new theories which were beginning to take hold. There were two main rival schools of linguistics. The new Parisian universities which had been created after the passing of the Edgar Faure law were divided between the two camps. The first was the *functionalism* advocated by Martinet and his disciples, which still held sway in the old Sorbonne and certain provincial universities. This was being challenged by the *generative linguistics* elaborated by the American linguist Noam Chomsky, which had first taken root at Vincennes. It was from the first camp, the functionalists, that the attack on Barthes came. Two of Martinet's students, Luis Priéto (an Argentinian who had settled first in France and then in Switzerland) and Georges Mounin, had decided to take up Saussure's old idea of a science of semiology. By reworking the ideas of the Belgian linguist Eric Buyssens, whose *Les Langages et le discours* had been published in 1943, their aim was to map out the boundaries of 'orthodox' semiology, what Mounin termed 'the linguist's semiology'. In doing so, they tried to exclude Barthes's work from this field of study.

It was Mounin who led the attack in a book published in 1970 called *Introduction à la sémiologie*,[19] in which he insisted strongly that there was a distinction between what he called the 'semiology of communication' ('proper' semiology), which described different codes, and what he termed the 'semiology of signification'. According to him the latter functioned essentially on the level of metaphor by calling absolutely anything a language. He claimed that no one could be caught up in a process of communication unwittingly, and that in order to prove that an emission of meaning was taking place, one first had to prove the existence of both a code and a desire to communicate.

Naturally, this meant that the whole methodology and aim of a book like Barthes's *Mythologies* was called into question. Everything Barthes had said, for example, about wrestling, the Tour de France or steak and chips was not the product of a code, according to Mounin's definition of the term. In a chapter called 'The semiology of Roland Barthes', Mounin did not mince his words: 'Barthes's work cannot be discussed in scientific terms. He is regarded as a theorist whereas the reality of the matter is that he is merely an essay writer. He confuses everything, and in short his work is not semiology but "social psychoanalysis".'[20] True, the above diatribe does come just after a passage in which Mounin pays homage to 'the generous spirit in which he has carried out his struggles, the many stimulating aspects of his theories, his skill in framing vital questions and uncovering promising areas and perspectives'. Nevertheless, the excommunication remained irrevocable.

Thus Barthes, who had loyally drawn his inspiration from Martinet (even to the point of modelling the title of *Elements of Semiology* on Martinet's *Elements of General Linguistics*, the catechism of functionalism) and who regarded himself as a structuralist, paradoxically found his work refuted by the very branch of linguistics which was at the heart of that loose configuration known under the convenient label of 'structuralism'. As a result of this rejection, he moved further towards the analysis of narrative. If *The Fashion System* and *S/Z* can be taken as representative of two different strands in his thought, then henceforth he was to abandon the former in favour of the latter. Of course, this was partly a question of his own personal preferences, but the above criticisms must have played a part in his decision. Barthes never replied to Mounin's attack, but once again he changed his approach. From now on, he was to champion intertextuality, and the books which came after *S/Z* (*Sade/Fourier/Loyola*, *The Pleasure of the Text*, *A Lover's Discourse* and *Camera Lucida*) had no connection with the Saussurean heritage he had discovered through his friend Greimas at the beginning of the 1950s. Once again, Barthes changed theories.

9

Tel Quel

Changes were also taking place at *Tel Quel*. After the publication of Maria-Antonietta Macciochi's *Daily Life in Revolutionary China* and its subsequent banning from the book fair organized by *L'Humanité*, the 'movement of June 71' had broken with the Communist party and began flirting with Maoism. Prior to this, *Tel Quel* had been on good terms with the French Communist party and its theoretical organ *La Nouvelle Critique*. This page in the history of the journal's alliances was now brusquely turned and the group began to put all their energies into fighting against 'sinophobic revisionism'. Barthes went along with this position, of course, or at least gave the impression of agreeing with it. Some people, however, wondered what on earth he was doing mixed up with this bunch. Looking back, Jean-Paul Enthoven thinks it was a way for him 'to show his support for people who treated him well'. He adds that, as far as he can remember, Barthes never showed the slightest sign of any real conviction: 'He felt comfortable with Wahl and Sollers, they were family to him, and sometimes some members of the family act childishly. So he went along with it, rather indulged it.'

But as far as the outside world was concerned, the Maoist learnings of *Tel Quel* and the political positions of Roland Barthes were one and the same. In the autumn, part of a television interview he had given for 'the archives of the twentieth century' was published under the title 'Responses'. The interview was not broadcast in its entirety until 1988, after his death. In it, Barthes discusses his childhood, his time at the sanatorium and his intellectual trajectory. It was the first time he had spoken about his past and his background in public. However, what the published text of this interview did not contain was a certain passage in which he discussed his relationship with *Tel Quel*. This only came to light seventeen years later on the occasion of the television broadcast.

The interview took place in the autumn of 1970, that is before the change of direction of the 'movement of June 1971', or in other words when *Tel Quel* was in its staunchly pro-communist phase. Throughout the interview, Barthes's unease is evident. It is true that he did not like television, that he hated speaking off-the-cuff, even during the seminar. He hated speaking in public without a written text, and even wrote down carefully what he was going to say when taking part in vivas. During the interview, he glances only occasionally at the interviewer, keeping his eyes fixed on his notes: he has obviously written down his answers, since the questions were submitted to him in advance. Suddenly, however, he is asked: 'Would you like to say anything about *Tel Quel*, about your links with the journal, the group?' He does not look up, either at the interviewer or the camera, and he appears to be following his script carefully:

> Firstly, *Tel Quel*'s work is vital to me on a personal level. What I mean by 'vital' is that if it did not exist today, I personally would feel somewhat stifled by the current intellectual and ideological environment in Paris, and in France as a whole. Secondly, *Tel Quel* is vital because it is currently the only theoretical undertaking whose seriousness is incontrovertible, as is the lucidity of its analysis of the global political situation. Despite any problems that may exist in the articulation of its strategies, or differences on a tactical or strategic level, on the whole *Tel Quel*'s political stance seems to me to be correct. Thirdly, I believe that this struggle is undertaken without the slightest vulgarity or complacency on their part.

While he is reading this passage, Barthes's eyes are fixed firmly on his notes or script. In fact, his 'statement' might be a better way of putting it since, overall, its tone and his gestures remind one of an official spokesman reading a press release on how discussions at some international summit are progressing. He goes on: 'Fourthly, but this is my own personal interpretation' – he looks up at the camera as he says the word 'personal', as if he suddenly felt liberated from a speech which had been imposed on him by someone else – 'I believe the work of *Tel Quel*, no matter how serious it is, indeed precisely because of its seriousness, remains, so to speak, a great game, a fiction, in the Nietzschean sense.' As he concludes his remarks, he lowers his eyes to his notes again: 'For the first time in the intellectual history of the West, there have appeared a group of writers, or rather textual operators, who are seriously attempting to tackle the problem of the dialectical articulation of a revolutionary, Marxian political stance and a cultural activity that could be termed, crudely, avant-garde.'

Watching this part of the interview, one is always left with the same impression, or rather the same question: did Barthes write this text? And if he did not, then who did? Or perhaps, to frame the question slightly differently: if Barthes wrote it himself, then which Roland Barthes?

Biographemes

At the beginning of 1971, when *Tel Quel* was between its orthodox communist phase and its Maoist phase, Barthes published a book which was completely removed from all these political debates. In *Sade/Fourier/Loyola* he constructs a Sadean grammar comprising 'postures', 'figures', 'operations' and 'scenes'. He distinguishes in Loyola's *Exercises* four levels of signification, which he terms 'literal', 'semantic', 'allegorical' and 'anagogic'. All three writers are what he calls – thus coining yet another neologism – *logothetes* or founders of languages. But in the course of developing his analysis, Barthes raises a further question, the question of biography. The 'amicable return of the author' is posited, the author as 'the site of a few tenuous details, yet the source of vivid novelistic glimmerings'. His conception of biography is that of the *biographeme*, the short note, the brief sketch, in short the index card which, as has been seen, was his principal way of working. This is how he conceives his own biography, as he outlines in the preface, and the way he approaches the biographies of the three writers he is analysing. At the end of the book he lists a number of points under the heading 'Lives' (twenty-two for Sade, twelve for Loyola): 'Suddenly transferred from Vincennes to the Bastille, Sade made a great fuss because he had not been allowed to bring his *big pillow*, without which he was unable to sleep'; 'Fourier hated old cities: Rouen'; and so on.[1]

It was around this time that someone decided to jot down a few such 'biographemes' about Barthes himself, but without his good will towards his subject. In 1972, the publishers Christian Bourgois brought out a book called *Immédiatement* by Dominique de Roux. It was a kind of diary in which de Roux attacked a number of his contemporaries. Informed about Barthes's activities by Lapassade, he included a short passage about him in his book. Barthes telephoned Bourgois, who had the relevant page torn out of every copy already in the shops. Dominique de Roux, who was in the United States at the time, was so angered by his publishers' action that he broke his contract with them. A new edition of the book was not published until after the deaths of both Dominique de Roux and Barthes eight years later, by another firm, L'Age d'Homme. The incriminating passage was a mere eight lines long:

> Lapassade said to me:
> 'One day, when I was with Jean Genet, we were talking about Barthes and how he leads a double life, keeping the Barthes of the brothel boys separate from the Talmudist Barthes (as I called him). "Barthes is a drawing-room man, a table, an armchair," I said. "No," replied Genet, "*Barthes, c'est une bergère.*" '[2]

Why did Barthes intervene to get this passage removed, when it is obvious that in doing so he proved Lapassade right? Barthes's phone call made it seem as if Lapassade's claim that he was anxious to keep his sexual preferences secret was well founded. Was he trying to protect his mother? Although there was little likelihood of her reading a Dominique de Roux book, Barthes might quite rightly have been worried that the press could pick up the story. Whatever the case, Barthes did not forget this incident. At the time, de Roux was working on a special issue of the *Cahiers de l'Herne* dedicated to Queneau. Violette Morin was also involved in the project and Barthes telephoned her to ask her not to submit her article. She agreed and did not produce anything until Dominique de Roux had resigned from the editorial team.

Of course, Barthes also bore a grudge against Lapassade. Once, when he was having dinner with Hervé Landry, he bitterly attacked Lapassade, calling him a skinflint and accusing him of sponging off him while he was living in Rabat. At the time, Lapassade was teaching in Tours, Landry's home town, and so the latter listened attentively, especially since Barthes never usually spoke ill of anyone. Barthes said that Lapassade had abused his generosity rather too often, that in the brothels of Tangiers it had regularly been Barthes who had to foot the bill. In the end, Barthes had had enough. Whether that story was true or not, the fact remains that it shows how resentful Barthes felt.

His resentment can only have been exacerbated when Lapassade published a short story called *Le Bordel andalou*. The story begins in Tangiers, in a Moorish baths with two entrances, the lower one for the Arabs and the upper one for the Europeans who go there to cruise. Who are the characters in the story supposed to represent? Since their real identities are hidden behind pseudonyms, and they are all fairly one-dimensional, it is difficult to guess. But Lapassade implied that one of them was Barthes, and everyone tried to guess which one. Who was Armand Glaïeul? Jean Genet? And who were Scorp, Machaire, Pontalanche? And Roland Putois, was he Barthes? The thing that is certain is that one passage in the story contains an almost word-for-word account of what Lapassade had told Josette Pacaly about Barthes:

> Those who frequented the brothel veiled their true desires behind the steam. When they left the baths and emerged once more into the Place du Général-Franco, their faces and their appearance changed; they respected all the social rituals. The price society charged for their visits to the hammam was increased submission to its conventions.[3]

It was during this period that Jacques Le Goff, who had taken over from Fernand Braudel as head of the sixth section at the École Pratique des Hautes Études asked Barthes to join the team in charge of day-to-day administration at the École. Le Goff was convinced when he asked him that Barthes would refuse. However, to his great surprise, Barthes asked for a few days to think it over and then accepted. He took his new appointment very seriously and immersed himself in his administrative tasks. Le Goff had asked Barthes because he wanted him to 'devote his time and energy in particular to getting an overview, to thinking through the École's current and future direction'. He had intended the day-to-day tasks to be left to the other four members of the team. But he had a further surprise in store: Barthes assumed responsibility for these tasks. He scrupulously reread and corrected the minutes of the weekly meetings. He saw students who wanted to continue with their studies at postgraduate level but whose records were problematic. He helped draft new statutes for the college and he attended meetings with union representatives. In other words, over a three-year period, he revealed a different side to his character, what Le Goff called 'Barthes the administrator'.[4]

It was also during this period that he met Jean-Louis Bouttes at the home of the philosopher Henri Lefèvre. At the time, Bouttes was a student researching an article on Barthes. He was expecting to meet Barthes the theorist, but was immediately bowled over by the charm of Barthes the man. According to Bouttes he was taken with Barthes's way of 'making a theoretical relationship a friendship and making theory out of his friendships, out of dissensions and weaknesses, often talking about other people by allegorically addressing himself'. Like many others, he was struck by Barthes's tendency to devalue his way of expressing himself verbally, his conviction that he was 'stupid' when he spoke, whereas in reality what he said was always extremely subtle.

Jack Lang, the future Minister of Culture, had the same impression of Barthes the first time he met him. According to Lang, Barthes was 'a wonderful man, charming and extremely refined'. In fact, Lang had just been put in charge of the Chaillot theatre, and was looking for a new kind of writing for the theatre, one that would dramatize history and contemporary events, a theatrical interpretation of the world. He needed writers who were able both to express and to interpret the times they were living in. Remembering Barthes's articles in *Théâtre populaire* and his *Mythologies*, Lang hoped Barthes might be such a writer. In fact, despite their common interest in the theatre, it was Barthes's book on Japan, *Empire of Signs*, which had most impressed Lang. He still feels enthused by the book today: 'I don't know if it is fact or fiction, the product of an imaginary relationship with Japan, a fantasy, or a realistic account, but I loved his descriptions of Japanese cooking, of the crowds, of Tokyo.'

So he phoned Barthes and they arranged to meet in a café in Saint-Germain-des-Prés. They spent several hours discussing Lang's project. 'What you're really looking for', Barthes told him, 'are *scriptors*.' This neologism remained engraved in Lang's memory. He thinks Barthes had decided to write a theatrical piece for him, which is plausible, given Barthes's taste for commissions. Unfortunately, Lang was replaced as director of the Chaillot theatre and the project went no further. However, the two men kept in contact, meeting on several occasions, including a certain Monday in February 1980 . . .

In 1972, Roland went to spend his holidays at a friend's house on the Côte d'Azur. The Cannes film festival was on and he met a young film-maker called André Téchiné there. Téchiné had not yet turned thirty and he had only one film to his credit, called *Pauline s'en va*. For a long time, this film had remained unshown, but it was now being screened at the fringe festival in Cannes. Barthes did not manage to see it there, but he saw it on his return to Paris, at a screening in Studio 27 in Montmartre. Afterwards he and Téchiné had a long discussion, and this was the beginning of another important friendship. Téchiné, too, was fascinated by Barthes's complete lack of desire for power, his kindness and, of course, his voice. But, above all, it was Barthes's talent for listening that captivated the young man. Almost everyone who has spoken about Barthes has mentioned this ability. Téchiné began to attend Barthes's seminars and Barthes took an interest in his film projects. In 1979, Barthes wrote an article in *Le Monde* on his film *Souvenirs d'en France*, which had been selected for Cannes (the official competition this time): 'With Téchiné comes lightness: this is a significant event not just for the theory of film-making but also for the practice of film-watching.' Yet another example of Barthes's loyalty to his friends.

Painting

At the beginning of the 1970s, Barthes added a new touch to his palette. Along with music and writing, he began to take an interest in painting, or rather 'graphisms'. Once again, this new interest sprang from his experience, from his time spent in Japan and Morocco, where he had discovered calligraphy: an extension of writing, a transmutation of those hand movements that form letters in writing. In Japan (and in China, as he learned on his later visit there), handwriting and calligraphy were regarded as extremely important, to the point where to call someone's handwriting 'beautiful' was to pay them the ultimate compliment. In addition, the instruments used by calligraphers (ink, paper, brushes) were the same as those used by painters and often the poem merged into the drawing. In *Empire of Signs*, Barthes adds the following caption to a reproduction of a drawing in ink by Yokoi Yayû called 'Mushroom Picking': 'Where does the writing begin? Where does the painting begin?'

It was in Japan that Barthes first discovered this play of hand and brush in which the signifier is immediately more important than the signified. He encountered the same thing in Morocco, but multiplied. Islam prohibits the representation of the act of divine creation: the desire to represent in pictorial form what God has created is considered sacrilegious, and figurative representations are considered totemistic. Islamic cultures have therefore channelled the impulse to create figurative images into the art of writing. Barthes's stay in

Rabat was the longest time he had spent in Morocco, longer than any of his previous trips to Tangiers. It was during this period that he saw numerous examples of calligraphy, as well as abstract geometric designs on pottery.

So he began to experiment himself, letting his hand move freely across the page, extending his writing in an almost automatic fashion. The signifier, the form, far outweighed the content. At first, he considered this activity to be merely playful. He included three of his efforts in *Roland Barthes*, with the captions 'doodling', 'the signifier without the signified' and 'squandering'[5] (because his drawing was done on a piece of headed notepaper from the École Pratique des Hautes Études). In an interview in 1973, he referred to himself as a 'Sunday painter'. Nevertheless, one of his drawings was reproduced on the cover of *Roland Barthes* ('Souvenir de Juan-les-Pins') and painting became increasingly important to him. When he died, he left behind almost five hundred paintings, all of them dated and itemized, and many of them on sheets of headed writing paper from the institutions at which he had taught (the École Pratique or the Collège de France) or from Urt. Despite this, he always regarded his painting as a sideline and was astonished whenever visitors took an interest in his creations. He would explain how easy it was, that all you had to do was let your pencil wander across a sheet of paper.

It was also around this time that he began to write articles on painters. He had of course already written on Bernard Buffet, but the article had focused mainly on his reflections on New York. Now he began to analyse painters like Arcimboldo, André Masson, Erté, Cy Twombly or Réquichot, just as he had previously analysed Racine or Michelet. This might look a somewhat heterogeneous list, but the kind of art that three out of the five were producing is similar to his own production. Erté is an obvious choice, with his famous alphabet in which the female body becomes the shape of the letter, but there are even greater parallels with Réquichot or Cy Twombly. Like these two painters, Barthes liked to extend writing until it became drawing, and, by adding colour, to transform it into its own negation, to dissolve it into vague, meaningless forms. For example, he found echoes of Chinese painting in Twombly's work: 'Chinese painters . . . must triumph over the line, the form, the figure, at the first stroke, without being able to correct themselves, by reason of the fragility of the paper, the silk; this is painting *alla prima*.'[6] He goes on to state clearly the influence Twombly's work has had on him:

Thus this morning, December 31 1978, it is still dark, it is raining, everything is still when I sit down at my work table again. I look at *Hériodiade* (1960), and I really have nothing to say about it, except the same platitude: that I like it. But suddenly something new appears, a desire; the desire to do the same thing; to go to another table (not the one where I write), to choose colours, to paint, to draw. Ultimately the question of painting is: 'Do you want to do a Twombly?'[7]

Réquichot interests him because he produces an 'illegible writing' or represents 'a total language: in his letrist poems and in his snout collages'.[8]

Once again, as always, the interest here is in language. However, in his writing on Arcimboldo, who produced heads composed of vegetables, objects and animals, there are some of the same tics as in his *Mythologies*, which lead him to draw some rather rash conclusions. He distinguishes, for instance, a 'linguistic basis' in the painter's work, giving as an example the prune which represents the eye in Arcimboldo's picture 'Autumn': 'In the figure of "Autumn", the (terrible) eye consists of a little prune. In other words – in French at least – the botanic *prunella* becomes the ocular *prunelle*, our word for eyeball.'[9] The difficulty with this interpretation, of course, is that Arcimboldo was Italian. Despite Barthes's qualification, the linguistic fact remains: in the language of Dante, *prugnola* has only one meaning, that of the fruit. The word for pupil is *pupilla*.

But despite the tenuous nature of the links he makes, what emerges clearly from these analyses is Barthes's conception of painting: painting is an extension of writing, of language. Furthermore, when he discusses a painter's work, he never refers to the material, the texture of the paint, its thickness. He always confines himself to images. In fact, he could just as well have used two-dimensional reproductions for the purposes of his analyses. For Barthes, Arcimboldo produced rhetorical figures rather than canvases, and this is precisely what he himself was trying to produce. Thus among the collection of Barthes's paintings and drawings belonging to Romaric Sulger-Büel, there are pastel drawings, watercolours, ink drawings, but no oil paintings. The same applies to the exhibitions of his work, both those held during his lifetime, in 1976 and 1977, and those held posthumously, in 1980 and 1981. Barthes painted in two dimensions.

This is not to say that his work lacks interest. It is the expression of his dream, the dream which also carried him away when he was writing about other painters. There are lines, colours, but no depths.

If his texts can patently be treated as texts, discussed as writings
where the medium of language has been worked on, then equally
they cannot be called paintings, if by this one means a work in which
the medium of paint, its texture is worked on.

It's not for nothing that I'm a structuralist

At the beginning of July 1973, Kristeva had her Ph.D. viva at
Vincennes, before a very Parisian audience. In accordance with
tradition the candidate spoke first, and in the conclusion to her
defence of her work she paid tribute to Roland Barthes, whom she
said had always tried 'to ensure that avant-garde research remained
communicable and intelligible'. This provoked a somewhat surprised
response from the audience, since Barthes's texts were not exactly
renowned for their clarity. She went on to conclude, 'this is what I
myself have always strived to ensure.' After the two linguists on the
jury, Jean-Claude Chevalier and Jean Dubois, had spoken, it was
Barthes's turn. His tone resembled that of a pupil addressing a
teacher, rather than the other way around: 'On several occasions,
you have helped me to evolve my ideas, in particular to move from a
semiology of products to a semiotics of production.' He added that
through her research, Kristeva was in the process of writing the
modern novel. As usual, Barthes read from a carefully prepared text
and contrary to tradition, he did not ask the candidate any
questions. His ability to summarize brilliantly the main points of
theses he had only looked at cursorily, without reading them
properly, was a talent which had always fascinated Bernard Dort,
who had often sat on juries with Barthes. But on this occasion, no
one could claim that Barthes had not read the text to which he was
referring. For the past seven or eight years he had followed Kristeva's
work closely. She was the foreigner, the 'stranger' he had written an
enthusiastic article about in 1970.[10]

Edgar Morin also has a story about Barthes's performance at a
viva. Once he asked Barthes and Henri Lefèvre to sit on the jury for
a Master's thesis which, in his view, was 'hopeless'. The subject was
the secondary school newspapers which had sprung up during 1968.
Morin says, 'I had warned them about it, but at the time I thought
one should try and remove the sacred aura from academic
institutions and help make good natural inequalities. Brilliant people
don't need Master's degrees.' Lefèvre took a bit of persuading, but
Barthes agreed immediately, perhaps out of friendship, perhaps

because, as usual, he was incapable of saying 'no'. On the day of the viva he read from a prepared text as usual and, according to Morin, 'he gave a brilliant speech analysing a non-existent thesis, transforming it with his words, like an alchemist, from something that had previously been mediocre and inept into something interesting.' Furthermore, in none of the numerous vivas in which he took part did he ever treat a candidate 'nastily'. He was never aggressive, or even critical, which both testifies to his gentle nature and perhaps at the same time relativizes the seriousness of the event itself, the conferring of degrees and the academic authority which confers them.

The care taken by Barthes when preparing even the most insignificant speech, the panic which having to improvise aroused in him, is only one aspect of his working methods. An interview he gave to Jean-Louis de Rambures, published in September 1973,[11] gives a fair idea of how he worked. He said that he was almost fanatical about his pens, pencils and felt-tips. He owned a huge number, and he was continually buying more and changing them. At the same time, he had just bought an electric typewriter, and he had carefully set aside a fixed time each day to practise his typing: 'Every day I practise for half an hour.' He meticulously kept his different activities separate; for example he never mixed reading for work and reading for pleasure. He reserved his work reading for the mornings, spent at his desk, and he read for pleasure at bedtime. His answers in this interview contain a good many such 'biographemes', and they speak for themselves:

> I find it impossible to work in a hotel room. It's not so much the hotel itself which bothers me, the atmosphere or the decor, but the way the space is organized. (It's not for nothing that I'm a structuralist, or rather that I'm labelled as such!)

> To function properly, I need to be able to reproduce the structure of my normal workspace. In Paris, this is my bedroom (which is not the space where I wash or have meals). I work every day from 9.30 a.m. to 1 p.m. (this regular timetable, that of the professional writer, suits me better than the irregular working hours that suggest a continual state of excitement). This workspace is completed by a place where I can play music (I play the piano every day at around 2.30 p.m.) and somewhere I can 'paint'. (I say paint in inverted commas because I'm really a Sunday painter, I paint about once a week, so I need a place I can mess around in).

> In my house in the country, I have reproduced these three spaces exactly. It makes no difference that they're not in the same room: it is not the partitions which count but the structure.

This is not all. My workspace must itself be subdivided into a number of functional microspaces. Firstly, it must contain a table (I prefer wooden tables, I feel comfortable with wood). There must be a space for overflow next to this table, that is, another table where I can spread out the different bits of my work. Then there has to be somewhere for my typewriter and a lectern for my various different 'memory aids', my 'microschedules' for the next three days and my 'macroschedules' for the whole term (I never look at them, mark you, it's enough to know that they're there). Finally I have a system of index cards. These must be of an exact format: a quarter of the size of my normal writing paper; at least that's the size they used to be until sizes were changed and standardized by the European Community (for me, that was one of the hardest blows inflicted by the Common Market!). Luckily I am not a complete obsessive, otherwise I would have to write them all out again on new cards, and they go back twenty-five years to when I first started writing.

Roland Barthes, published in 1975, gives the same information but in a more condensed form. Barthes likens his two workspaces in Paris and Urt to the Argonauts' ship, the *Argo*, each piece of which was gradually replaced, so that finally it was a completely different ship and yet still the same one:

> Between them there is no common object, for nothing is ever carried back and forth. Yet these sites are identical. Why? Because the arrangement of tools (paper, pens, desks, clocks, [ashtrays]) is the same: it is the structure of the space which constitutes its identity. This private phenomenon would suffice to shed some light on Structuralism: the system prevails over the being of the objects.[12]

Four years later, he returned to the same theme in an interview, making more or less the same point. He concluded by joking that he was a good structuralist because his rooms in both Paris and Urt had the same structure, and this meant that when he got off the train he could get down to work without feeling unsettled by unfamiliar surroundings.[13] There is something triumphantly smug in this parading of his old-maidish, pernickety habits. He must have smiled to himself at the thought of revealing them, laughing both at himself and at us. Once again, the preface to *Sade/Fourier/Loyola* comes to mind, in which he (for once) confronts the problem of biography head-on, describing how his own biography might and should be written. Or rather, how he would like it to look:

> For if, through a twisted dialectic, the Text, destroyer of all subject, contains a subject to love, that subject is dispersed, somewhat like the

ashes we strew into the wind after death (the theme of the *urn* and the *stone*, strong closed objects, instructions of fate, will be contrasted with the *bursts* of memory, the erosion that leaves nothing but a few furrows of past life): if I were a writer, and dead, how I would love it if my life, through the pains of some friendly and detached biographer, were to reduce itself to a few details, a few preferences, a few inflections, let us say to 'biographemes'.[14]

He gives a wealth of examples of these 'furrows' left on life, as if on a piece of clothing moulded into a particular shape by wear, by the endless repetition of some habitual gesture, or carelessly creased and still retaining the traces: the pencils, the table, the relative positions of objects and different areas, the index cards, all things which would probably be considered insignificant, and yet he himself set such store by them. Describing in this way the functioning of a mythical being, the writer (the series of interviews in which this one figured was called 'How writers work'), he is adding one more touch to a mythology that has been sketched and resketched so many times:

Gide was reading Bossuet while going down the Congo.[15]

To endow the writer with a good fleshly body, to reveal that he likes dry white wine and under-done steak is to make even more miraculous, for me, and of a more divine essence, the products of his art.[16]

I have got into the habit of saying *migraines* for *headaches* ... whoever heard of the proletarian or the small businessman with migraines? The social division occurs within my body: my body itself is social.[17]

These small, seemingly insignificant details accumulate to form a self-portrait, one which is found in the margins of the text. For someone who was anti-biography – or so he would have had us believe – Barthes certainly left behind a lot of clues.

So, China

Peking, Shanghai, Nanking, Xian: in April 1974, a delegation from *Tel Quel* spent three weeks travelling through China. The country was in the throes of the Cultural Revolution, a campaign in which Lin Biao and Confucius were denounced in the same breath. The

Chinese had invited the group at the suggestion of Maria-Antonietta Macciochi. Philippe Sollers had been in charge of organizing their trip, and he had selected those who would make up the delegation apart from himself: Barthes, Kristeva, Wahl, Marcelin Pleynet and Lacan. The latter was very taken with the idea, explaining that he had studied Chinese at the École des Langues Orientales during the war, and that he was keen to go and take a closer look at the Chinese unconscious, which he believed to be structured like a form of writing rather than a language. At the last moment, however, he changed his mind, for reasons that remained unclear, and the party was reduced to five.

On their arrival, the group went along quite happily with the official rhetoric of friendship, sometimes wearing 'Mao costume' and asking serious questions, even though they received only bureaucratic formulae in reply. To begin with, Barthes merely laughed at these rituals and played the game like the others. On factory visits, he would take out his notebook and jot down the tons and tons of steel or rice which Mao Zedong's teachings had produced. He appeared interested in the nursery schools they were shown around, and he listened to the explanations about contraception. Then gradually he lost interest in trying to decode what was going on around him and imperceptibly withdrew into himself, making plain his indifference and voluntarily excluding himself from the group. On one occasion, when Philippe Sollers and François Wahl were involved in a heated discussion about Buddhism and the Cultural Revolution, he went off to his room, not wanting to witness (according to Sollers) such a confrontation between his friends. He did not take part in the group visit to see the Guardians of the Tombs of Xian, preferring to stay behind on his own. He refused to bathe in the hot springs of the Black Horse mountain above Xian.

Julia Kristeva's account of their visit, written in 1982, is confirmed by the others:

> In China, in 1974, a bus took us through millennia of history which, at the time, was inaccessible to most Westerners. We pored greedily over each stone, each statue, each jewel, each character. As for Barthes, he often stayed in the bus or waited for us at the museum door. He was bored by this commemoration, this linearity, this dream of filiation.[18]

Today she adds to the above account that when Barthes arrived in China he found everything 'insipid', the colours, the people. He did not feel the enthusiasm he had expected to feel and he showed a complete lack of curiosity for everything they saw. Nevertheless, on his return to France, he agreed to write an article about his experience for *Le Monde*. He produced a brief, subdued piece called *Alors, la Chine* ('So, China').[19] The article is really a series of formulae which give the impression that he does not want to say anything: 'China is not *coloured in*', 'China is peaceful', 'China is prosaic', etc. However, the initiated will recognize the enormous compliment implicit in the final sentence: 'A people . . . go about their business, drink their tea or do their solitary exercises without any drama, without noise, pretension, in short, without hysteria.'

It seems strange, however, that Barthes paints a picture of a China that is so 'colourless' at the precise moment when the country was actually being thrown into turmoil by the activities of the Red Guards. It is true that 1974 was not a year of spectacular events in China: the critique of Lin Biao and of Confucius continued, the number of young people going into the countryside increased and gradually army officers were ousted from provincial organizations, but then perhaps all this escaped the eye of the tourist. Nevertheless, the majority of the *Tel Quel* group were pro-Chinese, even if today Kristeva claims that she was merely interested in the ancient China, and the possibility of a 'national alternative to communism'. China was still a 'mythology' in France, a fact Barthes must have been aware of, just as he must have realized that his reactions to the visit were eagerly awaited.

Philippe Sollers believes that 'recognizing the demand, he didn't want to fulfil expectations, a fairly Taoist gesture on his part.' 'And yet,' as Bernard-Henri Lévy remarked to Barthes in an interview, 'China is certainly full of signs!' Barthes replied that this was true but 'signs are only important to me if they seduce or irritate me. Signs in themselves are never enough for me, I must have the desire to read them.' He expanded further on this last point: 'In China, I found absolutely no possibility of erotic, sensual or amorous interest or investment. For contingent reasons, I agree. And perhaps structural ones as well. I mean in particular the moralism of the regime there.'[20] China was not Japan.

In the meantime, however (speaking in the third person, as we shall see), he had given another explanation for the 'neutral' article he had written. It was that, at the time, he did not want to *choose* China, but simply to *acquiesce* in it:

On the occasion of a trip to China he tried to use the word *assent* again, to explain to the readers of *Le Monde* – in other words, of his world –

that he was not 'choosing' China (too much was missing for him to shed light on such a choice) but merely acquiescing in silence (what he called 'insipidity') . . . This was not understood at all. What the intellectual public wants is a choice: one was to come out of China like a bull crashing out of a *toril* in the crowded arena, furious or triumphant.[21]

Once again, there emerges through these differing, inconsistent explanations one of his most consistent character traits: his faithfulness to his moods – even if, with great bad faith, he tried retrospectively to give them a theoretical gloss. But there is a further possible explanation to consider. Shortly before his departure for Peking, Barthes went to London to give a seminar at University College. While he was there, he explained to Annette Lavers that he had to go to China for reasons that were to do with his media image. He thought he would never be forgiven if he did not. A year later, when Claude Roy was asked by *Le Monde* to define 'his' Barthes, he returned to the subject of this bizarre trip:

It is strange that his gentle, patient and insatiable mania for *unveiling* seems to have come unstuck on his recent visit to post 'Cultural Revolution' China. The same Barthes who decoded *Paris-Match* and the Tour de France, the 'vestemes' and 'anti-vestemes' of fashion, Balzac, Sade and Réquichot, found nothing to decode in China, no Unconscious to render conscious, no enigma to decipher, no depths to penetrate. This silent Prince of the 'Order of Sarcasm' summed up his Chinese quest and the outcome of his enquiry in a single word: *nothing*.[22]

In all likelihood, Barthes found China boring and was exasperated by the Maoist fervour of his companions. He was bored, so he transformed his boredom into a theory of 'insipidity'. He could not stand the factory visits, the official rhetoric, the sight of the operation performed while the patient was under acupuncture to which all 'visiting foreign friends' were subjected. Above all he could not bear the atmosphere of rigid austerity. According to Kristeva, the only time during the whole three weeks of the visit when his interest seemed to be aroused was one evening when they were at the ballet and Barthes was seated next to a young man. He tried to approach him, but it was a timid and probably unsuccessful attempt. So on his return to France he had written an article which was colourless, subdued, half-hearted, whatever adjective one wishes to apply to it. An article which said that he had nothing to say, an exercise in style written in order to avoid a breach with his *Tel Quel* friends, whose passions probably bothered him less than they amused him. Then came the questions and he had to come up with an explanation: he had to transform his initial bad mood into a theory.

The whole episode would be almost without significance were it not for the fact that it highlights one of the ways he functioned. The *Le Monde* article bears the same relation to the explanations that followed it as his 'little mythologies' of the 1950s bore to the final text in the book of *Mythologies*, 'Myth today'. After the moods come the *a posteriori* construction of a theoretical discourse which takes them in hand and makes sense of them. He also acquiesced once again, not to China this time, but to what his friends said about it. When Kristeva published her book on *Chinese women*, he asked Jean-Louis Bouttes to review it in *La Quinzaine littéraire*. Bouttes found the book rather boring and a bit pious, but he did not tell Roland what he really thought. Instead he got round it by a sleight of hand. He wrote that instead of discussing Maoism like everyone else, Kristeva talked about women. However, one evening he and Barthes were discussing China and Kristeva's book with Taïeb Baccouche when Barthes declared: 'Mao has liberated women.' Baccouche disagreed, saying that Mao had achieved no more than Bourguiba, who had managed to introduce contraception and give women equal divorce rights in an Islamic country. Did Barthes take this as an implicit criticism of Kristeva's book? Whatever the case, he suddenly got extremely angry. He stood up, purple with rage, and exploded: 'What, so little Tunisia is a worthy example for great China!'

Such militancy on his part regarding China seems somewhat surprising, given that he had not spoken out in 1973 when Pinochet had taken power in Chile, or during the Lip factory movement in Besançon, which had mobilized the whole of the French left. In fact, it is obvious that what he was defending was not China so much as Kristeva's book on China, a book in which she discusses the subject with an enthusiasm Barthes had scarcely shown and certainly never felt. An obvious parallel here is Gide's trip to the Soviet Union. Gide probably went for much the same reasons as Barthes, swept along on a wave of enthusiasm by friends who had stronger convictions, acquiescing at first, then later withdrawing. On his return, Gide reassessed his visit critically in *Retour d'URSS*. But Barthes felt no need to compensate for an 'acquiescence' which did not commit him in any way.

It was the early 1970s, a period of prosperity for Barthes, and he seemed content. He was recognized, respected and sought-after, and even if he still complained about the 'pains-in-the-neck' who pestered him and prevented him from getting on with his work, he was acutely aware of this perception that other people had of him. He organized his working day (which, as has been seen, was highly structured) in such a way as to be free from about seven in the evening onwards. This was an inviolable principle, a way of making the transition between work, the puritan tradition, and friendship. Jean-Louis Bouttes remembers the systematic way he organized his life during this period: 'Throughout the day there were meetings, arranged so that as the day wore on and evening approached, meetings about work would gradually give way to eroticism or intellectual intimacy.' For their part, Sollers and Kristeva confirm that after the three of them had had dinner together, which was a frequent occurrence, Roland would usually leave them around eleven to go in search of other pleasures. He went out every evening, with different friends, and before leaving he always made sure that he had the Havana ciger he liked to smoke after dinner. Hervé Landry remembers these cigars and also another of Barthes's habits: he never carried his cheque book on him, just the single cheque he needed to pay his share of the bill. This seems like a wise precaution given how he would normally end his evenings – and in whose company. Since being robbed on the beach at Biarritz, he had grown more circumspect.

At last, however, he was able to enjoy all the comforts that came with having money, and to do things that would have been unthinkable fifteen years before, when he had constantly had to struggle to make ends meet – even if he still complained about his low salary and the poor revenues from his books and articles: 'Mine is a qualitative, not a quantative success,' he would say. Nevertheless, he could now permit himself the luxury of turning down a particular well-paid commission if he so wished, for instance the article *Paris-Match* asked him to write on Brigitte Bardot.

Moreover, he could afford to eat out in a restaurant every evening, leaving generous tips in a rather ostentatious manner, like a Russian prince. As the evening wore on, its tone would change, one network of friends replacing another, even if their focal point remained the same. Some of those of his friends who were 'in the know' left, preferring not to risk seeing him looking ridiculous as he chatted someone up, while others stayed, and still others arrived later. Then, at the end of the meal, freed from the day's various constraints, a quite different Barthes would make his appearance. Over the coffee, his language would become almost crude, in singular contrast to his normal, reserved way of speaking. Once, taking advantage of this atmosphere, Hervé Landry asked him a rather strange question: 'If

Julia Kristeva implied that she wanted more from you than friendship, would you make an exception to your usual sexual preferences?' Barthes laughed and replied that he probably would: 'She's the only person I'm really in love with, the only woman who could make me change my sexuality.'

Kristeva, on being informed about this incident, did not simply dismiss it: 'I don't know if things could have gone further, but think he really did love me, and it was mutual.' She adds that he was probably referring to the deep affection they felt for one another, as well as their closeness on an intellectual level. According to her, in his relationships with younger people he often found intellectual compatibility a big problem: 'Even towards the end of his life, when the fact that someone found him physically attractive gave him great pleasure, he felt that a relationship based on this kind of attraction was inferior to one which was based on a deeper form of communication and involved intellectual understanding.'

Often, Landry would talk to him about the Situationists, the group of students from Strasbourg with whom he was involved. But Barthes hated these residues of May '68. On another occasion, Landry asked him if he wanted to try some acid or LSD. Barthes jokingly got out of it by remarking: 'That would be like putting someone who hasn't passed their driving test at the wheel of a racing car.' Both these examples involve a glaring misconception of what Barthes was like. A whole generation of young people regarded him as the cutting edge of a certain form of social subversion. This generation, who read *Tel Quel* and Castanedas, but who also listened to the Rolling Stones or the Beatles and took drugs, imagined his life to be like theirs in all respects. In fact, he led a life of exemplary prudence. The only non-conformist thing about him was the form in which he got his sexual pleasure.

Images of these evenings remain in the memories of Barthes's friends. The cigar and the single cheque have already been mentioned. Then there was his habit of choosing other people's food for them. In affectionate and humorous fashion, Jean-Paul Enthoven ad libs a Perec-style poem on the subject: 'he happened from time to time – although he hated Cocteau – to order my dishes like him.'[23]

It is time to return to 1973, when Barthes published *Le Plaisir du texte (The Pleasure of the Text)*[24] – or his 'mini Kama Sutra', as Bertrand Poirot-Delpech referred to it in *Le Monde*. This book, or at least the idea of it, had been around for some time. In 1972, in reply to a question about *Empire of Signs* he mentioned the title of a future book 'which will deal with the problem of the pleasure of the text'.[25] *Problem* is the right word, since his austere education and upbringing had for years been pitted against his voracious approach to life, his gourmet's desire to savour each moment to the full. Nevertheless, such questionings about pleasure and desire were also signs of the times. In 1972, Gilles Deleuze and Félix Guattari had published *L'Anti-Œdipe* ('Anti-Oedipus'), a sort of manifesto for a 'philosophy of desire', and *The Pleasure of the Text* dealt with similar sorts of issues.

In a sense, the book can be seen as the pinnacle of Barthes's production, the end point of a trajectory which can be divided into three distinct phases (even though this kind of exercise is, by its nature, oversimplifying and artificial). He had begun by thinking about textual production in *Writing Degree Zero*, and this had led at the beginning of the 1960s to the distinction between *écrivain* and *écrivant*. Then in *Sade/Fourier/Loyola* he had studied the different modes of reception and evaluation of a text, and had proposed a distinction between a writerly (*scriptible*) text, which the reader can rewrite, or desires to rewrite, and a readerly (*lisible*) text, which can only be read. Finally, in *The Pleasure of the Text*, he turned his back on theory, in one sense, and looked at the relationship between pleasure, ecstasy (*jouissance*) and desire. At the same time, he maintained a constantly ambiguous conception of the relationship between the text and the body. In his own view, he shifted from textuality to morality, and from a phase of being influenced by Kristeva or Derrida to a phase influenced by the work of Nietzsche.

In *Roland Barthes*, under the heading 'Phases', he draws up the table given opposite. Below this table he remarks: 'as one nail drives out another, so they say, a perversion drives out a neurosis: political and moral obsession is followed by a minor scientific delirium, which in its turn sets off a perverse pleasure (with its undercurrent of fetishism).'[26]

There is a three-stage stratification at work here (Barthes distinguishes four stages, but in terms of the relation to the text there is no need to distinguish between the first two). Each stage has a positive term, and this Barthesian triology (*écrivain*, writerly, pleasure) represents the successive criteria he used to evaluate texts.

In 1975, *Roland Barthes by Roland Barthes* appeared, a 'Roland Barthes to the power of two' as it were, a jokey allusion that was immediately picked up and continued by Maurice Nadeau, who asked Barthes to review the book himself in *La Quinzaine littéraire* and called the review 'Barthes to the power of three'. Barthes loved this kind of task – commissions, exercises in style, the challenge of

Intertext	Genre	Works
(Gide)	(desire to write)	—
Sartre		*Writing Degree Zero*
Marx	Social mythology	'Writings on the theatre'
Brecht		*Mythologies*
Saussure	Semiology	*Elements of Semiology*
		The Fashion System
Sollers		*S/Z*
Kristeva	Textuality	*Sade/Fourier/Loyola*
Derrida		*Empire of Signs*
Lacan		
(Nietzsche)	Morality	*The Pleasure of the Text*
		Roland Barthes by Roland Barthes

producing ten pages of intelligent, incisive text on a subject set by someone else. Just like François Villon, at Blois, who entered Duke Charles's competition and wrote a ballad on the set theme of water: 'I am dying of thirst beside the fountain.'[27] In his review, Barthes wrote: 'I imagine if one asked Barthes for a review of his own book, he would have to decline . . . How could he agree to give a meaning to a book which in its entirety is a rejection of meaning, which seems written expressly to reject meaning?' The heavily ironic tone of the piece is thus established from the outset, and Barthes thoroughly enjoys playing the critic. He concludes that, in comparison to *The Pleasure of the Text*, the *Roland Barthes* is outmoded, a regression. It is a disappointing book because the author, constrained by the rules of the genre to narrate his life, 'has only been able to say one thing: that he is the only person who is unable to speak *truthfully* about himself'.

In *Le Monde* of 14 February, two full pages of the paper were devoted to Barthes's book: On the left was a piece on the book by Jacques Bersani in which he asked:

What stage is Barthes at in 1975? Contrary to the claims some would like to make for him, he has moved beyond Gide or Valéry. Neither is he in the Lacan or Derrida camp, as his avant-garde friends think, nor even with Nietzsche, as he himself seems to be suggesting. Barthes is with Barthes.

On the right-hand page, under a general heading 'Barthes by others',

Alain Robbe-Grillet, Philippe Sollers, Claude Roy, Michel Butor and Pierre Barberis gave their 'judgements' of the man and his work. What a media hit!

Three days later, on 17 February, Jacques Chancel interviewed him for the French radio station France-Inter. In his opening introduction, Chancel conveyed an impression of Barthes as someone difficult to define, someone who could only be described by a network of converging characteristics: 'You are a sociologist, a writer, a teacher, a critic, a semiologue, but it should also be immediately added that in all these roles you have been concerned with the same kinds of issues.'[28] As a whole, the interview developed into a sort of balance sheet, first and foremost of his relationship with writing, from *Writing Degree Zero* or *Mythologies* to *The Pleasure of the Text*:

> Writing can take on different disguises, different values. At times one writes because of a belief that by doing so one is participating in a struggle. This was the case at the beginning of my career as a writer . . . Then, gradually, the truth emerges, a more naked truth, if I can call it that: one writes because, at heart, one enjoys it, because it gives one pleasure. Ultimately, the motivation behind writing is one of pleasure [*jouissance*].

Does this mean that Barthes no longer feels he is taking part in a struggle? Quoting the singer Georges Brassens's remark that one should die for one's ideas, but slowly, Chancel tries to steer him towards this subject, but Barthes evades the question. He argues in favour of Marx and Freud because they 'brought about a kind of rupture in Western language', and of intellectuals in general, saying he feels solidarity with them, especially when they are attacked. He explains that even if French is a single language, it is divided into different and conflicting discourses. He mentions his preference for fragmentary forms of writing, like Pascal's *Pensées*, the writings of Nietzsche and the Japanese haiku.

Chancel then asks why the photographs on the opening pages of *Roland Barthes* only go as far as his adolescence. Barthes replies: 'Once I started to write, my body was no longer present in images or in photographs but in my writing.' He then quotes Mallarmé's comment that one should not present a writer as 'Mr X' because he does not really exist, except in his writing. In fact, throughout this hour-long interview, writing is really the only thing he talks about, apart from mentioning a few memories from his childhood and his illness. He defines writing as 'an aimless pleasure, and therefore a perversion'. He also discusses reading. At the end of the interview, Chancel returns to the subject of politics. Barthes says that he is 'a very bad political subject', and admits that he feels a great resistance to political discourses. The only kind he would be able to relate to, the kind he would like to see replace the political discourses that currently exist, would be a form of analysis. Doubtless he is thinking of a discourse which would foreground the whole question of meaning, but then hadn't he already done this himself in his *Mythologies*?

In the concluding minutes of the interview, replying to a question about his books, he says that his own favourites are the *Michelet* and *Empire of Signs*. This may have come as something of a surprise to those intellectuals who saw him as a leading light of semiology. Why Japan? 'Because for me it's a space that's both extremely sensual and extremely aesthetic, an extraordinary lesson in elegant sensuality.' He adds that in the book he is referring to Japan as a space and not a country, in the sense of its economic and political structure. Here, in a nutshell, is the real balance sheet or state of play: at the beginning of 1975, Roland Barthes quite openly acknowledges his hedonism.

Roland Barthes was written during the summer of 1974, when he was staying at the house of Daniel Cordier, an art dealer who had worked with Jean Moulin during the war, at Juan-les-Pins. During his stay Barthes had met Casimir Estène, the owner of a large hotel who spent his summers on the Côte d'Azur and his winters in Paris. About six months later, at the beginning of the winter of 1975, Estène held a dinner party in his Paris flat. The guests included several intellectuals and a young student of law and history called Romaric Sulger-Büel. He was seated opposite Barthes, the star guest of the party. Barthes was bombarded with questions, much to his dislike, since he hated being the centre of attention in a large group. Romaric, perhaps because he was feeling shy, behaved towards the distinguished guest in a very different, slightly facetious manner.

The two men ended up spending most of the evening laughing together, although some people around the table found Romaric rather iconoclastic. After dinner, they carried on talking and decided to walk from Estène's flat in the Rue Vaneau to Barthes's flat in the Rue Servandoni, in spite of the cold weather. This meeting was the start of a great friendship between the two, who began to see a great deal of one another. Romaric Sulger-Büel was soon admitted to the 'inner circle' of Barthes's friends. Also, somewhat by chance, he became the owner of the largest collection of Barthes's drawings and the person who knew most about his graphic works. Barthes would often make presents to his friends of his drawings and paintings, interspersing the images with texts, a short sentence or a brief improvised poem.

Around this time a young student from Caen, Jean-Loup Rivière, was instrumental in reviving one of Barthes's great interests from the past: the theatre. Rivière asked Barthes to supervise a thesis on Antonin Artaud, but almost immediately Barthes persuaded him to work on the aesthetics of theatre instead. He joined Barthes's seminar, something which made him feel both proud and anxious. He was afraid of not coming up to scratch, since outside Paris the seminar was regarded as one of the summits of intellectual achievement. On top of this, Barthes did not fit the usual picture of a supervisor at all. One of the first things he did was to explain to what degree a 'thesis' was in fact a 'fantasy'. Jean-Loup Rivière had come in search of a 'scholar' but discovered instead a master in intellectual morality. A remark Barthes made in the first session of the seminar he attended made a particularly strong impression on him. Barthes was talking about censure, and he distinguished two kinds, 'negative censure', which prohibited, and 'positive censure', which obliged. He did this in order to show that neither kind was used in his seminar and that, in particular, no one was obliged to speak unless they wanted to. Rivière saw this as proof of Barthes's great generosity.

On another occasion, Rivière gave a paper on the importance of the 'corpus' in research. Despite its extreme technicality, his talk hinged on a fairly obvious metaphor: the 'corpus' as both the body of research and the body (*le corps*) itself. After he had spoken, it was Barthes's turn, as usual. He emphasized that the use of the metaphor was perfectly legitimate, but then added, quite brutally: 'However, you have spoken about everything, about other people's bodies, but not about your own.' It is this art of giving his students a jolt that Rivière believes was characteristic of the 'Zen master' side of Barthes. He never commented on or 'corrected' his students' work directly; he always influenced them through his incisive yet subtle hints about interpretation.

Above all, Rivière sometimes took Barthes with him to the theatre. He could not believe that anyone who had once been so passionately interested in the genre could turn their back on it altogether. He remembers how often the former editor of *Théâtre populaire* would leave the theatre in a bad mood, even feeling angry. The same Barthes who had put all his energies into defending the TNP or Brecht now found live theatre uninteresting and was bored by it.

The summer holidays arrived, and Barthes retreated to Urt to work. At the end of the summer he was planning to go to Tunisia with Jean-Louis Bouttes. He got in contact with Philippe Rebeyrol, who at the time was French ambassador in Tunis, and explained that he wanted to have a week's proper rest before the winter. He fancied spending five or six days at the luxurious Sahara Palace hotel in Nefta, in the south of Tunisia, a place he had been told was peaceful and beautiful. This meant he could stop off in Tunis on his way and see Rebeyrol. The trip went ahead as planned, and Barthes travelled to Nefta via Carthage and Tunis. He did a bit of writing, and he spent hours talking to Bouttes and the group of young Tunisians who gathered around them. His behaviour was a mixture of epicurism and attentiveness to others, to people he would probably never see again, but to whom, for the time being, as always, he attached the greatest importance. His short stay in Nefta was a happy one, a brief respite which allowed him to forget, or at least pretend to, that back in Paris his mother was unwell.

10

The Collège de France

Over the past few months, the atmosphere of euphoria which normally characterized the seminar seemed to have vanished. The students were unanimous in their opinion that Barthes's mother's illness was behind the change. From 1974 to 1976 he lectured on 'The lover's discourse', and the subject of the seminar was 'Bouvard and Pécuchet' and then the following year 'The intimidations of language'. During the same period he also made the necessary overtures to be put forward as a candidate for the Collège de France. Despite what has been implied in some quarters, it seems that the initiative for his election came from Barthes himself, and not from Michel Foucault, with whom he had been on bad terms for over ten years. Barthes went to see Foucault, who had been elected to the Collège seven years previously, and the latter agreed to support his candidature. Didier Eribon heard the following description of their meeting from Pierre Nora:

> Pierre Nora remembers that Foucault said to him one day: 'I'm really put out, I have to see Barthes. He wants to put himself forward for election to the Collège de France. I haven't seen him for ages, will you come with me?' The meeting between them went fine, and Pierre Nora left them alone after the first ten minutes.[1]

Foucault presented a report on the candidate, one passage of which might seem rather ambiguous:

> His appeal might seem to be limited to the trendy, as they say. But any historian would accept that fashions, enthusiams, fads, or even exaggera-

tions can, at a given moment, reveal the existence of more deep-rooted and fertile cultural phenomena. These voices, these few voices heard today outside the universities, do they not form part of contemporary history? And should we not welcome them among us?

Foucault's peers followed his lead, and on 14 March 1976 the assembly of the professors elected Barthes to the Collège de France, and informed the Secretary of State responsible for universities of their decision. Finally the day was approaching when Barthes could claim victory over the numerous obstacles, his illness, the sanatorium, academic institutions, which had prevented him from fulfilling his childhood vocation of going to the École Normale, passing the agrégation and becoming a fully fledged academic. He could not have known that this victory also marked what was to be the final phase of his life.

Ever since its establishment by François I in 1530, the powerful 'college of three languages', as it was then known (the three languages being Greek, Latin and Hebrew), had been an institutional counterbalance to the power of the Sorbonne. Indeed, François had created it for Guillaume Budé precisely for this reason. It was not incorporated into the national education system until 1852. Members were elected in the same way as to the Académie Française, after a campaign which paved the way for their election. Thus it was Michel Foucault, who was already a member, who put Barthes forward for a chair in 'literary semiology', specially created for the occasion. His election in 1976 was not simply a revenge on academe, but also a kind of reinstatement. For the first time he believed he had been forgiven for not having passed the agrégation – even if he was only elected with a majority of one. Finally he had been recognized by the academic system, even if only just. Since he himself did not have a Ph.D., he had been unable to supervise doctoral theses. His only qualification was a literature degree. He had always been in a marginal position in relation to academic institutions, and as a result had suffered a great deal. Previously his books had been his main qualifications, but now he held a chair, and at one of the highest academic institutions in France. His life and his own view of it were completely transformed.

The lecture

For the time being, while he was waiting for the usual procedures to be completed, he carried on teaching at the École Pratique des

Hautes Études. Life seemed to follow its usual course; work, music, friends. One spring evening, while he and Romaric Sulger-Büel were having dinner at the Closerie des Lilas, he ran into Patrice Chéreau, who was staging a production of Wagner's ring cycle with Pierre Boulez. Chéreau came over to their table to say hello and Barthes, who did not like Wagner but liked Chéreau and Boulez, asked him how to get hold of tickets for Bayreuth. Chéreau said they were in great demand, but that he would try to see what he could do. A few weeks later he dropped by the Rue Servandoni and left some tickets in Barthes's letterbox. So in August Barthes and Sulger-Büel made their Wagnerian pilgrimage, for which they had prepared themselves with great seriousness by reading the scores and studying the text in German. Without being a real fan of Wagner's music, Barthes knew it had influenced the music of Gabriel Fauré and Emmanuel Chabrier, two composers he did like and he spent the whole train journey to Bayreuth talking about the subject with skill and conviction. Romaric Sulger-Büel also remembers that as soon as they arrived in the small Bavarian village, Barthes went to an art shop in search of pens and paints. In his hotel room he reconstructed part of his working space in Paris and would spent the mornings painting while Romaric explored the region.

The day of his official entrance to the Collège de France was fast approaching. In the autumn the future professor dined with Maurice Nadeau at the home of some mutual friends. Nadeau proposed to Barthes that he should let him publish the text of his inaugural lecture and Barthes jumped at the suggestion: of course, what a good idea! It was Nadeau who had helped him to get his career started in *Combat* so it was only fitting that he should publish the text which represented its culmination. Later, when the lecture was published by Seuil, Nadeau somewhat resentfully reminded Barthes of his promise. Barthes retorted that Nadeau must have misunderstood: he would never have contemplated publication with any other publisher. In fact, it was more likely that it was Seuil, and François Wahl in particular, who had prevented Barthes from publishing with Nadeau.

He was in the process of finishing *A Lover's Discourse* and was unsure what order to give these fragments, how to organize them into chapters. He and Romaric would amuse themselves by choosing fragments at random and ordering the headings in all kinds of different ways, as Barthes used to do with his index cards on Michelet. He also made a sketch for the cover of the book, using one of his drawings. However, just as he found ordering his chapters by a process of random selection unsatisfactory, he finally decided to use a detail from a painting of the Verrocchio school, 'Tobias and the Angel' on the cover, rather than one of his drawings.

There had also been a change in his domestic arrangements. In October 1976, Roland and Henriette had moved from their fifth-floor flat into one they had rented on the second floor. Their building did not have a lift and Henriette was no longer able to climb five flights of stairs. Michel, who had got married three years before, would stay in their fifth-floor flat with his wife Rachel and it was hoped these changes would make Henriette's old age more comfortable.

The year of 1976 ended on a strange, rather discordant note. On Thursday, 9 December, Lucie and Edgar Faure hosted a lunch party at the Hôtel de Lassay. On the menu was caviar, a 'chic' starter, followed by a more 'popular' main course of stew. The guests were the President of the Republic Valéry Giscard d'Estaing and his wife, Gisèle Halimi, Claire Brétécher, Jean-Louis Bory, Emmanuel Leroy-Ladurie, Dominique Desanti, Philippe Sollers, and Roland Barthes. It was a strange mix of people, and the reasons behind this guest list were known only to the Faures. Sollers remembers that Barthes, over coffee, summoning up his Marxist culture, asked Giscard if he was in favour of the decline of the state. 'Why not?' the President replied. Edgar Faure declared his support for the death penalty and Giscard declared himself against it, even though he was to do nothing during his period in office to abolish it (Michel Foucault had also been on the guest list, but had declined the invitation precisely because Giscard d'Estaing had refused to commute Christian Ranucci's death sentence). The President also revealed something of his animosity to Jacques Chirac, implying that he wanted to distance himself from the Republican party, and that he himself was a real liberal. Sollers remarked 'I'm on the left or a liberal, but I'm certainly not a socialist or a fascist.' Barthes complimented the cartoonist Claire Brétécher on her work, telling her she was the best sociologist of contemporary life. In return, she later paid him an implicit compliment by showing him a drawing of a lonely, loveless girl sitting crying as she reads *A Lover's Discourse*. And so the social chit-chat continued.

A few days later Jean-Luc Pidoux Payot, at the time the managing director of the Payot publishing house, bumped into Dominique Desanti. 'So, how was the soup?' he quipped. Desanti, furious, turned her back on him and walked off. Nevertheless, Pidoux-Payot's gibe is representative of how many people felt: what were they doing getting mixed up with that bunch? In an interview with Bernard-Henri Lévy in *Le Nouvel Observateur* in January 1977, Barthes was asked the same question. At first he gave an almost technical reply: 'I went out of curiosity, a taste for hearing things, a bit like a myth-hunter on the prowl. And a myth-hunter, as you know, must hunt everywhere.'[2] When Lévy reminded him of the left's unfavourable reaction to the lunch party, he went on: 'There are, even on the left, people who substitute facile indignation for difficult analysis: it was shocking, incorrect, it's just not done to chat with the enemy, to eat with him. One must remain pure. It's all part of the left's *good manners.*'[3] What were they doing getting mixed up with that bunch? For his part, Sollers explains today that *'Tel Quel*'s brand of left politics and its Maoism have never been anti-democratic,' and that in his view Giscard wanted to find a foothold on the left and that they had to go and see what it was all about, not just refuse to meet him on principle.

On 7 January 1977, Barthes gave his inaugural lecture at the Collège de France. The hall was jam-packed for the occasion: François Châtelet, Gilles Deleuze, Lucie Faure, Algirdas Greimas, Alain Robbe-Grillet, Philippe Sollers, Edgar Morin, Bernard Dort, Jean-Marie Benoist even Louis Leprince-Ringuet were all among those present. The only person missing, as *Le Monde* pointed out, was Jacques Lacan. Apart from those privileged enough to have received an invitation and get a seat, there were others standing, sitting on the floor and spilling out into the corridor. Suddenly the noise died down and Roland came from the back of the hall and walked towards the platform, Henriette on his arm as if a marriage was about to take place. Henriette took her seat in the front row while her son took his place behind the microphone on the platform. As was his habit, he read from a written text: 'Monsieur the Administrator, dear colleagues, I would like to thank you for welcoming me among your ranks. I should probably begin with a consideration of the reasons which have led the Collège de France to receive a fellow of such dubious credentials.' He then went on to thank all those who for so many years had believed in him, and gave a brief sketch of his career:

Philippe Rebeyrol, who appointed me to the post of lecteur at the French Institute in Bucharest after a long period of illness; Julien Greimas, who gave me my initiation into linguistics while we were both teaching at Alexandria University, where we translated Jakobson's then little-known article on metaphor and metonymy; Lucien Fevre and Georges Fried-

mann, who enabled me to acquire a training in research methods at the
CNRS; and Fernand Braudel and my colleagues at the École des Hautes
Études, who over the past fifteen years have given me the greatest
opportunity a man can have: the opportunity to combine a profession and
a passion.

Among this list, there are no teachers, no mentors to thank (apart
from Greimas, more a friend than a teacher), only people who have
helped him. Of course the unconventional and uneven nature of his
career is partly responsible for this, but only partly. Having reached
the summit of academic achievement, the new professor at the
Collége de France did not profess any intellectual debt to academic
institutions. The only teacher he had ever acknowledged was the
Hellenic scholar Paul Mazon, whose name was inexplicably absent
from Barthes's list. Strangely enough, the whole of this introduction
was cut from the published text of the lecture, as if such public and
affectionate displays of gratitude did not deserve publication, as if a
distinction had to be made between the spoken and the written
word, with the written precluding unsuitably direct displays of
emotion.

Barthes went on to express how delighted he was to be entering an
institution which was 'outside the bounds of power',[4] having
reminded his audience that although his had been an academic career
he was nevertheless 'without the usual qualifications for entrance
into that career'.[5] It was half-way through the lecture that he made
the much-quoted remark that has become so famous: 'But language
. . . is never reactionary nor progressive; it is quite simply fascist; for
fascism does not prevent speech, it compels speech.'[6] An example
illustrating this claim that language forces one to speak was the use
of 'tu' or 'vous' in French, indicating one's relation to the person
being addressed: thus 'social or affective suspension is denied me.'[7]

Even if it was the expression 'language is fascist' which was to be
remembered – either as a source of ridicule or of sadness that such
an intelligent man could come out with such a meaningless phrase –
the lecture in fact went on to offer a long exposition of the principles
of semiology: after all, this was the subject in which he had been
given a chair. Barthes's definition of the subject was far from
technical:

There has come a time when, as though stricken with a gradually
increasing deafness, I hear nothing but a single sound, that of language
and discourse mixed. And linguistics now seems to me to be working on

an enormous imposture, on an object that it makes improperly clean and pure by wiping its fingers on the sheen of discourse like Trimalchio on his slaves' hair. Semiology would consequently be that labour which collects the impurity of language, the waste of linguistics, the immediate corruption of the message: nothing less than the fears, the appearances, the intimidations, the advances, the blandishments, the protests, the excuses, the aggressions, the various kinds of music out of which active language is made.[8]

Fears, appearances, intimidations, advances, blandishments, protests, etc. His audience had just had what they could not know was a foretaste of the book he had just completed and would publish three months later with the title *A Lover's Discourse*. He then came to the end of his speech on a note which also echoed his current line of thinking: 'There comes another age at which we teach what we do not know; this age is called *research*. Now perhaps comes the age of another experience: that of *unlearning*.'[9] And, with his taste for etymology, he concluded that this experience can be summed up in a single word, '*Sapientia*: no power, a little knowledge, a little wisdom, and as much flavour as possible.'[10]

However, as a whole his speech left some people dissatisfied. As the audience were leaving the hall, and as Alain Robbe-Grillet was expressing his admiration for what Barthes had said, a woman journalist from *Les Nouvelles littéraires* challenged him angrily: 'But what did he say? In fact, he didn't say anything at all!' Robbe-Grillet laughed it off, but this incident can be seen as something of a sign of the times: Barthes annoyed a section of his audience.

Yet, despite this, there was a very special atmosphere in the hall that day. Representatives from all his different 'families' were present and several people had tears in their eyes as they listened to his speech, keenly aware that they were witnessing an extraordinary event. This emotional response from his friends, sharing his joy quite spontaneously and unconditionally, is ample proof of Barthes's generous spirit and warm heart. His election to the Collège de France obviously represented promotion for Barthes, and a vindication of him by an academic system which previously had spurned him. It was also the beginning of a new life or *vita nuova*, as he put it, quoting Michelet. However, despite this, he was to find it increasingly difficult to put up with the crowds which flocked to his lectures. His new-found fashionability became ever more difficult to live with, and he missed the more intimate atmosphere of the seminar, of small groups where a different sort of communication and interaction were possible.

Thoughts on photography

Around this time, Barthes did a series of radio interviews for France-Culture with Bernard-Henri Lévy and Jean-Marie Benoist.[11] In these interviews, Barthes stood back and took stock of several things. Firstly, of the avant-garde which, according to him, had for the past fifteen years been involved in 'dismembering language', in the footsteps of Joyce and Lautréamont, and deconstructing syntax. He thought that perhaps the avant-garde might now evolve more discreet and subtler forms: 'I think we may see a return to what I would call a writing of the imaginary.' Secondly, he took stock of reading, claiming somewhat provocatively that the best way to read a book was not to read it all the way through but to skip parts of it, 'lifting fragments, samples of writing out of it'. He also admitted once again that there were few authors whose works he himself had read all the way through, with the exception of Michelet.

In the second interview he again discussed literature, but from the writer's perspective this time, not the reader's. He launched into a defence of the necessity for the writer to be involved with worldly and commercial matters, since for him being a writer was not a kind of honour sufficient unto itself but a 'profession', which meant that he or she necessarily depended on the support of other people and was part of an economy. Since a writer wrote in order to sell books, he or she also had to sell themselves, which meant taking part in television or radio programmes and giving interviews. Such a justification seems somewhat strange coming from someone who was continually complaining about how boring such activities were, and how much time and energy they took up. Then, referring to his own writing, he once again mentioned his preference for concise, fragmentary forms: in poetry, the nineteen-syllable classical Japanese form of the haiku and in music the short pieces of Anton Webern or Schumann's *intermezzi*.

In retrospect, however, it is the third interview on the subject of 'the pleasure of the image' which is most revealing. Speaking about his interest in photography, Barthes explained that for a long time it had been one of his dreams to 'take a look' at the subject, and then went on to outline the ideas which were subsequently to appear in *Camera Lucida*. In his view, art photography was of no greater theoretical interest than documentary photography, and what was really fascinating about a photograph was that it said, 'this has existed'. In other words its interest lay, quite simply, in the fact that it immortalized a significant moment or person: 'In the final analysis, what I really find fascinating about photographs, and they do fascinate me, is something that probably has to do with death. Perhaps it's an interest that is tinged with necrophilia, to be honest, a fascination with what has died but is represented as wanting to be alive.'

Such a fascination would hardly have been news to his friends, who had often heard him talk about his interest in the Turin Shroud, which could still be believed at the time to bear the imprint of Christ's face. But it was the first time he had spoken in public about it, and he concluded by giving a definition of the image as 'that which excludes me'. *Camera Lucida*, his last book, will be discussed in due course, but it is evident that the themes Barthes deals with in the book were already present here – except that the event which was to precipitate its writing had not yet taken place.

In the spring of 1977, Barthes published a book based on his lecture series on 'A Lover's discourse'. The book is a kind of structural portrait of the lover 'who speaks and says'.[12] It consists of a series of fragments arranged according to the aleatory order of the alphabet. Barthes both stages and dramatizes the lover's discourse through a series of 'figures' which give each of the fragments its title and beneath which there is a kind of definition or 'signboard à la Brecht', as he calls it. Thus one piece of discourse follows another, all 'impure' fragments of language like those he had referred to in his inaugural lecture. They are rooted, as the headings show, in the lover's day-to-day experience: absence, anxiety, declaration, drama, jealousy, letter, crying, encounter, remembrance, suicide. First of all, there is the name of the figure ('Waiting') then below it the 'signboard à la Brecht', rather like a slightly unusual dictionary definition:

Waiting Tumult of anxiety produced by waiting for the loved being, subject to trivial delays, rendezvous, letters, telephone calls, returns.[13]

Then come the fragments of the waiting lover's discourse:

The setting represents the interior of a café; we have a rendezvous, I am waiting. In the prologue the sole actor of the play (and with reason), I discern and indicate the other's delay; this delay is as yet only a mathematical, computable, entity (I look at my watch several times); the prologue ends with a brain storm: I decide to 'take it badly', I release the anxiety of waiting. Act I now begins; it is occupied by suppositions: Was there a misunderstanding as to the time, the place? I try to recall the moment when the rendezvous was made, the details which were supplied. What is to be done (anxiety of behaviour)? Try another café? Telephone? But if the other comes during these absences? Not seeing me, the other might leave, etc. Act II is the act of anger; I address violent reproaches to the absent one . . .'[14]

The reader can react in different ways to these fragments. In the preface, Barthes says he hopes the reader will exclaim: 'That's true, I recognize that language scene,'[15] their intuition in this area of experience confirming the truth of his figure in the same way that linguists use people's linguistic 'intuition' or 'sense' to validate a form or expression. On the other hand, the reader may choose to look at them more analytically, treating them as fragments of a synopsis, extracts from a script, complete with stage directions and notes on shots and dialogue. Finally, in keeping with this interpretation, the reader may see them as a writer's sketches for characters. Already, on the inside cover of the *Roland Barthes*, a handwritten sentence had warned: 'It must all be considered as if spoken by a character in a novel.' This prefatory remark partly explains why the narrative voice constantly shifts between 'I' and 'He'. Barthes was both referring to himself in the first person and talking in the third person, that is, from a distance, about a certain character, an *R.B.* In *A Lover's Discourse* he employs a similar technique. In fact, he seems to be slipping, almost unwittingly, towards writing a novel himself. He is literally taking notes for a novel he will never write, notes which are also a transcription of his own discourse of love, and which become a book which is not itself a novel.

A Lover's Discourse brought Barthes unexpected fame. It was the first of his books to sell in big numbers, and it brought him large sums in royalties. On 22 April 1977 he appeared on television on the literary discussion programme 'Apostrophes'. Along with Barthes, the presenter Bernard Pivot's other guests were Françoise Sagan and A. Golon. The subject of the discussion was 'love talk' and Barthes proved to be quite a hit, both with the viewers and with the other guests: Françoise Sagan in particular seemed fascinated by what he had to say. On the following Monday bookshops in both the capital and the provinces flooded Barthes's publishers Seuil with orders for the book. It sold faster than any of his previous publications, and in much greater numbers. Seuil was caught on the hop by the demand, in all likelihood because they had been overcautious: the first print run had been only 15,000 copies, and was quickly exhausted. In the space of a single year, there were seven more print runs, a total of 79,000 volumes. Nor did the book's popularity decline. In 1979, there was another reprint, then two more in 1980 and further reprints in 1981, 1983, 1985 and 1987, until in 1989 the sixteenth edition of the book was published, bringing the total number of copies to 177,000. With this book Barthes had, for the first time in his life, a publication which was almost in the 'bestseller' league. And, with a few exceptions, aren't most bestsellers novels?

For the time being, he had no plans for other books, which perhaps explains why he agreed to Jean-Loup Rivière's suggestion that he be allowed to put together a collection of Barthes's articles on the theatre and publish them in a single volume. Rivière, who was in the middle of finishing his thesis on the aesthetics of theatre, had already set up a new journal on the theatre called *L'Autre scène*, and his idea was to publish a book series with the same name. Barthes's collected writings on the theatre would be the first volume in the series. He had intended to publish with a small firm, L'Albatros, but Seuil would not agree to any work by Barthes being published elsewhere, so he was offered a contract for the book. What became of it will be seen in due course.

A French-fried

A few months later, from 22 to 29 June, a week-long conference was held in the international cultural centre at Cerisy-la-Salle with Barthes as its 'pretext'. It was organized by Antoine Compagnon and brought together around fifty 'Barthesians'. Their papers and discussions were later published,[16] and together they constitute an extremely valuable document on what would retrospectively be called 'the final Barthes'. In fact, Barthes found himself confronted by numerous different Barthes which his friends, students and disciples reflected back at him like images from so many distorting mirrors. Patrick Mauriès implicitly compared the teacher's power to that of the analyst, and the seminar to the psychoanalytic cure. Barthes himself said that if there was an analysis taking place, then it was the teacher who was the analysand, since it was he who spoke in front of an audience which constituted a collective analyst. But he let the discussion continue. Jacques-Alain Miller began to recount his memories of Barthes's first year of teaching at the Hautes Études in 1962 . . .

It soon became apparent that there was a gulf at the conference between his Parisian followers, those who had attended the seminar and were familiar with his latest ideas, and his followers from abroad. The latter group were rather confused by a language they did not always understand and which made them feel excluded. On the one side, there was the almost familial intimacy of the Parisian circle, and on the other, the distant American cousins. Barthes was aware of this divide and tried to do his best to soften its effects: 'It would appear that there was a danger that some people would feel excluded from, or alien to, the proceedings, or unable to communicate.'[17] He also compared, not without a touch of humour, the social image he had become to the fate of a potato being turned into a French-fried:

> In the skillet the oil spreads, smooth, flat, matte (barely any smoke): a kind of *materia prima*. Drop a slice of potato into it: it is like a morsel tossed to wild beasts only half-asleep, waiting. They all fling themselves upon it , attack it noisily: a voracious banquet. The slice of potato is surrounded – not destroyed, but hardened, caramelized, made crisp; it becomes an object: a French-fried potato.[18]

He attributes this transformation to a 'dandiacal . . . Parisianism', but the use of this metaphor can also be interpreted as his way of distancing himself from those students who were closest to him and who had appropriated him, transforming him into their object, their property. Later, in his closing remarks to the conference, he returned to the subject of the foreign participants: 'You may perhaps, on occasion, have felt isolated, even excluded or perhaps even disappointed by these proceedings and the language in which they have been conducted.'[19] He went on to explain that the conference was allusive, that it revealed how the discourse of modernity was itself changing. What he did not say was that this allusiveness had revealed itself even in the form some of the papers had taken, which must have come as quite a surprise to the 'foreigners'. In fact, with *Roland Barthes* and *A Lover's Discourse*, Barthes's writing had entered a new phase. He was now writing without any of his former theoretical props, without recourse to any grand theory like Marxism, psychoanalysis or semiological theory. Some of the speeches – usually those of his closest disciples – were written in a 'fragmentary' style that imitated this new departure.

The conference brought together many of the disparate groups or networks of friends which Barthes had previously kept separate, with the result that they had never interfered with one another.

There was the group from Morocco, the Robbe-Grillet 'network', the André Téchiné 'network', the current worshippers from the seminar, and former seminar students who had gone their separate ways but were now reunited for the occasion. The atmosphere between these various subgroups was charged, almost as if there were electric currents passing between them – and with the occasional short-circuit. For while it was obvious that there was a Barthesian 'tribe', it was divided into different clans whose members were either completely unaware of one another's existence, or who watched one another, or who were jealous of one another. Now, suddenly, they had all been thrown together. As for Barthes, who already felt embarrassed by the influence he had, and who had a recurring dream in which he was an imposter pretending to be a bishop, he was somewhat disconcerted by this 'High Mass' in which different sects worshipped their own, widely divergent images of him.

At no time were these differences more evident than when the speakers gave their own affectionate and ironic views of this 'French-fried'. When Barthes voiced his dislike for the adjectives that had been applied to him, and said that he refused to be pinned down in such a way, Jacques-Alain Miller pointed out that throughout the conference he had in fact managed to wriggle out of any adjectives applied to him and make his getaway. Miller therefore proposed his own definition: 'This shows, then, that in your own way you're a slippery customer.' Of course, everyone burst out laughing, but some of the laughter was through clenched teeth. There was even more discomfort when, in a felicitous speech, Alain Robbe-Grillet said that Barthes was a man of the past who pretended to be interested in modernity, and that the conference was so hushed that when he arrived he thought he had forgotten to take out his ear plugs.

Another theme running just below the surface at the conference was the relationship between Barthes's writing and fiction. In his response to a paper given by Frédéric Berthet ('Ideas on the novel'), the conference's 'pretext', the 'French-fried' or the 'slippery customer' implied that his writing was fictional in the sense of being 'the desire for a novel, its postulation'. But the previous day Robbe-Grillet had asserted that as far as he was concerned, Roland Barthes was *the* modern novelist because, 'unlike the Balzacian novel, which fits together nicely around a solid kernel of truth and meaning, the modern novel . . . is a text which is purely fragmentary and these fragments, into the bargain, always describe the same thing, which is almost nothing.'[20] Someone in the audience, taking this as a reference to *A Lover's Discourse*, suggested that perhaps Barthes had just published his first novel. 'Nonsense,' replied Robbe-Grillet, 'he's just published his fifth or sixth.'

The first death

All in all, R.B. must have left the conference feeling reassured, as if such reassurances were needed, that his disciples cared about and respected him. But he had other more worrying things to think about. André Téchiné remembers being struck by the way in which Barthes, as he was leaving Cerisy to return to Paris, where he would be reunited with his mother after his week's absence, bought himself a buttonhole, as if he were smartening himself up to go and meet a lover. The summer of 1977 was to be the most painful time of his life. Henriette, who was nearly eighty-four and who had been ill for a long time, was not getting any better. For part of that summer, while he was in Urt, Barthes kept a diary:

> Depression, fear, anxiety: I see the death of a loved one, I panic. (13 July)

> Mother feeling better today. She is sitting in the garden wearing a big straw hat. As soon as she feels a little better, she is drawn by the house, filled with the desire to participate; she puts things away, turns off the furnace during the day (which I never do). (16 July)

> Mother's birthday. All I can offer her is a rosebud from the garden; at least it's the only one, and the first since we've been here. (18 July)[21]

Nevertheless, he carried on working. He was writing an article for the communist daily paper *L'Humanité* called 'La lumière du Sud-Ouest' ('The light of the south-west'), which was finished on 17 July but not published until 10 September. In the autumn he returned to Paris and on 25 October 1977 the day he had been both dreading and expecting arrived: Henriette died in their flat on the Rue Servandoni. The following day, her death was registered at the municipal offices of the sixth arrondisement by a certain 'Dominique Lane, twenty years old'. The name Dominique is ambiguous, since it can be either masculine or feminine, even if from the death certificate it appears masculine. But the person whose name appears on the death certificate is merely an employee of the funeral parlour. Henriette's birth had been registered by her father; her death was registered by an undertaker. Michel and Roland decided to give their mother a discreet burial in Urt. The service was conducted by a Protestant minister, since she had been born a Protestant and remained one all her life. They chose a simple headstone and a grave in a quiet corner of the graveyard. The minister unwittingly upset Roland when he apologized on behalf of the Protestant community for the bigotry she had encountered during her life. He expressed his regret that some people should have seen fit to ostracize her because of a certain event in her life – an obvious allusion to Michel Salzedo's birth.

After the funeral, the two brothers returned to Paris. Barthes began to inform his friends of his mother's death. The first person he phoned was Robert David, and then he informed his friends who were living abroad. Singevin, who was working in Naples, received a letter which said, 'I wouldn't want you to hear about Mother's death from anyone else.' Greimas, who was in the United States, wrote to him from New York: 'Roland, what's going to become of you?' To him it was obvious that Barthes would be lost without Henriette. 'I have never seen a finer love,' he comments today. According to Edgar Morin, Henriette's beauty and kindness were the reasons, 'the almost miraculous reasons, if any are needed, for her son's attachment to his mother'. All his friends had sensed for a long time that Henriette's death would be a catastrophe, that she played an essential, irreplaceable part in his life. As he was to write in *Camera Lucida*: 'For what I have lost is not a figure (the Mother), but a being; and not a being but a *quality* (a soul): not the indispensable but the irreplaceable.'[22]

What, then, was this extraordinary bond that existed between them? Julia Kristeva recalls a scene which occurred frequently, and which casts a strange light on their relationship. She would often drop by the Rue Servandoni to leave books, manuscripts or a thesis while Barthes was out. Madame Barthes would always greet her by saying, 'Ah, mademoiselle, he's not here, he's gone to Vincennes and he's going to come back to me with his shoes all muddy and his trousers too. He's gone to Vincennes again.' According to Kristeva, Henriette always regarded him as her little boy. She did not realize that not only was he a grown man but an important one. For his part, Roland had for many years believed he was responsible for his mother, and perhaps he too, saw her as a little girl, his little girl. So, did they both equally treat the other like a child?

Alone in their second-floor flat, Barthes gave in to his grief, brooding over photographs of Henriette. This long meditation was to result in his final book, *Camera Lucida*. However, to the outside world, he appeared even more active, more vital than ever – and more frivolous. André Téchiné offered him the role of William Thackeray in his film of the Brontë sisters, *Les Soeurs Brontë*, also starring Isabelle Adjani as Emily, Isabelle Huppert as Anne and Marie-France Pisier as Charlotte. The film came out in 1978, and Barthes only appeared in two scenes. One is a street scene in which he speaks his lines rather self-consciously. The other is set at the opera, and he has practically nothing to say in it. His screen debut was hardly a revelation. Of course, he had never really been interested in the cinema. In an interview for France-Culture, he remarked that he did not find the cinema upsetting – it merely bored him. However, he immediately qualified his statement by adding, 'not all cinema, of course; there are some film-makers whose work I love; mine's a resistance which allows for exceptions.' He said that the cinema made him feel stubborn: 'I find it difficult to make myself go and see films and I find it difficult to talk about them.'[23] He explained that the mobility of a film exhausted him, that he preferred 'interruptions, fragmentary forms, litotic and elliptical representations, brevity, the momentary flash, the sudden spark'.

According to Téchiné, Barthes 'didn't like movement unless it was highly codified and controlled, as in Brechtian theatre or in Kabuki'. In short, he preferred photographs, because they are brief, like flashes of lightning. Neverthelesss, he did not hesitate for long before accepting the part in Téchiné's film. He did not even ask to see the script before accepting. He went to Leeds, in Yorkshire, to act his minor role, probably because he wanted to help his friend Téchiné, and also because he knew several of the actors and felt comfortable with them. Marie-France Pisier was a neighbour of his in Paris, and he also knew Isabelle Adjani and Isabelle Huppert. Then there was Jean-Louis Bouttes, who also had a minor role playing a publisher.

There were a few problems with the actual shooting of the film, particularly since Roland was unable to memorize the few lines that he had. He asked if he could have them written up on a board, but this was impossible since the street scene (in which the town hall in the background was to be transformed into the opera house) involved a long tracking shot, and the camera had to be mounted on a rail. Because he kept forgetting his lines, the scene had to be shot many times, and in the end required fifteen takes. Barthes was sorry about this, since he realized how expensive it was and knew he was keeping the technicians waiting and that the night was wearing on. But Téchiné wanted this particular scene to be recorded live, unlike the rest of the film, where the actors were asked to dub their own voices. This was an unusual aesthetic decision, designed to give their voices a slightly muffled, almost sing-song quality, like an old newsreel. On the other hand, Barthes's tone of voice and his slow delivery – slow because he kept on forgetting his lines – was exactly what Téchiné wanted for Thackeray.

Finally, the shooting was finished, but Barthes's workload did not ease. In March he took part in a session at IRCAM[24] with Michel Foucault and Gilles Deleuze. Then, wanting a break from Paris, he went to Tunisia for a week's holiday, and stayed with Philippe Rebeyrol in the ambassador's residence in La Marsa, just outside Tunis. The two spent hours every evening talking. During one of these conversations Rebeyrol asked Barthes why he had never openly admitted his homosexuality, especially since Gide was such a frequent point of reference for him – the world had changed and many things that had formerly been taboos were now socially acceptable. Barthes replied that: 'I have always made it a matter of principle never to deliberately conceal it, but also never to publicize it.' Tunis and La Marsa were linked by a much-used train, the TGM (Tunis-La Goulette-La Marsa). Rebeyrol remembers that Barthes would never use the ambassador's car but always preferred to take this train so that he might have the chance of picking someone up.

Of course, this was not his first trip to Tunisia, and even if he preferred Morocco, he was quite happy to be staying in the ambassador's beautiful villa once again. He was also happy to have the chance to talk over old times with his friend, whom he had known for over fifty years, and to make plans for the future. He said he planned to come back and visit Rebeyrol and his wife as soon as he could. Rebeyrol reminded him that in a few months time his posting would change, so Roland would have to make it soon. Barthes promised he would, but he could not have known as he left Tunis that it was for the very last time.

11

———

An Unqualifiable Life,
a Life without Quality

———

It was the autumn of 1978, and Barthes was at the height of his fame. He was much in demand: he was asked to give interviews, write prefaces, do lectures and radio programmes and invited to dinner parties. He was so successful that Burnier and Rambaut even produced a quite witty parody of his writing: *Le Roland Barthes sans peine* ('Roland Barthes without tears'). He appeared in the book alongside parodies of other celebrities such as François Mitterrand and André Breton, in a piece called 'Zero level'. As was only fitting, it consisted of a series of fragments with titles such as 'The angular flight of flies', 'Butter and jam' and 'Silent speech'. Barthes himself, however, was far from impressed, despite his friends' assurances that being parodied was the very stuff of stardom. He regarded it as an attack on him, like the pamphlet Picard had published years before. He moaned about it to anyone who would listen, complaining that he was being attacked and that they had something against him. 'Moaning' was in fact one of his principal 'biographemes', and the subject of his complaints was usually his body, his headaches. Antoine Compagnon, for one, remembers him thus:

Meeting Barthes after work, I would ask how he was. He would always start moaning that he had a headache, that he felt sick, that he had a cold or a sore throat. Then one day the complaints stopped. I was really delighted that he was feeling better, and I told him as much. But it wasn't that he was feeling better. If he no longer moaned it was because on one occasion I had told him he was always moaning. So he started up his little number again, what he called his 'moan'. It was always the first thing he talked about whenever he met you.[1]

After going on about his body and the physical pain he was in, Barthes would get on to the subject of the image people had of him, or the image they tried to give of him. He regarded the *Roland Barthes sans peine* as an act of spite, even though it was more like a schoolboy prank than anything. He got into a huff over it, he moaned on and on.

Another newspaper column

One of the people Barthes complained to about it at the time was Jean Daniel, editor of *Le Nouvel Observateur*. Daniel says that it was then he discovered that 'even people at the height of stardom can feel vulnerable, feel themselves undermined.' During a discussion which lasted for several hours, Barthes put himself through a kind of self-interrogation. Was this caricature of his style really, in fact, the way most secondary school pupils or university students understood and used his methods? Had his interpretations been over-exaggerated? Basically, hadn't Picard been right in his criticisms of Barthes's approach to Racine? Then, in the midst of his confusion, came an attack from another quarter: René Pommier published a book called *Assez décodé!*('An end to decoding!'). It was a light-weight book, written in an unnecessarily aggressive, hectoring, bad-tempered tone:

> How one longs to write a 'Roland Barthes/Fed up to the back teeth', which would be the first volume in a new series on 'pretentious prigs of our time'. For when it comes to the art of dazzling cretins with a clever mix of jargon and claptrap, Roland Barthes is the undisputed master. Nothing is more indicative of the current crisis of critical thought than the fact that someone with such a muddled mind is regarded by many as the very embodiment of clarity; that someone with such clouded thoughts is seen as one of the leading intellectual lights of our times; and that the avant-garde has chosen for its leader someone whose ideas are so hard to pin down.[2]

Why did Barthes inspire such hatred? Was Pommier, who dedicated his book to the memory of Raymond Picard, completely mistaken? Or did there lie behind such questions, as Jean Daniel suspects, a desire for a return to classicism? He was not surprised when Barthes told him that he needed a platform from which to defend himself against these unjust caricatures of his work, that he needed a bastion. Years ago he had written a column in *France-Observateur*; why shouldn't he take up the idea again and begin writing a new series of 'mythologies', this time in *Le Nouvel Observateur*? Of course, Daniel took him up on it immediately, and Barthes began to write a weekly column in an attempt – abortive, as it turned out – to revive the style of his 1950s *Mythologies*. His column ran from 18 December 1978 to 26 March 1979, and this episode is an interesting one, because most people thought he had agreed to write the articles at the magazine's request. Did he really think he was under attack? Did he really need to defend himself? Or was he just trying to kill time by taking on demanding tasks?

Norbert Bensaïd, who was in charge of the magazine's coverage of medical issues, quotes the opinion of a psychoanalyst friend on the subject. Every evening, Barthes had always talked over the day's events with his mother. Once she was no longer there, he needed to replace her by keeping a diary or a notebook. Jean-Paul Enthoven has another explanation. According to him, Barthes wanted to 'take up arms again' for three different reasons. Firstly, because Sollers was urging him to keep a high media profile; secondly, because he found the idea of being obliged to produce short pieces which could eventually be turned into a book appealing; and thirdly because he wanted to set himself a challenge. However, it was 1978, and more than twenty years had passed since the appearance of the first *Mythologies*. The condition of the intellectual was very different from what it had been. In the mid-fifties things had seemed quite straightforward: the function of the intellectual was to denounce consumer society and its appearances and to lay bare its shams. The thinker could therefore have the final word, and a project like Barthes's *Mythologies* had made sense. But in the late 1970s, the situation was not so clearcut: there no longer seemed to be any viable options on the left and the 'critical' intellectual – if such a person still existed – lived in a society whose principles he or she accepted.

Indeed, Barthes used to say to his friends that there were two ways for an intellectual to criticize society. Firstly, it could be criticized in the name of the Third World or of a utopian future. Alternatively, there was criticism in the name of a tradition – the reactionary kind of criticism practised by the likes of Joseph de Maistre. Between these two alternatives there was nothing else, and he was interested in trying to develop a new kind of discourse and new angles of attack.

Under the generic heading 'The Roland Barthes column', he began writing his articles for *Le Nouvel Observateur*. For a period of fifteen weeks he wrote his fragments on subjects such as Nureyev, Sollers, a dinner in town, the first record release of a young singer. In each weekly column he would tackle three or four themes, but he was unable to find the right 'tone'. As a result, everyone felt disappointed: the readers, his fellow journalists on the magazine and Barthes himself. However, one significant incident did take place during this period. One evening, Enthoven took him to the printers to see them 'putting the paper to bed', as they say in the trade. The typesetter was right in the middle of arranging the page layout of one of Barthes's articles. 'You put the photo here, the title here and the text there,' he commented. In fact the term he used for 'the text' was 'le gris' (the grey) and immediately Barthes was fascinated by the term. He talked of nothing else all evening, in all likelihood wondering how he could use it as a metaphor in the future.

All in all, Barthes was continually on the go, seemingly everywhere at once, on the radio, on television, in the papers. In May 1978, he had published an article on Le Palace nightclub in *Vogue Homme*, and he also gave an interview to *Playboy*. The interview was published in 1980 when he was already in hospital. Moreover, he was often to be seen at Le Palace, 'putting himself about,' as Greimas says, living his life to the full without inhibition. He had met the club's owner, Fabrice Emer, through François-Marie Banier, and Youssef Baccouche. From now on, he went there almost every evening, enjoying the comfortable surroundings and amusing himself by watching people, half playing the voyeur. For instance, he was probably amused at drinking champagne with the Shah of Iran's family at the very moment Khomeini's followers were seizing power in Iran.

Yet he may have felt rather embarrassed by this double life he was leading, and he was careful to keep his professional life and his nights on the town distinctly separate. If it had been respect for his mother which had prevented him from being open about his homosexuality, then things should have changed after her death. It should have enabled him to admit publicly that he was gay, as Michel Foucault suggested he did. In fact, he did nothing of the sort, which begs the question of whether his mother had simply been a kind of alibi – an alibi that had just been blown. Free as he now was to be open about his homosexuality, he seemed to feel no need to

change his behaviour. On the contrary, he even seemed to find his
new-found freedom frightening, as can be seen particularly clearly in
the case of his domestic arrangements. Some of his friends believed
he would now begin to live with someone, but in fact he carried on
as he had before his mother died. He merely increased the amount of
time he set aside each night for his pleasures, and more often than
not he came home alone.

In November he went to New York for eight days at the invitation
of Philippe Roger. He gave a lecture with a title that can hardly be
called humble, 'Proust and I', the same lecture he had given at the
Collège de France under a different title, 'Longtemps je me suis
couché de bonne heure' ('For a long time I used to go to bed early'),
the opening line of Proust's *Remembrance of Things Past*. On 12
November, he celebrated his sixty-third birthday at the White Horse
in Greenwich Village, whose claim to fame was that it had been
Dylan Thomas's favourite bar. The group of friends who took him
there included some of his former students from the seminar, and
they all wanted to mark the occasion and give him an enjoyable
time. Barthes felt happy and relaxed, surrounded by friends. He
launched into an improvised speech in which he tried to guess the
hopes and plans of those present, wishing them well and making
predictions about the future, all of which was done with his usual
kindness.

With friends, he discussed plans for new books on Schumann and
Chateaubriand. Was it at this point that, looking back over the
books he had written, he began to have doubts about them?
According to Alain Robbe-Grillet, 'in the last stages of his life,
Roland Barthes ... seemed obsessed with the idea that he was
merely an imposter: that he had spoken of everything from Marxism
to linguistics, without really knowing anything.' Robbe-Grillet
reassured him in a far from ambiguous fashion: of course he was an
imposter, because he was a real *écrivain*. As Robbe-Grillet saw it, the
only ambiguity in his friend's position was that people wanted to see
him purely as a thinker and refused to see him as a creator. Later, he
would remark that Barthes was a 'fluid thinker':

> for, slippery as an eel . . . his shifts are not simply the result of chance, nor
> do they come from a weakness in judgement or character flaw. Messages
> that change, branch off, veer in other directions – this is what he teaches.
> So it follows that our last 'real' thinker will be the one who preceded him:
> Jean-Paul Sartre.[3]

On 21 November 1978, a few days after his birthday party in

New York, a party was held at the Maison d'Amérique Latine to celebrate the twenty-fifth anniversary of Barthes's collaboration with Seuil, their 'golden wedding anniversary' as he put it. Those present included old friends and acquaintances such as Paul Flamand, one of the founders of the publishers, who had retired in 1976, Jean Daniel, François Wahl, who was in charge of the human sciences list, and also Philippe Sollers, Jean-Louis Bouttes and Bernard-Henri Lévy, who was wearing his usual open shirt, his 'look', as it came to be called. The whole of intellectual Paris was present, and Barthes seemed happy, feeling loved as he moved from group to group, embracing Sollers, chatting with Jean Daniel, as usual making sure everyone was enjoying themselves.

A few months later he did what Sollers had been pestering him to do. He revised and expanded some earlier articles and turned them into a book, *Sollers, écrivain* (*Sollers, Writer*). This public defence of a writer and a man who was at the time under attack left some of his friends wondering. The person at the centre of it all, Sollers, says today that the publication of the book got caught up in a complex power struggle that was taking part between different factions at Seuil: 'The reason *Tel Quel* was tolerated by Seuil – and I stress tolerated, since when was the last time you saw a publishers create at least two new reviews, *Change* and *Poétique*, in order to get rid of a third? – was because it was supported by some of Seuil's star authors, in particular Barthes and Lacan.' Was the publication a strategic move on Barthes's part? It is more likely to have been a gesture of friendship, but even so it was still a slightly sly move on his part: after all, the use of the word *écrivain* might be taken as an indication that he preferred Sollers's 'fictional' writings, a way of distancing himself from Sollers's theoretical writings.

Olivier Burgelin, after receiving the book from Barthes, wrote to him to tell him that although *Tel Quel* did not mean much to him, he had enjoyed the book a great deal. This had led him to the conclusion that it was a fictional work about the avant-garde along the lines of Flaubert's *Madame Bovary*. Barthes replied, 'Well, yes, it's a work of fiction, but don't forget that as far as I'm concerned, every discourse is fictional, even the most serious discourse!' Today Burgelin comments that 'by appearing to agree with me he prevented me from altering his way of thinking, and in a way that seems to me extremely skilful and stylish.' Violette Morin, for her part, thinks that Barthes could only write about someone if they were being criticized, and says that he often told her, 'I can only discuss someone properly if they are being attacked.' She adds that she sometimes suggested that he should write an article on Queneau or Edgar Morin, but he had always replied, 'but no one's attacking them!' Of course, this could have been an ethical principle of his, but it was also part of his project to always side with the avant-garde against his old enemy, common sense.

Whatever the case, work had once again become the centre of his life. His articles in *Le Nouvel Observateur*, which definitely failed to recapture the tone of his 1950s *Mythologies*, were an accumulation of impressions gleaned from his daily experience. In March he wrote about a dinner party at which he had felt bored, and once again drew a comparison between boredom and hysteria: 'I gradually fell silent: it was impossible to get a grip on anything: I was bored of seeming bored. Which shows that boredom is really a form of hysteria.'[4] Nevertheless, according to Edgar Morin he was expert at concealing his boredom. He would nod his agreement with the most inane remarks made by his fellow guests, smiling and murmuring periodically 'yes, yes'.

Camera Lucida

A fortnight after his account of the dinner party, on 26 March 1979, he announced that he was going to give up his newspaper column, or rather that he was taking a break from it. Was he bored? Did he have too much on his plate? In fact, he was paving the way for a new project, a book he had been wanting to get on with for several months. He reduced his workload, tired of always having to interrupt his writing in order to write a lecture or a preface, or to supervise a thesis. From the outside, it appeared as if his mother's death was now a distant, forgotten event. But he thought about it constantly, and it was at the heart of his new project. He told Philippe Rebeyrol in March that this new project was absolutely essential to him. He had also promised to write a short piece on photography for *Les Cahiers du cinéma*, for their new series. However, the text he planned to write was too deeply bound up with images of his mother, and for months these images had stirred up dormant feelings of grief which had prevented him from beginning work on the text. Now that he had freed himself from his numerous obligations, including his lectures at the Collège de France, he was ready to get down to work.

He wrote the whole of *La Chambre Claire* (*Camera Lucida*) at one go, or almost, during the period between 15 April and 3 June 1979.

The subtitle of the book was 'note sur la photographie', and its declared aim was to keep his mother's memory alive for as long as his own fame lasted. In it, he writes poignantly about absence: 'My mother. It is always maintained that I should suffer more because I have spent my whole life with her; but my suffering proceeds from *who she was*; and it is because she was who she was that I lived with her.'[5] Later he writes:

> It is said that mourning, by its gradual labour, slowly erases pain; I could not, I cannot believe this; because for me Time eliminates the emotion of loss (I do not weep), that is all. For the rest, everything has remained motionless. For what I have lost is not a figure (the Mother), but a being; and not a being, but a *quality* (a soul): not the indispensable, but the irreplaceable. I could live without the Mother (we all do, sooner or later); but what life remained would be absolutely and entirely *unqualifiable* (without quality).[6]

There is nothing more to add to this muted and harrowing expression of grief. On the other hand, it is interesting to analyse how the book came about, since it helps destroy the myth that Barthes thought it up as a way of commemorating his mother, an idea he himself put in circulation. In fact he was asked to write a book on the seventh art by *Les Cahiers du cinéma*. 'I've got nothing to say about film,' he told friends, 'but photography, on the other hand . . .' Thus the origins of the book are doubly anecdotal. Firstly there was the request by *Les Cahiers du cinéma*, and secondly his grief over the death of his mother, the only woman he had ever loved. However, as has been seen, he was already outlining the ideas which would eventually appear in the book in February 1977 – that is, several months prior to her death – in an interview with Bernard-Henri Lévy and Jean-Marie Benoist. So it may be that he could only realize his desire to write about photography after he had experienced the death of a loved one and been through a genuinely distressing bereavement. His mother's death did not create the need to write the book, but it provided him with an opportunity to produce a book he had already felt a need to write.

Over half of the book, the first part, is devoted to photographs of public events. In this section, Barthes elaborates his distinction between the *studium*, by which he means a kind of 'general enthusiastic commitment' to a large number of photographs for political or cultural reasons, and the *punctum*, which is the way a particular photograph 'pricks' you, the way it seeks you out, pierces you, wounds you. This distinction was already familiar to those who had heard the radio interview which was broadcast in February 1977, even if it had not been formulated in these precise terms. He then proceeds to examine private photographs, those of his mother, and the tone of the book tips in a completely different direction. But even if this second half represents the *affective* or emotional centre of his project, it is in *effect* the application to a particular case of the general theory he has outlined in the first hundred pages of the book.

The book was written in under two months, but this speed does not seem so surprising if we assume that he had worked out his ideas long before Henriette's death. All he had to do was ask himself a few secondary questions such as whether he should publish the 'winter garden photograph', which showed his mother at the age of five with her seven-year-old brother. He told Michel Bouvard: 'I think the text must replace it, be a substitute for it.' Later Martin Melkonian, in his book *Le Corps couché de Roland Barthes*, comments on this absence: 'at the heart of the book there is thus a blind spot . . . To say everything and yet to conceal it, to conceal everything while saying it, this is what the characters in a bourgeois drama do, when they enjoy remaining aloof.'[7] To an outside observer, the photograph is a cliché, a commonplace, but for Barthes it is 'like the last music Schumann wrote before collapsing, that first *Gesang der frühe* which accords with both my mother's being and my grief at her death.'[8]

In fact, his treatment of photography resembles his treatment of painting. He regards it as having a linguistic basis, an image which 'pricks' the person looking at it. He remains faithful to his old position, the idea that behind a sign there is always a language. This is why he reversed Ferdinand de Saussure's claim that linguistics forms part of a more general science of semiology. If he chooses not to reproduce the winter garden photograph but to replace it with words, it is because he believes – with a rather casual rejection of theory – that what matters in a photograph is what it shows, its content, and not how it shows it, how it is framed, its formal composition. Naturally, this means that the art of the photographer becomes irrelevant: all he or she does is produce images, just as all a writer does is tell stories.

And now a novel?

In his novel *Women*, in which Lacan and Althusser appear thinly disguised as the characters Fals and Lutz, Philippe Sollers also describes Barthes (under the pseudonym Werth) as he was in the last stages of his life. Or perhaps *his* version of the final Barthes:

> I can still see Werth at the end of his life, just before his accident . . . His mother had died two years before . . . The great love of his life, the only one . . . He let himself drift more and more into complications with boys; that was his penchant and it suddenly grew more marked . . . He thought of nothing else, although he dreamed all the time about breaking off, abstinence, beginning a new life, the books he ought to write, a fresh start . . .[9]

One might find this passage disagreeable, but it has to be admitted that in tone it is very similar to Barthes's own observations. After the publication in *Tel Quel* of 'Délibération', where he discusses the possibility of keeping a diary and includes the notes he made during the summer of 1977, Barthes did begin to keep a diary of his evening activities (what he referred to as his reward for a day's work).[10] This journal reveals a new Barthes, one without inhibitions or reserve. Naturally enough, he writes about missing his mother and recounts how, returning home one evening, he had instinctively gone up to the fifth floor, where their old flat was, 'as if it were the old days and mother were waiting up for me'.

But mainly the diary contains descriptions of his nights on the town and of his bedtime reading. Jean-Louis Bouttes, who saw a great deal of him during this period, and with whom he would spend hours talking, believes that these notes were part of an outline for a novel. Barthes used to jot down notes about characters he had met on index cards. He also used to sketch verbal portraits of these characters for his friends. These portraits of real-life 'characters' were succinct, humourous, ironic in tone and often tinged with malice. For instance, on numerous occasions he told them about the woman with long brown hair and tons of jewellery who had sat down at his table in the Café Flore and tried to start up a conversation. Antoine Compagnon is even more convinced that Barthes was planning to write a novel: 'It had got to the notes stage. He had a whole mass of index cards, there were a hellish amount. He'd tried several times to put them into some kind of order, but hadn't managed to. They remained without any definite shape.'[11]

So he had been making notes and wondering how to sort them out, torn between the idea of two different kinds of text. Either he could attempt to write a 'great novel', along the lines of Tolstoy, or he could retreat strategically and write a novel about the process of writing a novel. He was so carried away by this project that he even contemplated reorganizing his life, moving to Urt in order to write, and making only occasional trips to Paris to see friends and give his lectures at the Collège de France. It was also at this time that he discussed making a film biography of Marcel Proust with André Téchiné. Both the novel and the film were, for the first time in his life, projects he had not thought up because someone had asked him to. At the end of his lecture on Proust at the Collège de France, he had wondered out loud: 'Does this mean I am going to write a novel? How should I know? I don't know if it will be possible still to call a "novel" the work I desire and which I expect to break with the uniformly intellectual nature of my previous writings.'[12]

Of course, fate was to decide otherwise, but it still remains possible to ask just how plausible these projects were. In his reading of fictional texts, he had always concentrated on functions and not on characters. Was he in fact the prisoner of his own theory, condemned to being unable to produce a novel, or rather to only being able to write one in the autobiographical mode? Or was he aiming with this new project to transform his life, to start again from scratch, as if it was a way of removing a section of his life which had ended unhappily?

Part of the material for his new book, his diary, was later published thanks to François Wahl. This text, *Incidents*, is surprising on two counts. First and foremost, because he claims that for bedtime reading he much prefers Pascal's *Pensées* or Chateaubriand's *Les Mémoires d'outre-tombe* to the more recent publications he is sent to review. Of the latter he comments: 'but they're like little homework exercises and once I've paid my debt (by instalments), I put them down with a sigh of relief and get back to *Les Memoires d'outre-tombe*, the real book.' He finds these modern works 'nice' or 'well written', but he confesses that all he has to say about them is 'yes, that's all very well.' This worries him, and he asks himself: 'What if the Moderns were mistaken? What if they didn't have any talent?'

This passage hardly comes as a surprise to those who were closest to him. According to Jean-Paul Enthoven:

He was like those fifteenth-century Spanish Jews whom the Spanish referred to pejoratively as *marranos*, which means 'pigs' and comes from an arabic term meaning 'something forbidden by religion'. Forced by Queen Isabella either to renounce their faith or leave the country, they converted to Catholicism. Outwardly, they displayed great piety but they secretly maintained their own religious practices, handing their faith down from generation to generation.

So Barthes was a modern-day 'marrano' who had converted to the twentieth century, to modernism, to *Tel Quel*, but who secretly hankered after Saint-Simon or Chateaubriand. Enthoven goes even further, claiming that:

> He did not want to miss out on any opportunity of being modern, of being in the swing of things. It was inconceivable to him that a young writer's career could take off without his seal of approval, his complicity. This was probably symptomatic of a profound contempt, an indifference to other human beings, a deep loneliness.

Contradictions? In fact, in his strategy of being an important person in the world, paying compliments did not cost him anything. If he continually complained about being asked to write prefaces and letters of recommendation, then it was he himself who had chosen this role. His behaviour was an ambiguous mix of great kindness and also, perhaps, general disdain, which he converted into blessings.

The second reason *Incidents* is surprising is because in this text Barthes describes in straightforward, simple terms how he used to pick up boys. His descriptions are also extremely poignant, and contain a faint echo of Sollers's description of him in *Women*.

> It became patently obvious to me that I had to give up boys, both because they no longer desired me and because I was too scrupulous or too clumsy to impose my own desire upon them. I saw this as an unavoidable fact, proved by all my attempts at flirting, that it makes my life unhappy and that, finally, I am bored and that I need this hope or this interest in my life. (If I take my friends one by one – apart from those who are no longer young – each relationship has been a failure: A., R., J.-L. P., Saül T., Michel D., R. L., too brief, B.M. and B.H., no desire, etc.). The only thing left to me will be gigolos.[13]

He recounts how he meets these gigolos or 'gigs' as he sometimes refers to them, in the Rue Bernard-Palissy, in the Café Flore, or in a bath-house, where he meets 'Arabs'. He also relates how, one evening, after taking a herbal tea in a café near the place du Châtelet, he walks back along the Rue Saint-André-des-Arts or the Boulevard Saint-Michel just to get a glimpse of 'boys' faces' before going to bed. His accounts of these evenings out may seem of little interest, and perhaps that is true, except if one remembers the discretion he had previously shown in such matters. Then they appear truly remarkable, and it is difficult to believe that he really intended to publish this journal. Romaric Sulger-Büel for one believes that Barthes had no intention of doing so, particularly not in this form.

Nevertheless, François Wahl seems convinced he did intend to publish, even if he knew the reaction to such a publication would be spiteful and ungenerous. However, he explains, Barthes was not someone 'who would have shrunk from making a statement if he thought it justified, that is, if he thought it justified itself as a piece of writing: which is why these pages are also exemplary in an ethical sense'.[14] The overwhelming impression one gets from these 'Parisian evenings' is of his deep sadness, a desolation which this time does not stem from the absence of his mother but from the negative balance sheet of a love life that is going nowhere. There is an all-pervasive sense of failure and regret in this text. Is it really necessary to mention that this diary was written shortly after he had finished *Camera Lucida*? It seems as if Barthes had no other writing project in mind, and that he was feeling directionless, bored with his semi-holiday. He says as much in the last entry to the diary: 'From now on (22 September 1979) no more fruitless evenings on the town; (1) so as not to waste time and get lecture preparation over with as quickly as possible; (2) so as to go over my notes – and write everything on cards from now on.' Is this a reference to his novel? Or to a literary form halfway between the production of the *écrivain* and that of the *écrivant*?

Does the opposition between *écrivant* and *écrivain*, which had been theorized when he was a contributor to *Arguments* and put into practice in the two phases of his writing exemplified by *The Fashion System* on the one hand and *A Lover's Discourse* on the other, represent an irreducible antagonism? On 26 May 1977, in the midst of the polemic over the 'New Philosophy', which had been exacerbated by the publication of Bernard-Henri Lévy's book *Barbarism with a Human Face*, in which he stated his radical rejection of Marxism, Barthes had published a 'Letter to Bernard-Henri Lévy' in *Les Nouvelles littéraires*. This letter is worth mentioning on several counts. Firstly, because in it Barthes managed by his usual method of turning ideas on their head to introduce into what had been an extremely confused debate a dimension which had previously been overlooked. It was a debate in which 'New Philosophy' was accused both of being 'media philosophy', and of representing a shift to the right. Barthes wrote: 'You have added to some important ideas – which will definitely be seen to fall within the field of politics – that rare thing, the grain of a writing.' Secondly, because, as the rest of the text of his letter shows, this was no mere hasty formal act of acquiescence on Barthes's part, an act of politeness designed to let him off the hook, so that he is not forced to take sides in what was a bitter polemic. It was a genuine reflection on the reemergence of language as a form of passionate engagement:

> I would therefore suggest that today writing is an act of militancy . . . and in no sense a decorative activity . . . It seems to me that by staging a certain historical pessimism, especially as regards the relations between power and language, you have engendered a genuine writing – writing in all the stylistic plenitude of the term.

As Barthes rightly asserts, as it were in passing, the importance of Lévy's work would be located in the 'political' content of his ideas, rather than in the 'stylistic plenitude' of his writing, and mistakenly, since the latter is the sign of an *écrivain* not an *écrivant*, and because this book 'of positions, of arguments' bears the mark of 'the written, not the merely transcribed'.

Barthes's analysis is remarkably accurate. For even if, with hindsight, it seems astonishing that Levy's text provoked such a violent reaction (such 'political backbiting', as it were) given that its ideological thrust is located on a quite different level, then the claim of 'New Philosophy' to be 'philosophical' seems to be equally in doubt. On the contrary – and again Barthes was one of the few people to recognize this – Lévy's text in fact heralded a quite different kind of watershed: the return of literature, of 'style' to the human sciences. It was precisely in that same year, 1977, that Barthes published *A Lover's Discourse*, which was heralded as a sign that he was branching into fiction. The conclusion to his 'Letter to Bernard-Henri Lévy' went as follows: 'I have thought it . . . only fair to point out to you how much I think this book hangs upon and is itself articulated around the *ethics of writing* with which it is *currently concerned*.' This ethical dimension, which is produced by reintroducing literature into analytical thinking, could well be the alternative to the opposition between *écrivain* and *écrivant* which Barthes had been looking for, an opposition whose relevance is belied by the path his own writing took.

The 'pains-in-the-neck'

Once again, work had become the centre of his life. There were the usual obstacles and interruptions; the phone calls, the requests, the visitors of all kinds who continually pestered him – the 'pains-in-the-neck' as he referred to them. Words like 'pains-in-the-neck', 'prattle', 'hot air', came up constantly in his conversations with friends. Jean-Paul Enthoven supplies the following identikit picture of the average 'pain-in-the-neck': 'First of all he would be got up disgracefully. He would be neither handsome nor attractive nor charming, nor a charmer, just highly intelligent, a teacher for instance.' In *Women*, Sollers gives the following description of Barthes's predicament:

> Werth was at the end of his tether ... Everything bored, wearied and disgusted him more and more ... The demands of some people, the entreaties of others ... The atmosphere of unremitting malice in which amateur prostitution is shrouded ... The stupid dependency of boys always wanting to be helped, mothered, pushed, have strings pulled for them ... What a price to pay for a few pleasant moments (if that) ... The phone calls to make, letters to write, favours to ask, quarrels to settle ... The advice, the endless making allowances, the responsibility, the tips disguised as something else ... By dint of all this resignation, Werth had become a kind of saint in spite of himself, though he remained very reserved, with sudden bursts of rage.[15]

Thus Barthes complained that people were continually pestering him, that they wanted to 'sign him up' when he did not want to belong. In fact, he had only himself to blame. He had never done anything to prevent others from reaching him. He had never, for example, had any kind of secretary. He had refused to get his number put on the answering service, for fear of missing a friend's call. He had always answered the phone himself, and since he was incapable of saying no to anyone – as Sollers says, 'it wasn't part of his rhetoric' – he put himself at the mercy of the ubiquitous 'pains-in-the-neck'. All his close friends have tales to tell of his recriminations: 'so-and-so has managed to extort a letter or a reference, so-and-so has wormed a preface out of me.'

The fact of the matter is that, in this respect, he showed a great deal of bad faith. He tended to write prefaces for friends, not for books, and it has been claimed many times that he willingly wrote prefaces for books he had never read, which would of course be impossible to prove. However, on one occasion, Renaud Camus did set a trap for him. In his book *Tricks*, which is a series of stories about ultra-fast gay relationships, most of which are one-night stands, there is a scene in which a discussion takes place about a text Barthes has written for the magazine *Créatis* on D. Boudinet's photographs. A character asks: 'Does he often do this kind of thing?':

> Yes, there are lots of little texts by him lying around. He has a whole perverse theory of professional misconduct, he told me about it one day. For instance, he likes the idea of writing a preface to a book he wouldn't like or might like but which would be indefensible. Writing something out of friendship or love. A kind of present.

Of course, the preface to *Tricks* itself is written by Barthes. Reprinted in *The Rustle of Language*, the preface makes no allusion to this slightly ironic passage and it begins as a kind of dialogue:

> — Why did you accept to write a preface for Renaud Camus?
> — Because Renaud Camus is a writer and his text is part of literature.

Because Renaud Camus is a writer. Not 'because he is a friend.' The passage about 'the little texts' comes near the end of a book that is over four hundred pages long, and one may indeed wonder whether Barthes had read it.

However, what matters here, more than any possible lapses in professionalism, which he was fully conscious of, are Barthes's good manners. In his case, what is normally a way of establishing a bond with someone was a way of keeping people at a distance, at least according to his closest friends. There was one phrase in particular which he would use – 'how kind of you' – which apparently really meant 'you're bothering me, leave me alone.' Those who worked with him knew when they heard this phrase that they had to tie things up quickly and disappear. Yet, at the same time, he agreed to every request. He would draft a preface, a letter of recommendation, a note or a few lines whenever asked to. Jean-Paul Enthoven says that 'he did not want to run the risk of upsetting anyone, that was his weakness.' This short explanation probably says more than any lengthy analysis of Barthes's behaviour could. It was this kind of behaviour which swelled the ranks of the 'pains-in-the-neck' he complained about all the time. The Barthes who moaned about society life and its demands and claimed he felt extremely bored at the dinners he was invited to was the same Barthes who sought out such invitations and who could not bear being alone. Yet as a consequence he often ended up regretting not being alone.

His Parisian friends were probably less aware than other friends who lived abroad and who consequently did not see him so often of how much his behaviour had changed. Previously, he had always arranged to meet in small bistros where he could talk undisturbed. Now he would arrange to meet in the fashionable cafés of Saint-Germain-des-Prés, places with mirrored walls into which he would be continually glancing, trying to catch a glimpse of someone he knew: 'his head turning constantly from side to side, like a lighthouse,' as Annette Lavers put it. She found a very different Barthes from the one she had met in the early 1960s, who had been a less affected, more discreet person. But not everyone would agree with this view. Violette Morin, for one, remembers Barthes as someone whose celebrity got on his nerves: for her he was 'the degree zero of vanity'.

Around the same time, Norbert Bensaïd was invited to a birthday party which Marie-France Pisier was giving for her brother. There were lots of young people there, dancing, and two 'old folks', Bensaïd and Barthes, who were both standing watching. Bensaïd, feeling a bit out of place, went up to Barthes, whom he had seen once or twice before, and by way of striking up a conversation said: 'We don't know one another, but a lot of mutual friends say we look alike' (it was true they had the same profile and head of hair, but Bensaïd was taller and thinner). Barthes looked him up and down and then, without replying, turned back towards the dance floor.

In the autumn, in October, he recorded a radio programme lasting two hours for France-Musique on Schumann. By way of an introduction, he read a text by Nietzsche, a 'cruel' text in his view, because it involved 'the execution of someone I love, Schumann, by someone I admire, Nietzsche'. As opposed to Chopin, whose works could only be attempted by pianists who were technically brilliant, Schumann's works were not written for virtuosos and could be played by almost anyone. Barthes said that as he fell into the latter group, he was a fan of Schumann and explained how much he loved his works: Schumann was the musician of the night, of melancholy, a melancholy to which Barthes was himself prone. For while it was true that he was now a celebrity, success had perhaps come too late for him, at a time when his life lacked any flavour, or when he himself no longer had any great taste for life.

A lesser desire

For several months, Barthes had been planning another trip to Tunisia to see Philippe Rebeyrol. However, he kept putting it off. He was due to go at the beginning of December, but he postponed it, saying he was trapped in Paris by too many trifling tasks, that the days kept slipping by and he found himself unable to stop time marching on. He wondered out loud whether it was old age. Or whether since his mother's death he had lost his desire for things. Finally, he compared himself to Proust's aunt Léonie, who always believed, quite sincerely, that she was about to get up and go for a walk but who never left her room.

In the middle of January 1980, he put off his trip to Tunisia yet again, this time using as his excuse the fact that he had to correct the proofs for *Camera Lucida*, which were due to arrive during his only free week, the week he had set aside for his trip. Besides, he had to give his lecture every Saturday. He said he regretted that he would not be able to see the ambassador's splendid residence in La Marsa again, as Rebeyrol's posting would soon be changing. In all likelihood Barthes was obliged to stay in Paris because once again he had made too many promises and had agreed to do too many things, and so he had decided to tell a half-lie: the printing of *Camera Lucida* was complete by 25 January, so the proofs must have been corrected a few weeks prior to this. Review copies of the book were sent out to the press and Barthes wrote his usual series of dedications: as always he assured his friends of his 'loyalty', and as always he wrote the dedications in blue ink. In those dedications he wrote to friends he no longer saw much of, because their paths had diverged, he wrote, 'I am certain we will meet again.' To others he promised 'eternal friendship'.

The reaction from the press was not what he would have liked, and he was extremely disappointed, since this book meant more to him than any of his previous publications. On 23 February he told Kristeva over the phone that he felt like 'burying his head in the plaster'. She found this expression strange and asked Philippe Sollers if in French the correct form of this expression wasn't 'to bury one's head in the sand, not the plaster'. 'You can say whatever you like if you're Barthes,' Sollers replied with an ambiguous smile. Kristeva thought that if he had got an expression wrong, then he must really be depressed.

Nevertheless, he had anticipated that the book would not get a favourable reception, and he explained why to Michel Bouvard, who was still teaching in Rabat. Photographers would not like his book because he was only interested in the referent, not in photography as an art form. The previous day, Friday, 22 February, Philippe Rebeyrol, who was back in Paris, had phoned him and found him feeling exhausted. He had complained about being plagued by requests, trapped by all his engagements. In short, he was suffering from the 'pains-in-the-neck', as usual. As if this were not enough, he had accepted an invitation to go to a lunch party which was being given by François Mitterrand on the following Monday, 25 February. So the two friends arranged to meet later in the week.

He had hesitated for a long time before accepting Jack Lang's invitation to have lunch with the First Secretary of the Socialist party. He still had memories of the lukewarm reaction to his lunch with Giscard d'Estaing and Edgar Faure. He was afraid that if he accepted this time, it would be seen as an attempt to move 'to the left' in order to offset his previous move 'to the right'. Besides, since his election to the Collège de France he had received numerous invitations along the same lines. But he had been on friendly terms with Lang for eight years – in fact, since the time Lang, as the newly appointed director of the Chaillot theatre, had asked him to write a piece for it. Finally, his friends insisted he go, so in the end he accepted the invitation. As Julia Kristeva says, he always ended up accepting, 'because he was an ambiguous character, on the side of order and also on the side of difference at the same time'.

He had just finished a draft of the paper he was due to give at a conference on Stendahl in Milan. He had given it the title 'On échoue toujours de parler de ce qu'on aime' ('One always fails to speak about the things one loves'). The manuscript was lying on his table and all he had to do was type it up; in other words, rewrite it, as he always did, transform it. On the morning of 25 February 1980 he put a piece of paper in his typewriter and began to type: 'A few weeks ago, I made a brief trip to Italy. When I arrived at Milan station, it was a cold, foggy, filthy evening . . .' Having finished the first page, he took it out of the typewriter and put in a fresh sheet, then he glanced at his watch: he had run out of time, he was due at his meeting, his lunch party. He got up, leaving what was to be his final text where it lay. Then he slipped on his overcoat and left. At about the same time, Bernard Dort found a copy of *Camera Lucida*, with a dedication in the front written by Barthes, in his letterbox.

The lunch was being held in the Rue des Blancs-Manteaux, in the Marais, in a flat belonging to Philippe Serre, a former Popular Front member of parliament who had lent it to Lang for the occasion. Lang and he had met in Nancy and become close friends. For quite some time the future Minister of Culture had been organizing regular lunch parties with artists and intellectuals for François Mitterrand. They were usually held in Lang's flat in the sixth arrondissement, but on this occasion a lot of people had been invited, and Serre's flat was larger and more luxurious. Since he was going to be away, he had offered to let Lang borrow it. Seated around the table with François Mitterrand and Jacques Lang were Jacques Berque, Danièle Delorme, Pierre Henry and Rolf Liberman. Mitterrand and Barthes had met one another a few times, but hardly knew each other. However, the future president had found Barthes's *Mythologies*, his critical readings of everyday events and phenomena, extremely interesting. Above all, he was fascinated by Barthes's style, 'his taste for words, for expressions'. Today, he still believes that Barthes's style was the perfect vehicle for his thought. The elections that would bring Mitterrand to power were due to take place the following year, and one would be correct in thinking that these lunches had a specifically political function. Today the President denies this, saying, 'I enjoyed and still enjoy meeting creative people, and I trusted Lang to organize these contacts for me.' Lang echoes this when he says, 'Those lunches with François Mitterrand were not public events. The President enjoys meeting people and it's not his usual custom to issue a press release to say he has had lunch with so-and-so.'

The conversation covered different topics; culture, music, literature were all touched on; and the guests left feeling quite happy with one another. Barthes decided to walk a little, to return home on foot. At about 3.45 p.m., when he had reached 44, Rue des Écoles, according to witnesses he looked left, then right, before crossing. Was his mind on something else? Was he, as some have claimed, feeling exasperated by the lunch party he had just left, bored by the conversation of those political 'pains-in-the-neck'? Whatever the case he did not see the van coming towards him, despite its size, and it ran him over. Unconscious and bleeding from the nose, without his identity card or any other form of identification, he was taken to the Salpêtrière hospital by ambulance. No one knew who he was, which is why the media did not get hold of the news until much later. On 25 February, at 8.58 p.m., Agence France Presse issued the following bulletin:

> The academic, essayist and critic Roland Barthes, 64, was involved in a traffic accident in the Rue des Écoles in the fifth arrondissement this afternoon. According to the hospital authorities, Roland Barthes was taken to the De la Pitié-Salpêtrière hospital. At 8.30 p.m., no further information as to the writer's condition was available.

The following day, 26 February, his friends were relieved to hear the statement on the 12.37 p.m. bulletin to the effect that: 'Roland Barthes is still in the Salpêtrière hospital. According to a statement issued by the hospital authorities, Barthes is under observation and his condition is stable. His editor has indicated that the writer's condition gives no cause for concern.'

The initial news from relatives and close friends implied that he was not in any serious danger, and that he simply wished to be left alone to rest. As Philippe Sollers was later to say, it was 'a discourse of intensive minimization.'[16] At Seuil, the talk was of a few grazes, and it was implied that he was fine but that for the time being he did not want anyone to visit him. In fact, François Wahl had taken charge of the situation and was keeping a tight rein on what information was released. Alerted by other sources that Roland was not in fact as well as he was said to be, Kristeva and Sollers went to the hospital, where a crowd had gathered – students from the seminar, friends and boyfriends. They practically forced down the door, and according to them found Barthes a dying man. In an extremely anxious and emotional state, they began to envisage all kinds of scenarios, some of which were highly improbable. Had there been an effort, deliberate or not, to prevent there being any connection made between the lunch party with a top politician and the running over of one of France's most important intellectuals? Was there a fear that Mitterrand might be thought of as having the 'evil eye'? Why say someone was fine when they were dying? Was the left-wing press carrying out a form of self-censorship during this period? Or was it disinformation? Today Sollers still thinks that 'it seems a strange business.' But was there anything more to it than this?

It is true that a certain sense of doubt reigns over the accident. First of all there is the strange, faltering way the story began, this lapse or 'successful failure'[17] on the part of a van driver which transformed Barthes's death into an ironic little mythology. A witness on a motorbike claimed at the time that, before crossing the road, Barthes had looked right in the direction of the oncoming van. Were his thoughts elsewhere? According to friends, he loathed Saint-Germain-des-Prés on Saturday nights when the traffic was very heavy. He was always afraid that other people were going to be run over and would tell them to be careful when they were about to cross the street. André Téchiné remarks: 'It's children you tell to be careful when they cross the street and his mother was no longer there to remind him.'

Whatever the case, Barthes was still in hospital and at first his condition did not give the doctors or those closest to him any cause for concern. Of course he had bumps and bruises, but he could speak and he could reassure his visitors, greeting Jean-Louis Bouttes, Youssef Baccouche and Michel Foucault with the words, 'how stupid, how stupid', a hint of anger in his voice. He was traumatized by the accident, unhappy and annoyed at being in such cold and anonymous surroundings. But even so, at first the doctors genuinely thought he had nothing seriously wrong with him. So when Jean-Louis Bouttes asked one of the doctors whether he should bring in recent X-rays of Barthes's lungs for them to examine, he was told that he did not need to. However, one month later, after Barthes had died, another doctor told Bouttes that the X-rays should have been examined immediately.

The real and exhausting problem for the time being was who he should see from all the different networks of his friends and acquaintances. Jean-Louis Bouttes remembers that 'trying to work out who he should see and who not was like working out the moves in a chess game. Everyone wanted to see him, and no one knew how to sort it out properly.' When Michel Salzedo tried to discuss the matter of his mail or his phone calls, Roland would simply shrug his shoulders, apparently indifferent to it all, as if it was of no importance. His regular visitors, or rather those who were allowed to visit him, were Évelyn Bachelier, Youssef Baccouche, Philippe Rebeyrol, Severo Sarduy, Daniel Percheron, and some of his students from the seminar. Violette Morin went to the hospital every day, but did not want to go in to see him, thinking he would prefer her not to see him in his current state. André Téchiné felt the same. He went often to the hospital but did not want to see Barthes. He felt overwhelmed by the crowd of people blocking the corridor and felt that it was all too much for a sick man who, above all, needed peace and quiet. All his friends were astonished by the way François Wahl took over control of the situation, practically confiscating Barthes and making himself, as Romaric Sulger-Büel puts it, the 'master of ceremonies' of his last days.

The first visit to the hospital by Philippe Sollers and Julia Kristeva is interesting from this point of view. Roland's brother, Michel Salzedo, helped by François Wahl, had taken charge from the beginning and it was Michel who acted as intermediary between his brother and the outside world. It was he who, after consultation with Wahl and Roland himself, would decide which visitors to let in and which to turn away, plus the duration of the visit. When Sollers arrived, Michel asked him what he wanted and went to see if Roland felt up to seeing the two visitors. 'Who's he?' Sollers asked Wahl. 'That's Michel Salzedo, Barthes's brother,' Wahl replied. 'What, that's him?' said Sollers, astonished.

Barthes and his brother had lived together for practically the whole of their lives, for many years in the same flat, then three floors away from each other. Sollers was one of Barthes's best friends. Yet although he was vaguely aware that Barthes had a half-brother, he had never met him. The fact that the two brothers led completely separate lives and had separate groups of friends has been highlighted before, and it will come up again later, but this particular incident makes it glaringly obvious.

Barthes drifted between periods of unconsciousness and periods of feeling better. He had had a tube inserted into his windpipe to help him breathe more easily, but this also meant that he could no longer speak and was only able to communicate by means of gestures or by writing things down. He seemed to be feeling better, but his body was not responding to treatment: it was as if his body could not get going again. He recognized his visitors, would shake hands with them, smile and nod his head or write a few lines, but he did not seem to have the will to carry on living. A psychologist friend was even asked to try and find out what was happening, but to no avail. Was it his usual tiredness that was preventing him from fighting? Or was it rather, as Sollers suggests, that since his mother's death he no longer had any desire to live? Perhaps the most likely explanation is that he had lost his appetite for life in general, and his mother's death was not the only factor involved in this.

Here, one must go back to the final sentence of *Incidents*, the entry for 17 September 1979, in order to see that Barthes had been confronted with the fact that he was no longer desired: 'I sent him away, saying I had work to do, knowing it was over and not just over with him: the love of *any* boy was no longer possible.' To the conclusion of this possibly unreliable journal can be added a passage from Martin Melkonian's book:

> When he happened to recognize a spark of desire in the eyes of the other, he made a half-movement towards the pure circle of the room. Then desire eluded him, as did the other in his luminous nakedness. The habitable space of the other. Invariably it was impotence, death which triumphed, until the arrival of death itself.[18]

Did Barthes believe that from now on, with all hope of love closed to him, all that was left to him were the gigolos?

During the months preceding his accident he had often spoken of the 'projects' he had for 'the end of his life'. He was going to write such and such a book, perhaps a novel, and retire to Urt to get away from it all. Olivier Burgelin comments that:

> He thought death was approaching long before the accident which killed him. I don't know what was at the root of it all, after his election to the Collège de France I didn't see much of him. But whenever I did, I was struck by the way he used the term 'end of life' when referring to his plans for the seminar. As soon as the accident occurred, I knew he was lost, I was convinced of it. It probably sounds irrational, but I believed he was going to die. I'm telling you this only because it's the truth.

Yet during the period just prior to his accident, Barthes had also had new projects in mind: he was thinking of living with Romaric Sulger-Büel and co-writing a book with him on 'the art of living', an art which according to him meant combining the pleasures of study and reading with a certain attitude towards food, travel and friendship. Are these really the plans of someone whose life is about to end, or do they represent the start of a new life? It remains unclear, and different people have different versions of events.

As has been said, Philippe Rebeyrol was in Paris, between postings. He had just left Tunis and had been appointed ambassador to Athens. He was a frequent visitor to the hospital, where he came across Sollers and Kristeva, of course, but above all the members of Barthes's 'family' or the 'inner circle' of Jean-Louis Bouttes, Éric Marty and Youssef Baccouche. The tube which had been inserted into his windpipe was proving a constant irritation to Barthes, since it not only prevented him from speaking but also meant eating was difficult. The doctors decided to carry out a tracheotomy, that is, to open up the trachea to allow tubes to be inserted, a minor operation which would alleviate the patient's condition. But Barthes felt threatened by this operation, taking it as a sign that he was going to die. Rebeyrol tried to reassure him, but his friend remained panic-stricken and made a sweeping gesture with his hand across his throat, as if to say, 'they are going to cut my throat.'

The operation went ahead, but Barthes was still unable to speak; he had collapsed in a state of complete exhaustion. Some visitors felt that the doctors were annoyed by his resistance or his refusal to get better. The question still remains: was this a form of suicide? The view of the doctors at the Salpêtrière was more qualified: Barthes's tuberculosis had left him with a severe 'respiratory inefficiency'.

With the shock of the accident, his lung had 'de-compensated', in other words his breathing had become even less efficient, which is why he had had to have the tube inserted into his windpipe. This process of 'intubation' was difficult to reverse: 'extubation' required that the patient make a vigorous effort; he had to force himself to breathe and cough. In short, he had to fight. Barthes had probably seen patients who had undergone tracheotomies during his time at the sanatorium. He had witnessed these struggles to breathe through a tube, a machine, struggles which all too often proved fruitless. If this were the price of being able to breathe, of life, then it may have seemed too high, too heavy a burden to bear.

However the term 'suicide' is too strong; perhaps it is better to say that he was aware that what awaited him at the end of a long and uncertain struggle would mean that he could never again live a 'normal' life. His last happy moments must have been when his brother Michel brought him a tape of the Brandenburg concertos, which he listened to with a broad smile on his face. Once again, for the last time, music.

Barthes died on 26 March 1980 at 1.40 p.m. The forensic surgeon's report concluded that 'the accident was not the direct cause of death, but it led to the development of pulmonary complications in a patient who was particularly handicapped by chronic respiratory insufficiency.' It was as if, thirty-five years later, Saint-Hilaire-du-Touvet and Leysin had finally taken their revenge on the body that had escaped them.

The paying of the last respects took place on Friday, 28 March at the morgue in the rear courtyard of the Salpêtrière hospital. Greimas and Italo Calvino both arrived too early, met in the courtyard and went off to wait in a café for an hour. Then they returned to the courtyard, which was now filled with around a hundred people: there were students from Barthes's seminars, the editorial teams at Seuil and *Tel Quel*, François Wahl, Michel Foucault, André Téchiné, Roland Havas, Michel Salzedo and his wife Rachel. Someone announced that the coffin had arrived: 'Roland's on his way down,' and Rachel jumped, as if he were about to appear. One by one, they filed past the coffin. Dead bodies shrink and Greimas contemplated the body of 'little Roland, quite tiny, as if he had shrivelled up.' Everyone felt useless, helpless. Nothing had been planned or arranged, there was no ritual, no ceremony, only what our society has developed for this sort of occasion: a laid-out body which was momentarily rendered invisible by the shadows of those who filed past it quickly, almost shamefacedly. Then the coffin lid was shut and it was taken to the station, where it was loaded on to a train bound for Urt. A handful of Barthes's friends travelled down to Bayonne overnight on the same train: Bernard Dort, François Wahl, Philippe Rebeyrol, Violette Morin, Youssef Baccouche, Jean-Louis Bouttes, Robert David and André Téchiné. They all met up at the house in Urt, then went on to the nearby cemetery for a service which was as brief as the one in the courtyard of the Salpêtrière hospital had been.

In *Le Monde* of 28 March, Jacques Cellard paid hommage to 'Barthes l'émerveilleur' ('Barthes who filled us with wonder'), and Bertrand Poirot-Delpech raged against the stupidity of his death: 'True, the car forms part of our mythology, but it is scarcely twenty years since Camus met his death in the front seat of a car, and during this time literature has paid a rather harsh tribute to the chrome goddess.' Was he aware that in expressing his regret for these deaths, he was bringing together two men who in 1955 had been at loggerheads with one another? On 5 April, again in *Le Monde*, it was Jean-Marie Benoist's turn to praise Barthes in an article called 'Roland Barthes ou la délicatesse' ('Roland Barthes: a lesson in delicacy'). Tributes to Barthes poured in from all quarters and he was given a second burial. Then there was a third and final burial when the Public Prosecutor's office decided on 17 April that proceedings would not be instituted against the driver of the van which had run Barthes over since, as the forensic report had stated, 'the accident was not the direct cause of death'.

In the meantime, another death had occurred which had eclipsed that of Barthes. On 15 April, Jean-Paul Sartre had died in the Broussais hospital. Barthes's funeral in the cemetery at Urt had been attended by a mere handful of his friends, but Sartre's funeral in Montparnasse was to attract a crowd of over fifty thousand people. Moreover, the tenth anniversary of Barthes's death in 1990 was hardly given a mention in the media, whereas the anniversary of Sartre's death was marked by tributes to him on both radio and television.

Two very different kinds of farewell ceremony, bringing to a close two parallel destinies. Parallel, as geometry tells us, does not mean convergent, of course, or at least only very rarely, and it takes two to bring about a meeting. Barthes had read Sartre and defended his views, but Sartre in a now famous interview in 1966 had definitively rejected those human sciences which, according to Sartre, wanted to make mankind into a set of structures, whereas it was mankind who made history.[19] Yet among those attending Sartre's funeral on 17

April there were readers of both *Mythologies* and *Situations, A Lover's Discourse* and *The Critique of Dialectical Reason*, people who had been influenced just as much by Barthes's ideas as by Sartre's. But these two different kinds of ceremony, these two very different ways of handling death, are indicative of two very different attitudes to life. At his death, Sartre was accompanied by 'the people', his people, who had gathered together in one final act of militancy. Barthes on the other hand, even in his death, demonstrated his refusal of 'hysteria'.

12

The 'After Death'

After his death, there were dozens of people who claimed that they had been Barthes's best friend, the person who was closest and dearest to him. Dozens of people sent letters of condolence to Michel Salzedo. The fact that there were so many is proof of the pretension of these self-proclaimed friends, some of whom had probably been in the 'pains-in-the-neck' category. It is also symptomatic of Barthes's lifestyle, his ability to compartmentalize his life and of his preference for seeing people on a one-to-one basis, which meant that all his friends were under the impression that their relationship with him was unique. He felt different with everyone he saw on a regular basis, and he wanted to give his all to each and every one of them. Because he believed in the virtues of dialogue, he cultivated numerous quite separate friendships. On top of this, the different areas of his life hardly ever overlapped. He carefully divided up his groups of friends according to the categories they fell into, be it professional, literary, homosexual, old friends, etc. His reluctance to let these different networks overlap could be seen as a hangover from the days when homosexuality was a social taboo and was forced underground. However, perhaps this does not explain his behaviour fully, and Philippe Sollers may be right in interpreting the way he organized his life as an 'aesthetic gesture'. For his part, Olivier Burgelin believes that it stemmed from 'a desire not to impose people on one another'.

In addition, his kindness, his capacity for listening, and listening with such attentiveness, made everyone he talked to feel extraordinary and special. Obviously this was the case with his students, most of whom must have felt at one time or another that they were his intellectual heir, the person who would carry on his work. Barthes protected himself, withdrew sometimes, but being afraid of loneliness or boredom the protection he sought was in a complex and contradictory network of affective relations. A network of friends, lovers, contacts, of preferences which were quite temporary or perhaps wholly provisional, but which were experienced by those involved – or perhaps imagined by them – as being absolute and definitive.

The 'toilette of the dead'

Posthumous works are also part of the 'after death' and they were numerous. Between 1981 and 1987, no fewer than five books were published by Seuil under the name of Roland Barthes. The first of them, published in 1981, was *Le Grain de la voix* (*The Grain of the Voice*), which consisted of a collection of thirty-eight interviews which he had given to various newspapers and magazines from 1962 to 1980. An unsigned introductory note, which was in fact written by François Wahl, stressed that this volume brought together 'most of the interviews given in French by Roland Barthes', and it went on:

> The best possible preface would have been a description by Roland Barthes himself of what an interview is. We will never have such a description now, but we do have a few pages where Roland Barthes analyses, with admirable clarity, the passage of the spoken word to the word transcribed: we thought it fitting to begin with these pages, where the style of writing interlaces with the grain of the voice.[1]

These few pages, which were written in 1974 as the preface to a series of dialogues published by Grenoble University Press, are an incisive reflection on the process of transcription, on the transference of the spoken word into writing:

> We talk, a tape recording is made, diligent secretaries listen to our words to refine, transcribe and punctuate them, producing a first draft that we can tidy up afresh, before it goes on to publication, the book, eternity. Haven't we just gone through the 'toilette of the dead'? We have embalmed our speech like a mummy, to preserve it forever. Because we really must last a bit longer than our voices.[2]

Barthes asks himself what is lost and what is gained in this process.

What is lost is 'an innocence', the material presence of two bodies facing one another, what linguists call the *phatic* function of language: the tags, the 'isn't that so?' or the 'you see' which are a kind of appeal to the other person, which punctuate a communication and ensure it gets across. What is gained is the more logical organization of the discourse, which occurs when, for example, the 'but's' and the 'so's' are replaced by 'although' and 'therefore', with the written preference for subordination. A more ordered, hierarchical structure is imposed on the ideas. Thus, when spoken language is transformed into written language, the body gives way to the mind.

The following year, 1982, a new collection of essays appeared under the rather bizarre title of *L'Obvie et l'obtus* [3] subtitled *Essais critiques III*.[4] It contained twenty-three texts, prefaces and articles, on the subjects of the theatre, painting and music. Again, it was prefaced by an introductory note by François Wahl outlining how at the end of his life Barthes had wanted to publish a new series of 'critical essays'. On the back panel of the cover there was a blurb signed 'R.B.', comprising twenty-two lines of quotes explaining the meaning of the book's title. On closer examination it turns out to be a surprising montage extracted from the third essay in the collection, 'The third sense: research notes on several Eisenstein stills', which has been edited and presented in this strange fashion. To let the reader judge, here is the blurb:

> I believe I can distinguish | three levels of sense. An informational level, | this level is that of *communication*. | A symbolic level | and this second level, in its totality, is that of *signification*. Is this all? | No, I read, I receive | a third meaning, erratic, yet evident and persistent, I do not know what its signified is, at least I cannot give it a name, | this third level | is that of *signifying* [*signifiance*]. | The symbolic meaning | compels my recognition by a double determination: it is intentional (it is what the author has meant) and it is selected from a kind of general, common lexicon of symbols: it is a meaning | which *moves ahead of me* | I propose to call this complete sign *the obvious meaning*. | As for the other, the third meaning, the one which appears 'in excess', as a supplement my intellection cannot quite absorb, a meaning both persistent and fugitive, apparent and evasive, I propose calling this *the obtuse meaning*.[5]

The vertical lines added here mark the cuts which are nowhere mentioned on the cover of the book, the first line marks a cut of three words, the second a cut of twenty-six words, the third a cut of thirty-three words, and the fourth a cut of fourteen lines. This process of cutting adds up to a total of seventy lines: the mind boggles! Particularly since this is a mutilated version – in which the use of the scissors is not indicated in any way, either by brackets or ellipses – of the text where Barthes explains the two terms which go to make up the title of the book, 'the obvious' and 'the obtuse'. For obvious: '*Obvius* means *moving ahead* which is just the case with this meaning, which seeks me out' and for obtuse: 'This word comes readily to my mind, and miraculously, on exploring its etymology, I find it already yields a theory of the supplementary meaning; *obtusus* means *blunted, rounded.*'[6]

Two years later the same thing occurred in *Le Bruissement de la langue* (*The Rustle of Language*), which is subtitled *Essais critiques IV*. It consists of a collection of forty-six texts, all of which again are prefaces or articles. Plus, by way of a blurb, there is the same kind of mutilated extract. In quotation marks and signed 'R.B.', ninety-two lines of an original Barthes text have been condensed into twenty-seven lines, that is, three pages have been turned into a half-page extract![7]

The same thing occurred yet again in *L'Aventure sémiologique* (*The Semiotic Challenge*), which was published in 1985. Collected together in this volume were fifteen previously published texts, most of them available in the form of reviews, and some of which had already been republished several times (for instance, 'Elements of semiology', 'Introduction to the structural analysis of narrative', etc.). Again, included on the back panel of the cover was a chopped-up extract from one of Barthes's texts – although this time three out of the five cuts had been indicated by ellipses.

Of course, Barthes's heirs or executors have every right to do if not absolutely everything, then at least a great deal with his writings. And of course it makes good commercial sense to republish previously published texts, add a couple of unpublished ones, give the whole thing an attractive title, and thereby produce a 'new' book. But perhaps it is worth asking whether the publication of *Incidents* in 1987 was not overstepping the mark. This slim volume, in total 116 pages of large type, brought together four texts: 'La lumière du Sud-Ouest' ('The light of the south-west'), published in *L'Humanité* on 10 September 1977; 'Incidents', a series of notes Barthes had made while he was in Morocco in 1968–9; 'Au Palais ce soir' ('At the Palace tonight'), published in *Vogue Homme* in May 1978; and finally 'Soirées de Paris' ('Parisian evenings'), a diary Barthes had kept between 24 August and 17 September 1979. Thus two out of the four texts had already been published elsewhere. In his 'Editor's note', François Wahl wrote that it was only right to publish 'Incidents' because 'the text was ready for the printer and because Barthes was considering publishing it in *Tel Quel*.' As for 'Soirées de Paris', he said that 'the manuscript is titled, the pages are numbered and, as the reader will see, it contains several corrections in the margin which make it quite clear that it was intended for publication – one day.'[8] Then he added the following:

> Is it right to pretend that we do not know what in fact we know only too well – the total lack of generosity, in all senses, with which the doubts Barthes occasionally expresses in these pages about modern forms of writing or his despair over desire will be received? R.B. was not someone who would have shrunk from making a statement if he thought it justified.[9]

Rather than speculating about a possible lack of generosity on the part of the readers, it might be worth asking whether Barthes would really have wanted these pages to be published. In 1979, he had published an extract from this 'diary' in *Tel Quel*, the first part of which had been written in Urt between 13 July and 13 August 1977, and the second part in Paris on 25 April. He had also added a 'deliberation' on whether or not one should keep a diary. But even though this was published after his mother's death, it still made no allusion to his homosexuality. It is principally because of the explicit references to homosexuality it contains, and not because of his comments on modern writers – echoes of which were already present in *Roland Barthes* – that the publication of *Incidents* might be considered to represent the breaking of a tacit agreement. Hasn't *Roland Barthes* been rather too heavily made-up in this 'toilette of the dead' than he would have wished?

Additionally, and in contrast, François Wahl had explicitly declared his intention not to let even the smallest unpublished text by Barthes be published without his say-so. The same applied to any republished texts. It will be recalled that Barthes had agreed to let Jean-Loup Rivière put together a collection of his writings on the theatre and publish them together with his own preface. As Barthes was putting the final touches to *Camera Lucida*, Rivière was also finishing the editing of the collection and his own preface. He then submitted the whole thing to Barthes. Naturally, the text, which to this day remains unpublished, highlighted the fact that during the period when Barthes had become its chronicler, the theatre had been a site of struggle. But it also raised the question of why he had stopped writing for the theatre and asked how can one simply give up what has once been a real passion, how can one leave the theatre?

Today Rivière explains that 'this gesture of his both disturbs and intrigues me. In *Roland Barthes*, he writes: "At the crossroads of the entire oeuvre, perhaps the Theatre." So why did he abandon it?' And Rivière suggested in his preface that perhaps this paradoxical shift from passionate engagement to disappointment was in part connected with the rise to power of De Gaulle: 'In May 1958, there was a brutal change from a system in which the head of state *represented* France to a system in which he *incarnated* it. Barthes published an article on *Ubu Roi* and gradually withdrew.' The seventy articles which he selected for the book spanned a seven-year period from 1953 to 1960 and were mostly taken from *Théâtre populaire*. Since they were all written in the 1950s, Barthes felt somewhat embarrassed by their dated style on rereading them, especially since he was about to publish a new book which bore hardly any resemblance to any of his previous texts. He explained to Rivière that they must make a few cuts, leave out a few articles, perhaps add a couple of new ones, but that at present he had no time to write them. Besides, he probably did not want the two books to come out at the same time, and *Camera Lucida* naturally took precedence. So together he and Rivière agreed to postpone the publication of 'Writings on the theatre' until later. But then Barthes died.

A few months later Rivière, who had signed a contract for the book with Seuil, sent his manuscript to François Wahl. Wahl opposed its publication strongly, just as he had opposed the publication of any of Barthes's letters, especially his voluminous correspondence with Robert David and Philippe Rebeyrol. His argument for not publishing the 'Writings on the theatre' was, of course, that Barthes had not wanted the project to go any further. In fact, all Barthes had wanted to do was take a look at the articles Rivière had selected and make a final choice on what was to be included later, after the publication of *Camera Lucida*. So the manuscript was dropped. As for Barthes's letters, Wahl's arguments against their publication were different: Barthes had not approved of biography, so he could not under any circumstances give his blessing to a project which came close to biography. In both cases, Wahl's clampdown, his determination to stand in the way of any publication which he would not have final control over, meant he was in a key position of power. It was a position some people thought he had usurped: Romaric Sulger-Büel says he behaved as if were the executor of Barthes's will, which he was not. The novelist Max Genève, who had run up against similar problems while making a series of radio programmes on the author of *Mythologies* for France-Culture, wrote to Wahl: 'Stop thinking you're Barthes.'

Jean-Loup Rivière, unable to publish the book he had been commissioned to produce, found his own oblique and poetic way of paying homage to Barthes. Several years before, Barthes had got him taken on at the Beaubourg centre as leader of a research group on the image. In particular, the group had come up with the idea of an exhibition on cartography, which was put on in the main gallery of the Pompidou Centre in 1980 under the title 'Maps and figures of the earth'. A huge catalogue was published to accompany the exhibition a few months after Barthes's death. Inside, on the first page, there is a reproduction of an ordnance survey map and superimposed on to this sober background is a text by Gilles Deleuze and Félix Guattari. Few people can have realized that the map showed the Urt region and that on the right bank of the Adour river, opposite the village and slightly downstream, was an area marked 'The Barthes'.

A character in a novel

Along with these posthumous publications (and withholdings), Barthes was also about to embark on a new career which he could hardly have imagined for himself – as a fictional character. Philippe Sollers was the first to 'open fire' in 1983 with the publication of his novel *Women*, in which Barthes appears in the final stages of his life as a character called Werth, along with Lacan and Althusser. In the same year Renaud Camus published *Roman Roi*, in which Barthes had a somewhat minor role playing a librarian in Romania. Of greater interest is Norbert Bensaïd's *Le Regard des statues*, which was published eight years after Barthes's death. Michel Laporte, an academic, writer and intellectual guru is run over by a car. A crowd gathers round his hospital bed, mostly women (his lovers) and disciples. Then there is Antoine, the young man who ran him over, who comes to visit him regularly, worries about him and eventually develops a bizarre relationship with him. 'Did Laporte cause the accident, consciously or not?' he wonders. 'Is he possessed by an obscure death-wish?' worries a psychoanalyst friend. Whatever the case, Laporte's condition does not improve and he eventually dies, not from the effects of the accident but from a heart-attack.

There are obvious parallels here between the Laporte character and Barthes. There is the accident, of course, but there is also the fact that both are famous intellectuals, that both have suffered from tuberculosis, and finally that both have complicated love lives (except that Barthes is homosexual and Laporte heterosexual). In addition, like Barthes, Laporte seems not to want to get better and he has just recently been bereaved, although in his case it is his former mistress, Anna, who has died, and not his mother. Moreover, both have just finished a book: Barthes's *Camera Lucida* came out a few days before his acccident, Laporte is correcting the proofs for his book in hospital. In short, everything leads one to the conclusion that the novel is a *roman à clef*.

However, according to Norbert Bensaïd, this is not the case. He claims never to have known Barthes, or only to have met him briefly a couple of times: 'My book has nothing, or very little to do with Barthes. There's the accident of course, but that's a common news item. No, what I was interested in was the Antoine character, and the idea of guilt. I found it astonishing to think that one could be guilty of causing the death of someone else without it really being your fault. Guilt without having done anything wrong.' He adds that none of the characters are disguised portraits of real people. Even if Laporte is a combination of Althusser, Sartre and Barthes (he has the former's physical appearance, Sartre's political activism and Barthes's death): 'all the other characters are completely fictional.' However, it still seems likely that it was this little supplementary mythology – one too many – putting a violent full stop to Barthes's deliberations (to write or not to write a novel) which led to his being transformed without wishing it into a fictional character.

Then in 1980, Julia Kristeva published *Les Samouraïs*, which comes with the disclaimer 'novel' on its front cover. Faced with such a title, it becomes difficult to avoid comparisons with De Beauvoir's *The Mandarins*, which deals with similar themes. Kristeva's novel, like Sollers's *Women*, is obviously partly autobiographical. She narrates her arrival in France, her Paris, which is inhabited by a good number of famous intellectuals including Lacan, Sartre, Goldmann and Roland Barthes (or Armand Bréhal as he is called in the book). The novel contains many of the same anecdotes which appear in the present biography (which it should be pointed out come from different if convergent sources). Among these are Barthes's behaviour during the events of May '68, Sollers's invention of the title for *S/Z*, the trip to China and his accident and death. Evidently Kristeva has invented very little and her 'novel' is really an autobiography. Nevertheless, the fact remains that for reasons of her own, she felt the need to add a fictional flavour to this chronicle of her adjustment to life in France and, once again, Bréhal/Barthes became a character in a novel.

To this list of Philippe Sollers, Renaud Camus, Norbert Bensaïd and Julia Kristeva can be added another name, Philippe Roger, whose book on Barthes, although not a novel, was entitled *Roland Barthes, roman* ('Roland Barthes, a novel'). Few theorists have so haunted the pages of works of fiction – or works which claim to be fiction – after their deaths. So much so that one is bound to ask just what will Barthes have left behind? Is his legacy limited to these allusive apparitions in the pages of a few dubious scenarios?

The Barthes system

The 'after death' is also the time for assessments. This is not the time or place to attempt to evaluate Barthes's theoretical legacy. It is too soon to assess his influence on contemporary research and, in any case, this would require a different genre, a different kind of book. Nevertheless, I shall attempt to outline briefly what could be termed 'the Barthes system', the system he has bequeathed not just to a handful of theorists, but to thousands of ordinary readers. How did this man whose life, friendships, travels, feelings, work and publications have been chronicled in this biography function intellectually? It could be said, perhaps rather provocatively, that his main talents and innovations fall within the field of literature, and that his principal contribution was to bring literature into the human sciences. Let us be frank about this: from *Writing Degree Zero* to *Camera Lucida*, Barthes contributed a great deal to semiology, textual analysis and, more indirectly, his work also has repercussions on linguistics or sociology. But his principal contribution was not a systematic theory but a certain way of looking at things, an intuitive approach.

It was this approach which taught thousands of readers to regard the scraps and ephemera of social life (news items, photos, posters, daily customs) as signs: in other words, he made his readers aware of the question of meaning. Some of the detail of his interpretations in *Mythologies* can be challenged or relativized, as has been seen, but this does not affect the import of his work, the fact that his interpretations of the Dominici affair, literary criticism, colonial discourse, the poster for Panzani pasta, the Tour de France, wrestling and the Abbé Pierre have changed the way thousands of people look at things. He showed his readers what a society could reveal about itself through the signs it produced. It would be wrong to think that Barthes introduced semiological theories to a wider public, even if some passages in his texts give this impression. In fact he did much more: he helped to create a semantic reflex by showing us that we live in a world charged with meaning. According to Olivier Burgelin, 'he was a mystic':

> Not an ascetic of course, but a sensual mystic, who practised a cult of sensuality. He was a mystic because the whole of his work was an exploration of the same vital question, and his whole life, which was continually being taken back to the drawing board, was engaged in this exploration. The question he explored was that of meaning, of language, of literature.

To this Violette Morin adds: 'He was like a Beethoven symphony, with a powerful central theme and lots of tiny variations and desires to write all kinds of things. So he would veer off in this or that direction, but he always returned in the end to the same theme'.

This is the real lesson Barthes taught us: we live in a world teeming with signs. Veiled by their signifiers, by writing, by the false obviousness of the 'natural', by pseudo 'common sense', clothing or theatre, we had almost no idea how to decode these signs. We did not know how the town plan, the discourse of literary criticism, the meal of steak and chips or the treament of a news item could conceal a social meaning. It was Barthes who made us aware of their existence.

If he was able to achieve this, it was mainly through his style, his writing. At a time when linguistics (centred around Chomsky and his generative grammar) was elaborating increasingly sophisticated models and when linguistic texts were becoming increasingly unreadable, Barthes mastered these theories and made them both *readable* and *crystal clear*. Even today, if one wants to introduce students to the concepts of connotation and denotation, one recommends Barthes, not Hjelmslev. But he also used these theories to develop his own line of thought and to support his own intuitions. For there are two ways for the researcher to proceed. The first is through slow and rigorous elaboration of a line of thought, which at times involves a certain amount of drudgery. The other way is by means of lightning flashes of intuition. In the former case, what is discovered is the end result of a methodological process and its proof is already present in this methodology. In the second case, *a posteriori* methodological justifications are needed. Barthes's great talent was to absorb contemporary theories and use them to shore up his own intuitions.

There are numerous examples of this way of working in his texts.

In *Writing Degree Zero* there are his discreet allusions to Marx and Sartre, in *Mythologies* the way he used concepts taken from Saussure and Hjelmslev to write his theoretical postscript. Then there is his use of Brecht, not just in his articles on the theatre but also in *A Lover's Discourse*, and the adaption of phonology to serve his own ends in *The Fashion System*. Finally, there are his borrowings from Lacan, Bakhtin and also the young authors who gathered around him and were busy constructing what has been labelled, rather meaninglessly, *modernity*. Barthes was continually subjugating other people's theories to his own moods, his own instincts. In order to carry out this theoretical re-routing, to concoct his own brew from all the diverse ingredients he collected, he needed more than talent: he needed to have his own way of looking at the world, his own voice and style. If Barthes is not a theorist, then neither is he simply an essay writer who used other people's theories.

Of the two important French intellectuals who died in 1980, Sartre is of course the theorist and Barthes the writer. However, somewhat paradoxically, their impact on society is the reverse: the theorist will be remembered for his actions and the writer for his interpretation of the world. Jean-Paul Sartre was a witness, someone who would always sign a petition, hand out a pamphlet, stand on the street and sell a banned newspaper or take over as its editor, and go to court to defend the causes he believed in. For thousands of people, both prior to and after 1968, these are the traces he has left behind, and this activism is at least as important as his theoretical texts, which are difficult to read and even controversial. Barthes, on the other hand, who never went on demonstrations, never handed out pamphlets, never, in short, became 'militant' for a cause, will be remembered by the same generation for his texts, for the way he deconstructed the signs our society generates. Because he taught us how to decode these signs.

As these lines are being written, the societies of Eastern Europe are being shaken by momentous changes. It is pointless trying to imagine the content of what these two thinkers, Sartre and Barthes, might have had to say about such events, but it may be possible to sketch the form their thoughts might have taken.

Sartre would most probably have attempted to theorize this object lesson of a system collapsing like a house of cards. For his part, Barthes would probably have analysed the different discourses on these events, the way they were being discussed. He would have given us his interpretation of the ambiguous reactions to German reunification in Western Europe, and in the case of Romania and

Poland he would have pointed out what, in the euphoria of the process of democratization, no one wanted to acknowledge. He would probably have proffered readings of topics such as the rise of Muslim fundamentalism and the reemergence of nationalism which, although opposed to the commonsense view of events, would nevertheless not be misreadings. This kind of intervention, characteristic both of the Barthesian universe and of his readers' expectations, meant that he fulfilled a vital critical function in a world which has become so full of signs that it sometimes appears devoid of sense. No one today has replaced Barthes in this role as reader and interpreter of social life. As Olivier Burgelin says:

> His death left a void totally out of proportion to anything I could have imagined. An original voice had fallen silent, a voice which had more to say than any other I have ever heard. The world seemed to have become a definitively duller place. We would never again hear Barthes's opinion on any topic.

It is a silence which leaves us in the grip of mere noises themselves.

Notes

Translator's note (TN): All translations are mine if no English edition is cited. Fuller details of the books and articles by Barthes referred to in the text can be found in the bibliography.

Preface: The Genealogical Silence

1 *Ronald Barthes by Roland Barthes* (1975), trans. R. Howard (London, 1977), p. 12.
2 Ibid., p. 44.
3 Ibid., p. 3.
4 *On Racine* (1963), trans. R. Howard (New York, 1983), p. vii.
5 'Réponses', *Tel Quel*, no. 47, 1971, p. 89.
6 Ibid., p. 94.
7 *Roland Barthes by Roland Barthes*, p. 163.

Chapter 1   A Ward of the Nation

1 *Roland Barthes by Roland Barthes*, p. 3.
2 'From the Niger to the Gulf of Guinea through the country of Kong and the Mossi'.
3 *Haut-Sénégal Niger* (Paris, 1912).
4 *Roland Barthes by Roland Barthes*, p. 13.
5 'Réponses', p. 81.
6 *Roland Barthes by Roland Barthes*, p. 44.

7   Ibid., p. 45.
8   'Réponses', p. 90.
9   *Roland Barthes by Roland Barthes*, p. 8.
10 Ibid., p. 6.
11 Ibid., p. 17.
12 Ibid., p. 8.
13 Ibid., p. 24.
14 Ibid.
15 Ibid., p. 122.
16 'La lumière du Sud-Ouest' ('The light of the south-west'), *L'Humanité*, 10 Sept. 1977, republished in *Incidents* (Paris, 1987).
17 Ernest Hemingway, *The Sun also Rises* (New York, 1954), pp. 90–1.
18 'Radioscopie', 17 Feb. 1975, Radio France cassette K 1159.

Chapter 2   A Little Gentleman

1   *Roland Barthes by Roland Barthes*, p. 50.
2   Ibid., p. 109.
3   In particular, he made her out to have been Valéry's mistress. This seems unlikely given that Valéry mentions her only once in his *Carnets* and refers to her by the first letter of her surname, R: 'At R's. Seignobos – eloquent on the history of women in the Middle Ages – Lancelot – the lady. Langevin. I shouted him down over Heisenberg' (entry for 16 May 1929). This is the only reference, and it's very brief.
4   *Esprit*, May 1965, p. 834.
5   Interview with Bernard-Henri Lévy, *Le Nouvel Observateur*, 10 Jan. 1977; in English as 'Of what use is an intellectual?', in *The Grain of the Voice: Interviews 1962–1980* (1982), trans. L. Coverdale (London, 1985), p. 266.
6   *Roland Barthes by Roland Barthes*, p. 45.
7   *Prétexte: Roland Barthes*, conference at Cerisy (Paris, 1978), p. 249.
8   The 'École normale' is one of the 'grandes écoles', which are equivalent to universities but more prestigious; it is much more difficult to get a place in them, since they have extremely competitive entrance exams. The École Normale is primarily for the training of teachers. (TN)
9   *Roland Barthes by Roland Barthes*, p. 31.
10 Translator's note: My translation of the following from *Roland Barthes par Roland Barthes* (Paris, 1975), p. 36:

> J'ai lu dans un livre qu'on nous apprend à vivre quand la vie est passée. La leçon fut cruelle pour moi, qui après avoir passé la première partie de ma jeunesse dans l'illusion trompeuse d'être un homme invincible parce qu'instruit, me vois aujourd'hui grâce au hasard des mouvements politiques, réduit à un rôle secondaire et fort décevant.

Issu de l'honorable bourgeoisie d'autrefois, qui ne prévoyait certes pas qu'elle touchait à sa perte, je fus élevé par un précepteur à l'ancienne mode, qui m'enseigna beaucoup de choses; il croyait qu'il . . .

11 *Roland Barthes par Roland Barthes*, p. 36.
12 Ibid.
13 Ibid.
14 *L'Arc*, no. 56, first quarter 1974.
15 In France the agrégation is the highest competitive exam for teachers. (TN)
16 Interview with Jean Thibeaudeau broadcast in 1988 on the third channel in 'Océaniques'.
17 *Roland Barthes by Roland Barthes*, p. 33.
18 Ibid., p. 183. A 'lecteur' is a native speaker language assistant at a university. (TN)
19 *L'Obvie et l'obtus* (1982), p. 248; see 'Music, voice, language', in *The Responsibility of Forms*, trans. R. Howard (New York, 1985), p. 280.

Chapter 3   In Limbo

1 'Of what use is an intellectual?', in *The Grain of the Voice*, p. 259.
2 Ibid., p. 260.
3 'Pédale' is a pejorative way of referring to a homosexual (like the English term 'queer'); there may also be a connotation of the French 'pédé' which is an abbreviation of 'pédéraste' (pederast). (TN)
4 'La nostalgie de l'eau chez Baudelaire' ('The nostalgia for water in Baudelaire'). It is not coincidental that Gaston Bachelard had just published *L'Eau et les rêves*.
5 A complete list can be found in *Communications*, no. 36, 1982, with one mistake: 'Culture et tragédie' ('Culture and tragedy') was not published in *Existences* but in a special issue of *Cahiers de l'étudiant* in spring 1942 – among the other signatories were Paul Louis Mignon and Edgar Pisani. It was republished in *Le Monde*, 4 Apr. 1986.
6 *A Lover's Discourse; Fragments* (1977), trans. R. Howard (London, 1979), p. 13.
7 Ibid., p. 158.
8 Ibid., p. 146.
9 Ibid., p. 41.
10 *Roland Barthes by Roland Barthes*, p. 61.
11 Partido Obrero de Unificación Marxista, a Trotskyist grouping supporting the Republican government. (TN)
12 Jean-Paul Sartre, 'Présentation des *Temps modernes*', in his *Situations II* (Paris, 1948), pp. 16, 17.

13 Stendhal, *Scarlet and Black*, trans. M.R.B. Shaw (Harmondsworth, 1953), p. 484.
14 'Radioscopie', 17 Feb. 1975.

Chapter 4   Paris–Bucharest

1 *Roland Barthes by Roland Barthes*, p. 4.
2 Philippe Roger, *Roland Barthes, roman* (Paris, 1986), p. 334ff.
3 At least this is what Nadeau wrote in his introduction to Barthes's first article on 'Le Degré zéro de l'écriture' in *Combat*, 1 Aug. 1947.
4 'Of what use is an intellectual?', in *The Grain of the Voice*, p. 260.
5 *Roland Barthes by Roland Barthes*, p. 184.
6 'Of what use is an intellectual?', in *The Grain of the Voice*, p. 260.
7 Extract from an unpublished text by Maurice Nadeau to be issued by Albin Michel under the title *Le Livre des autres* and which the author kindly gave me.
8 *Combat*, 1 Aug. 1947.
9 'La marquise sortit à cinq heures'; *Writing Degree Zero* (1953), trans. A. Lavers and C. Smith (London, 1984), p. 27.
10 'What is writing?', in *Writing Degree Zero*, p. 15.
11 Ibid., p. 64.
12 Jean-Paul Sartre, 'Explication de *L'Étranger*', reprinted in *Situations I* (Paris, 1947) without any reference to its place of publication and dated 'February 1943'; in English as 'Camus' *The Outsider*', in Sartre, *Literary and Philosophical Essays*, trans. A. Michelson (London, 1955).
13 For the following, see Barthes, *Le Degré zéro de l'écriture*, pp. 54, 26, 55, 56 respectively, and Sartre, 'Camus' *The Outsider*', pp. 33, 38, 40.
14 Sartre, 'Camus' *The Outsider*', p. 34.
15 Ibid., p. 35.
16 *Writing Degree Zero*, p. 3.
17 Louis Hjelmslev, *Prologomena to a Theory of Language*, trans. J. Whitfield (Madison, Wis., 1963).
18 Jean Mouton in *Hommage à Guiraud* (Nice, 1985), p. 25.
19 *La Chambre claire* (1980), p. 36; in English as *Camera Lucida: Reflections on Photography*, trans. R. Howard (London, 1982), p. 18.
20 An amusing evocation of this period, and a direct allusion to Barthes, is to be found in *Roman Roi* by Renaud Camus (Paris, 1983), p. 498.

Chapter 5   From Alexandria to *Writing Degree Zero*

1 In *L'Aventure sémiologique* (1985), in English as *The Semiotic Challenge*, trans. R. Howard (Oxford, 1988), p. 5.

2 *Roland Barthes by Roland Barthes*, p. 110.
3 Interview with A. Greimas.
4 Ibid.
5 *Mythologies* (Paris, 1957), p. 206.
6 *Leçon* (1978), in English as 'Inaugural lecture, Collège de France', in *A Barthes Reader*, ed. Susan Sontag (New York, 1982), p. 271.
7 Centre Nationale de Recherche Scientifique, a prestigious research institute not just for the sciences but also for the humanities. (TN)
8 *Les Lettres nouvelles*, July 1953, p. 599.
9 *France-Observateur*, 11 June 1953.
10 *Le Monde*, 3 Oct. 1953.
11 *Carrefour*, 8 Apr. 1953.
12 *Les Temps modernes*, Nov. 1953, pp. 934–8.

Chapter 6   The Theatre Years

1 *Existences*, no. 33, 1944.
2 'Radioscopie', 17 Feb. 1975.
3 Alain Robbe-Grillet, *Ghosts in the Mirror*, trans. J. Levy (London, 1988), p. 34.
4 Letter from Alain Robbe-Grillet to the author, 8 Oct. 1988.
5 *Michelet* (1954), trans. R. Howard (Oxford, 1987), pp. 33, 27, 84, 150.
6 *Le Monde*, 10 Apr. 1954.
7 *Michelet*, p. 17.
8 Ibid., pp. 18, 20, 22, 23.
9 Ibid., pp. 33, 41.
10 Ibid., pp. 65, 90, 95, 150.
11 Ibid., p. 3.
12 Ibid., pp. 203–6.
13 *Roland Barthes by Roland Barthes*, p. 84.
14 *Michelet*, p. 87.
15 *Essais critiques* (Paris, 1964), p. 115.
16 Letter from Françoise Giroud to the author, 20 Jan. 1990.
17 Simone de Beauvoir, *The Force of Circumstance*, trans. R. Howard (London, 1965), p. 334.
18 *Théâtre populaire*, no. 14, July–Aug. 1955.
19 *Bulletin du club du livre français*, 12 Apr. 1954.
20 *Club, bulletin du club du meilleur livre*, Feb. 1955.
21 'Réponse à Camus', *Club*, Apr. 1955.
22 'Suis-je marxiste?', *Les Lettres nouvelles*, July–Aug. 1955.
23 *Writing Degree Zero*, p. 60.
24 *Mythologies* (1957), trans. A. Lavers (London, 1972), p. 11.
25 Page numbers from *Mythologies* (Paris, 1957); extract from 'Le guide bleu' from the English edn, trans. Annette Lavers.

26 From 'Myth today', in *Mythologies* (London, 1972), p. 116.
27 Umberto Eco and Isabella Pezzini, 'La sémiologie des sémiologies', *Communications*, no. 36, 1982, p. 25.
28 *Mythologies* (London, 1972), p. 48.
29 Ibid., pp. 48–9.
30 'The Romans in films', in ibid., p. 27.
31 *Le Monde*, 3 Aug. 1957.
32 *Rivarol*, 28 Mar. 1957.
33 *L'Écho du Centre*, 31 Mar. 1957.
34 *Arguments*, no. 20, fourth quarter 1960.
35 All the issues were republished by Privat in 1983.
36 'Les tâches de la critique brechtienne' ('The tasks of Brechtian criticism'), *Arguments*, no. 1, Dec. 1956–Jan. 1957.
37 'Il n'y a pas d'école Robbe-Grillet' ('There is no Robbe-Grillet school'), *Arguments*, no. 6, Feb. 1958.
38 'New York, Buffet et la hauteur', *Arts*, 11–17 Feb. 1959; in English as 'Buffet finishes off New York', in *A Barthes Reader*, ed. Sontag.
39 'Buffet finishes off New York', in *A Barthes Reader*, pp. 158, 160.
40 Ibid., pp. 160–1.
41 Ibid., p. 161.
42 Claude Lévi-Strauss, *De près et de loin* (Paris, 1988), p. 107.
43 In a lecture given much later (in 1974) which was published in *Le Monde*, 7 June 1974, and then republished in *L'Aventure sémiologique*; see 'Introduction: the semiological adventure', in *The Semiotic Challenge*, p. 6.
44 'Histoire et sociologie du vêtement', *Annales*, no. 3, July–Sept. 1957.
45 'Langage et vêtement', *Critique*, no. 142, Mar. 1959.
46 'Tricot à domicile', *Les Lettres nouvelles*, no. 5, 1 Apr. 1959.
47 'Pour une sociologie du vêtement', *Annales*, Mar.–Apr. 1960.

Chapter 7   The École, At Last

1 Intervention during the conference at Cerisy, June 1977, reprinted in Roland Barthes, *Le Bruissement de la langue* (1984); see 'The image', in *The Rustle of Language*, trans. R. Howard (Oxford, 1986), p. 357.
2 'Littérature et signification', *Tel Quel*, no. 16, Winter 1964; see also Roland Barthes, *Essais critiques* (1964), in English as *Critical Essays*, trans. R. Howard (Evanston, Ill., 1972).
3 'Drame, poème, roman' ('Drama, poem, novel'), *Critique*, no. 218, July 1966.
4 'Savoir et folie' ('Wisdom and madness'), *Critique*, no. 17, 1961.
5 Letter to the author 22 Aug. 1988.
6 In an interview with Michel Delahaye and Jacques Rivette, *Cahiers du cinéma*, no. 147, Sept. 1963.
7 *France-Observateur*, 16 Apr. 1964.

8   Georges Perec, *Les Choses* (1965), pp. 35–6; in English as *Things, a Story of the Sixties*, trans. D. Bellos (London, 1990), p. 34.
9   He admitted as much in a private conversation with R. Sorin.
10   *L'Humanité*, 10 Sept. 1977.
11   In a broadcast on France-Culture, 16 May 1986.
12   *Roland Barthes by Roland Barthes*, p. 82.
13   *The Rustle of Language*, p. 106.
14   Ibid.
15   Interview with Bernard-Henri Lévy and Jean-Marie Benoist on France-Culture, Feb. 1977.
16   Letter to Maurice Nadeau, 21 June 1965.
17   Raymond Picard, *New Criticism or New Fraud?* (1965), trans. F. Towne (Pullman, Wash., 1969).
18   *On Racine*, p. vii.
19   'Une lumière nouvelle sur l'univers racinien', *La Tribune de Genève*, 3, 4, 5 Aug. 1963; 'Pour mieux aimer Racine', *France-Observateur*, 6 June 1963; 'Quand la nouvelle critique s'attaque aux classiques', *La Croix*, 17 June 1963; 'Roland Barthes et le mythe de Racine', *Le Figaro littéraire*, 10 Aug. 1963.
20   *La Pensée*, Feb. 1964.
21   *Critique*, June 1964.
22   *Le Monde*, 14 Mar. 1964.
23   Ibid., 23 Oct. 1965.
24   Ibid., 9 Apr. 1966.
25   *Le Nouvel Observateur*, 3 Sept. 1965.
26   *Le Monde*, 6 Nov. 1965.
27   Robbe-Grillet, *Ghosts in the Mirror*, p. 50.
28   *Le Monde*, 3 Nov. 1965.
29   Ibid., 28 Mar. 1964.
30   On 2 Jan. 1966.
31   *La Gazette de Lausanne*, 26 and 27 Mar. 1966.
32   *La Tribune de Genève*, 9, 10 and 11 Apr. 1966.
33   *Notre République*, 20 May 1966.
34   *Le Nouvel Observateur*, 13 Apr. 1966.
35   Ibid., 30 May 1966.
36   Pierre Bourdieu, *Homo Academicus* (1984), trans. P. Collier (Cambridge, 1988).
37   'New criticism's greatness lies in what it seeks and its frequent absurdity in what it finds.' 'Crisis in criticism', *Times Literary Supplement*, 23 June 1966.
38   *Le Monde*, 19 Apr. 1980.
39   Republished in *The Rustle of Language*, p. 122.
40   'L'ancienne rhétorique, aide-mémoire', *Communications*, no. 16, 1970; in English in *The Semiotic Challenge*.
41   'La voix de Barthes' ('Barthes's voice'), *Communications*, no. 36, 1982.

42 Julia Kristeva, in *Textuel*, no. 15, 1985, p. 5.
43 'Radioscopie', 17 Feb. 1975.
44 *The Fashion System* (1967), trans. R. Howard (London, 1985), Foreward, p. ix.
45 See *The Responsibility of Forms* (1982), pp. 107–8.

Chapter 8   Structures Do Not Take to the Streets

1 France-Culture broadcast, 14 May 1986.
2 *Sade/Fourier/Loyola* (1971), trans. R. Miller (London, 1977), p. 85.
3 Ibid., pp. 84–5.
4 'Les structures ne descendent pas dans les rues.' (TN)
5 This interview was recorded on 23 and 24 November 1970 and on 14 May 1971. It was not broadcast until much later, in 1988. Extracts from the interview were published in 1971 in *Tel Quel* under the title 'Réponses'.
6 Ibid.
7 Julia Kristeva, *Les Samouraïs* (Paris, 1990), pp. 37–8.
8 Such contracts were arranged through the Ministère de la Coopération and funded by government aid. (TN)
9 His paper and the ensuing discussion were published in *Exégèse et Herméneutique* (Paris, 1971). Ten years later, again at the invitation of Edgar Haulotte, he was to attend the inaugural session of a seminar on the *Epistle to the Romans*.
10 *Roland Barthes by Roland Barthes*, p. 47.
11 In the sense of Lévi-Strauss's concept of *bricolage*, that is making use of whatever implements or conceptual tools are at hand; see Claude Lévi-Strauss, *The Savage Mind* (Chicago, 1966), ch. 1. (TN)
12 In *The Rustle of Language*, p. 121.
13 *Camera Lucida*, p. 21.
14 *Sade/Fourier/Loyola*, p. 131.
15 In his introduction to *Incidents*.
16 *Incidents*, pp. 53, 54, 56.
17 *Roland Barthes by Roland Barthes*, pp. 63–4.
18 In the television programme 'Océaniques', see note 5 above.
19 Georges Mounin, *Introduction à la sémiologie* (Paris, 1970).
20 Ibid., p. 189.

Chapter 9   *Tel Quel*

1 *Sade/Fourier/Loyola*, pp. 8, 181–3.
2 Dominique de Roux, *Immédiatement* (Paris, 1980), p. 187. (A 'bergère' is a large and decorative armchair.)

3 Georges Lapassade, *Le Bordel andalou* (Paris, 1971), p. 32.
4 *Communications*, no. 36, 1982.
5 *Roland Barthes by Roland Barthes*, pp. 188, 113.
6 *The Responsibility of Forms*, p. 174.
7 Ibid., p. 192.
8 Ibid., p. 210.
9 Ibid., p. 130.
10 'L'étrangère', *La Quinzaine littéraire*, 1 May 1970, pp. 160, 176–7, 192, 193.
11 'Comment travaillent les écrivains' ('How writers work'), *Le Monde*, 27 Sept. 1973.
12 *Roland Barthes by Roland Barthes*, p. 46.
13 Interview on France-Culture with Bernard-Henri Lévy and Jean-Marie Benoist, Feb. 1977.
14 *Sade/Fourier/Loyola*, p. 8.
15 *Mythologies* (London, 1972), p. 29.
16 Ibid., p. 31.
17 *Roland Barthes by Roland Barthes*, p. 124.
18 *Communications*, no. 36, 1982, p. 121.
19 *Le Monde*, 24 May 1974.
20 'Of what use is an intellectual?', in *The Grain of the Voice*, p. 265.
21 *Roland Barthes by Roland Barthes*, p. 48.
22 *Le Monde*, 14 Feb. 1975.
23 'Je me souviens qu'il lui arrivait – lui qui haïssait Cocteau – de commander comme lui mes plats.' (TN)
24 *The Pleasure of the Text* (1973), trans. R. Miller (Oxford, 1990).
25 *Lettres françaises*, 9 Feb. 1972.
26 *Roland Barthes by Roland Barthes*, p. 145.
27 'Je meurs de soif auprès de la fontaine.' (TN)
28 'Radioscopie', with Jacques Chancel and Roland Barthes, 17 Feb. 1975.

Chapter 10   The Collège de France

1 Didier Eribon, *Michel Foucault* (Paris, 1989), p. 104.
2 Interview reprinted in *The Grain of the Voice*, p. 269.
3 Ibid., p. 270.
4 'Inaugural lecture, Collège de France', in *A Barthes Reader*, ed. Sontag, p. 458.
5 Ibid., p. 457.
6 Ibid., p. 461.
7 Ibid., p. 460.
8 Ibid., pp. 470–1.

9   Ibid., p. 478.
10 Ibid.
11 Five interviews broadcast on 5 and 6 Dec. 1977 and 23, 24, 25 Feb. 1978; they were repeated on France-Culture from 28 Nov. to 2 Dec. 1988.
12 *A Lover's Discourse*, p. 9.
13 Ibid., p. 37.
14 Ibid.
15 Ibid., p. 5.
16 Cf. *Prétexte: Roland Barthes*, papers and discussions from a conference on Barthes at Cerisy-la-Salle, published by Éditions 10/18 (Paris, 1978).
17 Ibid., p. 146.
18 Ibid., pp. 248–9; reprinted in *The Rustle of Language*, p. 355.
19 *Prétexte: Roland Barthes*, p. 436.
20 Ibid., pp. 257–8.
21 See 'Deliberation', in *The Rustle of Language*, pp. 362, 364, 365.
22 *Camera Lucida*, p. 75.
23 Interview on France-Culture, Feb. 1977.
24 Institut de Recherche et de Coordination Acoustique – the centre for modern music in Paris. (TN)

Chapter 11   An Unqualifiable Life, A Life without Quality

1   *Critique*, nos 423–4, 1982, p. 676.
2   *Assez décodé!* (Paris, 1978), p. 9.
3   Robbe-Grillet, *Ghosts in the Mirror*, pp. 50–1.
4   *Le Nouvel Observateur*, no. 748, 12–18 Mar. 1979.
5   *Camera Lucida*, p. 75.
6   Ibid.
7   Martin Melkonian, *Le Corps couché de Roland Barthes* ('The sleeping body of Roland Barthes') (Paris, 1989), p. 38.
8   *Camera Lucida*, p. 70.
9   Philippe Sollers, *Women* (1983), trans. D. Bray (London, 1991), p. 116.
10 Published in 1987 in *Incidents*.
11 *Critique*, nos 423–4, Aug.–Sept. 1982, p. 673.
12 In *The Rustle of Language*, p. 289.
13 *Incidents*, pp. 115–16.
14 Ibid., p. 10
15 Sollers, *Women*, p. 121.
16 'Nuits magnétiques', France-Culture, 15 May 1986.
17 Jacques-Alain Miller, ibid.
18 Melkonian, *Le Corps couché*, pp. 90–1.
19 *L'Arc*, Oct. 1966.

Chapter 12   The 'After Death'

1 *The Grain of the Voice*, p. 3.
2 Ibid., p. 5.
3 Literally, 'The obvious and the obtuse', but translated as *The Responsibility of Forms*. (TN)
4 Called *Critical Essays III* because after *Essais critiques* of 1964 Barthes published a second set of essays, 'Nouveaux essais critiques', in 1972 (*New Critical Essays*, 1980), included in the Seuil edition of *Writing Degree Zero*.
5 The blurb does not appear on the translation, *The Responsibility of Forms*. (TN)
6 *L'Obvie et l'obtus*, p. 45. The twenty-two lines which comprise the blurb are in fact a condensation of three pages of text, pp. 42–5 (pp. 41–4 in *The Responsibility of Forms*).
7 Taken from pp. 94–6 of *Le Bruissement de la langue* (Paris, 1984).
8 *Incidents*, pp. 8–9.
9 Ibid., p. 10.

Bibliography of Roland Barthes

Books and articles by Roland Barthes referred to in the text are listed below, in chronological order, with English-language editions.

'En marge du Criton', 1933, published under the title 'Premier texte' in *L'Arc*, first quarter 1974.
'Essai sur la culture', *Cahiers de l'étudiant*, Spring 1942.
'En Grèce', *Existences*, no. 33, 1944.
'Réflexions sur le style de *L'Étranger*', *Existences*, no. 33, July 1944.
'Le Degré zéro de l'écriture', *Combat*, 1 Aug. 1947.
'Responsabilité de la grammaire', *Combat*, 26 Sept. 1947.
'Triomphe et rupture de l'écriture bourgeoise', *Combat*, 9 Nov. 1947.
'L'artisanat du style', *Combat*, 16 Nov. 1950.
'L'écriture et le silence', *Combat*, 23 Nov. 1950.
'L'écriture et la parole', *Combat*, 7 Dec. 1950.
'Le sentiment tragique de l'écriture', *Combat*, 16 Dec. 1950.
Le Degré zéro de l'écriture, 1953, reprinted in the Points series, Seuil, Paris, 1972. Trans. as *Writing Degree Zero* by Annette Lavers and Colin Smith, Cape, London, 1984; this edition includes a translation of 'Éléments de sémiologie'.
'*L'Étranger*, roman solaire', *Bulletin du club du livre français*, April 1954.
Michelet par lui-même, Seuil, Paris, 1954. Trans. as *Michelet* by R. Howard, Blackwell, Oxford, 1987.
'*La Peste*, annales d'une épidémie ou roman de la solitude?', *Club*, Feb. 1955.
'Réponse à Camus', *Club*, Apr. 1955.
'Nekrassov juge de sa critique', *Théâtre populaire*, no. 14, July–Aug. 1955.
'Suis-je marxiste?', *Les Lettres nouvelles*, July–Aug. 1955.
'Les tâches de la critique brechtienne', *Arguments*, no. 1, Dec. 1956–Jan. 1957.

Mythologies, Seuil, Paris, 1957. Trans. as *Mythologies* by Annette Lavers, Cape, London, 1972.

'Histoire et sociologie du vêtement', *Annales*, no. 3, July–Sept. 1957.

'Il n'y a pas d'école Robbe-Grillet', *Arguments*, no. 6, Feb. 1958.

'New York, Buffet et la hauteur', *Arts*, 11–17 Feb. 1959. Trans as 'Buffet finishes off New York', in *A Barthes Reader*, ed. Susan Sontag, Hill & Wang, New York, 1982.

'Langage et vêtement', *Critique*, no. 142, Mar. 1959.

'Tricot à domicile', *Les Lettres nouvelles*, no. 5, 1 Apr. 1959.

'Pour une sociologie du vêtement', *Annales*, Mar.–Apr. 1960.

'Écrivains et écrivants', *Arguments*, no. 20, fourth quarter 1960.

Sur Racine, Seuil, Paris, 1963. Trans. as *On Racine* by Richard Howard, Hill & Wang, New York, 1983.

'Éléments de sémiologie', *Communications*, no. 4, 1964; republished in *L'Aventure sémiologique* (1985). Trans. as *Elements of Semiology* by Annette Lavers, ed. Susan Sontag, Hill & Wang, New York, 1968.

'Littérature et signification', *Tel Quel*, no. 16, Winter 1964.

Essais critiques, Seuil, Paris, 1964. Trans. as *Critical Essays* by Richard Howard, Northwestern University Press, Evanston, Ill., 1972.

'Drame, poème, roman', *Critique*, no. 218, July 1966.

Critique et vérité, Seuil, Paris, 1966. Trans. as *Criticism and Truth* by Katrine Pilcher Keuneman, Cape, London, 1987.

Système de la mode, Seuil, Paris, 1967. Trans. as *The Fashion System* by Richard Howard, Cape, London, 1985.

'L'étrangère', *La Quinzaine littéraire*, 1 May 1970.

'L'ancienne rhétorique: aide-mémoire', *Communications*, no. 16, Dec. 1970. Trans. as 'The old rhetoric: an aide-memoire' by Richard Howard, in Barthes *The Semiotic Challenge*, Blackwell, Oxford, 1988.

S/Z, Seuil, Paris, 1970. Trans. as *S/Z* by Richard Miller, Blackwell, Oxford, 1990.

L'Empire des signes, Skira, Paris, 1970. Trans. as *Empire of Signs* by Richard Howard, Cape, London, 1983.

'Réponses', *Tel Quel*, no. 47, Autumn, 1971.

Sade, Fourier, Loyola, Seuil, Paris, 1971. Trans as *Sade/Fourier/Loyola* by Richard Miller, Cape, London, 1977.

Le Plaisir du texte, Seuil, Paris, 1973. Trans. as *The Pleasure of the Text* by Richard Miller, Blackwell, Oxford, 1990.

'Alors, la Chine?', *Le Monde*, 24 May 1974.

Roland Barthes par Roland Barthes, Seuil, Paris, 1975. Trans. as *Roland Barthes by Roland Barthes* by Richard Howard, Macmillan, London, 1977.

Fragments d'un discours amoureux, Seuil, Paris, 1977. Trans. as *A Lover's Discourse: Fragments* by Richard Howard, Cape, London, 1979.

'La lumière du Sud-Ouest', *L'Humanité*, 10 Sept. 1977.

Leçon, Seuil, Paris, 1978. Trans. as 'Inaugural lecture, Collège de France', in *A Barthes Reader*, ed. Susan Sontag, Hill & Wang, New York, 1982.

Sollers, écrivain, Seuil, Paris, 1979. Trans. as *Sollers, Writer* by Philip Thody, London, 1987.

'Déliberation', *Tel Quel*, no. 82, Winter 1979. Trans. as 'Deliberation' by Richard Howard, in *The Rustle of Language*, Blackwell, Oxford, 1986.

New Critical Essays, New York, 1980. Trans. from 'Nouveaux essais critiques' included in the French 1972 edition of *Le Degré zéro de l'écriture*.

La Chambre claire, Cahiers du cinéma-Gallimard-Seuil, Paris, 1980. Trans. as *Camera Lucida: Reflections on Photography*, by Richard Howard, Cape, London, 1982.

Le Grain de la voix, Seuil, Paris, 1981. Trans. as *The Grain of the Voice* by Linda Coverdale, Cape, London, 1985.

L'Obvie et l'obtus, Seuil, Paris, 1982. Trans. as *The Responsibility of Forms* by Richard Howard, Hill & Wang, New York, 1986.

Le Bruissement de la langue, Seuil, Paris, 1984. Trans. as *The Rustle of Language* by Richard Howard, Blackwell, Oxford, 1986.

L'Aventure sémiologique, Seuil, Paris, 1985. Trans. as *The Semiotic Challenge* by Richard Howard, Blackwell, Oxford, 1988 (omitting 'Élements de sémiologie').

Incidents, Seuil, Paris, 1987.

Index